Decision Support Systems: Th

INFORMATION SYSTEMS SERIES

Consulting Editors:

D. E. AVISON BA, MSc, FBCS
Department of Accounting and Management Science
University of Southampton, Southampton, UK

G. FITZGERALD BA, MSc, MBCS
Department of Computer Science
Birkbeck College, University of London, UK

This series of student texts covers a wide variety of topics relating to information systems. It is designed to fulfil the needs of the growing number of courses on, and interest in, computing and information systems which do not focus purely on the technological aspects, but seek to relate these to a business or organisational context.

INFORMATION SYSTEMS SERIES

DECISION SUPPORT SYSTEMS:
Theory and Practice

PAUL C. RHODES B.Sc., Ph.D., C.Eng., MBCS
Department of Computing
University of Bradford

ALFRED WALLER LIMITED
HENLEY-ON-THAMES

To my late wife Jill

Published by
Alfred Waller Ltd, Publishers
Orchards, Fawley, Henley-on-Thames
Oxfordshire RG9 6JF

First published 1993
Reprinted 1994

Copyright © 1993 Paul Rhodes

British Library Cataloguing-in-Publication Data
A catalogue record for this book is available from the British Library

ISBN: 1-872474-07-1

All rights reserved. No part of this publication may be reproduced, stored in a retrieval system, or transmitted, in any form or by any means electronic, mechanical, photocopying, recording and/or otherwise, without the prior written permission of the publishers. This book may not be lent, resold, hired out or otherwise disposed of by way of trade in any form of binding or cover other than that in which it is published, without the prior consent of the publishers. The book is sold subject to the Standard Conditions of Sale of Net Books and may not be resold in the UK below the net price.

Produced for the publishers by
John Taylor Book Ventures
Hatfield, Herts

Printed and bound in Great Britain
by Hollen Street Press Ltd, Berwick-upon-Tweed

Contents

Foreword		x
Preface		xii
1	**Setting the Scene**	1
1.1	Introduction	1
1.2	Why Support Decisions?	2
1.3	Problems Facing Decision Makers	2
1.4	Decisions and Choices	3
1.5	The Answer	4
1.6	What is a Decision Support System?	5
1.7	The Role Of Decision Theory	6
1.8	Desiderata	7
1.9	About This Book	8
1.10	Summary	9
1.11	Case Studies	9
1.12	Points To Ponder	13
1.13	Further Reading	14
1.14	References	15
2	**The Role of Decisions in the Business Environment**	
2.1	Introduction	16
2.2	A Model Of Industry	16
2.3	Company Planning And Control	17
2.4	A Model for Planning and Control	21
2.5	Testing The Planning Model	27
2.6	Other Models	30
2.7	The Scope Of Decision Support	31
2.8	The Desirability Of An Architecture	33
2.9	Summary	34
2.10	Case Study: R, B & H Revisited	35
2.11	Points To Ponder	42
2.12	Further Reading	42
2.13	References	44
3	**The Decision Making Process**	
3.1	Introduction	45
3.2	Feasibility Of Decision Support Systems	45
3.3	Neutrality Of Decision Support Systems	47
3.4	Industrial Decision Making	52

3.5	The Decision Making Process	54
3.6	Supporting The Decision Making Process	59
3.7	Summary	69
3.8	Case Study: The R, B & H Transport Problem	69
3.9	Points To Ponder	77
3.10	Further Reading	77
3.11	References	78

4 Decision Support and the Working Environment

4.1	Introduction	79
4.2	Decision Support Systems And Productivity	80
4.3	Decision Support Systems and the Company Organisation	80
4.4	Motivation Theories	83
4.5	Review Of Cognitive Methods	85
4.6	Socio–technical Approach	89
4.7	Work Redesign And Decision Support Systems	90
4.8	The Impact of Work Redesign on Decision Support Systems	91
4.9	Summary	92
4.10	Case Study: Cognitive Practices at R, B & H	93
4.11	Points To Ponder	99
4.12	Further Reading	99
4.13	References	100

5 The Information Gathering Task

5.1	Introduction	102
5.2	The Nature of Information	103
5.3	Management Information Systems	105
5.4	The Information Gathering Task	109
5.5	The Demands on Information Gathering Systems	117
5.6	Summary	121
5.7	Case Study: A Management Information System For R, B & H	122
5.8	Points To Ponder	125
5.9	Further Reading	127
5.10	References	128

Contents

6 Summary of the Probability Theory Required for Supporting Decisions
- 6.1 Introduction — 130
- 6.2 Inadequate Information, Uncertainty and Decision Support — 131
- 6.3 Probability Theory — 135
- 6.4 Conditional Probability — 147
- 6.5 Probability And Logic — 154
- 6.6 Cumulative Probability Distributions — 155
- 6.7 Expected Values — 156
- 6.8 Relevance Of Probability Theory to Decision Support Systems — 157
- 6.9 Estimating Probabilities in the Presence of Dependencies — 158
- 6.10 Summary — 160
- 6.11 R, B & H Case Study — 160
- 6.12 Points To Ponder — 164
- 6.13 Further Reading — 165
- 6.14 References — 166

7 Structuring The Decision
- 7.1 Introduction — 167
- 7.2 Payoff Tables — 167
- 7.3 Decision Diagrams — 171
- 7.4 Node Substitution Methods — 177
- 7.5 Decision Diagrams within Decision Support Systems — 184
- 7.6 Strategies — 186
- 7.7 Influence Diagrams — 189
- 7.8 Summary — 191
- 7.9 Case Study: The R, B & H Strategic Plan — 192
- 7.10 Points To Ponder — 198
- 7.11 Further Reading — 198
- 7.12 References — 199

8 Allowing For Risk
- 8.1 Introduction — 200
- 8.2 Risk and Corporate Managers — 200
- 8.3 Ordering Preferences — 201
- 8.4 Evaluating a Utility Function — 204
- 8.5 Interpretation of the Utility Function — 208
- 8.6 Multidimensional Utility Functions — 211

8.7	Utility Functions and Business Decisions	212
8.8	Utility Theory and Decision Diagrams	215
8.9	Assumptions used by Decision and Utility Theory	220
8.10	Corporate Attitudes to Risk	225
8.11	Summary	225
8.12	Case Study: A Utility Function for R, B & H's Strategic Decisions	226
8.13	Points To Ponder	228
8.14	Further Reading	228
8.15	References	229

9 Making Decisions with Incomplete Information

9.1	Introduction	230
9.2	The Principle of Insufficient Reason	231
9.3	Maximum Entropy	232
9.4	Maximising Entropy	235
9.5	Maximum Entropy in Practice	235
9.6	Minimally Prejudiced Distributions	239
9.7	Maximum Entropy on a Manager's Desk	239
9.8	Summary	240
9.9	Case Study	241
9.10	Points To Ponder	244
9.11	Further Reading	244
9.12	References	245

10 Choosing the best Possible Outcome

10.1	Introduction	246
10.2	The Type Of Choices	247
10.3	Ordering the Possible Outcomes for Atomic Decisions	247
10.4	Ordering Possible Outcomes for Compound Decisions	249
10.5	Search Trees For Ordering Possible Outcomes	251
10.6	Compound Decisions with Dependent Continuous Sub–decisions	256
10.7	Other Algorithms For Ordering/ Choosing Possible Outcomes	266
10.8	Summary	267
10.9	Case Study	267
10.10	Points To Ponder	274
10.11	Further Reading	275

11 Validating The Decision
11.1	Introduction	276
11.2	The Use Of Models	277
11.3	Numerical Models	279
11.4	Probabilistic Models	280
11.5	Simulation	288
11.6	Expert Systems	297
11.7	The Human Computer Interface	301
11.8	Summary	301
11.9	R, B & H Case Study: The Use Of Models	302
11.10	Points To Ponder	303
11.11	Further Reading	304
11.12	References	304

12 Concluding Remarks
12.1	Introduction	306
12.2	Feasibility of Decision Support Systems	306
12.3	Viability of Decision Support Systems	308
12.4	Usability of Decision Support Systems	309
12.5	Constructability of Decision Support Systems	309
12.6	Future Developments	311
12.7	Summary	313
12.8	Case Study: Outline Decision Support System For R, B & H	313
12.9	Further Reading	316

FOREWORD

This Series on Information Systems contains student texts covering a wide variety of topics relating to information systems. It is designed to fulfil the needs of a growing number of courses on, and interest in, computing and information systems which do not focus on the purely technical aspects, but seek to relate these to the organisational context. There are also titles which deal with topics in greater depth and are more research oriented.

Information systems has been defined as the effective design, delivery, use and impact of information technology in organisations and society. Utilising this fairly wide definition, it is clear that the subject is somewhat interdisciplinary. Thus the series seeks to integrate technological disciplines with management and other disciplines, for example, psychology and sociology. It is felt that these areas do not have a natural home, they are rarely represented by single departments in polytechnics and universities, and to put such books in a purely computer science or management series restricts potential readership and the benefits that such texts can provide. This series on information systems now provides such a home.

The books will be mainly student texts, although certain topics may be dealt with at a deeper, more research-oriented level.

The series is expected to include the following areas, although this is not an exhaustive list: information systems development methodologies, office information systems, management information systems, decision support systems, information modelling and databases, systems theory, human aspects and the human-computer interface, application systems, technology strategy, planning and control, and expert systems, knowledge acquisition and its representation.

A mention of the books so far published in the series gives a 'flavour' of the richness of the information systems world. *Information Systems Development: Methodologies, Techniques and Tools* (D.E. Avison and G. Fitzgerald), looks at many of the areas discussed above in overview form; *Information and Data Modelling* (David Benyon), concerns itself with one very important aspect, the world of data, in some depth; *Structured Systems Analysis and Design*

Methodology (G. Cutts) looks at one particular information systems development methodology in detail: *Multiview: An Exploration in Information Systems Development* (D.E. Avison and A.T. Wood-Harper) looks at an approach to information systems development which combines human and technical considerations; *Software Engineering for Information Systems* (D. McDermid) discusses software engineering in the context of information systems; *Information Systems Research: Issues, Techniques and Practical Guidelines* (R. Galliers, ed) provides a collection of papers on key information systems issues; and *Relational Database Design* (P. Benyon-Davies) looks at relational database design in detail. New titles include *Business Management and Systems Analysis* by Eddie Moynihan; *Why Systems Fail* by Chris Sauer; *Systems Analysis Systems Design* by David Mason and Leslie Willcocks.

Paul Rhodes' book demonstrates the ways in which computer information systems can be used to support management decision-making. Paul has been lecturing at Bradford University for some years and he has also been a practitioner and evidence of this is found throughout. It is a very practical book, relating the theory to the real world, and it abounds with examples and two ongoing case studies. This should prove very helpful to all students, but particularly those who have not had significant real-world experience; those with practical experience will readily value its content. Very often, texts on decision support have been so theoretical that it is difficult to see their relevance and this text redresses the balance. Although the subject of decision support systems can be complex and difficult, this book is written in a very friendly and helpful style and the examples bring the material to life. We think that this deserves to be considered for adoption as the main text on courses in decision-support for management, computing and information systems at both undergraduate and postgraduate level.

David Avison and Guy Fitzgerald

PREFACE

This book has been written to try to demonstrate that practical computer support for business decisions is both desirable and feasible. There are excellent texts which propound decision theory; there are excellent books which explain how to support a particular type of decision; there are excellent books which explain how to use a particular type of decision supportive method; there are also many books which cover the whole subject rather superficially. However, books which try to explain how the theory can be used to support a whole spectrum of every day decisions are hard, if not impossible, to find.

When I first taught this course, some seven years ago, I was concerned that students were unable to relate the material presented in the text books to the real world. In fact, one mature student, who had comfortably passed the course and had many years of industrial experience, told me that he could not see how the material presented in the text books was of any practical use whatsoever. I found this very disappointing but also rather mistifying because, with eighteen years industrial experience myself, I found the material both stimulating and applicable.

After discussing the problem with several classes, I came to the conclusion that the problem lay in the diversity of the subject. Presumably, this is why other authors either cover a small part in detail or the whole subject rather vaguely. I decided to overcome this problem by taking a specific conceptual design for a Decision Support System so that I could show students how the existing theories could be used with at least one design. This approach would have the disadvantage that the students would only ever see the one conceptual design but it would have the advantage that they would see how to tie the theory and practice together. This approach proved to be quite successful. All students rated the new course more highly and those with industrial experience thought that the contents would be relevant to the workplace.

This book is a consequence of the continuing evolution of the above course. I have used the notes, on which the book is based, to teach both undergraduate and postgraduate students. I have also used the same material to teach both computing/information technology students and business/management students. I vary the emphasis according to the discipline of my class and the degree of self reliance according to the level of the course. I do, however, require all students to read widely to gain a fuller understanding of the subject and a broader perspective of it. This overcomes the 'one conceptual design' drawback mentioned above.

The material in this book should be of interest to any business/management student or practitioner who wishes to understand what decision support has to offer, how it could affect everyday life and what can be expected of a computer system. It will also be of interest to any computing/information technology student or practitioner who is interested in providing practical decision support using computer systems.

Readers who do not have a basic grounding in mathematics may find parts of this book to be rather formal. However, as long as these readers do not panic at the first sight of mathematics, they should be able to emerge from these sections with at least an appreciation of how the mathematics is used to tackle the problems. I have taught students with sketchy or ageing mathematical knowledge who, with a bit of patience on both sides, have easily grasped the principles embodied in this book.

This book falls roughly into two parts. The first five chapters address decision–making in general terms and have a business/management bias. The next six chapters review those theories which are pertinent to decision making and explain how these might be used in Decision Support Systems. These chapters will be of interest to anyone wishing to implement a Decision Support System but also to anyone wishing to have an understanding of how they might work and what they would have to offer. The final chapter looks at the feasibility, viability and usability of Decision Support Systems and should be of interest to all readers.

Two case studies thread their way through the book. One, a fictitious textile company, is used extensively for worked examples within the book. The other, choosing a holiday, is provided primarily to give the reader the opportunity to try supporting a different type of decision. Other sources are also used for examples when appropriate.

I am not the most lucid of writers so I am indebted to Dr Ron Thomas for reading and re–reading this text in an attempt to ensure that it enlightens, rather than confuses, the reader. I am also indebted to him for checking the worked examples.

I would like to thank my late wife, Jill, for typing large parts of the original text in spite of suffering from cancer at the time. She showed great courage but unfortunately did not live to see the fruits of her endeavours. I would also like to thank Gillian Clements for taking over the typing and for producing the word processed form of this book. Finally I would like to thank José Smith for her support and encouragement whilst I ported the book into a desktop publishing package and hence completed it in its present form.

I hope this book will raise the expectations of decision makers for better support from their computer systems. Equally, I hope the book will provide some of the inspiration for the computing and information technologists who may be required to satisfy that hightened expectation. But, most of all, I hope that readers will find the book both interesting and stimulating and that they will view decisions in a different light thereafter.

Paul C Rhodes

January 1993

Chapter 1
Setting the Scene

1.1 INTRODUCTION

In the competitive and fast moving environment of a modern day business everybody would benefit from assistance with making decisions whether they be members of the board of directors trying to make long term, strategic decisions or a salesperson trying to decide what price to quote for a job. In reality, however, the actions of either one of the aforementioned persons influence the actions of the other. Consequently, their respective decisions cannot be considered in isolation. Any attempt to assist with business decisions should, therefore, be integrated into the corporate decision making activity.

Almost all business decisions are complex and inter-related. Consider the following example. Mr Keith and Mr Philip are two brothers who run a family textile business. The textile trade has been in decline for many years but is currently going through a particularly severe depression. The company, R, B & H, has always had its own transport for collecting and delivering goods but their present vehicle is overdue for replacement and is, in any case, too expensive to run.

One alternative is to use a carrier. Carriers run fleets of vehicles and collect and deliver on a daily basis. It is, however, very difficult to get a carrier to collect/deliver at very short notice because the efficiency of their business relies on ensuring that their vehicles always carry economic loads. This means waiting until several items have to be delivered to the same place before making the journey. A further disadvantage of using a carrier is that the R, B & H driver would have to be made redundant.

The other possibility is to replace the ageing vehicle. The money could be found but other parts of the business would then be deprived of funding. It would keep the driver employed, however, and in addition provide maximum flexibility. There is a very wide choice of size and type of vehicle and they should be able to find a vehicle which would be significantly cheaper to run than their present one. However, whether or not this would be cheaper than using a carrier would depend on the quantity of goods they have to deliver.

The viability of R, B & H may not depend on a good solution to this problem but, on the other hand, it may do. The business could easily be in seriously difficulties if a few such decisions were badly made.

However, the situation is even more complex than it appears. Buying a new vehicle impacts on the financing of the rest of the business so they should be making more strategic decisions prior to this one. The complexity of any decision is increased many fold if other decisions, which constrain the one in question, have not been resolved first. This situation can only be recognised if the decision making environment is properly structured.

How then should the brothers go about making this decision and recognising those which should go before it? This book examines ways of providing support for business decisions like these.

1.2 WHY SUPPORT DECISIONS?

If businesses are to invest in ways of improving decisions they have to be convinced that their investment will be worthwhile. Consequently, the benefits which accrue from making better decisions need to be quantified.

Companies have good reason to be concerned about the quality of decisions because their prosperity relies on good decisions being made. For example, good strategic decisions help to ensure that the company will be well placed in the future and good day to day decisions go some way to guaranteeing that the company is still in business to enjoy that future. Unfortunately, nobody can ensure a good future because there is always an element of uncertainty and risk in any business and nobody is ever in possession of all the facts.

These two points almost go without saying but both require further thought because they conceal the fundamental problems which beset decision makers. They also conceal the true reasons for supporting decisions, namely that business decisions are too complex to be reliably made without some procedural, informational and computational support.

1.3 PROBLEMS FACING DECISION MAKERS

1.3.1 Incomplete Information

If all the information which is required to make a decision is available at the time the decision is made then the decision is deterministic.

Deterministic problems can be solved using deductive logic, i.e. a solution can be found for a general case and any particular case is merely one instance of this general solution. Consequently, many people do not consider deterministic decisions to be true decisions.

Business decisions are rarely deterministic. Invariably the information which is available is inadequate and/or incomplete. Non–deterministic problems such as these require inductive logic, i.e. a logic which looks at several examples and tries to generalise these to provide a solution to a similar particular problem. In other words, a formalism which learns by experience.

The average person is not particularly skilled at the former but is quick to observe patterns and trends which form the basis of the latter. Computers, are excellent at the former but poor at the latter. There are, therefore, obvious grounds for co–operation between decision makers and computers.

1.3.2 Uncertainty and Risk

If a decision involves no uncertainty or risk then it is not really a decision at all; it is merely a case of choosing between a set of possible outcomes. For the purposes of this book, this general statement will be made very specific by building it into the definition of 'decision' and 'choice'.

1.4 DECISIONS AND CHOICES

1.4.1 Definition of a Decision

A decision requires a person to express a preference between two or more possible outcomes where at least one of the possible outcomes has consequences which cannot be determined for certain, e.g. express a preference between paying £1 for a raffle ticket which will either win a magnum of wine or win nothing, or keeping your £1.

1.4.2 Definition of a Choice

A choice requires a person to express a preference between two or more outcomes whose consequences are known for certain, e.g. express a preference between a pot of tea, a cup of coffee or a soft drink.

1.4.3 The Relationship between Decisions and Choice

These two definitions establish a relationship which will be exploited in later chapters. If a person can provide a certain outcome which is equivalent to a risky outcome, i.e. the person would be indifferent between the two, then the decision can be reduced to an equivalent choice. In business, the only grounds upon which to choose is to optimise the benefits to the company. The following transformations should, therefore, be possible:

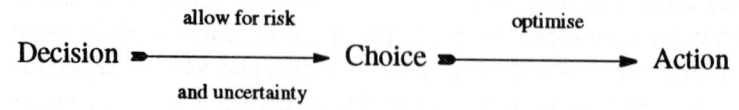

$$\text{Decision} \xrightarrow{\text{allow for risk and uncertainty}} \text{Choice} \xrightarrow{\text{optimise}} \text{Action}$$

The first transformation, allowing for risk and uncertainty, can only be done by a person or group of people. The second transformation is probably best done by machine. Here again there are obvious reasons for collaboration between decision makers and computers. Note, however, that the definition of both decision and choice leaves the final responsibility with a person (or group of people). This is entirely in sympathy with the idea of providing support, i.e. assisting people with a decision; not making it for them.

1.5 THE ANSWER

Having briefly discussed the issues underlying the question 'Why Support Decisions?' we are now in position to provide some answers. The reasoning proceeds as follows:

(1) Companies rely on good decisions for their well being.

(2) The company should be more prosperous, if better decisions are made.

(3) Business decisions are too complex to be made reliably without some support from experience, other people or a methodology.

(4) Business decisions are too important and too complex to simply hand over to a machine.

These four facts lead us to consider the following conjecture:

Perhaps a methodology could be defined to assist with decision making and machines could be used to automate the methodology.

The methodology referred to above could be called a Decision Support System. Notice, however, that the argument advocates a methodology which could be automated using computers. It does not state that it has to be automated.

1.6 WHAT IS A DECISION SUPPORT SYSTEM?

Having raised the prospect of a Decision Support System, it would be appropriate to define what one might be. A technical description is neither possible nor desirable at this juncture but a definition, couched in everyday language, is essential to concentrate our minds on the task in hand. The definition which will be used in this book is:

> A methodology, embodied in an organised group of people and machines, which is designed to assist, but only in a secondary role, one or more members of the organisation to express a preference for one action amongst the many which could be taken where at least one of those actions involves embarking on a sequence of events whose outcome cannot be precisely determined. The preferred action is deemed to be related to the person's job within the organisation and is deemed to influence and be influenced by the actions of others within the organisation.

This definition is very descriptive. It is true that a Decision Support System is a system in which an organised body of people and machines work together to achieve a common goal, i.e. the making of a decision. It is also true that the machine part of the system should take a subordinate role in assisting the people to settle or resolve issues with the added dimension of risk and uncertainty.

Note that the above definition encompasses support for all types of decisions. The term Decision Support System has been trivialised since it was first introduced and terms which focus on certain types of decision, e.g. Executive Support Systems and Organisational Support Systems, are now more popular. This book does not wish to make these distinctions because the material presented here is relevant to all business decisions. Consequently, the term Decision Support System will be used throughout the book with its original meaning, i.e. encompassing all types of system which support decisions.

Another point which should be noted is that decisions must be formulated and structured before they can be made. Mathematics cannot be used to solve problems unless the problem is expressed in mathematical terms. Similarly, a Decision Support System will not be effective unless the decision is expressed in some sort of formal system. Often the most difficult part of using mathematics to solve a problem is expressing it in mathematical terms. However, it is often a most important step, not simply because it facilitates the use of mathematics, but also because it increases the user's understanding of the problem. With decisions too, expressing them in formal terms will be one of the major tasks and, consequently, when this book refers to Decision Support Systems it is referring to systems which are capable of providing support to both structure and resolve decisions.

1.7 THE ROLE OF DECISION THEORY

Decision Theory was established during the 1960s when classic work was done by people such as Cox [1], Jaynes [2] and Tribus [3]. These authors established the mathematics of making rational decisions in situations which were clouded by uncertainty and/or lack of information. Although their work is still relevant to students and researchers, their techniques have not yet found general acceptance in industry. The reasons for this are unclear. Industrialists may think that the methods are impractical or that they are too complex but a more likely explanation is that they have never been delivered to the industrialist in a palatable form.

In the 1960s and 1970s the technology to put the theory into practice was not widely available and was very expensive but modern computers do have this capability and are cheap. So why is support for decisions still largely either very low level or very complex and specialised? One answer lies in the preoccupation with information. The information is required to make decisions but, until the decisions have been analysed nobody can identify what information is needed, what part of that information is available and how best to make the decision without the information which is unobtainable.

This book will advocate starting with the decisions, deducing the information which is required to make them and then devising systems to collect the appropriate information. It will also advocate a return to more formal theories for making the decisions.

The 'decision first, information second' approach advocated above does not diminish the importance of current Management Information Systems, Executive Information Systems, Intelligent

Information Systems and the like. When the time comes to look for information it is to these systems that we will turn. That does not make them Decision Support Systems, however, and the difference between the two will be emphasised as the subject unfolds.

1.8 DESIDERATA

The emphasis of the book will be on expounding a tangible, practical methodology for assisting a collection of people working in a single enterprise to make rational decisions in their normal everyday working environment.

There is no better way to start expounding a methodology than by specifying a set of fundamental properties which are required of it. The fundamental properties proposed by the early workers in decision theory are excellent for this purpose. They are given by Tribus as a set of desiderata ('things lacking but needed or desired' – Concise Oxford Dictionary).

When these desiderata are expressed in appropriate terminology they become :

(1) Consistency:

   If two or more techniques, which are deemed legal within the methodology, are used by a person to make a decision, the possible outcomes chosen will be the same.

(2) Continuity:

   If the same person uses the methodology to make two closely related decisions, the possible outcomes chosen will also be closely related.

(3) Universality:

   The methodology will be generally applicable to a wide variety of business decisions and will not be specific to a particular decision or class of decisions.

(4) Unambiguous:

   The methodology will only be expected to work with unambiguous information. In general, a statement will be accepted as unambiguous if what it is, and what is it not, can be stated without duplicity or omissions.

(5) No information will be withheld:

> The methodology will be expected to work without access to total information and provide the best advice possible with the information given. However, if information is withheld initially and provided later (or new information becomes available) the advice given may change substantially.

The above desiderata will set the tone of this book. They will not be used formally as an axiomatic starting point for a theory but the principles embodied within them will govern the development of the methodology in both its general aspects and detailed operation.

1.9 ABOUT THIS BOOK

The first three chapters of this book look at the role of decisions within industry and at the variety of decisions and decision makers. They then ask whether or not such a wide diversity of activities can ever be supported by a generalised system. By concentrating on the commonality and in particular the aspect of control, a general system is proposed which embodies:

(1) A decision model for a company;

and

(2) A three part decision making process comprising:

   (a) Structuring the decision;
   (b) Choosing a possible outcome;
   (c) Validating the decision.

The fourth chapter concludes this general approach by looking briefly at the social consequences of such systems in terms of the impact that they could have on the everyday working environment.

The rest of the book examines in some detail the technical and theoretical problems raised by the desire to support decisions in the manner described in the earlier chapters. It does this by following the three stages of making a decision outlined above.

Chapter 5 examines the role of information gathering within a decision making strategy and compares this role with the Management Information System rationale.

Chapters 6, 7, 8 and 9 invoke probability theory, decision theory, utility theory and information theory to express uncertainty, to structure the decision, to make allowances for risk and to estimate missing information respectively. This reduces the decision to a choice.

Chapter 10 looks at several mathematically based methods for making optimal choices. This chapter also examines the problems which arise at the interface between mathematical methods and the person using the method, especially when that person is not mathematically inclined.

Chapter 11 examines the problems of validating a decision. In its extreme this can be a sophisticated model which, given a set of actions, will predict the likely consequences. At this extreme, the first two steps of the decision making process can be de-emphasised and the decision maker can try alternative strategies until a suitable one is found.

The book concludes with a short chapter which looks at the prospects and potential of Decision Support Systems.

1.10 SUMMARY

This chapter asked and answered the question 'Why support decisions?'. It briefly discussed the fundamental problems associated with any decision making, namely the problems of incomplete information and uncertainty about the possible outcomes. It drew a clear distinction between a choice and a decision and extended this until a definition for Decision Support Systems was possible. The chapter then specified those attributes of a decision supporting theory which are considered to be desirable, if not essential, for sound support.

The chapter concluded by briefly previewing the contents of the remaining chapters.

1.11 CASE STUDIES

The ideas and theories expounded in this book are reinforced by the frequent use of examples. In particular, case studies are used to build larger scenarios which have sufficient complexity to exercise both the methodology and the mind of the reader.

Two such case studies are provided and both are progressively developed as the book proceeds. The first case study takes a fictitious textile company faced with the problems of improving its effectiveness in the face of a declining manufacturing base at home and increasing competition from overseas. The second looks at the problems of choosing a holiday. This has been deliberately chosen to be slightly off the main theme of the book so that the reader has an opportunity to apply the knowledge gained to a significantly different problem. However, at this point, we need to familiarise ourselves with the activities of R,B & H, our fictitious textile company.

1.11.1 Introduction to R, B & H

The company, R, B & H, is a traditional English family firm run by two brothers, Mr Keith and Mr Philip. The brothers have run the firm for many years because their father died early and their mother, although still a director of the firm, is content to leave running the business to her sons.

Their business is in textiles. They are commission winders, warpers and sizers for the worsted trade. These are specialist tasks which play a vital role in the long process of getting wool off the back of sheep and onto the backs of fashionable men and women.

All woven fabrics are made from two sets of yarns one of them running lengthways, i.e. the warp, and the other running across the width, i.e. the weft. R, B & H are only concerned with the warp. In a piece of worsted cloth there are about 5000 strands of yarn which run its entire length. The length can be anything from 500 metres for samples to several thousand metres for production runs. All these yarns have to be assembled, equally tensioned, in colours dictated by the pattern, on a large bobbin known as a beam which is mounted in the back of the loom. Any mistake on the beam, be it in the pattern or in the tension, will almost certainly result in the loss of hundreds of yards of very expensive cloth.

R, B & H make warps (the yarns on the beam) for very fine and/or very intricate fabrics. It is a highly skilled operation, requiring experienced staff under close supervision. In addition, R, B & H is subject to all the business problems which beset the textile industry as a whole.

They began using computers some time ago. Mr Philip had traditionally undertaken the administrative work and was finding that the payroll took a lot of time. This was a labour intensive task which appeared to lend itself nicely to new technology and the cost of the equipment could be justified in terms of the amount of Mr Philip's time which would be freed to do more important things. The brothers were given good advice by a competent supplier and soon had a small but effective computerised payroll system in their office.

Having successfully established a payroll system the next obvious candidate for computerisation was the book keeping, payment of bills, the issuing of invoices and statements and the identification of outstanding accounts. The computer salesman had packages which would do these jobs so Mr Philip bought one of these systems too.

The brothers quickly realised that, because the computer was fast, they did not have to wait until the end of the quarter before they knew whether or not they were operating profitably. Basically, they realised that it was advantageous to know about the company's performance as soon as possible, in fact, the sooner the better. But, in order to acquire this knowledge, they needed to gather data and quickly process it into information. In other words they were aspiring to have an ever increasing availability of information.

By now the brothers realised that they were becoming involved in a major new technology and they both decided that they should take stock of the situation. They agreed that Mr Philip should conduct a fact finding exercise and report back to the other two directors. They would then decide collectively what they should do in response to this new technology. Several months later Mr Philip was ready to give his report.

1.11.2 Mr Philip's Report

R, B & H was still near the beginning of the computer/management revolution and had just about reached a management style known as Management by Exception. This meant that a company set a variety of financial targets for each manager and then informed all the managers how they were progressing towards their targets. In particular a company could highlight for the manager those areas which were clearly going to fall below target, i.e. the exceptions.

Mr Philip explained that in the larger companies these methods spread from the purely financial aspects of the company to almost every other industrial activity. Many targets were now no longer fiscal and data had to be collected from diverse sources to provide the information required for this type of management control. The collection of this quantity of data, its storage, processing and compilation into the many reports required by the various managers was done by computer software known as a Management Information System.

Computers were buckling under the stress imposed on them by this huge demand for information. They were no longer required to run particular programs. They now had to run suites of programs which all wanted access to the same information. These changes brought about the advent of the database as computer scientists realised that providing information for managers was going to be a science in its own right.

Mr Philip explained that the pressure for change did not stop there. Management by Exception was suffering from a major drawback. Many managers who had failed to meet targets were simply arguing that the target was unrealistic in the first place. As targets at that time were largely set by senior managers this excuse was hard to refute.

As far as Mr Philip could ascertain, the answer to these problems came in the form of Management by Objectives. In this system each manager agreed a target with a superior. All the individual targets were collected together and collated to see how the company would perform if these targets were met. If the predicted performance was not satisfactory some corrective measures could be taken. These corrections may be to simply increase the targets of individuals but there was now some measure of how realistic this might be.

Together with these changes in management style came further pressure on the computer system. This had to be a concern for a small company like R, B & H because large computer systems are expensive but the computer is the obvious choice for collecting the plans of individuals and collating them into an overall plan. It is also the obvious piece of equipment to use for a refining process which, after several repetitions, produces an agreed plan for all to work to.

If the computer is to play this role, however, it will have to collect much more data and produce a new type of information. The new information which will be required is about the future and not the past. Mr Philip explained to the others that this seemingly trivial change is actually crucial. This is because decisions are about the future and, although the experience gained in the past is useful for making predictions, an estimation of what might happen in the future is essential.

Such a system would correlate agreed targets based on predictions of the future. The difference between the target and the actual would then be computed within the system. This meant that the computer could provide feedback, the essential component to control. They, as the managers, could have access to this feedback. They could see when things were running smoothly and when they were not. Management by Exception and Management by Objectives would become rolled into one as each of the managers, with their agreed objectives, would use the feedback to try to ensure that the objectives were met.

However, managers found it impossible to absorb all the information provided by the computer and unable to find the information of immediate interest amongst the mass of information available. Technology, however, had the answer which came in the form of Executive Information Systems. These differed from the previous systems in that the manager was provided with a terminal and a system which could answer a query within a few seconds but, far more importantly, the system could provide only that information which concerned the manager at the time.

This seemed to be the ultimate, or at least the current state of the art. But there was a problem. The technology was one with which they were unfamiliar and they could not afford to ignore its potential.

1.11.3 The Directors' Decision

After much thought and deliberation the two brothers and their mother devised a scheme to get them off the horns of this dilemma. In return for what was essentially cheap consultancy from a computing department in a local University, they would be prepared to have students, under instruction, working on their problem. They put this proposition to several Universities and waited for their reply.

1.11.4 Accepting the Challenge

This book will pretend that we have taken up the brother's offer and the Case Studies, at the end of each chapter, will use this general scenario to provide examples throughout the book.

1.12 POINTS TO PONDER

At the end of each chapter the 'Points to Ponder' section will invite the reader to consider certain issues which relate to the material which has been covered in the book. The aim is to encourage the reader to think about the issues involved. This, the first 'Points to Ponder' invites the reader to consider the following:

(1) We wish to support any and every decision. Consequently, we must concentrate on methods of making decisions which can be applied to any decision. Before reading further, consider how you decide which holiday to take. Ask yourself if you use a method or just adopt an ad–hoc approach. If you use a method ask yourself if you could use the same method for an entirely different problem. If you adopt an ad–hoc approach try to devise a method.

(2) Ask yourself if deciding which holiday to take is an easy or difficult decision. If you think it is easy, chose a decision which you find difficult instead. In either case, try to determine why the decision is difficult. Is it the complexity, is it lack of information or is it uncertainty about the outcome?

1.13 FURTHER READING

This book concentrates on showing how a generalised Decision Support System could be built. The advantage of this approach is that the reader is not confused by the diversity of the subject. The disadvantage is that the reader is not given an insight into all the issues and viewpoints raised by the other authors of books and papers on the topic. This shortcoming will be partially rectified by providing references in the 'Further Reading' section of each chapter.

- Alter, S. (1977) *A Taxonomy of Decision Support Systems*. Sloan Management Review, **1**, pp. 39–56.

- Alter, S. (1980) *Decision Support Systems: Current Practice and Continuing Challenges*. Addison–Wesley.

- Bonczek, R.H., Holsapple, C.W. and Whinston, A.B. (1981) *Foundations of Decision Support Systems*. Academic Press.

- Checkland, P. (1981) *Systems Thinking; Systems Practice*. J. Wiley & Sons.

- Fick, G. and Sprague, R.H. (eds.) (1981) *Decision Support Systems: Issues and Challenges*. Pergamon Press.

- Ginzberg, M.J., Reitman, W.R. and Stohr, E.A. (eds.) (1982) *Decision Support Systems*. North–Holland.

- Keen, P.G.W. and Scott–Morton, M.S. (1978) *Decision Support Systems: an Organisation's Perspective*. Addison–Wesley.

- Keen, P.G.W. (1981) Value Analysis: Justifying Decision Support Systems. *MIS Quarterly*, March.

- McLean, E. and Sol, H.G. (eds.) (1986) *Proceedings of the IFIP WG 8.3 Working Conference on Decision Support Systems: A Decade in Perspective*. Noordwijkerhout, The Netherlands, 16–18 June.

- Sol. H,G (1985) DSS: Buzzword or Challenge? *European Journal of Operational Research*. pp. 1–8.

- Sprague, R.H. Jr., Ralph, H. and Carlson, E.D. (1982) *Building Effective Decision Support Systems*. Prentice Hall.

- Sprague, R.H. Jr. and Watson, H.J. (1986) *Decision Support Systems: Putting Theory into Practice*. Prentice Hall.

1.14 REFERENCES

(1) Cox, R.T. (1961) *The Algebra of Probable Inference*. John Hopkins University Press, Baltimore.

(2) Jaynes, E.T. (1969) *Probability Theory in Science and Engineering*. Physics Dept., Washington University, St Louis, Mo..

(3) Tribus, M. (1969) *Rational Descriptions, Decisions and Designs*. Pergamon.

Chapter 2
The Role of Decisions in the Business Environment

2.1 INTRODUCTION

Originally businesses used computers for mundane and repetitive tasks but it has been increasingly realised that they have the potential to be used to generally improve operational efficiency and in particular to support tasks which rely on information. There is no better example of this than the evolution of Decision Support Systems.

Decisions, from corporate planning to every day operational control, are an essential part of controlling a company so tomorrow's Decision Support System will have to be an integral part of the corporate activity. This can only be achieved by helping employees at every level to make their own decisions whilst at the same time ensuring that these decisions are not made in isolation but with due regard to company strategy. This chapter describes the sorts of methodology which will be required to provide a Decision Support System which is integrated into a company's corporate planning and control function.

In order to understand this role for Decision Support Systems, we must have a basic understanding of how industry works. So, before we become involved in Decision Support System issues, we must first build for ourselves a basic model of industry.

2.2 A MODEL OF INDUSTRY

This book will assume that industry exists to make money. This is an oversimplification but it will serve our purposes. In order to make money, companies must use some or all of four resources, namely people, money, machines and materials. These four resources are the basic ingredients of industry and its ability to use these resources efficiently governs its overall success.

The word efficiently in the previous paragraph is important because to use resources efficiently managers must control their use. Control implies gathering information, deciding how to proceed, implementing the decision and then acquiring feedback so that a refined decision can be made and the cycle repeated.

Notice that the discussion about what industry is has hardly started and yet both 'information' and 'decision' have already crept into the discussion. In fact information is now so important that most industrialists would accept that it is an important resource in its own right.

Using resources efficiently in order to ensure success is, however, complicated by the fact that industry exists in an environment that it cannot control absolutely. This environment, referred to here as the Business Environment, comprises many forces. Some of these, grouped in a way which emphasises the breadth and scope of the forces involved, are given in Table 2.1. Information about the Business Environment is essential to industry to enable it to make better decisions and the better these decisions are made the better the chances of survival, hence the emergence of Decision Support Systems.

Table 2.1. The Business Environment

Other industries	Customers
	Suppliers
	Competitors
Labour	Unions
	Employment/Unemployment
	Productivity
Finance	Financial institutions
	Shareholders
Government	Interest rates
	Community spending
	Inflation
Social	Environmental issues
	Equality of the sexes
	Child care
	Health care

2.3 COMPANY PLANNING AND CONTROL

The purpose of the infrastructure of a company is to plan and supervise the activities of the company in the pursuit of wealth and well being. Planning ahead ensures that the company is always directed towards a profitable existence or is at best prepared for hard times if these cannot be avoided. Supervision ensures that the day to day activities proceed in an orderly manner. The two functions of planning and supervision are enmeshed since, if new plans come into being, the supervision will have to supervise within the constraints of the new plans.

The relationship between the type of decision and the level in the hierarchy at which it is most likely to be made is shown in Fig. 2.1. The base of the triangle is intended to depict the many, mainly supervisory type, decisions that are made by operational managers whilst the apex represents the fewer, mainly planning type decisions which are made by senior managers.

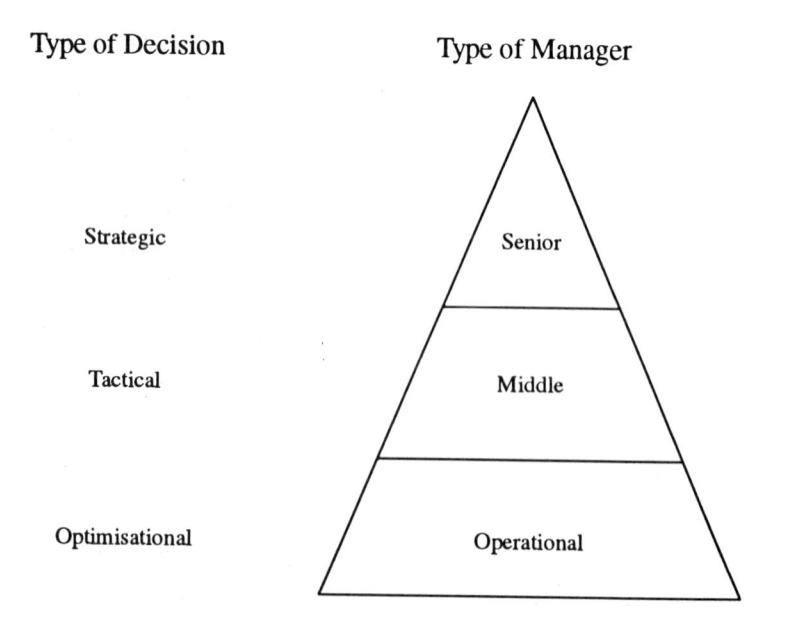

Fig. 2.1. Type of manager versus type of decision

The structure of decision making in industry is shown schematically in Fig. 2.2. It should probably be stressed that we are talking in general terms. It should also be noted that three tiers are not mandatory as any number could be used. In addition the top echelons may also have a pyramidal structure, i.e. a strategic plan feeding several tactical plans, etc.

If we now consider Fig. 2.2 in more detail we can note several of its properties. Firstly, it is a model of the planning and supervisory system of a company. Secondly it is composed of repeating entities which, although they have different names, appear very similar in structure. Finally each of the repeating entities has a single purpose, namely 'control', and two components, a supervisory component and a planning component.

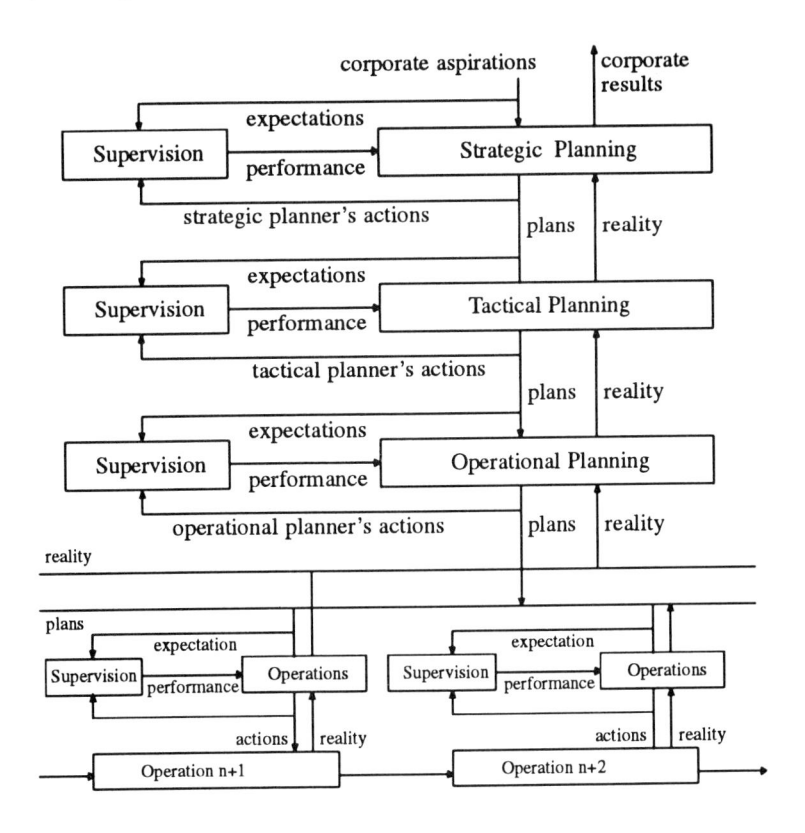

Fig. 2.2. Planning and control within a company

In order to emphasise this point consider for the moment a sales executive who is trying to gain an order. The customer has offered to buy the goods but has offered less than the price the executive's company is asking. What sort of decision is the sales executive faced with? Is it supervisory or planning? At first sight the answer would appear to be neither.

Consider the situation in a little more depth. The sales executive will have been given guidelines which lay down the rules for such an engagement, i.e. the company is trying to control its sales force. The guidelines will say, in effect, that if the deal conforms with certain constraints it can be accepted, if it does not then it must be referred to a higher authority.

In other words, the sales executives have certain targets to meet which are set by their management. They can plan their own campaigns within the constraints set by the targets but, if their plans fail, they will then have to make a planning type decision, e.g. 'do I modify my selling technique or stick to the original?', 'do I let this sale go or refer it to my management?', etc. However, if in order to gain a sale a sales executive breaks the company's guidelines then that executive's manager will be faced with a supervisory type of decision.

If, on the other hand, the executive returns to his company having failed to clinch the deal, someone in higher authority may be able to accept the customer's offer. If they do, they have modified their plans but they should in turn be working within more flexible guidelines. The senior management cannot hope to fulfil their plans if they do not discipline themselves to execute them properly, but equally they would be foolish to continue to execute a plan which had clearly become impractical. So, it is important to distinguish between ensuring that a plan is correctly executed, i.e. supervisory decisions, and modifying existing plans, i.e. planning decisions. It is also important to appreciate that both of these are an integral part of control.

Notice also that the purpose of the decisions in the higher echelons of the pyramid is to limit the scope of those lower down. The sales executives are not free to pursue any action they like because they have to conform to the guidelines imposed by the management. This limiting of the scope of lower decisions is essential. The lower decisions involve far more detail. If their scope was not limited, the number of possibilities which would have to be considered would be endless and they would be very difficult, if not impossible, to make.

Not all authors agree with this sort of analysis. Moore and Chang (1) argue strongly that Decision Support Systems should not use the structure of the decisions as a basis for the design of a Decision Support System. Mintzberg (2) also argues that managers spend a large proportion of their time on activities other than organising, planning and controlling operations. However, this does not invalidate the approach taken here. The planning and control function is essential to business and the sort of decision structures where the decisions high in the structure limit the scope of those below is typical of industry.

2.4 A MODEL FOR PLANNING AND CONTROL

In order to understand the nature of planning and supervision in depth we must understand control. Fortunately control is very common in life and is well understood. Furthermore, control possesses fundamental properties regardless of whether it is being used to fly an aircraft, to change a set of traffic lights or to influence human behaviour. In fact control is a specialised type of automated decision making in its own right. Other authors have also suggested adopting a control like closed loop decision process, e.g. Winograd and Flores (3), so let us look a little more closely at the fundamentals of control.

The absolutely essential ingredient of control is feedback. All attempts at achieving targets by dead reckoning have failed. Even with the precision which is possible today it still is not feasible to retain control over prolonged periods by dead reckoning alone. Control, therefore, relies on a knowledge of two fundamental pieces of information namely, the target which is to achieved and some form of feedback which provides information about deviations from the target. Both of these need further qualification.

2.4.1 The Target

An absolute target is unachievable so a degree of error has to be tolerated. The tighter these tolerances are, the more difficult the target is to achieve and hence more effort has to go into the control. Typically, the loosest tolerances commensurate with overall success should be chosen. In addition the target may not be a single dimensional object and the attainment of one aspect may be at the expense of another. Consequently the target has to be specified in terms of a set of standards which should be met. Frequently the standards involve cost, quality, quantity, time and materials.

2.4.2 Feedback

The feedback which is required is that which enables the supervisor to tell whether or not the standards have been met. It should also enable the supervisor to deduce whether or not the target is being achieved.

The distinction between the standards which are measurable entities designed to ensure a goal is met and the target which is the goal is important as we shall see later.

The final point to make about feedback is that it should be timely. Clearly the difficulty of hitting a target increases with increasing delay in receiving the feedback.

Control, as described so far can be depicted by Fig. 2.3. Note that the feedback is used in two ways. It is used to determine whether or not the standards are correct as well as to determine whether or not they are being met. The need for this dual role can easily be explained with an example.

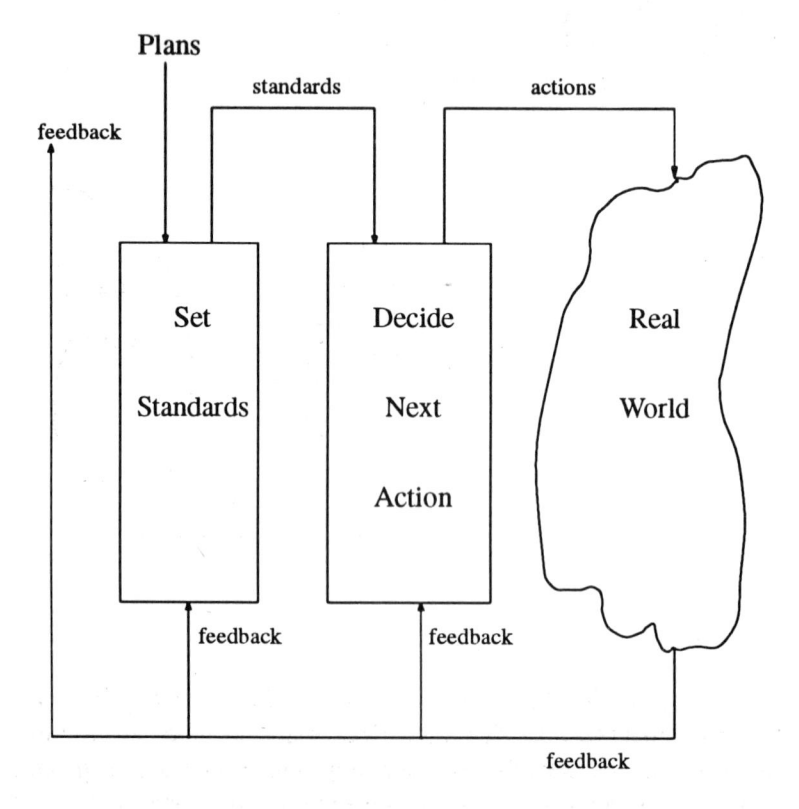

Fig. 2.3. The basic control loop

Suppose a clothing factory has several dresses returned because they tore for no apparent reason. The tears are diagnosed to be due to seams which have failed. These could have been sewn too near to the edge of the fabric but measurement of the seams confirms that they conform to the appropriate standards. The fabric concerned also meets the standards which cover it. In other words, quality control, i.e. supervision, was not at fault. In this case either the standards governing the seams or the standards governing the fabrics must be changed in order to achieve the target, i.e. a good quality garment.

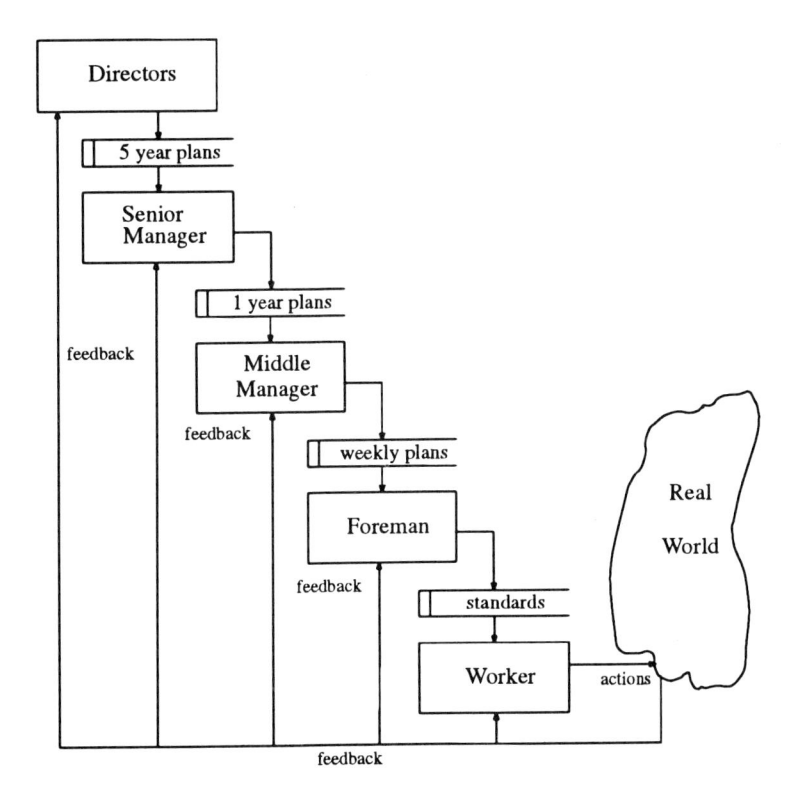

Fig. 2.4. A planning cascade

Note that in Fig. 2.3 there are two loops. The action loop is the one which compares actual with planned and makes changes accordingly. In the sense used here this is a planning function because it plans a new course of action given some feedback about the current level of success. The loop which modifies the standards is no different, however. If the standards do not produce the desired effect then the standards will have to be changed but they can only be changed within the constraints set by the plans. If the standards need to be changed more than is permissible under the plans then the plans themselves will have to be changed, so Fig. 2.3 can be incrementally extended backwards as shown in Fig. 2.4.

There is no point in planning if the plans are not implemented and this is the role of the supervisor. All the boxes in Fig. 2.4 represent planning type decisions, so where does the supervisor fit into the control model? The answer is depicted by Fig. 2.5.

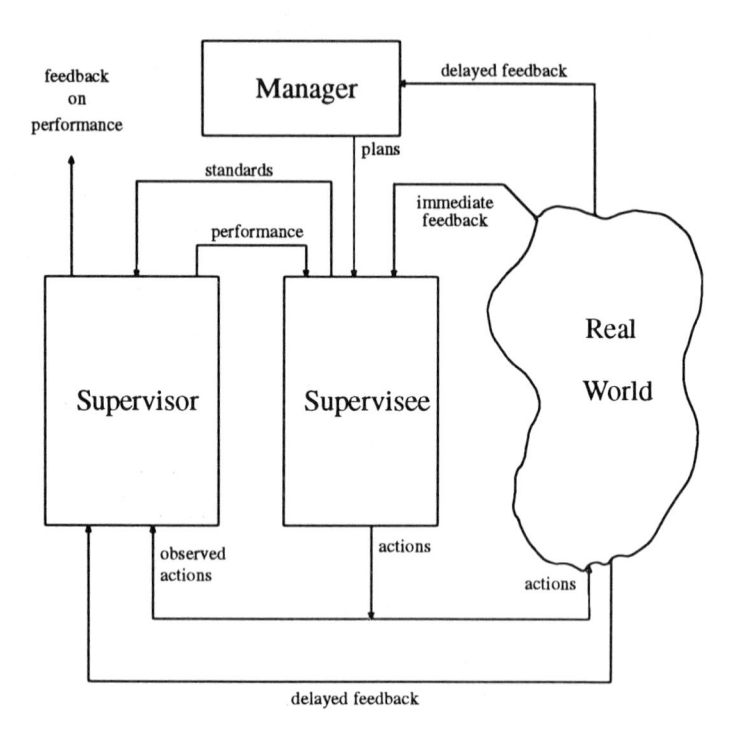

Fig. 2.5. The role of the supervisor

In Fig. 2.5 the role of the supervisor is clear. The supervisor decides whether or not the supervisee's actions conform with the standards. In other words the function of the supervisor is to raise the alarm if the supervisee is not actioning the plan properly, but, in human systems, the manager often plays the dual role of manager and supervisor as depicted in Fig. 2.6.

For our purposes it would be far better if these two functions were separated as shown in Fig. 2.5, although they could continue to be done by one person. A more interesting possibility, which will be discussed in a later chapter, is that everybody could take responsibility for ensuring the quality of their own performance, i.e. be self-supervising.

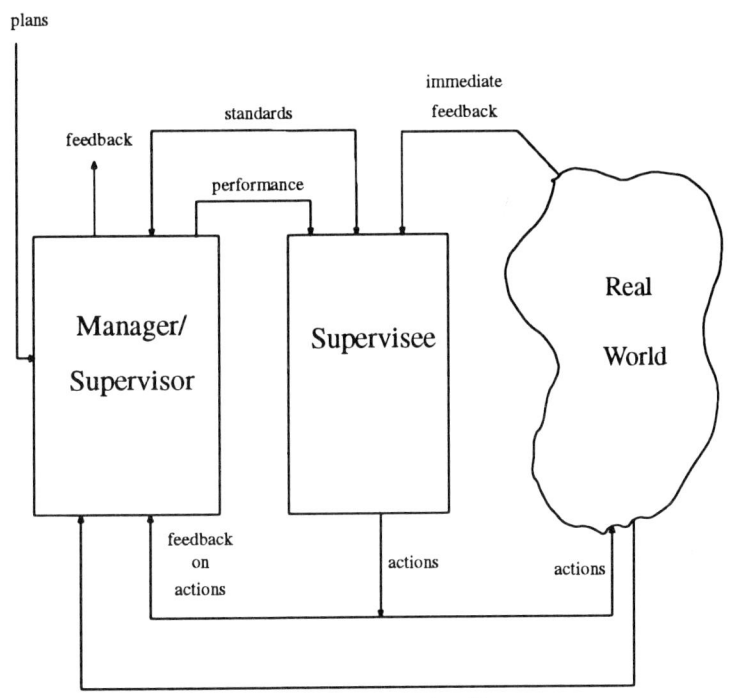

Fig. 2.6. The dual role of the manager/supervisor

Incorporating the ideas from Fig. 2.5 into those from Fig. 2.4 reveals that the Planning Model of a company has become a cascade type of model with level upon level of similar functions. Once we recognise that the plans of a planner are equivalent to the actions of a controller then the whole sequence of events is seen to be repeatedly using fundamentally the same process as it refines a strategy into operational details. Meanwhile, at each stage a supervisory function is checking the satisfactory execution of the plans for that stage. This is depicted by Fig. 2.7.

If the role of the supervisor is to check satisfactory execution of the plans then we must ask ourselves what type of decision a supervisory decision is. We do this by looking at the role of the supervisor. The role of the supervisor is simply to decide whether or not the supervisee is acting according to the plans. If the supervisor decides that the supervisee is not acting according to the plans then somebody has to plan what action to take to remedy the situation. But, the someone is not the supervisor. It is a line management or personnel problem. Thus the system is back in a planning mode but the context has changed. In computer parlance, the supervisor has raised an exception.

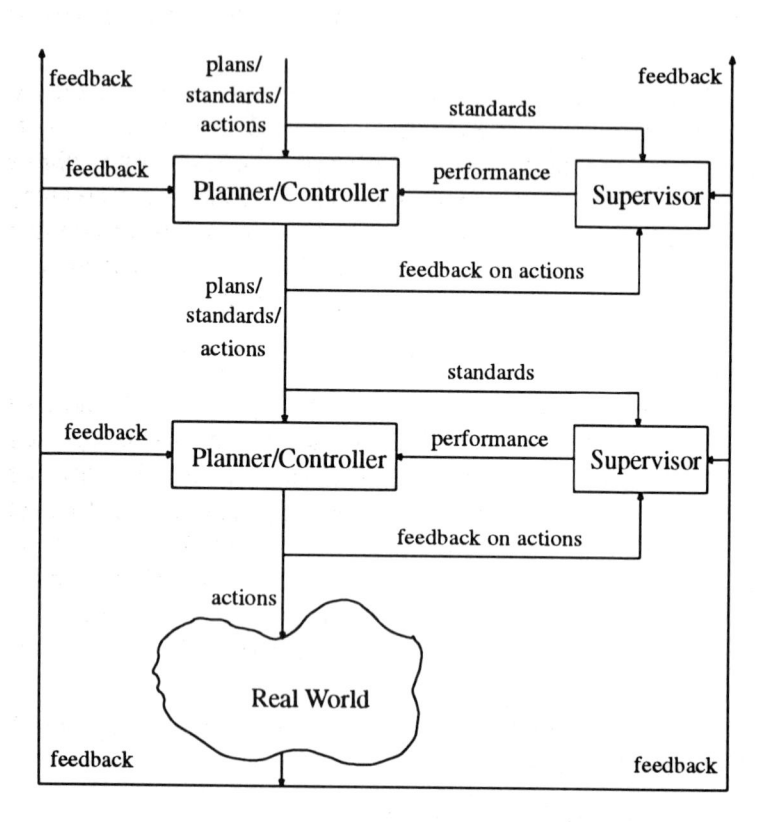

Fig. 2.7. The separation of supervision from planning

For clarification of this point consider a very simple controller which has to keep a tank of water at a pre-set temperature by switching a heater on and off. The controller is told what the temperature of the water should be and it also has feedback which tells it what the current temperature is. Its task is to devise a plan for the next increment of time. This plan should either be to switch on the heater or to turn it off.

Now suppose that nothing happens. The controller's supervisor detects and reports this fact and a whole new set of maintenance type plans are required to find and correct the fault.

From the above example it should be clear that the supervisor initiates a whole hierarchy of planning decisions in an entirely different domain from that in which the supervisor was working. This mechanism works from the highest levels of industry downwards. Consequently, industry is driven by planning decisions which decide what must be done and by supervisors who promote what is good and flag what is bad.

A Planning Model of a business can, therefore, be constructed from several cascade models each modelling one of the various functions within that business. The cascades will interact in places and will not be the same height or the same breadth but jointly they will model the activities of the company. The attraction of modelling a company in this manner is that each cascade, in isolation, will respond to analysis on a scale which is manageable.

2.5 TESTING THE PLANNING MODEL

If a cascade model of the type depicted by Fig. 2.4 could indeed be used to represent a Planning Model for a company it would greatly simplify the design of Decision Support Systems. There is a structure and a primitive sort of logic connecting this structure. The structure would depict the decisions and the outside world and the logic would represent the flow of information between decisions and between the decisions and the outside world. But, in order to discover if the model is adequate, we will have to examine the control loops used in industry.

Companies generally support three types of control loops which will be identified here as:

(1) Strategic/Tactical Control.

(2) Business Control.

(3) Operational Control.

In order to determine whether or not the model proposed is adequate we must test to see if it represents these functions.

2.5.1 Strategic/Tactical Control

Directors make strategic decisions with an eye on the business environment, both as it is and as predicted, and with a full knowledge of the performance of their company. The strategic decisions result in a set of directives, e.g. five year plans, which will be passed on to middle management. On receipt of the set of directives, middle management will start the task of transforming them into tactical plans. In order to do this they too will need information about the business environment and their company's performance but they will be interested in shorter timescales and higher levels of detail. The tactical plans will be passed to operational managers who will use very detailed information about the company's abilities, strengths and weaknesses in order to derive an actionable plan for the immediate future.

Consider an example of this process taken from a sporting background. The manager of a football or hockey team will decide whether or not the team should play a defensive or attacking game and choose the players accordingly. The trainer and the captain will work out a strategy for the type of game to be played, e.g. who will mark whom and whether to play open and fast or tight and slow. During the actual game the players must decide who to pass to, where to run to, etc. in accordance with the tactics dictated by the trainer and the immediate situation around them.

This whole process is one of corporately deciding what to do now in order to achieve a successful future and it is very much a top down process. As such it fits perfectly with the proposed Planning Model.

2.5.2 Business Control

Business Control, on the contrary, is a bottom up process. Operational managers predict what they could achieve in the future. For example, sales personnel forecast sales; production personnel forecast production details, i.e. capacity, raw material requirements, plant maintenance, etc.; research and development personnel forecast when new products, new processes, etc. could come on stream.

The forecasts at this level are combined and refined by higher levels of management each of which rationalises the information from below and passes it on upwards. Eventually, the most senior managers have a projection of how the company would perform if everybody proceeded along their proposed courses. The senior managers examine this projection to see how desirable it is and then devise their strategic plans.

Consequently, Business Control can be used as a precursor to Strategic Control in that it provides feedback on how things would turn out if the business proceeded with its present plans. The strategic planners thereby acquire both the feedback in what has happened in the past and what may happen in the near future. Both of these are useful for strategic planning.

The word 'feedback' in the previous sentence is the key to the role of Business Control. The proposed model requires feedback from every part of the operation back through the management levels right up to the most senior level. Business Control would provide this feedback and hence fits neatly into the model.

2.5.3 Operational Control

Many people view the two previous control loops as vertical control whereas they view operational control as horizontal, i.e. control of the day to day activities of the business. There is nothing wrong with this interpretation, particularly if it aids the understanding of the overall process, as long as it is not interpreted to mean that the decision processes involved are different.

Another reason for believing that this type of control is different from the previous two is through believing that a difference exist between deciding upon an action and devising a plan. But these two do not differ. There is no fundamental difference between deciding upon an action and then doing it and formulating a plan and implementing it. The decision mechanisms involved are exactly the same. The only difference which must be noted for Decision Support Systems purposes is that operational decisions must be made quickly, or at least with due regard to time, so very long protracted decision processes would be inappropriate for these decisions. In every other respect the Operational types of decision also fit the proposed model precisely.

Operational Control assures that a quality product is produced in the appropriate quantities, within target costs and at the correct time. The effectiveness of this is measured by gathering information from further downstream and providing this as feedback to those operations further upstream. The whole process absorbs quite a lot of effort, typically as much as the entire efforts of all higher levels of management put together. The only refinement to the model which might be necessary would be to add a facility for it to fan out as it descends the management levels and for there to be an identical structure across the horizontal layers. This is depicted by Fig. 2.8.

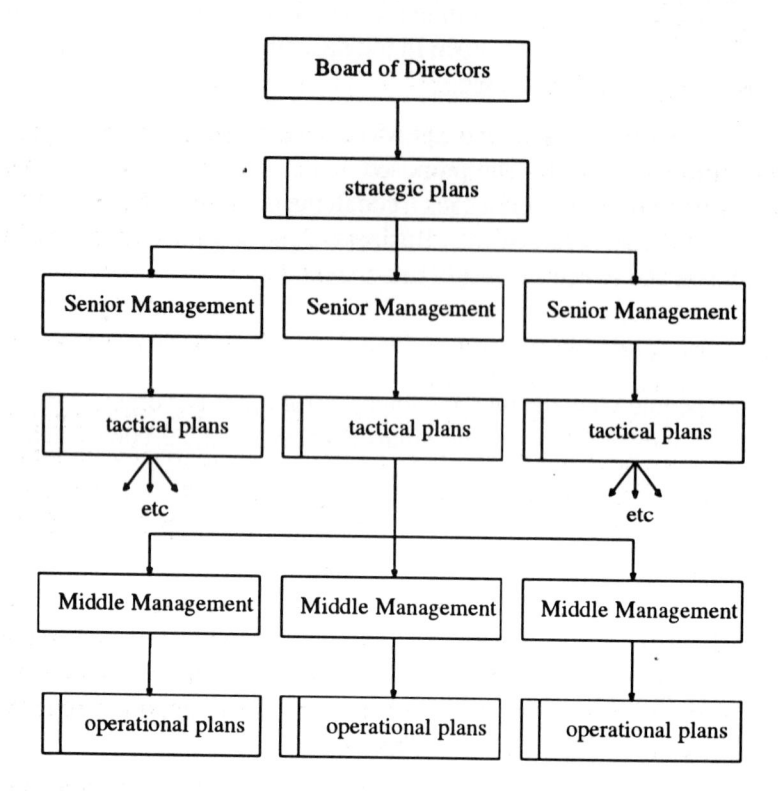

Fig. 2.8. A planning model of a company

2.6 OTHER MODELS

The model described above is not the only way to design a Decision Support System; e.g. Sprague and Carlson (4) propose four different types. However, any alternative model would need to conform to the same general principles, in particular it should:

(1) Be an integral part of the company's infra structure.

(2) Model the important decisions so that the broad nature of each decision is known.

(3) Model the relationships between the decisions and the order in which they will have to be made.

(4) Identify the main control loops and ensure that the associated decisions are in place.

This book, however, is going to concentrate on the model devised in section 2.5.

2.7 THE SCOPE OF DECISION SUPPORT

We have seen in the previous section that businesses use various types of control loops to maintain their well being. We have also seen that decisions are an essential part of any control loop. We have also suggested that a company's structure could be modelled in terms of a Planning Model which would link all the normal control processes of a business into a logical structure. We know that the control processes necessarily involve decisions and it is these which could be supported by a Decision Support System.

This does not preclude offering support to somebody wishing to make a decision which does not fall into the grand scheme of things but it does presuppose that Decision Support Systems will not really have an impact on business until they are an integral part of the company's infrastructure.

There is nothing in the immediately preceding discussion which precludes the very general model, depicted in Fig. 2.8, from being a satisfactory model on which to base a Decision Support System but before we do so we need to address the scope of the support and decide whether or not it is feasible to provide it.

In relation to feasibility, there seems to be one main problem, namely that everyday decisions are too complex to formulate using a handful of really rather simplistic concepts. There are two separate aspects of this complexity. The first aspect is to identify the many decisions which have to be made and the way that they interact with each other. The second is to actually make the decision.

In a business situation we can separate these two aspects. A company or business of any size or longevity has to have well established procedures for conducting their business. The decision structure and the form of the Planning Model should be identifiable from this. In addition the nature of the decisions which have been identified can be studied and appropriate tools devised for their support. There will always be many minute by minute decisions to make and these may or may not be supportable. The main point is that the really important decisions on which the well being of the company relies will be supported because it is these decisions which are embedded in the well established procedures which form the infrastructure of the company.

Consider for example the decisions surrounding a journey from one town to another some distance away. You would have to consider the cost of the journey in money and time and whether or not the rewards for making the journey were justified (i.e. strategic decisions). If you decided to go, you would have to consider whether to go by rail, 'plane or private car, for example. You would also have to decide when you had to be at your destination, how long it would take and hence when to leave (i.e. tactical decisions). You would then need to order a taxi, buy a train ticket, etc. (i.e. operational decisions). If you did this regularly it would be entirely feasible to provide support for all these decisions and hopefully to improve the effectiveness of your travels. The fact that you did not have support for deciding in which carriage to sit, whether or not to have a buffet lunch on the train, etc. would not detract from the usefulness of your Decision Support Systems. When designing business systems we must not allow ourselves to be blinded by the clutter of everyday life. The system will be more effective (and certainly much more cost effective) if it restricts itself to the important things and does these well.

The idea of restricting the manager to the important jobs is not new. Critical Success Factors (5) are a well established technique for trying to ensure that managers concentrate their efforts on those things which will make the company successful. They can also be used to assist in limiting the scope of Decision Support Systems. They are used as follows.

At the level of the individual, managers are asked to identify those parts of their jobs which are critical to the success of the company. Because only the critical parts are identified there should not be very many (if there was a genuinely large number the job could not be done well by one person and should be reappraised). The managers, having decided what the really important parts of their jobs are, can then concentrate on these parts thus ensuring that the job is done well.

The principle can be extended to company wide issues. For example, if a car manufacturer decided that stylish bodywork and well appointed interiors were the two critical factors in selling cars, then it would concentrate its efforts on these two aspects of the design and pay rather less attention to some of the others, such as performance.

It is a simple extension of these ideas to suggest that similar techniques could be used to identify critical functions within a company. Once the critical functions of a company have been identified then these are the functions which should be supported by a Decision Support System. The argument in favour of this is clear. If Decision Support Systems will improve decision making and the decisions which are being improved are part of the critical functions of a company then the company's business should be improved.

The complexity surrounding the plethora of decisions can, therefore, be contained. The same is true for the complexity within the decisions themselves but the details of how this is done must wait until later in the book.

2.8 THE DESIRABILITY OF AN ARCHITECTURE

We now have a method which identifies the important decisions within a company and the relationships between them. It is a way of analysing the decision structure by subdividing the company's activities until they become manageable, modelling them one at a time and then putting the individual models together to form a Planning Model of the company.

We have been fairly successful in putting together a framework for supporting decisions which was uniform across all decisions and all parts of the company. This is important to the designer of a system because, without these high level structures and protocols, activities do not merge into a system; they merely become a disjointed set of insular jobs which may or may not conflict with each other. The system designer is looking for coherence within the activities and easy communication between them. This leads to co-operation and a unified system.

Nobody, however, believes that every decision can be made using the same techniques. For example a financial planning package would not be able to solve a production scheduling problem. We have to choose a decision making method which is appropriate to the decision in hand. How then, if we have a uniform system architecture, are we going to insert into it very many different styles of package?

Computer scientists are used to this problem. In many application areas the same problem exists. For example consider databases. Once upon a time the only way to access a database was via the supplier's own query language and the user had to learn this language. This is no longer the case. By specifying the form of the query language and by specifying the way in which the databases should be queried, it is now possible to use any supplier's database so long as it conforms to the standards and you know the standard query language. The same is true of screen interfaces for interaction with the user. A user who knows how to use an Open Windows screen handler can run any package which offers an Open Windows interface.

Exactly the same is true of Decision Support Systems. If they are ever to become mainstream products some form of architecture will have to be devised and fixed as a standard. This standard will have to prescribe the framework for making decisions much as we have done in the preceding section with the Planning Model. It will also have to prescribe a framework for taking the decisions, which we shall do in the next chapter. Suppliers can then provide generalised Decision Support Systems which conform to the standards. A whole range of individual Decision Support Packages can then be provided which will all be usable from within the generalised Decision Support Systems as long as they also conform to these standards.

Any such Decision Support System Architecture could do with the full flexibility provided by, for example, the Open Windows architecture. Ideally decision makers should be able to proceed through the general process of making a decision and choose their preferred software for the task in hand. For example, a decision maker who is deciding on a 5 year plan should be able to choose the most appropriate decision structuring package. A person devising an operating plan at a lower level should be able to choose a different method if a different one is more appropriate.

It must be stressed that standards and fixed architectural models do not restrict freedom of choice, personal likes and dislikes, etc; databases, telecommunications and window managers are all proof of this. In fact it is now generally recognised that standards of this type are very beneficial and it is not easy to see true Decision Support Systems coming into being until some form of standard structure of this sort has been agreed.

2.9 SUMMARY

Decision making is a very important task within any business because decisions are an essential part of the business planning and control functions. Improving decisions should, therefore, improve the performance of the company but the decisions are not isolated events which can be treated as independent of each other. Consequently, it becomes necessary to build a Planning Model of a company which shows how the decisions relate to each other and to the well being of the business. This chapter described one such model to show that it is feasible and to demonstrate the properties which any Planning Model of a company should have. It then briefly discussed the use of such a model as an architectural prototype for a Decision Support System and examined the advantages of a generally agreed architecture.

2.10 CASE STUDY: R, B & H REVISITED

We will now apply the above ideas to our Case Study. In designing a Planning Model for R, B & H the following must be borne in mind:

(1) The hierarchical structure of the company.

(2) The fundamental subsystems of the company.

(3) The strategic/tactical, business and operational control loops.

In the R, B & H case there is an obvious way to start. They are commission warpers, winders and sizers and consequently must be oriented around doing these jobs so, if we follow a job from enquiry to completion, we should unearth a substantial quantity of information. If this is done for all three processes, i.e. warping, winding and sizing, a complete picture of the company could be built. This would establish the hierarchical structure of the company which would determine how high and wide the cascade model needs to be.

The next task is the identification of subsystems. Subsystems are of interest to us because it is highly likely that a cascade model can be drawn for every subsystem and they will be simpler to analyse if, at least initially, they can be treated independently. When cascade models exist for all the largely independent subsystems, the relationships between them can be determined and everything drawn together into one large Planning Model. Remember that the purpose of the model is to identify the important decisions, to ensure that the decisions are made in the correct hierarchical order and to ensure that the lower decisions observe the constraints imposed on them by the higher ones.

This brings us to the identification of control loops. The number of control loops at any given level will determine the breadth of the cascade at that level. The control loops are not so easy to identify so we will concentrate on the warping job itself. A warping job, as far as R, B & H is concerned has three components:

(1) A written specification giving details of the pattern, yarns to use, length of the warp, etc.

(2) The yarn which arrives wound on bobbins or cones which are packed into wicker skeps or cardboard boxes.

(3) The beam(s) onto which the completed warp(s) will be wound.

The amount of yarn on a bobbin is far longer than the length of the final warp and there are far fewer bobbins than the number of ends of yarn on the beam. The skill of the warper is to convert the long length on a few bobbins into a much shorter length of many more ends of yarn on the beam. This is done by repeatedly winding off sections of warp onto a swift (a large cylinder), placing them accurately side by side, and then winding the entire warp from the swift onto the beam. Not all jobs are suited to all machines so R, B & H have a selection of warping machines jointly capable of a wide variety of jobs.

In this scenario some control loops, i.e. the efficient use of the machinery, are general and familiar to any analyst. Other control loops, however, need specialist knowledge and emphasise the need for management to be closely involved in the design of a Decision Support System. For example, a warper is allowed some wastage of yarn; the job can be done more quickly if the allowed wastage is high but conversely wastage can be kept low if more time is spent conserving the yarn. Wastage is, therefore, a factor in two control loops, (i) getting the quotation right and (ii) doing the job in a cost effective way. This information could only come from the management of warping operations or the warpers themselves.

2.10.1 R, B & H's Decision Structure

We shall now take a very general look at the business guided by the three control loops described earlier. When we have a general picture, we will use the information we have to draft one of the cascade models and see if we can handle the complexity. Of course, R, B & H is a very small company and we will only have attempted to support a small fraction of their decision making activities. But, if we can design a Decision Support Systems Architecture for a small part of R, B & H, we will have established a principle which we can hopefully then apply more generally and to larger ventures.

2.10.1.1 R, B & H Strategic/Tactical Control

Mr Philip does most of the strategic planning and his plans are then vetted and checked by Mr Keith. When they have agreed these plans a full board meeting is called to ratify them.

In discussions with Mr Philip a strategic control model depicted by Fig. 2.9 emerges. Every year Mr Philip revises his 5 year plan and drafts out a twelve month plan for each of the activities within R, B & H. These plans are then given to the supervisor of each section as guidelines for the following year. This clearly establishes a hierarchy within the company.

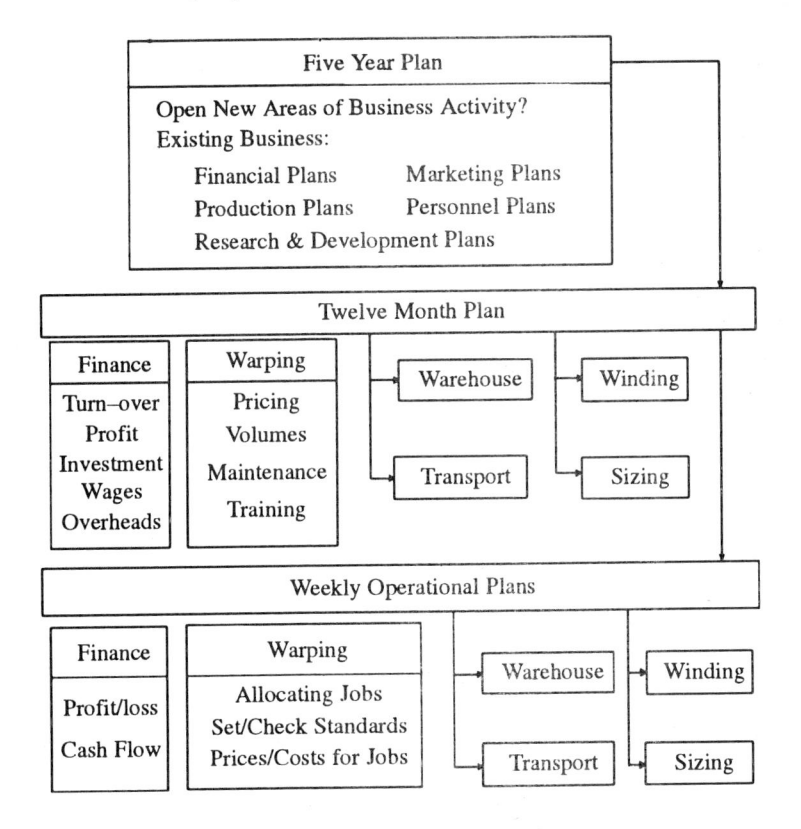

```
┌─────────────────────────────────────────────────┐
│                 Five Year Plan                  │
├─────────────────────────────────────────────────┤
│ Open New Areas of Business Activity?            │
│ Existing Business:                              │
│     Financial Plans      Marketing Plans        │
│     Production Plans     Personnel Plans        │
│     Research & Development Plans                │
└─────────────────────────────────────────────────┘

┌─────────────────────────────────────────────────┐
│                Twelve Month Plan                │
├──────────┬───────────┬──────────────┬───────────┤
│ Finance  │ Warping   │              │           │
│ Turn-over│ Pricing   │  Warehouse → │  Winding  │
│ Profit   │ Volumes   │              │           │
│Investment│Maintenance│  Transport → │   Sizing  │
│ Wages    │ Training  │              │           │
│ Overheads│           │              │           │
└──────────┴───────────┴──────────────┴───────────┘

┌─────────────────────────────────────────────────┐
│            Weekly Operational Plans             │
├──────────┬──────────────────┬───────────┬───────┤
│ Finance  │ Warping          │           │       │
│Profit/loss│Allocating Jobs  │ Warehouse→│Winding│
│Cash Flow │Set/Check Standards│          │       │
│          │Prices/Costs for Jobs│Transport→│Sizing│
└──────────┴──────────────────┴───────────┴───────┘
```

Fig. 2.9. R, B & H's strategic and tactical planning

Mr Philip's main strategic concern is the state of the textile trade in general. The textile trade has always had a cyclic nature, moving from boom to depression and back every 4 to 6 years, but the boom times have not been so good in recent times and the depressions have been getting worse. This situation has been compounded by the demise of several of their customers. For this reason Mr Philip is always looking for new business opportunities and his strategic concerns are:

(1) Determining how long their present business is likely to be viable.

(2) Searching for and evaluating new opportunities as they arise.

In the meantime their present business must be run as efficiently as possible.

Mr Philip is suspicious of banks after several of his associates have gone out of business due to the bank calling in the receiver. He, therefore, tries to run the business so that it funds itself and does not rely on overdraft facilities. Mr Philip must consequently invest capital when it is available and be able to free it again if it is needed.

Mr Philip is also aware that he must cut his operating costs and maximise his revenue. One way to cut operating costs is to mechanise production and reduce staff but in a small company losing staff, other than by natural means, is a painful business. Another option is to mechanise and increase business, but to increase market share in a declining business area is also difficult, if not impossible. Yet another option is to invest time and money in attempting to break into new business areas.

All these are considered in Mr Philip's five year plan which contains:

(1) Financial plans including level of investment outside the business, level of investment within the business (this includes whether or not to invest in information technology and what benefits it might bring), policy on wage settlements, predicted turnover, predicted costs, predicted profit and predicted return on investment, etc.

(2) Marketing plans including pricing policy, which area of the market to concentrate on, plans for promoting the name of the company, etc.

(3) Production plans including the type and mix of equipment which the company should have for the future, production targets in terms of both quantity and relative costs, maintenance targets, etc.

(4) Personnel plans including the number of people and the type of skills which would be required in the 5 year period.

(5) Research and Development plans including development of labour saving and quality improving devices for existing equipment, development of new techniques for doing present jobs, searching for new products etc.

The five year plan limits the scope of the 12 month plans by setting overall targets. The 12 month plans are constructed so that in their totality they conform with the five year plan. A similar relationship exists between the weekly plans and the 12 month plans. This ensures that the required level of control is maintained throughout the business.

2.10.1.2 R, B & H Operational Control

For the sake of continuity it is probably best to consider operational control next. For simplicity let us consider only the twelve month financial plan for warping. This plan sets targets for revenue, maintenance, production volumes (which may be linked to revenue) and running costs. Again for simplicity we will only consider running costs here. We will, therefore, examine the job of the warping supervisor in controlling the warping costs and keeping them within the plan.

Although, at this stage, we do not wish to get too closely involved in how such things are done and how they can be supported, it is instructive to outline practical techniques here so that we do not drift too far away from reality. One way to achieve cost control in a situation like this is to use a 'cost to complete' analysis. The supervisor would have to draft a budget in which the costs for each week were estimated and the sum of the estimates was the target figure. As each week passes the actual figures for that week are known and the actual figures for weeks gone by plus the estimates for weeks still to go must always add up to the target. If the supervisor overspends in one week, the budgets for the weeks to come have to be scaled down. This involves perpetually retaking the same decisions.

Do I authorise overtime? Can I use the machinery more effectively? How can I keep the staff well motivated? etc.

As the year progresses the supervisor will be well aware of how easily or how difficult it is to meet the targets. Maintenance jobs may have to be delayed to stay within budget; on the other hand it may be possible to give the staff an extra bonus. This information puts the supervisor in an ideal position to undertake the control process.

2.10.1.3 R, B & H Business Control

Although all three control processes should be running concurrently it is easiest to visualise them as being sequential, in which case business control is the final operation which ties the other two together.

Proceeding with our example, as the company's year enters its final quarter (or maybe much earlier with large companies) the supervisors must estimate the running costs for the next year and perhaps, in much less detail, for up to five years ahead.

Estimating staff costs, maintenance costs, cost of power and raw materials, etc. is a relatively straightforward task but the supervisors should be considering other factors as well. The stability of their staff and possible training costs would be an example. Another example is possible business opportunities or possible production savings. In general, the supervisors should be writing down their ideas for the most efficient and effective way of operating their activities during the next five years.

Once these plans have been drafted for each of the activities they are passed on to Mr Philip. All the plans can and should be viewed as feedback to the strategic/tactical decision making process even though much of it will be in the form of forecasts. If due regard is being taken of the foremen/women's views, there should be a strong resemblance between their feedback and the plans which the company produces for the forthcoming year.

2.10.1.4 Decisions Make the World go Round

We have now come full cycle and we should be able to see more of the detail. We should be able to identify the internal data which can be collected from within the company and provided as information for the decision makers. Some decisions will require a source of information which is outside the company. For example, the company's accountant is an external source of information. Strictly speaking the collection, collation and delivery of information is a Management Information System task. This is discussed in detail later in the book.

2.10.2 A Planning Model for R, B & H

Fig. 2.10 shows schematically a cascade type of Planning Model for part of the decision making processes within R, B & H. The rectangular boxes represent the decisions, open ended boxes represent the conclusions and the elliptical shapes represent supervisory functions which have been included to demonstrate control loops at the operational level.

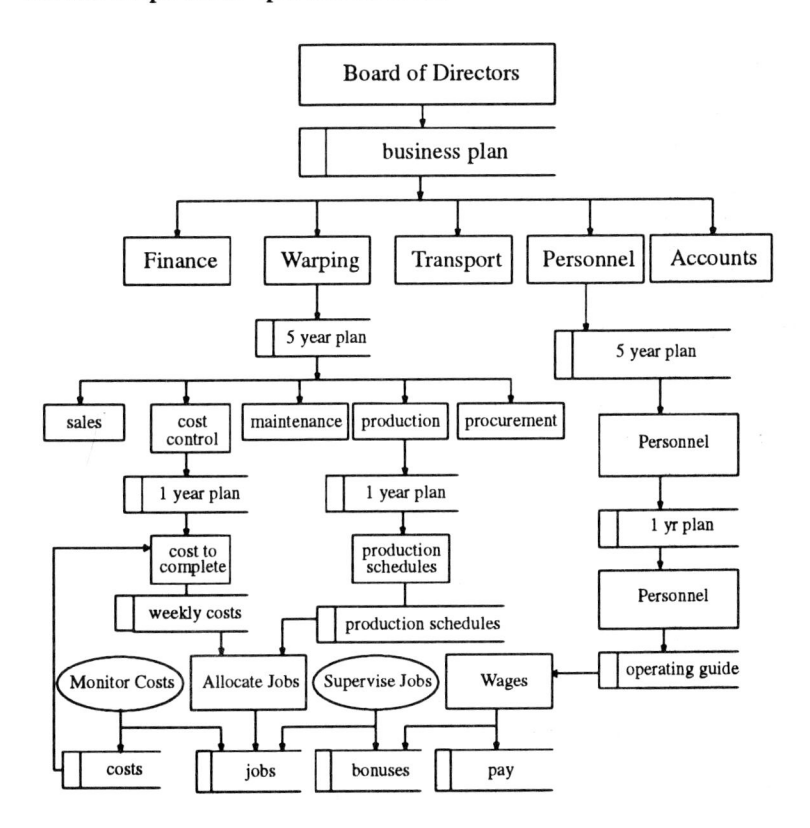

Fig. 2.10. Part of R, B & H's planning model

In Fig. 2.10, the rectangular boxes represent decisions which have to be made and the open ended boxes represent possible outcomes. The open ended boxes will, therefore, not contain anything until the decisions have been formalised.

2.11 POINTS TO PONDER

When it is pertinent, as now, the reader will be asked to ponder some of the issues raised by the second case study, i.e. choosing a holiday. In many cases the issues raised have no hard and fast answers so the process should stimulate individual thought or group discussion. Hence 'Points to Ponder'. In fact this very situation encapsulates one of the fundamental problems of Decision Support Systems, namely that people are different, having differing opinions, making decisions differently and coming to different conclusions. A Decision Support System has to be a single system which is capable of supporting the activities of many such people.

2.11.1 Choosing a Holiday

Consider the 'where to go on holiday' decision and try to set up a Planning Model including strategic/tactical control, business control and operational control.

2.11.2 Some Suggestions

Strategic decisions for holiday making may not be easy to envisage. If you have difficulty finding a structure for this, assume either that you have a strategic plan to visit all parts of the world over several summer holidays or that you have a strategic plan to try as many different types of holiday as possible during the next few years.

Concentrating on such things as accommodation may bring some meaning to tactical decisions such as whether or not to buy a caravan.

Asking yourself how you can ensure that you enjoy your holiday should provide an example of control. Planning costs and using estimated cost to complete the holiday should help bring some meaning to operational control.

2.12 FURTHER READING

- Ackoff, R.L. (1977) Optimization + Objectivity = Optout. *European Journal of Operational Research*, **1**, pp. 1–7.

- Anthony, R.N. (1965) *Planning and Control Systems: A Framework for Analysis.* Harvard Business School.

- Ariav, G. and Ginzberg, M.J. (1985) DSS Design: A Systematic View of Decision Support. *Communications of the ACM*, October.

Ayati, M.B. (1987) A Unified Perspective on Decision Making and Decision Support Systems. *Information Processing and Management*, **23,** no. 6, p. 615.

Bennett, J.L. (ed.) (1983) *Building Decision Support Systems*. Addison–Wesley.

Bonczek, R.H., Holtsapple, C.W. and Whinston, A.B. (1980) Future Directions of Decision Support Systems. *Decision Sciences,* **11,** no. 4, pp 616–631.

Brookes, C.H.P. (1986) Guidelines for Developing Effective Decision Support Systems. *The Australian Computer Journal* **18,** no. 4, pp. 186–190.

Dermer, J. (1977) *Management Planning and Control Systems: Advanced Concepts and Cases*. Irwin.

Doegun, J.S. (1988) A Conceptual Approach to Decision Support System Models. *Information Processing and Management* **24,** no. 4, pp. 429–448.

Finlay, P.N. and Forghani, M. (1987) The Concept of Management Intelligence Systems. *Journal of Applied Systems Analysis.,* **14,** pp. 41–51.

Gorry, G.A. and Scott–Morton, M.S. (1971) A Framework for Information System Design. *Sloan Management Review.* **13,** no. 1, pp. 55–70.

Hirouchi, T. and Kosaka, T (1982) An Effective Architecture for Decision Support Systems. *Information Processing and Management.* **5,** no. 1, pp. 7–17.

McGuire, J.W. (ed.) (1974) *Contemporary Management: Issues and Viewpoints*. Prentice Hall.

Ramish, R. and Sekar, G.C. (1988) An Integrated Framework for Decision Support in Corporate Planning. *Decision Support Systems* **4,** no, 3, pp. 365–375.

Shank, M.E. et al (1985) Critical Success Factor Analysis as a Methodology for MIS Planning *MIS Quarterly.*

Wang, M.S. and Courtney, J.F. (DATE) Conceptual Architecture for Generalised Decision Support Systems Software. *IEEE Transactions on Systems, Management and Cybernetics,* **14,** no. 5, pp. 701–771.

2.13 REFERENCES

(1) Moore, J.H. and Chang, M.G. (1983) Meta–design considerations in building DSS. In *Building Decision Support Systems.* Bennett, J.L. (ed), Addison–Wesley, pp. 173–204.

(2) Mintzberg. H. (1975) The Manager's Job: Folklore and Fact. *Harvard Business Review,* July–August, pp. 49–61.

(3) Winograd, T. and Flores, F. (1986) *Understanding Computers and Cognition: A New Foundation for Design.* Norwood N.J., Ablex.

(4) Sprague, R.H. Jr. and Carlson, E.D. (eds.) (1982) *Building Effective Decision Support Systems.* Prentice Hall.

(5) Rockart, J.F. (1979) Chief Executives Define their Own Data Needs. *Harvard Business Review,* March–April, pp. 81–93.

Chapter 3
The Decision Making Process

3.1 INTRODUCTION

The previous chapter outlined a Planning Model for a company. This model had boxes which represented planning decisions which would need to be made. It is now time to look inside these boxes and determine what they should contain.

In any company, however large or small, many different types of decision will have to be made and many different types of people will be making them. There must be some concern that it will not be possible to find a unified approach to supporting all types of people making all types of decisions. The use of the word 'support' lessens this concern, however, since it becomes clear that Decision Support Systems do not purport to make decisions, they only aim to support a human doing this task.

The need to analyse both the types of decision and the types of people making these decisions does not diminish just because the computer is only expected to provide support. Consequently this chapter discusses the types of decision that are made in industry. It also discusses the way in which the nature of the decision varies according to the role of the decision maker and the ways in which people approach the decision making task.

Surprisingly, out of all this diversity, some common threads emerge and those which lend themselves to computerisation are of particular interest within the context of this book. Not surprisingly, one of these common threads is the need for a structured approach to decision making, another is the need for information and yet another is the need to test the decision once it has been made.

3.2 FEASIBILITY OF DECISION SUPPORT SYSTEMS

One way to implement a Decision Support System would be to provide specialist support for all the decisions which have to be supported but this approach would present the following problem. There are many types of decision makers each with their own way of making any one of the many types of decision. If the system is to have many users and each user is to be able to apply their own method to each of many decisions, then the system would have to be very large and very complex. An alternative way would be to try to find decision support methods which were generally applicable to very many decisions and were flexible enough to be used willingly by many people.

This can be done if the decision making method is split into stages. Three possible stages have already been mentioned: a formulation stage, a choosing stage and a validation stage. If several methods were provided for each stage, i.e. one set for the formulation stage, one set for the choosing stage and one set for the validation stage, then it would be possible to allow a decision to be made using any combination of methods from each of the three sets.

Such an approach would give the decision maker considerable scope whilst not imposing impossible requirements on the Decision Support System. The whole approach depends, however, on being able to propose a small number of suitable stages for making a decision, on the availability of general methods for each of these stages and on our ability to present these, in a suitably usable form, to the decision maker.

If the above approach is adopted, designing a general purpose Decision Support System is feasible. However, in order to do so the application domain must be chosen carefully and defined precisely. In our case that means precisely defining a domain for general purpose decision making in an industrial environment.

Another important aspect of decisions is the matter of risk and uncertainty. Risk and uncertainty severely increase the complexity of decision making and a successful Decision Support System would have to handle these aspects as a matter of course.

Consider a toy maker who is trying to decide how many teddy bears to make prior to Christmas. If too few are made the stock will quickly be sold out and an opportunity to make more money will have been missed. If, on the other hand, too many are made the excess stocks may not sell until the following Christmas, forcing the toy maker to store them at considerable expense. The information required to make this decision is the number of teddy bears which will sell at Christmas but this is information which the toy maker cannot have. The toy maker could make an estimate but the estimate would be clouded by uncertainty. The decision will, therefore, inevitably involve risk. If the toy maker plays on the safe side, there is little to gain and little to lose. If the toy maker is ambitious, there is much to gain but also much to lose. A Decision Support System will obviously be of very limited use to the toy maker unless it can support this type of decision.

In industry, as with the toy maker, few decisions are completely devoid of risk but fortunately methods exist for assessing the risk and for making allowances for a decision maker's attitude to risk. Equally, few decisions are made under circumstances where all the required information is known but again methods exist for estimating missing information so neither of these problems are going to render Decision Support Systems infeasible.

3.3 NEUTRALITY OF DECISION SUPPORT SYSTEMS

Feasibility is not the only general issue which we must consider. Another essential property of Decision Support Systems is that they be neutral. It would be intolerable to have a Decision Support System which in any way influenced the decision maker. So, a Decision Support System should not favour any particular type of decision maker nor should it bias the outcome of the decision process. In order to ensure that the proposed system conforms to these requirements we need to look, in general, at mechanisms which influence the decision maker.

3.3.1 Neutrality and Personality

Fig. 3.1 is a model of decision makers which has been generalised from one published by McKenny and Keen (1). It represents a continuum of behaviour and we need to examine the neutrality of the proposed Decision Support System in this context.

Consider the information gathering axis first as this is clearly an important function to accommodate on a computer. Certainly a computer takes a totally unbiased attitude towards gathering data. In fact it goes further than this. Without some guidance it is incapable of gathering any information whatsoever. The gathering process is controlled either by the person directly or by the decision making process which will have been chosen by the user. The information gathering process is, therefore, unbiased.

Assume that the Decision Support System is designed so that it provides a facility for the user to suspend the present activity and move to an information gathering process. Once in that process the user would be able to request any information they wished and would not be constrained in any way. A receptive user would readily accept any suggestion arising from the decision support process, for example a suggestion based on a 'need to know' criterion, whereas a preceptive person would wish to state what information should be considered. Since either way has been accommodated, the proposed facility would meet the requirement to be neutral.

```
                    Information
                    Gathering
                        ↑
                    receptive/
                    unbiased
                                         Information
                                         Evaluation
    intuitive/                          systematic/
    feeling                             thinking
    ─────────────────────┼─────────────────────→

                    preceptive/
                    prejudicial
```

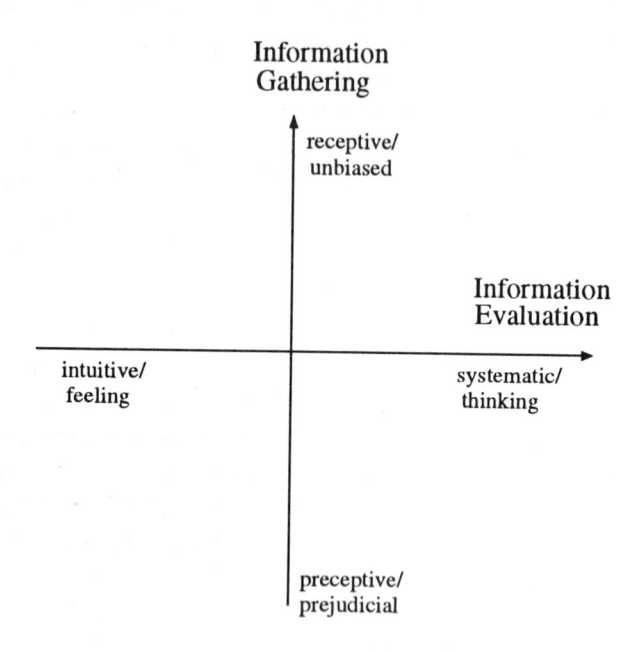

Fig. 3.1. A psychological model of a decision maker

However, it could be argued that the Decision Support System should be designed so that relevant data should be brought to the attention of the user. The counter argument is that some users may be simply containing the problem which could easily be so complex that they would quickly become swamped with data if some form of preceptive attitude was not adopted. In any case, users who are confronted with information which they do not wish to have would, at the very least, ignore it. If they are presented with unwanted information, they are likely to become agitated with the system and stop using it. This would clearly be counter productive and consequently the 'no influence' policy is the safest one for a Decision Support System.

Consider now the Information Evaluation axis. There is a strong correlation between highly structured decisions and systematic approaches to decision making. But, structured decisions are much easier to support, so we will have to exercise much more care to ensure that our Decision Support System does not favour the systematic decision maker. Consequently, it is the intuitive decision maker who poses a problem, so this type of decision maker will have to be examined rather more closely.

If we interpret information gathering as finding out what the possible outcomes are, we can immediately differentiate between two types of intuitive decision makers. The first type identifies all the possible outcomes, e.g. pursues a very receptive information gathering policy, and then chooses between the possible outcomes in a purely intuitive manner. This type of decision maker would not present a problem. The system would help identify the possible outcomes, allow the decision maker to select intuitively between the possible outcomes and then validate the decision.

The decision maker who might be difficult to support is the one who intuitively and instantly makes a decision without even considering all, or even most, of the possible outcomes. However, the Decision Support System proposed could even help such a person as long as we allow the decision maker to enter the Decision Support System at any of the three stages. In this case the decision maker would be allowed to enter the validation stage immediately and would be shown an estimate of the consequences of making the decision in this way. If the possible outcome proved satisfactory, intuition served a useful purpose. If not, the process must be repeated. If this approach is taken, the decision will be being made by trial and error. Alternatively, intuition having failed, the decision maker may decide to use the Decision Support System more fully, i.e. take more time to consider the decision.

An alternative scale for the Information Evaluation axis would be qualitative through to quantitative evaluation methods. The difficulty with this scale is defining a precise meaning for qualitative. Qualitative methods usually imply an imprecise measure, e.g. very good, good, not so good, bad, very bad. If this interpretation is adopted then qualitative will lie somewhere in the middle of the intuitive/systematic scale. The perceived wisdom is that the qualitative decision maker is looking for trends, pattern matching or reasoning with some form of imprecise logic. Support for all three of these can be provided, so a Decision Support System should be able to cope with all types of information evaluators. It would appear, therefore, that a general purpose Decision Support System can be designed to be completely neutral and not influence the decision maker.

3.3.2 Neutrality and Attitudes

People's backgrounds, views, attitudes and even their role in an organisation all influence the ways that they make decisions. In particular, their backgrounds, views and attitudes influence the possible outcome that they prefer. It is particularly important not to interfere or restrict these influences as to do so could seriously jeopardise the soundness of a decision. Generally speaking the values which cause these influences can be categorised into two classes:

(1) Personal values.

(2) Organisational values.

We will consider these now.

3.3.2.1 Personal Values

Personal values are those things which people consider desirable, for example:

(1) A theoretical, empirical or rational approach to life.

(2) The creation, use or preservation of wealth.

(3) A love of art and/or beautiful things.

(4) Harmony and the avoidance of conflict.

(5) To be socially accepted.

(6) Political expediency, e.g. power, influence or recognition.

(7) Comfort and/or security.

(8) Protecting the interests of others and/or the environment.

For example, different people buy different cars because they have different reasons for buying them. People who have a predominantly rational approach may carefully match the specification of a car with their requirements. People who are trying to preserve their wealth may well select a car which is good value for money etc.

3.3.2.2 Organisational Values

People are affected equally strongly by the role they play in an organisation and in industry this is important because it protects the various functions of the corporate body. For example:

(1) Production

primarily concerned with cost reduction, operating efficiency, schedules, etc.

(2) Research & Development

primarily influenced by technical Development superiority and the freedom to explore, innovate and pursue knowledge.

(3) Marketing

primarily concerned with sales volume, market share and profitability.

(4) Financial

primarily concerned with profits, return on investment, assets, cash flow and the orderly keeping of financial records.

(5) Personnel

Primarily concerned with organisational stability and matching available skills to required skills.

However, organisational values are not necessarily industrial. Consider the following example drawn directly from a real situation.

A group of eight friends, all students, had chartered a sailing boat and were planning a holiday cruising along the south coast of England. They were collectively trying to decide which were to be their ports of call. Only one of the students had a Yacht Master's certificate so, in the eyes of the owner and the insurers, he was responsible for the boat. One other student had extensive experience of racing sailing dinghys and had experience of crewing larger boats.

These two were the undisputed skipper and mate. The other six had never sailed offshore and four had never sailed before.

Normally all eight students were not opposed to the high life and the skipper and his mate were no more cautious than the rest. However, in their roles as skipper and mate they were placing severe restrictions on the aspirations of the others. They were obviously very aware that given bad weather and adverse tides they could be the only able bodied persons with the skills required to get the vessel onto safe moorings. Thus, their responsibilities as skipper and mate were making them far more cautious than they otherwise might have been. In other words, they were playing their skipper and mate roles and not their usual student ones. The safety of boat and crew would be greatly enhanced by this modified behaviour.

Organisational values are very important in industry. Since most people subordinate their personal values to the demands of their role, industry achieves a surprisingly high level of consistency. It is, therefore, essential that a Decision Support System does not disturb this. However, there is no reason why it should.

3.4 INDUSTRIAL DECISION MAKING

In order to be as specific as possible about decision making in the industrial environment we must consider why decisions are made, who is making them and how they are made. We will start by analysing the types of decision which are made and then examine how they can be made. This will enable us to establish a generalised framework for supporting industrial decisions.

The senior managers are typically trying to make decisions which would have to be challenged by using a 'why?' question, e.g. Why do we want to buy out XYZ? These are generally considered to be strategic decisions.

The middle managers are typically making decisions which correspond to the 'how?' question, e.g. How do we buy out XYZ? These are generally considered to be tactical decisions.

The operational managers make decisions which relate to the 'when?' and 'where?' questions, e.g. When do we buy out XYZ and where do the resources come from? It may be that XYZ is generic, i.e. an electrical contractor, in which case the operational managers may even be making decisions which relate to 'what, which or who' type questions as well. These are all considered to be operational decisions.

These three types of decision are all depicted by Fig. 3.2.

Attribute	Type of decision		
	Strategic	Tactical	Optimisational
Formalism	unstructured	semi-structured	structured
Questions	why	how	what when where
Timespan	5 years	1 year	this week
Type of Information	knowledge	information	data
Main Source of Information	external	internal/external	internal

Fig. 3.2. Type of decision versus attributes

In general the strategic decisions are unstructured, i.e. they cannot be formulated in terms of logic or some branch of mathematics. This makes them more difficult to support. The operational decisions (what?, when? and where?) are usually much easier to formulate mathematically. In fact, that is the role of the branch of mathematics known as Operational Research. In general strategic decisions are unstructured, not easy to formalise and not easy to support whilst operational decisions lend themselves to a structured approach, are relatively easy to formalise and supportive techniques largely exist already.

It is important to note, however, that not every strategic decision is unstructured nor is every operational decision structured. Consider, for example, the decision to make a takeover bid. If simple calculations concerning the strength of the opponent and the availability of resources make it clear that the takeover in question is impossible then the decision has been made in a totally structured way. On the other hand, if the manager of a shop floor is told by the shop steward that the staff do not like the new work schedules, the ensuing operational decision would be an unstructured decision, or at least one with an unstructured component.

However, the categories structured, semi-structured and unstructured do give some form of generality to work with.

Furthermore, if it can be shown that a semi-structured decision is one which can be divided into sub-decisions which are either structured or unstructured then our Decision Support System will need generalised methods for only two categories of decision, i.e. structured and unstructured ones.

Structured decisions present few problems because they can be formulated quantitatively but even an unstructured decision can still be formulated if only at the simple level of making a list of possible outcomes.

3.5 THE DECISION MAKING PROCESS

Having considered the multiplicity of factors in decision making, we will now look for the factors which most industrial decisions have in common. We shall begin by looking at the decision making process in more detail so that its component parts can be identified and matched with those parts of a Decision Support System which have already been proposed above.

In general terms, but particularly in an industrial setting, the decision making process consists of finding a series of actions which will lead to a desirable outcome and preferably to the most desirable outcome. From the definition alone it is clear that the decision making process must involve at least, finding a set of possible outcomes, allocating to each possible outcome a degree of desirability and choosing one which is at least as desirable as the rest. Add to this the need to gather information and the desire to validate decisions after they have been made and we are left with five steps:

(1) Gathering information.

(2) Finding an exhaustive set of possible outcomes.

(3) Allocating to each of these a degree of desirability.

(4) Choosing one which is at least as desirable as the rest.

(5) Validating the choice.

The five steps above are reminiscent of the scientific approach to problem solving and this may not be surprising. Many decisions are made against the background of a problem, consequently decision making has a strong element of problem solving within it. The scientific approach to problem solving was proposed by Francis Bacon in the sixteenth century and elaborated by John Stuart Mill in the nineteenth century (2). The five steps which they proposed, were:

(1) Observation.

(2) Definition of the problem.

(3) Formulation of a hypothesis.

(4) Experimentation.

(5) Verification.

The scientific approach to problem solving is a generalised method which, because it has distinct similarities to decision making and is well proven, has the potential to be modified to suit our purposes. This can be done as follows.

3.5.1 Observation

Consider the first stage of the scientific method, observation, and think of it in the context of decision making. It is just as important to observe any situation which is going to involve making a decision as it is to observe a problem.

One reason for this is that we must ensure that the correct decision is being addressed, i.e. that we are making a decision about the real problem and not one of the symptoms. If we have not identified the decision which must be made, we cannot expect to find a suitable possible outcome. Equally, if we have identified the decision wrongly, the wrong possible outcome is likely to be chosen. In both these cases a formal process for structuring the decision would reveal the shortcomings of the observation stage.

It should be noted that the observations continue throughout the decision making process. In the first place observations are made to establish what the decision is about. After that observations are made to find possible outcomes and then observations are made to attach a degree of desirability to the possible outcomes. Observations will also be needed for the validation step. Consequently, an information gathering facility, i.e. the decision making equivalent of observation, is required throughout the decision making process.

3.5.2 Structuring the Decision

This step is the equivalent of defining the problem and, like problem definition, it is a very important step. The discipline of defining the problem has long been known to be one of the major contributors to its eventual solution. The same is true of the decision making process. Nobody can expect to make a complex decision, especially one involving risk, as a single entity which has many facets requiring simultaneous assessment. A complex decision is much more likely to be made sensibly if it can be reduced to a series of sub–decisions, sub–sub–decisions, etc. in which the possible outcomes and risks can be assessed. Each sub–decision can then be made individually and the possible outcomes of all the sub–decisions can be combined together in some way to allow the overall decision to be made.

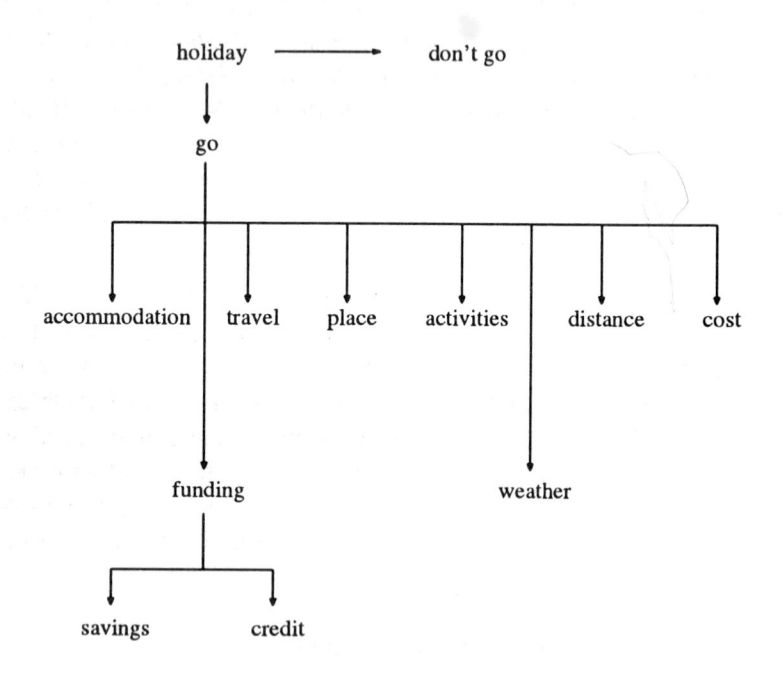

```
                holiday  ───────▶  don't go
                   │
                   ▼
                   go
    ┌──────┬───────┬──────┬──────┬──────┬──────┐
    ▼      ▼       ▼      ▼      ▼      ▼
accommodation travel place activities distance cost
           │                    │
           ▼                    ▼
        funding              weather
        ┌──┴──┐
        ▼     ▼
     savings credit
```

Fig. 3.3. Structuring the holiday decision

Consider the holiday decision. If you try to identify sub–decisions, sub–sub–decisions, etc. until no more sub–decisions can be identified, the result may well look something like Fig. 3.3.

Many other representations of decisions exist and some of these will be presented later in this book. Most formal methods of representing decisions were designed with the intention of processing the decision mathematically and we do not wish to push a reluctant user down this path. Fig. 3.3 does not have mathematical overtones and will serve as an example for the moment.

3.5.3 Identification of Possible Outcomes

This stage is loosely equivalent to the formulation of a hypothesis stage in problem solving but there is a significant difference. In the scientific method a hypothesis is formulated and then tested to destruction whereupon another is formulated and tested etc. In decision making all conceivable hypotheses, i.e. all possible outcomes, must be formulated simultaneously and then ranked according to their degree of desirability.

The approach to structuring the decision, outlined in Fig. 3.3, uncovers the scope of the decision and the large number of possible outcomes which may be available. This is a most important aspect of making a decision. An outstanding outcome will not get chosen if it fails to be identified as a contender at this stage. Failure to identify all the possible outcomes early in the process of making decisions is certain to jeopardise the chances of making a good decision. Given an open ended tree structure of the type shown in Fig. 3.3, most humans will happily identify very many possible outcomes.

Ideally, for probabilistic reasons, an exhaustive set of possible outcomes should be identified for each subdivision. When the possible outcomes shown in Fig. 3.4 are added to the tree shown in Fig. 3.3, the number of possible outcomes for the original complex decision is the product of the number of possible outcomes listed in each leaf of the tree. This is invariably a huge number and serves to emphasise the point made earlier that we cannot hope to find a good possible outcome for a complex decision without some analysis of this sort.

3.5.4 Evaluation of the Possible Outcomes

The purpose of this stage is to attach to each possible outcome a measure of its desirability and then to select one, presumably one of the more desirable ones. An alternative, which avoids the quantitative nature of allocating measures of desirability, is to simply rank the possible outcomes in order of preference. The latter is the only way to proceed if we wish to make decisions qualitatively. In business, the measure or the ranking will usually be financial, e.g. return on investment, but other measures are possible.

It may be necessary to search for additional information at this stage. For example, consider the holiday decision again. The possible outcomes that are given in Fig. 3.4 are only 'generic' in nature. It may well be that a particular user chooses a beach holiday with hotel accommodation in a faraway place. The decision maker would then have to find all possible holidays meeting this criterion and choose one of them.

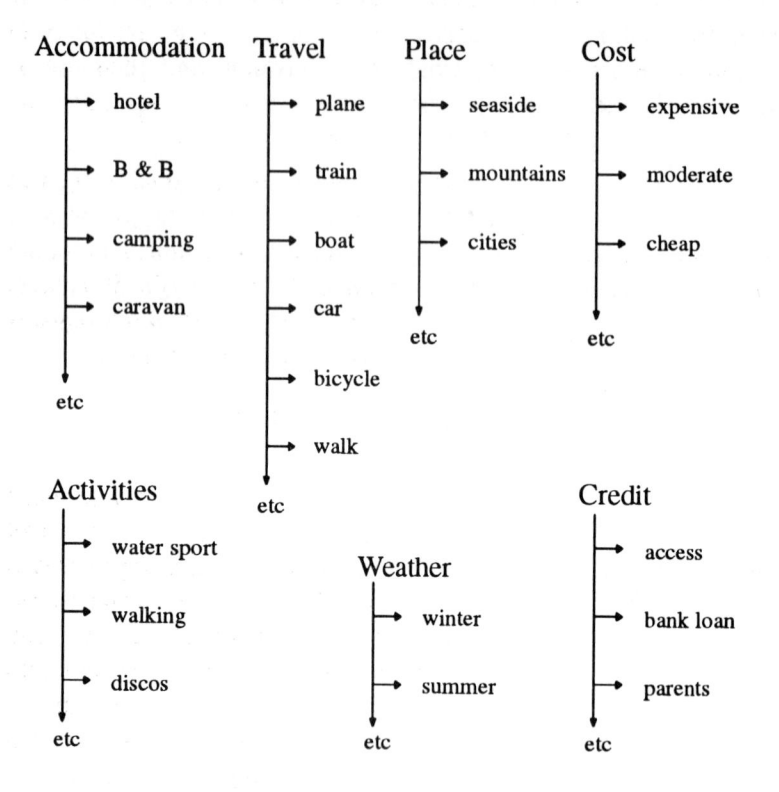

Accommodation
- hotel
- B & B
- camping
- caravan
- etc

Travel
- plane
- train
- boat
- car
- bicycle
- walk
- etc

Place
- seaside
- mountains
- cities
- etc

Cost
- expensive
- moderate
- cheap
- etc

Activities
- water sport
- walking
- discos
- etc

Weather
- winter
- summer
- etc

Credit
- access
- bank loan
- parents
- etc

Fig. 3.4. Possible outcomes for the holiday decision

3.5.5 Verification

The last stage of the scientific method is the verification stage. In decision making this can be interpreted in several ways, for example:

(1) Implementing the decision and observing the outcome.

(2) Simulating the chosen possible outcome.

(3) Analysing the chosen possible outcome for sensitivity.

All of these are appropriate at some time or another and the first will clearly have to be done eventually. Consequently, the perceived wisdom in industry, if the cost of reversing the decision is not high, is to implement a decision and observe the outcome.

On other occasions, however, such action would be foolhardy and some form of validation is required prior to implementing the decision. One such validation method is simulation. It is now the predominant method for training decision makers to act instinctively in dangerous circumstances, e.g. training a pilot, but it can also be very useful in any situation where the cost of making a wrong decision justifies its use. More will be said about this later.

Analysing decisions for sensitivity is also an interesting and potentially rewarding validation exercise. This involves trying to determine whether or not a slight change in circumstances could result in the chosen outcome becoming quite undesirable. If it could, an alternative outcome, which is less desirable but which remains attractive even if the circumstances change, is chosen instead.

3.6 SUPPORTING THE DECISION MAKING PROCESS

The method outlined above is a very general yet structured approach to decision making and is very similar to a well known model proposed by Simon in 1977 (3). It allows users to adopt any approach that they wish to take within the overall framework. It can be used to both direct a search for possible outcomes and to select between them. It positively encourages people to decompose their decisions into more manageable decisions and makes provision for validating the decisions once they have been made. Consequently, it can be viewed as a very general approach to decision making but it can also be viewed as a framework for supporting decision making. If it were used within the Planning Model described in the previous chapter, the two together would constitute a Decision Support System so we will develop these ideas further.

Fig. 3.5 portrays, in a very general manner, a possible structure for supporting a decision. This diagram will be steadily refined during the course of the book by thoroughly discussing what is required within the various boxes. In fact, from Chapter 6 onwards, this book will devote itself to a study of theories which provide relevant techniques for implementing various functions which can be used in the boxes shown in the diagram.

The general method portrayed by Fig. 3.5 will not be the only way to support decisions; there will be others. Certainly the one presented here would need tailoring to fit a given set of circumstances. The main point, however, is that this is a general method which transcends the differences described previously and, together with the Planning Model, it allows a framework for genuinely integrated decision support to be designed. We can then provide the sets of methods to plug into the various boxes/stages and we have a feasible Decision Support System.

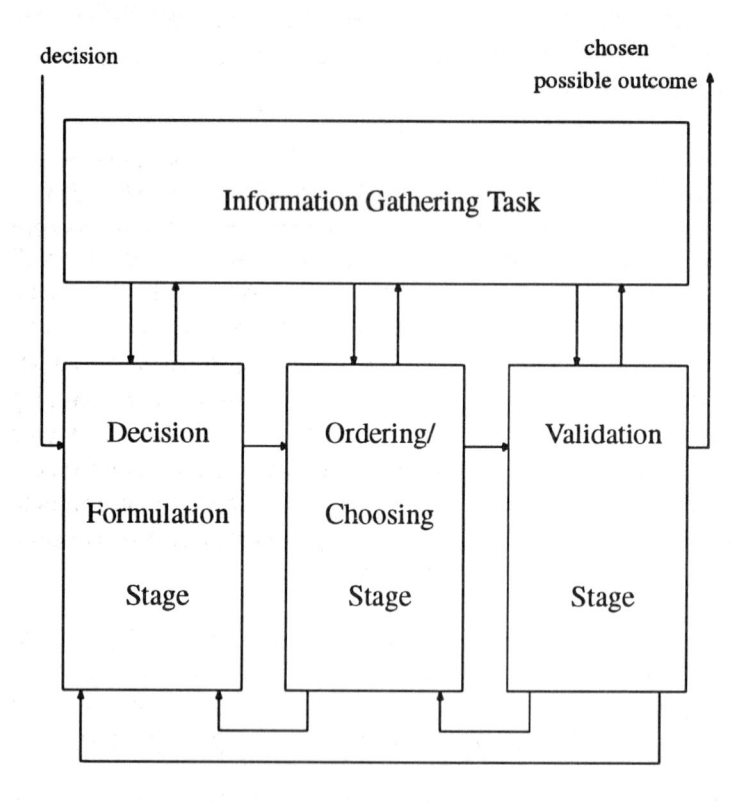

Fig. 3.5. Diagram of the decision making process

Equally, the Decision Support System proposed above is not specific to computers. The present tendency to think of all systems in terms of computers has its shortcomings. A good system is a good system whether or not it is operated totally by people or, at the other extreme, totally by machines. Consequently we should not envisage Fig. 3.5 as specifically a computer system. In fact, in the early stages of its development, it is far easier to think of it in human terms because this avoids the problem of being very explicit about the interfaces between the boxes. The interfaces between the boxes cannot be forgotten, however, because defining the interfaces is extremely important for any computer implementation of a system.

For the time being, therefore, imagine the system depicted by Fig. 3.5 to be a totally human system and think of the boxes in Fig. 3.5 as representing people who will help you, the decision maker, with your specific task. In making your decision you move from box to box, i.e. person to person, but you must take with you a specific request in a specific format. For example, if you wish to see the information gatherer then you must take with you a description of the information you require.

The only person who will be prepared to help you with a non-specific request is the person whose job it is to help you to formalise your decision. Given this help, you will request and get information from the person who helps gather information and will work at your decision until you get at least some part of the decision formalised to the extent that you have to choose between a set of possible outcomes. You will then take your set of possible outcomes to the person who helps you to order/choose between them. Having ordered your possible outcomes you can move on to the person who verifies decisions to see if the possible outcome you have chosen is a good one. If the verification process requires some more information you would have to go to the information gatherer to help you to get it and so on until your decision was finally resolved.

In human terms this may seem to be a very bureaucratic system but our concern is how well it would work, Computer systems require a high degree of structure, i.e. bureaucracy, and so this is being deliberately built into the system even at this very early stage.

One final point relates to the information which you are gathering to help you make your decision. It would be very much easier for everybody if you carried this around with you. You, and a person helping you, could then easily check whether or not you currently possess a particular piece of information or whether it has yet to be gathered. You can imagine, therefore, that you have a clip board and you jot down on the clip board all the information that you are using or have used for the current decision. In addition we will assume that if you personally can supply a piece of information then there is no point in going to ask the help of the information gatherer; you will simply jot it down on your clip board and proceed.

We will now proceed by looking at the various tasks depicted by Fig. 3.5 in more detail.

3.6.1 The Information Gatherer

The information gatherer may have two different tasks to perform, one being the actual retrieval of information and the other being a browser–like task which will assist users who do not have a precise definition of the information they seek. It would also benefit from a third task, namely forecasting. Forecasting is simply an attempt to get information which is not yet available. In a decision making sense it is clearly part of the information gathering function as it does not belong to any of the other tasks. The information gatherer, when faced with a request for future information, would gather historical and current information and, with the help of the user, would predict values for the future. There will be more about this later in the book.

More should be said at this juncture about the way in which the information gatherer is prepared to respond to the rest of the system. Our concern is whether or not we should insist that the information which the gatherer has acquired should be added to the user's 'clip board'. The alternative is to permit any of the three. stages, i.e. formulation, decision making and verification to request and receive data directly from the information gatherer. In order to maintain the spirit of support the user should always have the facility to override the system. If the only way in which information moves around the system is on the user's 'clip board' and the user is free to accept, reject or modify this information then control of the decision making process remains firmly in the hands of the user. In addition, it helps to facilitate the receptive/preceptive range of information gatherers and ensure that any bias which does creep in is either a direct consequence of user action or at least with the collusion of the user. The user's 'clip board' is, therefore, a good mechanism for moving information around the system.

The information gathering task described above can be depicted by Fig. 3.6.

3.6.2 The Decision Formulation Stage

The first step in making any decision is to establish that the problem behind the decision is being properly addressed. You are unlikely to enjoy a holiday if you do not really want to go. You would be better employed deciding what to spend your money on instead.

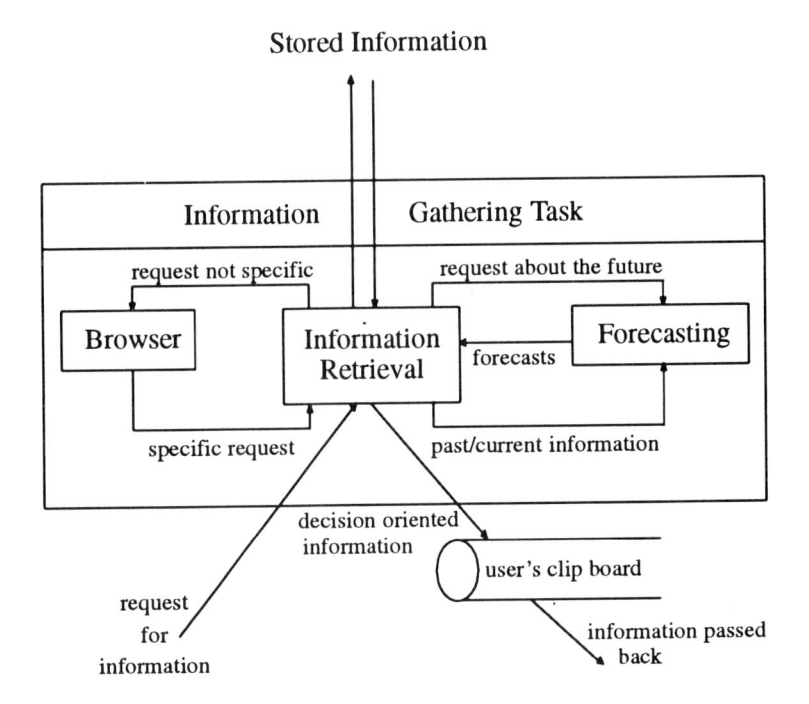

Fig. 3.6. Diagram of the information gathering task

In the business world this point is easier to illustrate. Consider a company where productivity is low due to low morale amongst its workers. If the management is trying to decide whether or not to buy new machinery in order to improve productivity it is unlikely to be addressing the correct problem. The initial assistance given by a Decision Support System to structure a problem should discreetly prompt the user to check that the decision is well founded before proceeding to the next step.

The second step is to decide whether or not the decision is comprised of sub–decisions. It is folly to attempt to make a compound decision without first breaking it up into sub–decisions and this would be one of the main roles of the assistance given to help structure the problem.

Consider the holiday decision. If you are deciding where to go on holiday there are a host of sub–decisions; how much you can afford, what sort of accommodation you want, the type of destination, the sort of activities available, the mode of transport etc. There is no point in trying to make the main decision without first addressing the subordinate ones.

Once we are certain that the correct decision is being made, we can continue to subdivide it until we have identified subdivisions which cannot be further divided. At this stage we can proceed with the text book method of making decisions (3).

An effective starting point for any decision is a Critical Success Factor analysis (4). The Critical Success Factors are those things which are critical to the success of any outcome and should be few in number. For example, if your idea of a good holiday is to get a dark brown sun tan all over, then you should declare this as a Critical Success Factor. The moment you do this your mind focuses on what you require of a holiday and the decisions which have to be made to make it happen.

But, suppose you don't really want to go on holiday and we try to get you to give Critical Success Factors for your intended holiday. In your search for the non–existent Critical Success Factors you are likely to realise that you do not really wish to go at all. The only Critical Success Factor you are likely to identify is the desire to derive satisfaction from the money, or the time, you would save by not going and presumably, in this scenario, you would have other ideas about how better to spend your money or your time.

An approach like this would be relatively easy to set up on a computer. The user could easily be asked to provide the Critical Success Factors which pertain to the current decision and/or to provide objectives which should lead to the same thing. Note that if the decision is one which is made regularly, or even one which has been made before, then the Critical Success Factors may already exist in the system. This would be particularly easy to do if the user had a different 'clip board' for each decision and each user had a different set of 'clip boards'. A user remaking an old decision could find the old 'clip board' for that decision and rework the old decision.

The Critical Success Factors should, either directly or indirectly, lead to the identification of sub–decisions. Having identified the sub–decisions, each sub–decision should start at the beginning of the decision support process, maybe even with its own page on the 'clip board'. In other words the sub–decision should have Critical Success Factors defined for it and then be examined to see if it, too, is comprised of sub–sub–decisions. Eventually, a collection of small indivisible decisions will be obtained, i.e. atomic decisions. A set of all possible outcomes for each of these atomic decisions must then be acquired. This task is the role of the penultimate activity within the decision formulation stage which, in its simplest form, needs to do no more than ask the user to provide a list all the possible outcomes.

Once the user has a list of all possible outcomes, the most desirable one must be chosen but, in any practical situation, some if not all of the possible outcomes will involve risk or uncertainty. It is virtually impossible to choose the best option in these circumstances so some technique is required to allow for the risk and uncertainty. This is the job of the last step in the decision formulation stage. It can be done using sophisticated mathematical techniques or it can be done by simply providing a non–risky equivalent for each possible outcome, i.e. an outcome which does not involve risk which the user would just accept in preference to the risky one. Note that the non–risky equivalents will be less desirable in all aspects except risk but once they have been provided a straight choice between non–risky equivalents is possible. The risky outcome which should be chosen is the one which is equivalent to the most preferred non–risky equivalent.

If the decision develops with time, then it will need specialist techniques for formulating it. The decision formulation stage should, therefore, offer a range of more sophisticated methods for formulating decisions but, if these are to be used from within our Decision Support System, they must be tailored to fit into the general architecture described above. Both the techniques and tailoring will be discussed later in this book.

Fig. 3.7 is a schematic representation of the formulation stage. This shows quite clearly that the output from this is a set of possible outcomes which the user will have to choose between.

The next stage, i.e. the Ordering/Choosing Stage, will help the user to do this. Notice that when a user makes a sub–decision, a possible outcome or an ordered list of possible outcomes replaces the sub–decision in the original decision. This is done so that the original complex decision is eventually reduced to a choice between possible outcomes which are combinations of the possible outcomes from the various sub–decisions. In this way the complex decision has been reduced to a set of atomic decisions each one of which can proceed through the process to produce the final choice.

```
                    Decision Formulation Task
        ┌─ valid decisions ─┐ ┌─ atomic decisions ─┐ ┌─ all outcomes ─┐

        Identification    Identification    Identification    Allowance
        of Critical       of                of all            for
        Success Factors   Sub and           Alternative       Risk
        and Validity      Atomic            Possible          and
        of the Decision   Decisions         Outcomes          Uncertainty
```

non formalised complex decision   user's clip board   possible outcomes from a sub-decision   set of possible outcomes

sub-decision

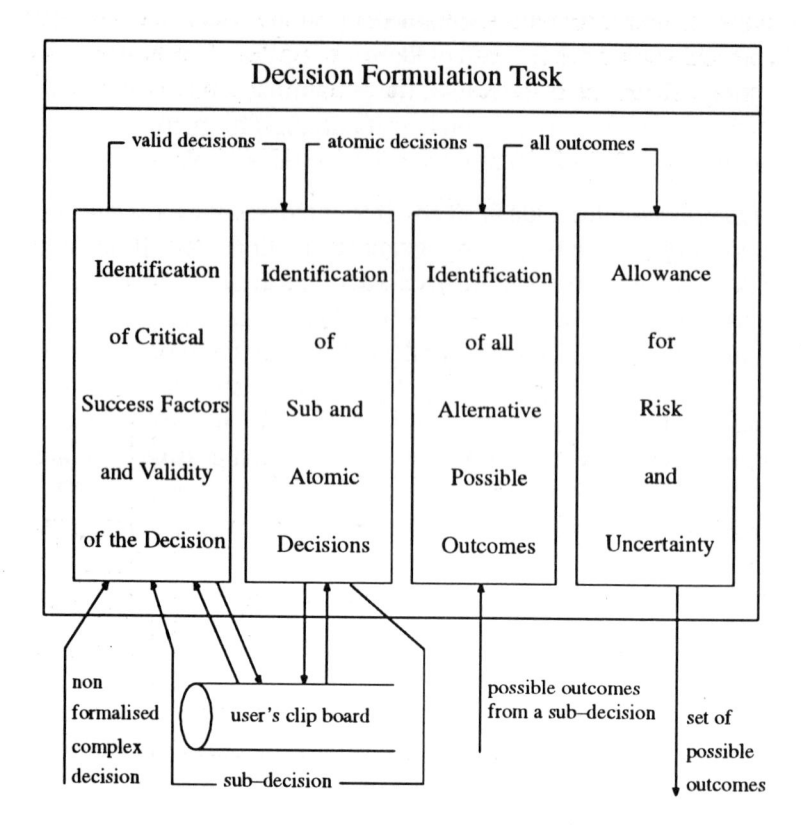

Fig. 3.7. Diagram of the decision formulation task

3.6.3 The Ordering/Choosing Stage

Once the possible outcomes for a decision have been identified the next step in making the decision is to sort them into an order determined by their potential payoff. Helping the user to do this is the task of the Ordering/Choosing Stage.

Decisions have already been segregated into two classes, structured and unstructured. These two types of decision require different approaches to the way we choose between the possible outcomes, namely quantitative and qualitative ways. A structured decision can be made either way. Unstructured decisions, however, will have to be made qualitatively since, by definition, they lack the properties which allow them to be formulated in a quantifiable way.

If the decision making stage is to cope with these two fundamentally different approaches to decision making then it will have to provide programs to provide support for the users to proceed in whichever way they wish. For our purposes it would be worth making this distinction clear and this can be depicted as in Fig. 3.8.

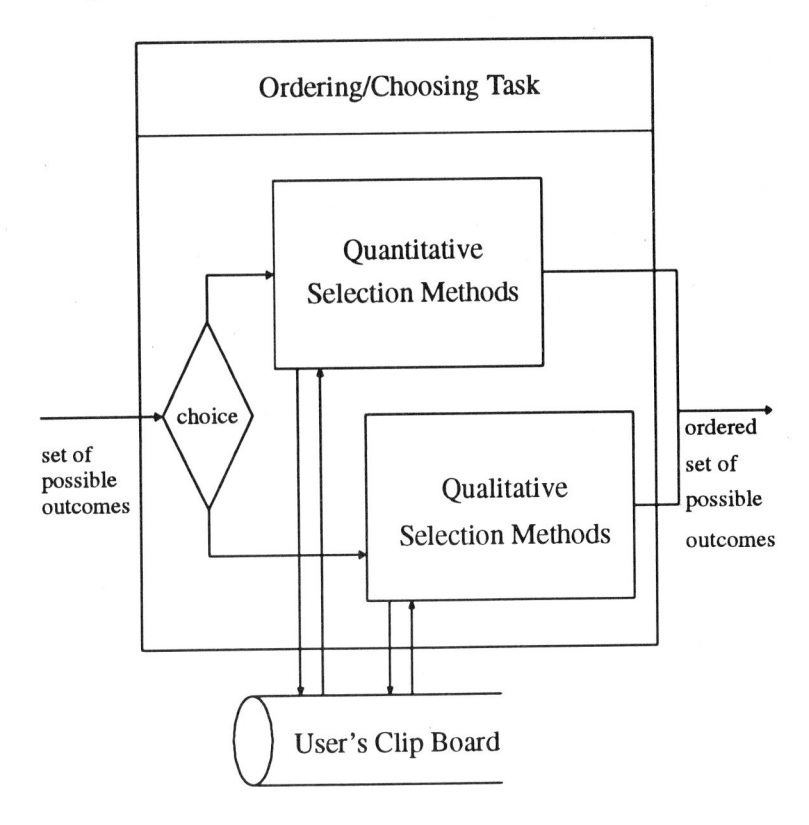

Fig. 3.8. Diagram of the ordering/choosing task

Note that the output of this stage is an ordered set of possible outcomes. The reason for this is that, if the validation stage rejects the first on the list, then the remaining possible outcomes can be considered.

If the set of possible outcomes can be assessed in terms of a single measure, e.g. money, then the Ordering/Choosing stage is a trivial sorting procedure. If, however, the possible outcomes are being assessed using several measures, more complex sorting methods are required and the Ordering/Choosing stage is far from trivial.

For example, each possible route for a new road can be assessed using cost, number of cars likely to use it, the number of people who will be displaced, the number of people who will be affected by noise and impact on the environment. Somehow the pros and cons of the various routes have to be weighed against each other and the best overall route chosen.

3.6.4 The Validation Stage

This stage should take the ordered list of possible outcomes and attempt to validate the first possible outcome on the list using one of the three methods outlined earlier, i.e. implementing the decision and observing the consequences, simulating the consequences of implementing the decision and testing the sensitivity of the decision. It should be noted that a user may wish to use any combination of these three and will ultimately have to action the first, i.e. implementing the decision. Given that there are several possible ways of validating decisions by simulation and that there are also various ways of assessing sensitivity, the validation stage could be represented by a block diagram like the one shown in Fig. 3.9

If the first possible outcome in the incoming set of possible outcomes is rejected then the entire list must be returned to a previous stage so that the reason for rejection can be included in the considerations for a new ordering of the set of possible outcomes. The list of possible outcomes will cycle round the Validation Stage and the Ordering/Choosing Stage until an acceptable possible outcome is found. It could justifiably be argued that the Ordering/Choosing stage should have correctly ordered the possible outcomes but this may not necessarily be the case. For good validation, the validation stage must not use a validation method which is based on the same techniques as the one used by the Ordering/Choosing Stage. To do so would render the validation stage impotent as the same result is to be expected from substantially the same techniques. Consequently, an alternative method should be used to check the decision. This approach is also useful for users who are making qualitative decisions. Having seen the results of the validation, they may well wish to re–order their list of possible outcomes.

It is assumed that the previous stage will order the possible outcomes according to some preference, i.e. return on investment, and that this stage will only overrule that order if some further investigation, of the environment say, shows this to be prudent. The validation stage, as envisaged here, would not be capable of establishing an order, its purpose is simply to determine how a given decision may work out in practice.

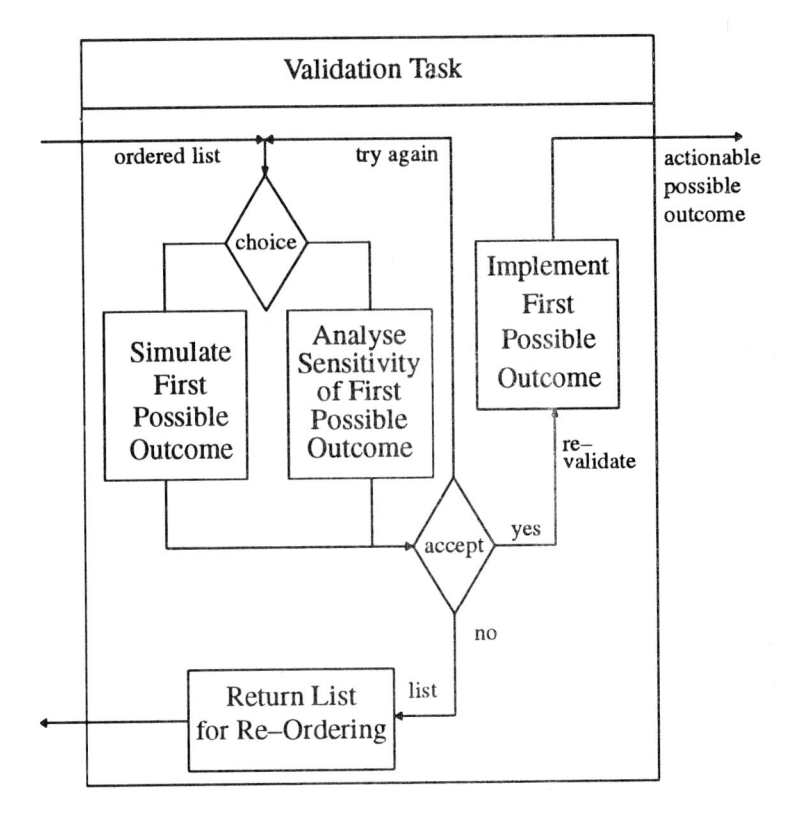

Fig. 3.9. Diagram of the validation task

3.7 SUMMARY

This chapter has examined the different types of decision, decision makers and decision methods and has proposed a general approach which should suit any combination of these. Furthermore it has demonstrated that, at least in outline, this approach is automatable.

3.8 CASE STUDY: THE R, B & H TRANSPORT PROBLEM

Consider again the problem posed at the very beginning of this book. The two brothers Mr Keith and Mr Philip were trying to decide what to do about providing transport to collect and deliver goods. When they were considering this decision in the original scenario, it was suggested that they were trying to make this decision too soon and other decisions needed to be made first. In order to remove this added complexity we will assume that they have formulated their five year plans and are now in a position to make the decision about transport.

3.8.1 Gathering Information: The Initial Observations

The decision about whether or not to buy a new truck is going to be affected by the following facts. The truck is not fully utilised and the driver, who is a willing worker, cheerfully lends a hand in the warehouse when all his other duties, e.g. cleaning the truck, are complete. Many carriers visit R, B & H delivering goods. Some of the drivers are cheerful and helpful but others are not. On occasions, if R, B & H run short of yarn for a job, their own truck is sent to collect some more yarn because it is cheaper to keep the machines running and pay for the transport than to wait for the supplier to deliver the shortfall. Consequently, the initial facts that could be noted on the 'clip board' are:

(1) Truck not fully utilised.

(2) Driver does other duties willingly.

(3) Carriers exist who could and would carry goods onward.

(4) Some of these carriers would be easy to work with.

(5) Occasionally goods have to be collected as a matter of urgency.

(6) Current vehicle needs replacing.

3.8.2 Structuring the Decision

The first step in structuring this decision is to identify the Critical Success Factors and ensure that the decision is bona fide and not symptomatic. The brothers agree that the Critical Success Factors for the overall carrying job are:

(1) There must be a significant cost saving over their present situation.

(2) The goods must be collected within two days of being ready, and delivered, in good condition, on the next day at the latest.

The Decision Making Process

(3) To find a solution which was acceptable to their present driver.

There is nothing about these Critical Success Factors to suggest that the decision is ill founded so it will be pursued in its present form.

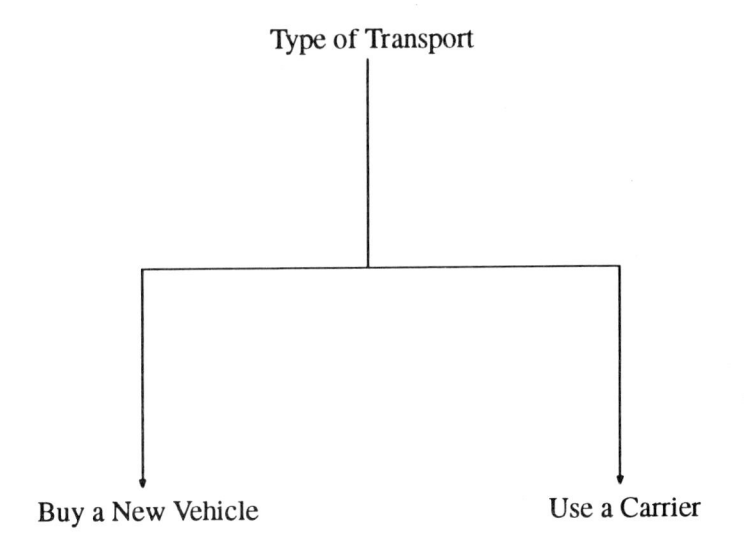

```
                    Type of Transport
                           |
            ┌──────────────┴──────────────┐
            ↓                             ↓
       Buy a New Vehicle              Use a Carrier
```

Fig. 3.10. Structuring the R, B & H transport decision:
The initial sub–decision

The decision does not immediately appear to have sub–decisions, it merely appears to have two possibilities, namely to use their own transport or to use a carrier. But, these two (exclusive and exhaustive) possibilities each raise their own questions. If the brothers are going to use their own transport they will have to buy a new truck. If they use a carrier they will have to choose one and find some way of redeploying the driver. Consequently, upon analysis, this decision does have two sub–decisions. This degree of structuring can be represented by Fig. 3.10.

In accordance with the procedures set down above, these sub–decisions must be individually put back through exactly the same procedure (called recursion in computing). Starting with 'buying a new vehicle' and identifying the Critical Success Factors the brothers decide that the vehicle should be at least large enough to deliver the materials from a single job in a single trip, that it must be reliable, it must be economical to run and it must be affordable (to purchase). The first three of these refer to the vehicle but the final one raises the question of finance. This leads us to consider two sub-decisions, one being the type of vehicle which is appropriate and the other being the type of finance which would be both available and appropriate.

Continuing the process (depth first) down the tree the 'type of vehicle' decision is processed using the same procedure. The Critical Success Factors for the vehicle have already been stated. The first of these suggests that the size of the vehicle would be a sub-decision. The second and third suggest that the type of fuel should be considered, diesel having a reputation for economy and reliability but being initially more expensive.

If this process is continued the 'size of vehicle' decision will be presented to yet another incarnation of the same procedure. The Critical Success Factors for this are that the truck should be able to carry at least one job in one load, be reliable, economic to run and affordable within the context of its size.

These suggest two further sub-decisions, the 'capacity of the vehicle' and its manufacturer. The sub-decision 'manufacturer' being introduced to embody reliability and price. One more cycle of the procedure and 'capacity of the vehicle' emerges as an atomic decision. At this stage the structure will look like that shown in Fig. 3.11.

The next stage is to identify all possible outcomes for 'truck capacities' which lie within the constraints set by the Critical Success Factors. The brothers do not know the capacities of vehicle which are available so they will have to indulge in some information gathering.

On metaphorically entering the information gathering task the brothers go in search of (external) information about the size of trucks. For the purposes of this case study let us assume that they return with information on 1.5, 2 and 5 tonne trucks and that these are the only possible outcomes which fit the Critical Success Factor criteria. These three possible outcomes form the set of all possible outcomes for the capacity decision and as such they are passed on to the next stage.

3.8.3 The Ordering/Choosing Stage

With only three possible outcomes this stage can be completed quickly. The brothers decide to make the decision quantitatively on the basis of running costs. It is clear that the vehicles are more expensive to own the larger they are, so the brothers rank them inversely in order of size. This produces an ordered list of possible outcomes which can be passed on to the next stage.

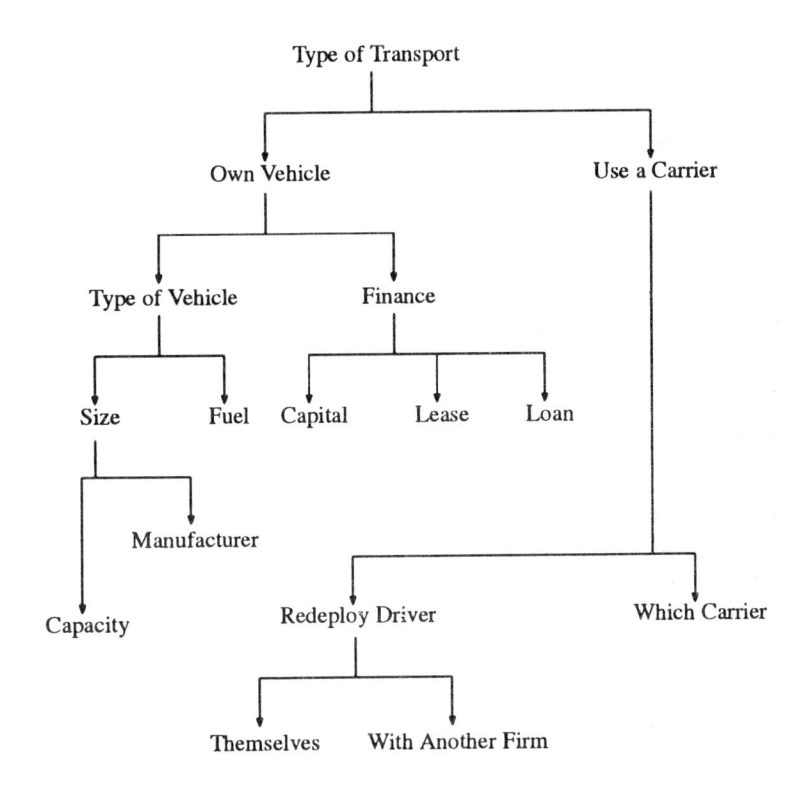

Fig. 3.11. Structuring the R, B & H transport decision: identifying other sub decisions

3.8.4 Validating the Decision

The brothers decide to search their records from the preceding year to prepare a list of load sizes and frequencies (information gathering again). They use this list to check whether or not the proposed truck would have been adequate. They discover that on two occasions the smallest truck would not have been able to carry a single job and on several occasions it would not have been able to carry sufficient goods to keep up with the demand. In the light of this knowledge they return to the previous stage and adopt their second choice, the 2 tonne truck, which subsequently validates without problems.

3.8.5 Continuing the Process

At this stage the procedure returns to the 'type of vehicle' decision but the 'manufacturer' sub–decision remains to be made. This decision will also be atomic so, when the brothers have chosen a manufacturer, the procedure returns, with a 'size', i.e. capacity, and a 'manufacturer' to the 'type of vehicle' level. At this level 'fuel' is an unaddressed sub–decision which we will also assume to be atomic and furthermore we will assume that a diesel vehicle is chosen and validated. By this time the sub–decision being reconsidered is the 'buy a new vehicle' one and the 'finance' sub–decision has still to be made. If we assume that leasing is chosen then we return to the main decision having chosen a vehicle and a method of financing it. The sub–decision 'use carrier' is still to be investigated, however, and Fig. 3.12 gives the reader an idea of what might occur when this is done.

The detail will be left as an exercise for the reader and we will simply discuss here the sub–decision 'redeploy driver'. The reason for doing so is because this is almost certainly an unstructured decision.

The brothers have the future well–being of the employee as one of their Critical Success Factors, partly from loyalty to the employee and partly because they have no wish to cause unrest amongst the other employees. This decision has two acceptable possible outcomes, one is to redeploy him themselves and the other is to persuade one of the carriers to offer him a job as a driver. The brothers return to the information gathering task to collect information regarding possible driving jobs and to use the forecasting facility to predict their likely staffing requirements. Using this information the brothers decide, by simply listing pros and cons, to offer the driver a job in their warehouse with direct responsibility for loading and unloading the trucks.

The brothers are now left with a straight decision between operating a specific truck and using a particular carrier with their own driver redeployed in the warehouse. These two possible outcomes are now the only possible outcomes associated with the original decision and the brothers decide, on purely financial grounds, that it is best to use a carrier.

This is passed to the validation stage where the brothers decide to utilise the information gathering task again to forecast the likely demands of transport for the next two years. This forecast predicts the need to do three emergency collections in the next two years. The brothers realise at this stage that 'emergency collections' should have been a subdivision under 'use a carrier' (shown as a dotted line in Fig. 3.12).

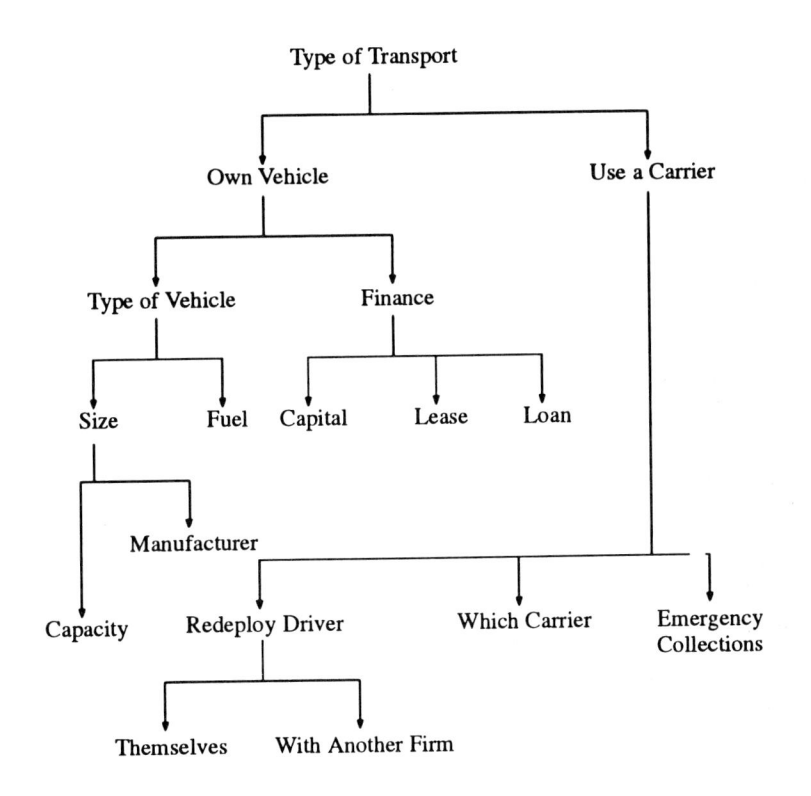

Fig. 3.12. Structuring the R, B & H transport decision: Adding a missing sub–decision

The brothers can easily backtrack and add this sub–decision to their previous structure. All the previous sub–decisions remain the same with the same possible outcomes. They decide that the 'emergency collections' can be most easily overcome by using an estate car as one of the director's cars. The extra cost of doing this does not tip the balance in favour of continuing to run their own transport so this is what the brothers decide to do.

3.8.6 Combining the Planning Model and the Model of a Decision

We are now in a position to combine part of the Planning Model for R, B & H and the decisions from the Transport Problem discussed

76   Chapter 3

above. Fig. 3.13 depicts this by tracing the appropriate decisions from the five year plan with those from the production plans through to the transport problem itself. Note that in this case transport is assumed to lie under the general jurisdiction of the Production subsystem.

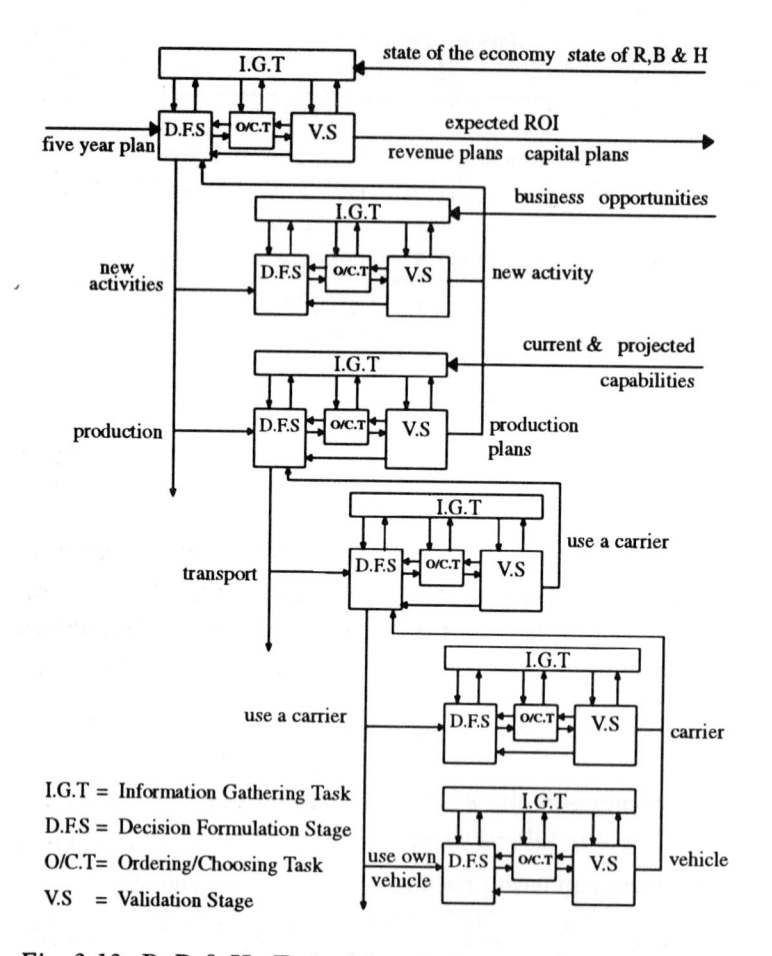

Fig. 3.13. R, B & H: Embedding decisions in the planning model

I.G.T = Information Gathering Task
D.F.S = Decision Formulation Stage
O/C.T = Ordering/Choosing Task
V.S = Validation Stage

3.8.7 Concluding Remarks

The previous case study is only fiction but it does demonstrate that decisions can be supported in a way which conforms to the architecture given here. The reader is invited to verify that the previous procedure is workable, is very general and is applicable to a wide range of decisions.

3.9 POINTS TO PONDER

Take the 'choosing a holiday' decision and break it down into sub-decisions which address the important aspects of enjoying a holiday. Try to keep the model generic, i.e. a beach holiday rather than a holiday in Blackpool.

Keep subdividing decisions until you can provide a list of possible outcomes for each of the 'atomic' decisions. The combinations of all these possible outcomes should then provide every conceivable holiday.

Try to establish control loops, i.e. how do you measure if you liked the hotel; if you did not, why not? how will you modify the choice of hotel next year to try to ensure that it is better?

Get a few brochures from the travel agents and see if you can find a holiday to match your preferred generic one.

3.10 FURTHER READING

- Ackoff, R.L. (1981) The Art and Science of Mess Management. *Interfaces*, **11**, no. 1, pp. 20–25.

- Eden, C., Jones, S. and Sims, D. (1983) Messing about in Problems: an informal structured approach to their identification and management. *Frontiers of Operational Research and Applied Systems Analysis*, **1**, Pergamon Press.

- Holtzman, S. (1984) On the use of Formal Methods for Decision-Making. Presented at the *ORSA/TIMS 17th Joint National Meeting*, San Francisco, May, Stanford, California: Department of Engineering-Economic Systems, Stanford University.

- Holtzman, S. (1981) *A Model of the Decision Analysis Process*, Stanford, California. Department of Engineering-Economic Systems, Stanford University.

- Howard, R.A. (1980) An Assessment of Decision Analysis. *Operational research*, **28**, no. 1, pp. 4–27.

- Howard, R.A. and Matheson, J.E. (eds.) (1983–84) *Readings on the Principles and Applications of Decision Analysis*. Menlo Park, California: Strategic Decisions Group, 2 vols..

- McMillan, C.J. Qualitative Models of Organisational Decision Making. *Journal of Management Studies*, **5**, pp. 22–39.

- Polya, G. (1945) *How to Solve It: A new Aspect of the Mathematical Method.* Princeton University Press.

- Raitt, R.A. (1974) Must We Revolutionize our Methodology? *Interfaces,* **4,** no. 2, p. 2.

- Shirley, R.C. (1975) Values in Decision Making: Their Origins and Effects. *Managerial Planning*, January–February, p. 1.

- Simon, H.A. (1976) *Administrative Behavior.* 3rd edition, New York: Free Press.

- Simon, H.A. (1977) *The New Science of Management Decision.* Prentice Hall.

- Stabell, C.B. (1979) *Decision Research: A Description and Diagnosis of Decision Making in Organisations.* Working Paper A79.006, Norwegian School of Economics and Business Administration, June.

3.11 REFERENCES

(1) McKenny, J.L. and Keen, G.W. (1974) How Managers Minds' Work. *Harvard Business Review*, May–June, pp. 79–90.

(2) Raitt, R.A. (1974) Must we Revolutionise Our Methodology?, *Interfaces*, **4,** no. 2, p. 2.

(3) Simon, H.A. (1977) *The New Science of Management Decision.* Harper and Row, 3rd edition.

(4) Shank, M.E. et al (1985) Critical Success Factor Analysis as a Methodology for MIS Planning. *MIS Quarterly.*

Chapter 4
Decision Support and the Working Environment

4.1 INTRODUCTION

Decision Support Systems will not only address the needs of the company, they will address the needs of the department and the individual as well. This will undermine the traditional power base structure where the person who controlled the information controlled the people who needed it. Consequently, as more and more employees are provided with wider access to information the need for a highly structured, many layered, pyramidal style of organisation will diminish and flatter organisations will evolve.

The provision of support for decisions will increase the scope of such changes. Control loops can be rethought so that people have access to feedback pertinent to their own actions. This, coupled with assistance in making decisions, provides the potential for employees to become self regulatory, further diminishing the need for layer upon layer of management. This will enable companies to move from complex reporting structures with restrictive, inward looking internal communications to a flatter, maybe even networked, organisation, controlled from the top but with distributed decision making and an outward looking, flexible approach to their businesses.

Commercial pressures for change also exist. If companies are going to invest in Decision Support Systems they will be wishing to see a return worthy of their investment. This return on investment can be in the form of productivity improvements, gaining a competitive advantage or the more usual cost savings.

Productivity improvements, if not accompanied by a subsequent reduction in staff, are a particularly palatable way to introduce new technologies into companies. Supporting people whilst they make decisions may not seem to have such potential but, as we shall see later, Decision Support Systems may be an enabling mechanism in the quest for a more dedicated work force and hence higher productivity.

Fortunately Decision Support Systems are not likely to make many people redundant as their use is much more likely to be justified through 'competitive edge' than cost saving but their impact on our lives might nevertheless be quite dramatic.

4.2 DECISION SUPPORT SYSTEMS AND PRODUCTIVITY

Decision Support Systems have the potential for improving productivity and the promise of better productivity is a strong incentive to industrialists because it is one of the few counter inflationary forces over which they have direct control.

Most of the things which cause inflation, e.g. an increase in the cost of raw materials, cannot be entirely controlled by managers. These inflationary forces form a vicious circle. If raw material prices rise, for example, then the cost of goods will rise. If the cost of goods rises then people want more pay so that they can maintain their purchasing power. If pay rises then the cost of goods rises again and so it goes on. The only way to stop this is to increase productivity since productivity increases are cost reductions in real terms.

Productivity improvements are not necessarily synonymous with making employees work harder, however. Productivity improvements can mean employees working more effectively. Put another way, it means 'more brains and less brawn' which in business means more ingenuity, more inventiveness and more appropriate equipment. In the context of Decision Support Systems it means taking forward looking decisions and handling risk better. To the employee it means job enrichment and more responsibility, i.e. less boredom, but it may also mean a different way of working.

4.3 DECISION SUPPORT SYSTEMS AND THE COMPANY ORGANISATION

In the past companies were organised on a fairly rigid hierarchical structure. Alternative structures have been tried but there remains, inherent in the system, a hierarchical mentality. In such an organisation, which is depicted in Fig. 4.1, staff look inwards and upwards because that is where the directives, the promotion and the rewards come from. This results in the archetypal 'company man'.

These organisations are also very restrictive in other ways. They lead to complex reporting structures, unnecessary layers of management and are a breeding ground for empire builders. They also lend themselves to a 'buck passing' system where decisions are not made at the level at which they arise but are pushed upwards. This can cause a situation where those who are technically competent to make the decision do not have the authority to make it and those who have the authority to make it no longer have sufficient contact with the everyday business to be able to make it competently.

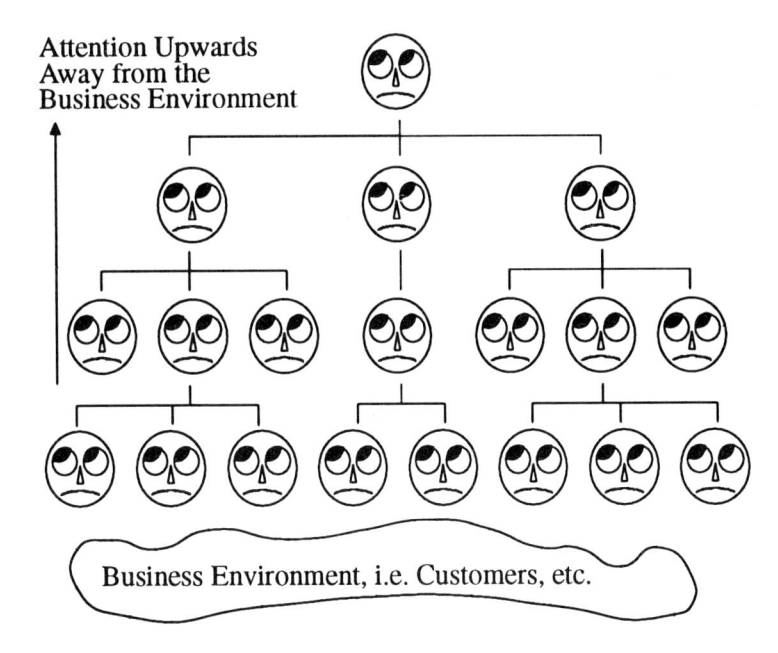

Fig. 4.1. Hierarchical reporting structures

If Decision Support Systems are brought into this situation many things could change. The people next to the business environment could have both the information and the support that they need to take their own decisions wisely. The company would then not require many layers of management because it would be possible for each manager to lead a far larger group of people. In fact it might even be possible for large groups of peers to work together, resolving their own conflicts and passing and receiving the information they need to do their job.

If this were possible companies would be able to adopt far flatter organisations and the organisations themselves would be more flexible, more willing and able to change, more innovative etc. and consequently more likely to be successful. Such an organisation is depicted by Fig. 4.2. In this organisation the bulk of the employees are concerned about the customer, the suppliers and the rest of the business environment. They have the information and the support they require from a networked Decision Support System. The managers have access to the same systems via a gateway. The purpose of the gateway is to prevent the managers from becoming overloaded with detail. When they need reports, they will have access to them and when they feel that they really need the detail, they will have access to that too. The gateways would also allow managers to pass down general directives so that they can retain strategic and tactical control of the business.

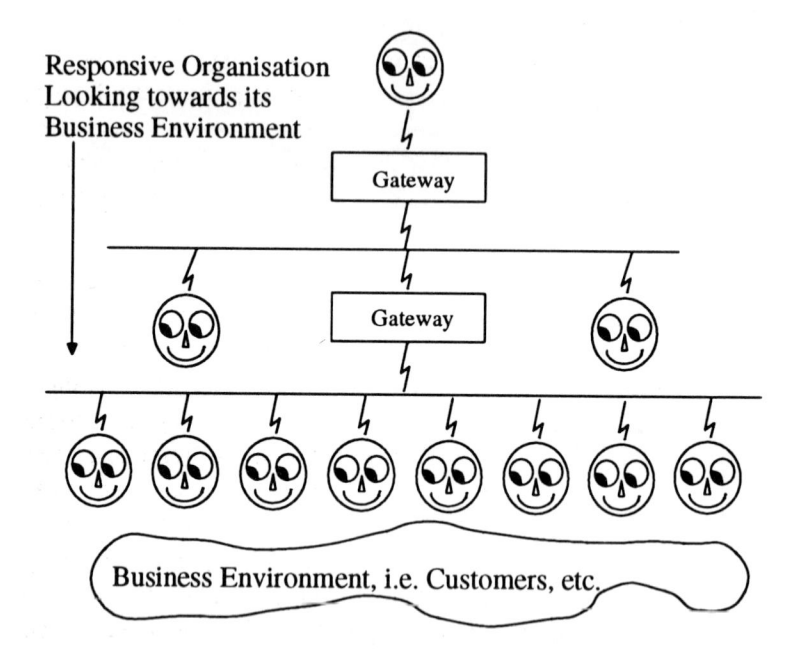

Fig. 4.2. Outward looking organisations

If such systems have obvious advantages why are companies not converting to them as quickly as possible? The answer, of course, is that they have equally obvious disadvantages. With an organisation like that shown in Fig. 4.2 what chance does one have of gaining promotion, power and influence? The answer is, very little, and if these major motivating forces are withdrawn something else will have to be provided which can satisfy the egotistic demands of the staff and their desire to succeed. In other words, an alternative motivating mechanism is required.

4.4 MOTIVATION THEORIES

Decision Support Systems may indirectly result in the removal of the present motivating forces but, ironically, they may also make a direct positive contribution to staff morale and motivation.

A Decision Support System will not be very effective unless management uses it to delegate decisions to employees who would not normally have been allowed to make them. Used correctly this could have a very positive effect on staff morale but used incorrectly it could leave them feeling overwhelmed with the technology and unable to help themselves.

Industrial psychologists believe that people can be motivated in two different ways, namely behaviouristically or cognitively. Behaviouristic methods encourage what the company or society view as good behaviour with praise, promotion and greater rewards whereas the cognitive methods seek to put 'meaning' into a job and increase a person's autonomy.

Industry has used behaviouristic methods for many years. If people work harder they expect to be paid more and if they are successful they expect to get promotion. But some people do not work primarily for such rewards and these people typically belong to the 'caring professions'. Nurses, for example, do a very demanding job with antisocial hours but they are not highly paid and their profession only offers limited promotion. Even the most senior posts in the nursing profession are still viewed as rather lowly within the social order of the medical profession. What is intriguing is that they get a lot of satisfaction from their jobs and are 'model' employees in spite of the apparently unattractive rewards. If all employees could be persuaded to be as tolerant, productivity would surely rise. So why aren't all employees like nurses?

4.4.1 Behaviouristic Approaches

One possible reason is that not all employees are treated like nurses in that most employees live under behaviouristic domains and not cognitive ones.

The outward signs of a behaviouristic domain are easy to detect. They invariably reward their workers with either bonus schemes, commission working, perks or promises of promotion. Unfortunately, these actions have undesirable side effects which can be so severe as to make the whole approach self defeating.

Whilst encouraging employees to work ever harder the behaviouristic approach does nothing to relieve the underlying boredom of a very repetitive job. The pressure to produce more and more, puts all the emphasis on quantity and not on quality which can quickly suffer. The attitude of both employees and management can become one of the 'sweat shop' with the employees feeling that there is never time for a break and management viewing any rest time as lost production. The scramble for promotion does not promote co-operation between peers and the giving of perks and status symbols can lead to petty jealousy. Clearly none of this does anything to promote a good working environment. Fortunately these things do not usually get out of hand and these methods have worked, for better or worse, for many years. They have, however, left us with one very inflationary side effect for which, as yet, there is no answer. The system of offering rewards has bred in all of us an expectation of ever increasing rewards to the extent that few people are satisfied unless they get a pay increase at least once per year.

4.4.2 Cognitive Approaches

The cognitive approaches were designed to avoid this trap and may yet allow industry to achieve a situation where wage settlements do not continually fuel inflation. They work by increasing the employees' self-esteem and making their jobs more worthwhile.

Cognitive methods are becoming more feasible with the onset of Decision Support Systems because the computer, rather than management, can be used to provide information and help with decisions. To a large extent, this frees the employee from direct supervision and frees management from its supervisory role with a consequential change in the working environment for all concerned.

The use of computers is not necessarily allied to cognitive approaches, however. Consider as an example the use of computers to automate very repetitive jobs. The idea is, of course, that once the most repetitive parts of a job have been removed the rest of the job, being less repetitive, will keep the employee more interested. The removal of boring parts of a job does not increase a person's self-esteem, however. It may not even make the job less boring. The reason for this is that human beings measure most things relatively and if the most boring parts of a job are removed the next most boring parts immediately take their place. For example, in most households washing up is always perceived to be a chore so many people buy a dishwasher only to find that emptying the dishwasher is then the task which is perceived to be the chore.

The assertion that workers necessarily find repetitive work boring can also be questioned. Many people do very repetitive activities for relaxation and much that is admired in art is often repetitive and tedious to do, e.g. veneer inlays in furniture. Repetition is, therefore, not at the root of the problem. Automation will proceed but it is being pursued for productivity reasons and not to directly benefit employees in their day to day work. In fact, automation, be it in the form of processing invoices, paying wages or building cars, is not a cognitive approach. It has not, therefore, fundamentally altered the relationships between people in the workplace.

This is in direct contrast, however, to the role played by Decision Support Systems. Decision Support Systems potentially help people to make good decisions and consequently could allow decisions to be made lower down the management structure and possibly by the workers themselves. They will require users to be provided with feedback enabling workers to take control of their own actions and free them from direct supervisory control. They could also be used to warn managers when things are going wrong. Managers could then take a lower profile or even concentrate on entirely different aspects of their jobs in the knowledge that their attention will be drawn to anything which needs their intervention.

Decision Support Systems could, therefore, change the working environment in a way in which the introduction of computer systems has not done so far. The impact of this technology should have a cognitive effect on employees. Cognitive approaches to management have already been tried but, although early successes were heralded and highly proclaimed, the methods have dropped out of the limelight. Some companies are now trying these techniques again but with much less fuss and firmly backed by computer systems. Consequently, it is pertinent to ask why it is that Decision Support Systems may revitalise cognitive approaches to improving productivity and motivating employees.

4.5 REVIEW OF COGNITIVE METHODS

Cognitive methods for motivating staff were first tried in the late 1960s and 1970s. At this time, however, they did not have the support of computer systems. Three basic types were tried:

(1) Job enlargement.

(2) Job enrichment.

(3) Socio–technical approaches.

All three are essentially the same approach to the problem but implemented in different ways. They all attempt to make the job more complete so that the employees see some final 'product' as a result of their endeavours. Consequently, the employees have to put more into the job and, therefore, get more out of it.

All three will now be briefly reviewed.

4.5.1 Job Enlargement

Job enlargement endeavours to enlarge a job horizontally to encompass more of a worker's capabilities. This is sometimes achieved by providing the employee with more varied tasks requiring the same level of skill or ability. Alternatively, it is achieved by providing the employee with more varied tasks with the same level of responsibility. In brief, the various job enlargement techniques are:

(1) Job Rotation.

(2) Advancement.

(3) The Addition of Duties.

(4) Making Entire Assemblies or Sub–assemblies.

The most classic example of job rotation is the worker co–operative in which every member takes it in turn to be the Managing Director, etc.. The problems encountered with this approach depend on the timescale of the rotation. If a long timescale is involved those doing the boring jobs have ample opportunity for getting bored and the prospect of a better job in the future does little to relieve the immediate problems. If the timescale is reduced to alleviate this there can be problems with continuity, with inefficiencies due to hand over times and nobody becoming expert at their job.

In the second technique, advancement, workers on a production line, for example, move along with the product. The problem associated with this is the cost of training as the employee has to be trained to do a whole series of jobs.

In the third case, duties can be added to the job remit of an employee; for example, machine operators can be given responsibility for setting up their machines and testing the components which are produced.

The fourth approach, making entire sub–assemblies, is really only an extension of advancement to the extent that a single worker can identify with an end product. This has been shown to be very good for quality but does suffer from the relatively high training costs.

4.5.2 Job Enrichment

Job enrichment as opposed to job enlargement makes a determined effort to extend a person's job by providing extra tasks which specifically include some managerial type decisions. This exercise is usually conducted as follows. Members of staff are asked to fill in questionnaires identifying:

(1) Those decisions which they feel their subordinates could take for themselves.

(2) Those decisions which their managers currently take which they feel they should be allowed to take.

The idea of this is that it makes every worker feel more responsible for their own actions and this brings with it three types of benefit, as follows:

(1) Workers can become self supervising. Consequently, a supervisory layer of management can be removed with associated cost benefits.

(2) New technology can be introduced as part of the job enriching process. This increases productivity and, if the new technology has been introduced as part of a job enrichment policy, it should also increase the level of skill required to do the job. The changes can then be made without meeting the sort of resistance that is often associated with the introduction of new technology.

(3) Most importantly, it should improve management. The delegation of responsibility frees time for the manager to do a better job (fewer interruptions). The relationship between

manager and employee should improve because it should become more co-operative and less supervisory.

Even these approaches run into difficulties, however. Some workers do not respond well to being given extra responsibility and prefer to be told what to do. There is no reason to despise this attitude because such workers frequently do their jobs well. They may well 'work to live' rather than 'live to work' and probably derive most of their satisfaction and fulfilment from other activities. People like this may prefer shorter hours to either pay or promotion. This is simply symptomatic of the fact that not all people are the same and indicative of the fact that any approach can never be totally applicable.

There are two other possible reasons for the failure of this approach. The first is that some people like the social pattern of their job. Many people can easily endure a boring job if the social contact is good. The second is the increased fear of failure that it can induce in some people and the increased chance of costly mistakes. In some environments a confident person who is short of experience is a liability and much more difficult to accommodate than an experienced person who is short of confidence. Job enrichment would probably be welcomed by the former who could easily make mistakes whilst it may be feared by the latter who would probably do an excellent job.

When viewed in the light of the preceding paragraphs the final disadvantage can be turned to advantage. Job enrichment is not only inappropriate for some people it is also inappropriate for some types of jobs. Clearly then, given sufficient freedom of movement and scope of employment, employees could transfer to those jobs which they prefer and staff morale and productivity should improve as a consequence.

4.5.2.1 *Example of Job Enlargement and Job Enrichment*

The example chosen here is taken from standard literature (**1**) and is a true case study.

A telephone company in the USA employed 33 people whose job was to recompile the telephone directories. The company was very concerned about the accuracy of its directories so the preparation of a directory was split into twenty one steps of which ten were to simply check that the previous task was done correctly, i.e. manuscript preparation, manuscript verification, key punch preparation, key punch verification, copy preparation, copy verification etc. An employee only did one of these steps. Approximately fifty different directories were recompiled each year.

After several cautious moves over a two year period the company achieved its final goal. Every employee was responsible for at least one entire directory or an alphabetic sub–section of a particularly large one. Some employees were responsible for more than one small directory. The number of steps was reduced from twenty one to fourteen and the employees did all fourteen steps including checking their own work. In addition to the directories, addenda were prepared on a daily basis and given to the operators to keep them up to date.

The experiment was a resounding success. Staff turnover decreased dramatically (initially 28 of the 33 staff left each year) and the company was pleased with both the productivity improvements and the quality of its product.

4.6 SOCIO–TECHNICAL APPROACH

The socio–technical approach is more radical than job enlargement and job enrichment in that it takes as its basic premise the postulate that man is a social animal and has a predominant need to be a member of a group. Furthermore, it assumes that everybody needs to feel socially accepted and recognised as useful within the group and that when this is so the whole group is well motivated. As a result, when the socio–technical approach is used, jobs are radically modified to facilitate group work.

The advantages of this approach are thought to be fourfold. Firstly, groups can be arranged to have the full range of skills required for a particular role so that the abilities of the group complement each other. Secondly, people are more inclined to regulate themselves within a group, making discipline easy to achieve. Thirdly, the company can assign entire jobs to the group leaving the assignment of individual tasks for the group members to sort out between themselves. Finally a group incentive scheme can be utilised and this does not have as many drawbacks as the personal incentives schemes used by the behaviouristic approaches.

Many of the advantages mentioned above arise because the management can step back from the individual and deal with a group. The accent has changed from the individual to the group. The goals are now group effectiveness, not selfish individual betterment and the organisation is more democratic and less authoritarian. All of these are properties which are likely to find favour in a modern society.

4.6.1 Example of Socio–technical Approach

The classic experiment in this area was done by Volvo (2, 3) in the early to mid 1970s. They built a car plant which enabled groups of people to do entire jobs. One such job was the assembling of engines. The plant was organised in such a way that each engine was entirely assembled by just one team. This team decided what to do and when. The experiment was very successful and received much acclaim.

4.7 WORK REDESIGN AND DECISION SUPPORT SYSTEMS

The modification of jobs in the way described in the previous sections is known as work redesign and Decision Support Systems have more in common with work redesign than is, at first, apparent.

The early euphoria about cognitive methods has passed. People have reaped the benefits or not as the case may be, but, in general, those cognitive techniques which worked have been absorbed into the traditional practices and the more extreme experiments have had their day.

This can be explained in part by reference to Fig. 4.3. The graph shows staff morale versus time when a person's job is changed. Initially there is a drop in productivity because the person is unfamiliar with the job. Productivity rises rapidly as the person learns how to do the job and confidence grows. This is usually associated with high morale and interest in the new job. As time passes, however, the new job becomes the norm, morale and degree of interest return to normal and productivity falls. This will eventually level out at a new sustainable level of productivity. If this new level is not higher than the old level, the new job is no more satisfactory or satisfying than the old one.

It should now be clear why Decision Support Systems have the potential to change the traditional management structures. Better informed employees, able to make their own decisions, will not require layers of management to supervise them. Senior managers will be aware of this and will reduce the number of layers of management to save costs. This they can safely do because the Decision Support System will quickly detect when things are going wrong and alert the appropriate people via the feedback mechanism.

As a by product of this cost saving exercise employees will have more influence over their day to day activities and, if the cognitive theories are correct, should be happier with their work, work better and hence be more successful.

This then is the crux of the matter. When cognitive approaches were tried in the 1970s they were tried for their own sake. They are now likely to be a side effect of change which is driven for other more commercial reasons. However, the reason for their re-introduction is immaterial. They are known to be beneficial to employees. They appear to be a side effect of the introduction of Decision Support Systems. The changes which Decision Support Systems will bring to the workplace should, therefore, be beneficial for the workforce.

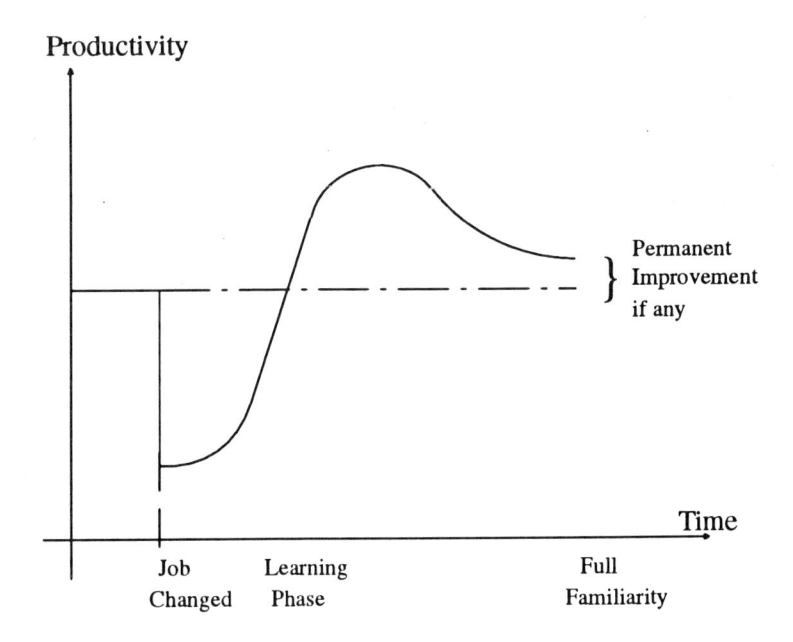

Fig. 4.3. Effect of change on productivity

4.8 THE IMPACT OF WORK REDESIGN ON DECISION SUPPORT SYSTEMS

Anyone who drives significant distances will be aware of the 'new road' problem. Planners design roads to be large enough to cope with expected levels of traffic and to have some spare capacity for growth. However, it always seems (and this may be illusory), that the very presence of a new road attracts many more travellers than the planners expected and so it instantly becomes congested.

Decision Support Systems could fall into the same trap. If the introduction of Decision Support Systems into the working environment is successful, it may well change the way people work to a way that they prefer. If the workforce prefer the new way of working, the desire to move increasingly to this new way will place extra demands on the Decision Support System. It is now a well established fact that if such additional demands are not anticipated at an early stage in the design of a computer system, they will be very expensive to provide later on. If these additional demands are foreseen, however, the design can be made to accommodate them so that even if not implemented initially they can be catered for without due expense in the fullness of time.

4.9 SUMMARY

Commercial pressures created by the emergence of Decision Support Systems are likely to change the working environment in a manner which happens to have been one which was advocated in the 1970s. These changes, the so called cognitive approach to work, will increase self determination in the workplace and should make work more rewarding for the workforce. In order to maximise the benefits which arise from this mode of working, management should consider manipulating the changes in accordance with cognitive ideals, i.e. redesign work so that:

(1) Every person is involved with a complete piece of work.

(2) A high degree of own decision making and self–control is permitted, i.e. people should be able to decide how best to do their jobs (after adequate training).

(3) All employees get sufficient feedback to know whether they are doing a good job. This is known as 'closure'.

(4) All employees get feedback about their productivity.

This should result in the majority of people getting on with their jobs, reporting their progress to the management and receiving appropriate feedback rather than asking for permission before undertaking each step of their job. This is known as inverting the delegation triangle (4).

The different methods of working will also have an effect on the number and style of managers. The number of layers of management will decrease and management styles are likely to change to:

(1) Demonstrate trust and confidence in the ability of the workforce.
(2) Listen to the ideas of subordinates when problem solving.
(3) Train the workforce well, allow it access to the data it needs and generally support its efforts to be more productive.
(4) Encourage co-operation between workers and between 'levels' of management.
(5) Promote egalitarian treatment for everybody.

4.10 CASE STUDY: COGNITIVE PRACTICES AT R, B & H

A design for a Decision Support System for R, B & H has already been proposed. What must be done now is to study the likely impact of this system on the working practices in R, B & H to see if good morale can be promoted by taking a cognitive approach to redesigning jobs. We must also ensure that the Decision Support System proposed will be able to support the extra decisions being made by the workforce due to the redesign of their jobs.

As an example, let us consider the warping function within R, B & H. The current management structure for the warping function is: Mr Keith who is the Production Director, Donald who is the foreman and the warpers who are Edith, Sally, Beth, Dolly and Stan. Donald's job is largely supervisory and that part of his job is vulnerable to job enrichment pressures. On the other hand he is the undisputed expert when it comes to knowing how to do the tricky and less frequent jobs, knowing how to rectify mistakes and knowing how to train new staff. His role as an expert is not vulnerable although the reliance of others on him decreases with time.

Sectional warping, the type practised by R, B & H, is conceptually a simple job but it has subtle complexities typical of traditional trades like the textile trade. The basic aim is to provide the weaver with a beam which has in the region of a thousand continuous lengths of thread wound onto it each of which is the same length and at exactly the same tension. The quality of the final warp is currently ensured by having Donald check each stage in the traditional 'ask, do, report' manner.

The warper is allocated a job by Donald, who asks the warehouseman to bring the baskets containing the packages of thread into the working area. The warper then prepares the job and asks Donald to check that the pattern and all machine settings are correct before proceeding.

The first section is then wound onto the swift and is measured for length. The length is checked by the foreman and when he is satisfied that this section is at least the length required by the customer a second clock is set. This ensures that all sections are the same length as the first. The warper then proceeds to wind the remaining sections onto the swift ensuring, in the process, that all threads are continuous and even in tension.

The final operation, that of winding the completed warp off the swift and onto the beam, is done by the foreman. This is called 'beaming off' and, doing it himself, allows the foreman to check that no threads are broken, that the tension is even and that the width is correct. Minor errors can be corrected during this stage but if major deficiencies are found the warp has to go through a further operation, called 'dressing', to be rectified. Dressing is expensive but R, B & H provide a quality product and prefer to dress a warp rather than send a poor quality one to a customer. When a job is complete all the remaining packages are removed from the creel, packed back into the baskets and both warps and baskets are returned to the customer.

Whilst the foreman is beaming off, which is a relatively slow process, the warper may be setting up the next job or helping another warper. R, B & H do not employ 'juniors' for their warpers. Juniors could help with the creeling part of the job, replacing packages which have run out and repacking the baskets after the job is finished. It is also one way of training warpers.

The warpers are paid a fixed weekly wage plus a bonus. The bonus is calculated from the number of warps they have completed and the complexity of those warps.

The management of this function could clearly be converted to a more cognitive style. The warpers could negotiate with the managers a price for preparing a warp. They could decide whether or not to employ a junior to assist them but, if they did, the cost of the junior would be deducted from their earnings. They could decide whether or not they required assistance from the foreman or whether to do the entire job themselves and they could be totally responsible for the quality of the warp produced and would have to pay, via deductions, for the cost of any dressing which was required.

If this was the way that things developed, the Information Gathering Task which R, B & H used would have to cope with collecting information at a lower level than otherwise might be necessary. They would require some facility for accounting for the costs incurred in producing a warp. Although this would only be for internal accounting, it would be important for everyone to be convinced that the system was fair and to have access to the information for their own accounting purposes. An Information System would be required which could provide feedback on the quality of the warps. This could only be achieved by attaching a reply paid questionnaire to each warp, asking the weaver to comment on how easily the warp wove into fabric. The replies could be typed into the system so that they were only available to the warper who had made the warp and not to the other warpers.

The Decision Support System would need to support Mr Keith and Donald too. They would probably need support to help them to decide which jobs should be given to which machine and when. The results of their decisions would need to be available on the system so that both the foreman and the warpers knew what the next job would be. It is difficult to envisage how any sort of production schedule could be maintained if the warpers were allowed to pick and choose between jobs. However, it would be possible for the warpers to have some sort of latitude to say how much they felt a particular job was worth. This would help Mr Keith and Donald to detect those jobs which everyone preferred, those which everyone hated and possibly, where some jobs were preferred by some people and not by others, to give jobs to people who preferred doing them. An exercise like this could be used to ensure that the jobs which were generally disliked and the ones which were preferred were shared out equally. It could also be used as feedback for Mr Philip, who fixes the price with the customer, to help him get a higher price for the less preferable jobs and consequently to be able to offer a higher bonus for them.

When one applies new technologies to situations like this there are endless possibilities. For example, one could fit the machines with electronic broken thread detectors. These would stop the machine and prevent the warper from proceeding until a new thread was knotted onto the broken one. This should improve the quality of the warps by ensuring that there are no broken threads. It should also improve life for the warper who would rely on electronics, rather than quick reactions, to catch a broken thread. It could also be used to measure the quality of the thread provided by the customer and hence measure how easily it could be made into a warp. This information could be used in deciding what price to charge for the work in the future and could also be passed back to the suppliers to give them feedback on their own quality.

Production Scheduling

1. Next Job

Setting up the Machines

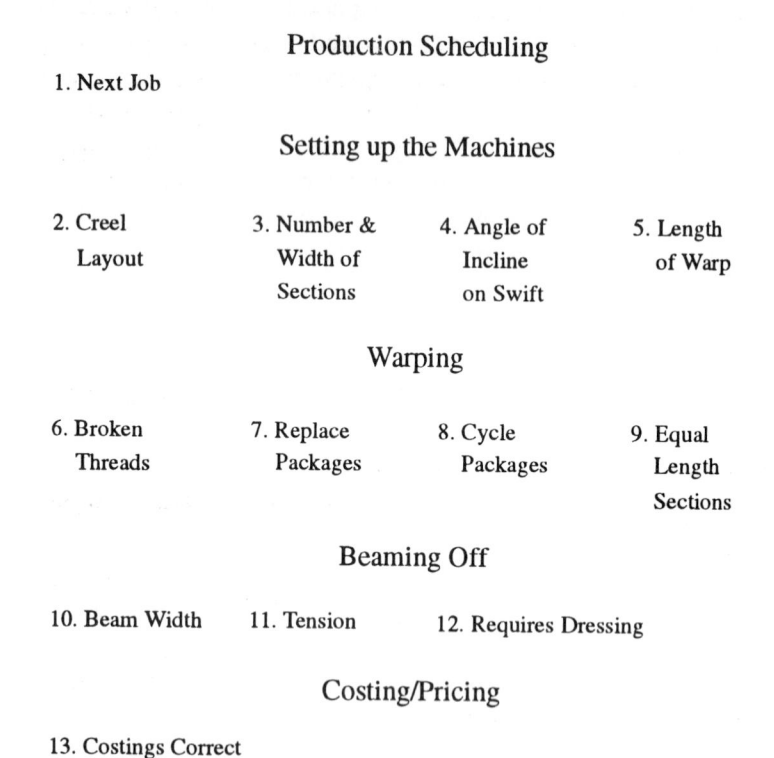

2. Creel Layout
3. Number & Width of Sections
4. Angle of Incline on Swift
5. Length of Warp

Warping

6. Broken Threads
7. Replace Packages
8. Cycle Packages
9. Equal Length Sections

Beaming Off

10. Beam Width
11. Tension
12. Requires Dressing

Costing/Pricing

13. Costings Correct

Fig. 4.4. R,B & H warping decisions

This demonstrates how, once information technology is utilised, decisions, information and automation become enmeshed into a complex web. If our systems are going to be effective this web must be studied, simplified and structured, to give maximum benefit for the investment involved. We therefore need to look at the warper's job, trace the decisions which have to be made, decide where the information for making these decisions comes from, what information will be generated, whether or not the information will be of use elsewhere and whether or not to support the decisions.

Fig. 4.4 shows, in tabular form, the decisions which a warper has to make and the order in which they are made. By no means would all of these be computer supported but many of them could be. At this stage one has to consider the relative merits of providing a terminal which is easily accessible to the warper and supports most of the decisions versus supporting most of the decisions some other way.

Let us assume that Mr Keith and Mr Philip decide that they would be prepared to provide a terminal for every warper and support the decisions listed above. We can then consider what would be involved in supporting two of the decisions shown in Fig. 4.4. We will choose decision 13 which interacts considerably with the rest of the business and decision 8 which is self–contained and private to the warper concerned.

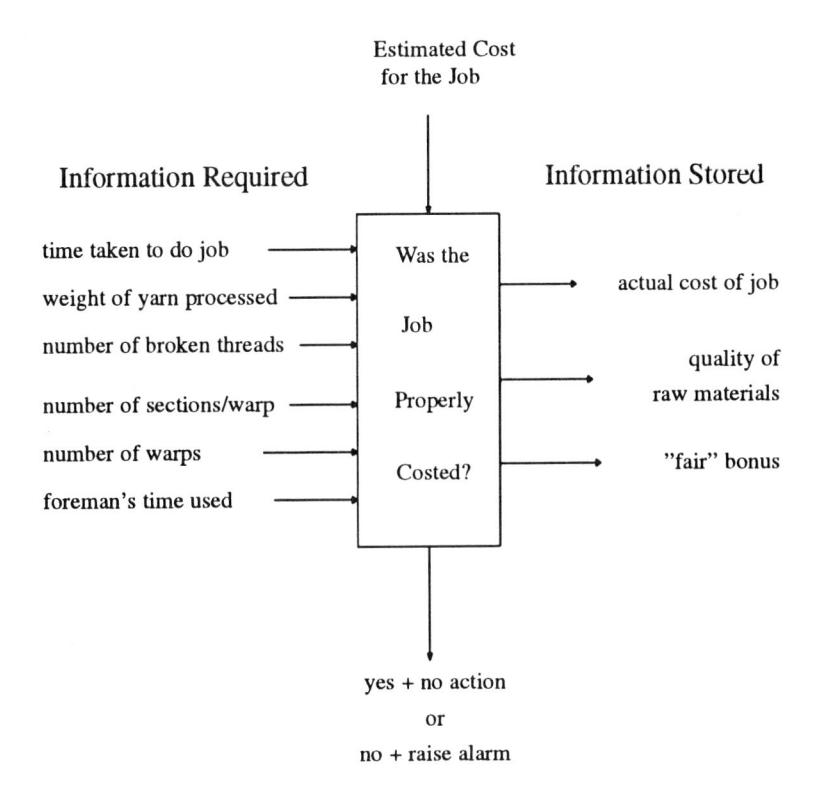

```
                        Estimated Cost
                          for the Job
                               |
   Information Required        |        Information Stored

 time taken to do job ─────┐  Was the ┌─────→ actual cost of job
 weight of yarn processed ──┤          │
                            │   Job    │
 number of broken threads ──┤          ├─────→ quality of
                            │ Properly │       raw materials
 number of sections/warp ───┤          │
                            │  Costed? ├─────→ "fair" bonus
 number of warps ───────────┤          │
 foreman's time used ───────┘          │
                               |
                        yes + no action
                               or
                        no + raise alarm
```

Fig. 4.5. The 'costed correctly' decision

Fig. 4.5 depicts decision 13, 'whether or not the job was properly costed'. This decision would probably be supported using a simple spreadsheet but our concern for the moment is that the decision exists and needs supporting and so requires information and will generate information. The information which the decision requires will have to be acquired from the warper but, most importantly, this information will not only be required by this one decision, some of it will also be required by production control, some for costing/estimating etc. The information should not be requested over and over again, however. It should be collected once and stored until a decision has need of it.

Much of the above is also true of the output shown in Fig. 4.5. The result of the decision is really only yes/no but a lot of useful information would be lost if it is not collected and stored. If the result of the decision is 'yes' then no intervention is necessary but if the result of the decision is 'no' then Mr Philip and Mr Keith should have their attention drawn to the fact. In the diagram this has been done by raising an alarm which can only be cleared by either Mr Philip or Mr Keith acknowledging that they have seen it. It would be implemented by having a message appear on the screen used by Mr Keith and/or Mr Philip which would only disappear when a predetermined key was depressed.

The other outputs are all things which the decision support procedure would have had to compute and which are going to be required elsewhere. Consequently they may as well be stored until required. For example, the actual cost of the job will be used for profit/loss calculations, as feedback to check the accuracy of the quotations and for forecasting the cost of jobs in the future. The quality of the materials received may be useful feedback for the supplier but will definitely be useful for costing future jobs which use materials from the same supplier. The 'fair' bonus for the warper will also be useful feedback for the decision which sets the level of bonuses in the first place.

It should be clear that the above decisions interact quite strongly with the whole company even though, superficially, they were only to do with warping. This emphasises the need for Decision Support Systems to be an integral part of the business. The next example, in contrast, is a largely self–contained decision which would be provided solely for the benefit of the warper.

Suppose that eight threads of a particular colour are required in the pattern and the supplier has provided ten packages of this thread. All ten packages will be required to complete the job so if eight are used exclusively two will be left and these will be too few to make up the pattern when the first eight are empty. The solution is to cycle the ten packages round the eight positions and use the packages evenly but it requires a lot of changing of packages particularly if there are several other colours which need the same treatment. A much more efficient way to do it is to compute how many sections to allow a package to run before removing it. That is where the Decision Support System can help because a package can easily be provided which computes a schedule of package changes which will ensure success.

4.11 POINTS TO PONDER

Consider the holiday situation and role play one of two parts. Either play a parent and think about which decisions the children should make for themselves for the better enjoyment of their holiday. Alternatively do the same thing from the child's point of view. Having tried to enlarge/enrich the children's role, decide what decisions they will have to make. Now consider each decision in turn and devise a method to help the child make the decisions. Then consider the information which the child will need and where it should come from. Follow this by considering what information the child might generate which would help in taking future decisions about holidays.

4.11.1 Some Suggestions

If you are unable to think of any decisions which could be handed down to children think of:

(1) Spending money.
(2) Activities.
(3) Which clothes they should take.

All these offer plenty of scope for exploring the concepts expressed in this chapter, albeit in an entirely different setting. The combination of the first two together provide an excellent set of examples of both fuller participation and the scope for supporting decisions which accompanies it.

4.12 FURTHER READING

- Bariff, M.L. and Lusk, E.J (1977) Cognitive and Personality Tests for the Design of Management Information Systems. *Management Science,* **23**, no. 8, pp. 820–828.

- Ford, R.N. (1973) Job Enrichment Lessons from A.T.&T. *Harvard Business Review*, January–February, pp. 96–106.

- Ginzberg, M.J. (1984) Redesign of Managerial Tasks: A Prerequisite for Successful DSS. *MIS Quarterly*, **2**, no. 1, pp. 39–52.

- Grote, R.C. (1972) Implementing Job Enrichment. *California Management Review*, **15**, no. 1, pp. 16–21.

- Huber, G.P. (1983) Cognitive Style as a Basis for MIS and DSS Designs: Much Ado about Nothing. *Management Science*, **29**, no. 5, pp. 567–582.

- Kilbride, M.D. (1969) Do Workers Prefer Larger Jobs? *Personnel*, September–October, p. 47.

- Paul, W.J., Robertson, K.B. and Hertzberg, F. (1969) Job Enrichment Pays Off. *Harvard Business Review*, March–April, p. 66.

- Reif, W.E. and Luthans, F. (1972) Does Job Enrichment Really Pay Off? *California Management Review*, **15**, no. 1, 1972, p. 36.

- Reif, W.E. and Tinnell, R.C. (1973) A Diagnostic Approach to Job Enrichment. *MSU Business Topics*, Autumn, p. 30.

- Trist, E.L., Higgins, G.W., Murray, H. and Pollack, H.B., (1965) *Organisational Choice*. Oxford University Press.

- Walton, R.E. (1972) How to Counter Alienation in the Plant. *Harvard Business Review*, November–December, pp. 70–81.

- Whitsett, D.A. (1975) Where are your Unenriched Jobs? *Harvard Business Review*, January–February, p. 75.

4.13 REFERENCES

(1) Ford, R.N. Job (1973) Enrichment Lessons from A.T.&T. *Harvard Business Review*, January–February, pp. 96–106.

(2) Gibson, C.H. (1973) Volvo Increases Productivity through Job Enrichment. *California Management Review*, **5**, no. 4, pp. 64–66.

(3) Gyllenhammer, P.G. (1977) How Volvo Adapts Work to People, *Harvard Business Review*, July–August, pp. 102–113.

(4) Grote, R.C. (1972) Implementing Job Enrichment, *California Management Review*, **15**, no. 1, p. 20.

Chapter 5
The Information Gathering Task

5.1 INTRODUCTION

The importance of information for making decisions was realised a long time ago, so it is not surprising that in Chapter 3 the Information Gathering Task was identified as a major contributor to the decision making process. This task continued throughout the entire decision making process and the user was allowed to enter it at any time. The details of the task were rather sketchy, however. It simply had several ways of accessing 'stored data'. The purpose of this chapter is to look at the Information Gathering Task and the 'stored data' in more detail.

Storing data is nothing new; nor is storing data for the purposes of making decisions. In fact, Management Information Systems have been in existence for many years and they are the obvious providers of information for the Information Gathering Task. Things might not be quite so easy, however. Management Information Systems collected that data which was easy to collect; Decision Support Systems want data which is relevant to the decision in hand and the two may not be the same.

This chapter highlights the potential mismatch by reviewing all the various types of Management Information Systems which have existed. Not surprisingly, the chapter concludes that the latest types of Real Time Management Information Systems are very good for this role but even these would benefit from a reversal of emphasis. The old idea of collecting that information which is easy to collect and then using it to make decisions if it happens to be applicable, is not adequate. In future it will be necessary to identify those decisions which must be supported and then gather the appropriate data if it is economic to do so.

This reversal of emphasis belies the idea that some of the most advanced Management Information Systems are, in themselves, Decision Support Systems, at least as they are defined here, but they are a very important part of the unified system. This is depicted by Fig. 5.1.

The respective roles of Decision Support Systems and Management Information Systems have been the subject of much debate (**1, 2, 3, 4,**

5, 6, 7), but the discussion must not start with lofty debates because, as yet, we have not even said what we mean by information.

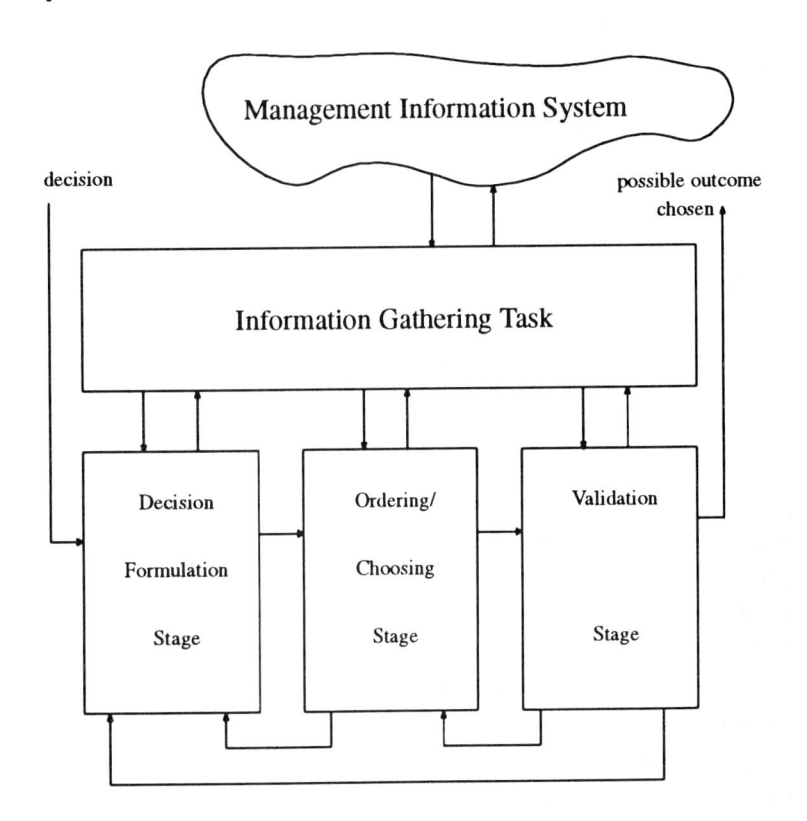

Fig. 5.1. The role of management information systems

5.2 THE NATURE OF INFORMATION

In the previous chapters the term 'information' has been used in a normal context without being explicit about its precise meaning. This chapter draws a distinction between data, information and knowledge so at this point we will pause a moment to define these terms more carefully.

Throughout the rest of this book data will be the term used for a single fact or an event, e.g. fact: Smith worked 40.5 hours this week, event: the moment when an invoice is sent. Information, on the other hand is an aggregation of data for a specific purpose. For example, Gillian, R, B & H's sales manager, does not want a list of individual sales at the end of a month, she wants totals for each member of the sales force and an overall total. In general, data is selected and processed in some way in order to turn it into information.

The word knowledge is more specialised, however. It will be used here to refer to a collection of related information but in particular to a collection in which some of the information has been deduced from the others. Information will have been analysed in some way before it became knowledge. For example: a list of dates stating when a remittance was received from A. Smith & Co, is data; the fact that they are large customers, pay well and complain little, is information; that A. Smith & Co are good customers, is knowledge. Knowledge will be largely the prerogative of human beings and will imply experience of a topic and intelligent interpretation of information about that topic but, in the closing chapters of the book, machine implementations of knowledge will be discussed.

Whilst discussing the topic of information it is worth noting that both data and information can be classified according to certain criteria. The classifications which are required for the purpose of this book are those of:

(1) Internal/external.

(2) Historic/futuristic.

These are defined as follows.

5.2.1 Internal/External Information

Internal data is data generated within a company. Because it belongs to the company it is relatively easy to collect since only the actual collecting mechanism requires attention. Consequently internal information is equally easy to collate. Any company which does not know all there is to know about itself has only itself to blame.

External data, however, is an entirely different matter. This has to be collected from outside the organisation and both the means of collection and the accuracy of data can be unreliable. All companies have to try very hard to collect adequate quantities of external data. This is a major concern to most companies since all the information about the Business Universe is external in nature.

5.2.2 Historic/Futuristic Information

Similarly information is easier to acquire the older it is. Even within an organisation it can take time to collect the data, process it into information and get it to the managers. The older information is, the less useful it is and consequently it is less valuable. The old adage 'yesterday's news is not news' is equally true for information. What everybody would like, but nobody can have, is a look at 'tomorrow's news'.

Information in the form of predictions is available for tomorrow, however, and whilst factual information about the future may be an impossibility, estimations about the future are available for those who try hard enough to find them. But accurate predictions are expensive, not easy to prepare and not entirely reliable.

The age and accuracy of the information available is vital to good decision making. This is because much of the information is for feedback and feedback must be both accurate and timely for good control, i.e. good decisions.

5.3 MANAGEMENT INFORMATION SYSTEMS

The problems associated with only collecting internal data and presenting this as information after some considerable delay can easily be seen from a review of the development of Management Information Systems.

The basic aim of Management Information Systems was to produce reports which were designed to provide relevant information for controlling current and future operations. The reports could be configured to provide general information. Human beings, by their very nature, would absorb this information and perform better.

But, human beings will only read reports when they need them and, even then, only if the information is relevant. Consequently, if Management Information Systems are to be effective they must provide only the information requested and they must provide it almost instantaneously, i.e. they must work in 'real time'. If 'browsers' and 'forecasting' are added to such a Real Time Management Information System it actually satisfies the requirements laid down for the Information Gathering Task. The latest types of Management Information Systems can, therefore, be integrated into the Decision Support System as shown in Fig. 5.2.

The reader should not be left with the idea that all of this is now established technology. It is not. Most, if not all, companies with Management Information Systems are constantly working to refine them and much has still to be learnt about how to design, build and operate them effectively. Since the concept of Decision Support Systems does not make Management Information Systems obsolete, Management Information Systems are likely to continue to be refined for some considerable time to come.

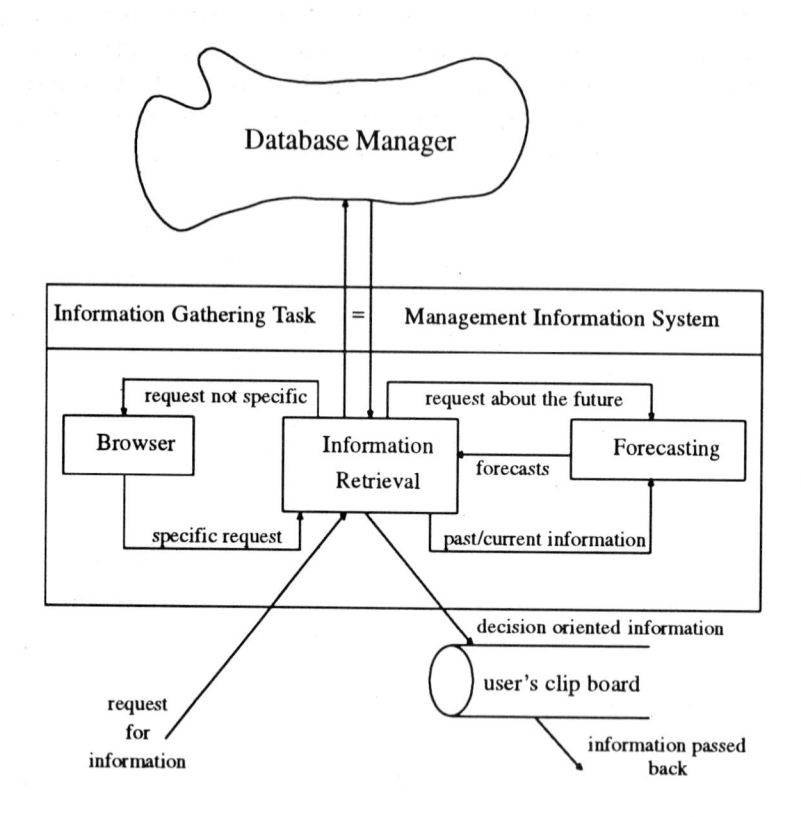

Fig. 5.2. Integrated management information systems

The twist which brought about a Decision Support System rather than a Management Information System was the realisation that decisions and not data lay at the centre of a manager's universe. Up to this point in time everyone had been obsessed with gathering data. The more data you gathered the more information you could generate; the more information you could generate the more information you could give to managers; the more information managers had the better informed they were and the better informed they were the better would be their decisions. Consequently, a whole generation of computer professionals grew up with an instinct to collect data from wherever it was available and to save it forever in case someone at sometime needed it.

As time progressed and databases grew larger and larger the above approach became more and more unrealistic and somehow decisions had to be made about what data should be collected and what data should not be collected. It was also necessary to decide how long to store data and when to discard it. The obvious way to tackle this problem is to ask who is using the data and for what. The answer to this question turned out to be that, by now, everybody in a management position was using data to help them make decisions.

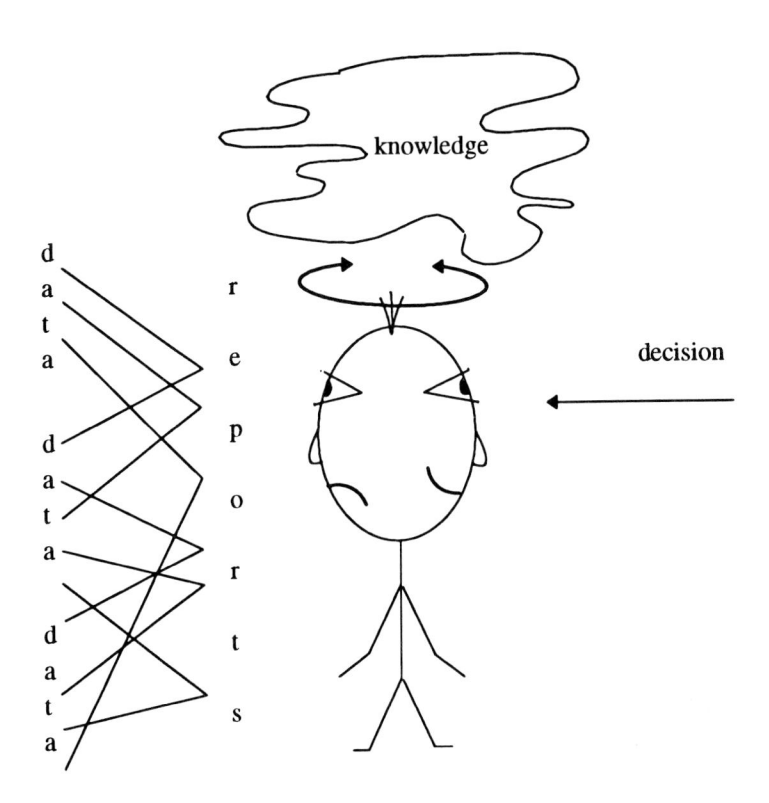

Fig. 5.3. Management information system rationale

This answer places the spotlight in the right place. Data should not be gathered just for the sake of gathering data, it should be gathered to help to make decisions. Consequently, if we wish to know what data to collect and what data to discard, the way to start is by asking what decisions have to be made. If we can establish what decisions are made, we can establish what information is required to make them. If we know what information is required, we can establish what data should be gathered in order to generate the required information. Consequently, the emphasis moves to the decisions.

Once the emphasis is on the decision it is a simple step to start to ask how else we can support decisions. Clearly providing information supports decisions but how do people know what information they want? Do people analyse a decision properly? Do they make decisions rationally? In how many other ways should we be supporting decisions?

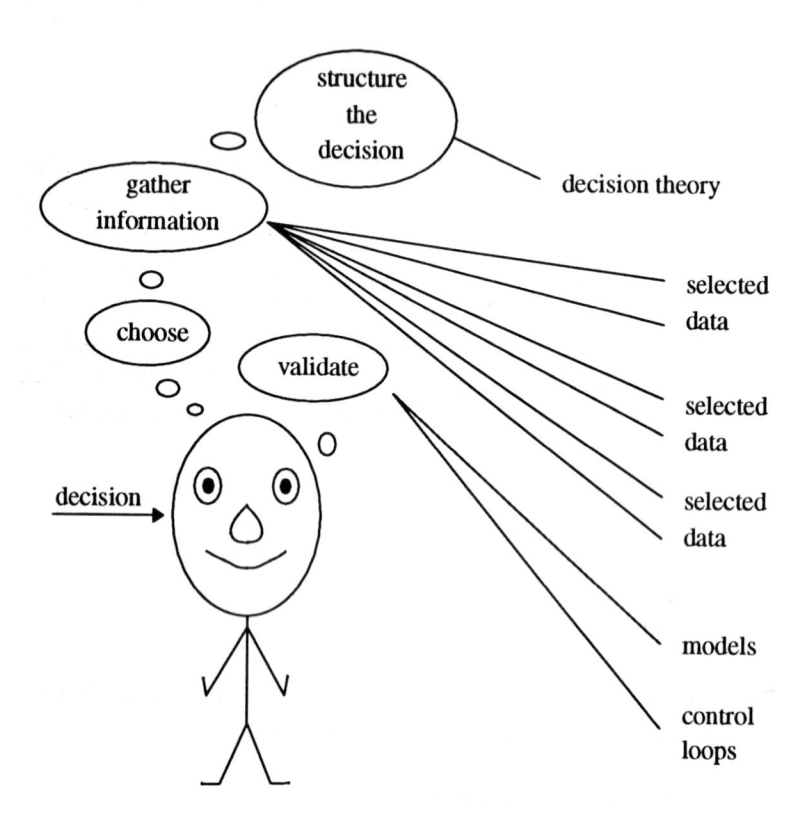

Fig. 5.4. Decision support system rationale

Traditionally, a Management Information System collected all the data it could, processed the data into information in the form of reports and disseminated this information so that managers could read it and be more knowledgeable. When managers needed to make decisions they were on their own, albeit much better informed. This is shown in Fig. 5.3.

Ideally a Decision Support System will turn this around. A person faced with a decision is in need of three types of assistance. Firstly they require help to structure their decision, secondly they require knowledge and information to help make the decision and finally they need some way of validating their choice so that the decision can be refined. This is depicted in Fig. 5.4.

The preceding chapters of this book have shown in general terms how this can be done. The remaining chapters will concentrate on the methods which are required to build a viable Decision Support System.

5.4 THE INFORMATION GATHERING TASK

If Decision Support Systems are to be effective the Information Gathering Task will have to overcome, or at least circumvent, the problems still inherent in Management Information Systems. In order to do this they will have to draw on expertise from various disciplines. This is actually a feature of Decision Support Systems and, as this book turns its attention to detail, it will become apparent that much of this detail is drawn from other disciplines. The disciplines which are used in the Information Gathering Task are:

(1) Databases.

(2) Information retrieval.

(3) Statistics.

(4) Telecommunications.

The following sections describe how these disciplines are used in the various parts of the Information Gathering Task.

5.4.1 The Information Retrieval Module

Fig. 5.2 shows the Information Retrieval Module as central to the duties of the Information Gathering Task. The purpose of this module will be to make a direct query for some data or some information which will probably be stored in a database somewhere.

The queries would have to be directed at a database manager whose role is to preserve the integrity of the database whilst allowing users to read from it and write to it. The database manager will only accept very precise, unambiguous instructions and Information Retrieval as a specialism is concerned about how these very precise instructions to the database manager can be constructed whilst at the same time providing the user with a facility for requesting information in a way which is both very flexible and easy to formulate. The accepted way to do this is to use a query language.

As an example suppose you have decided that you wish to have a holiday by the sea, in a hot sunny climate. A hypothetical query language might let you say:

> LIST ALL holidays IN ASCENDING ORDER OF price THAT HAVE location = seaside AND temperature = hot AND climate = sunny.

This might look very easy but the words in capital letters are keywords which the query language recognises and the words in lower case letters are names of fields which the database recognises. Unfortunately if you do not know which keywords to use, the order in which to ask for things and precisely what the database calls them, your request will not be granted. For example if you put 'location = by the sea', because 'by the sea' is unknown to the database, you will get a message back saying that there are no such holidays in spite of the fact that there may well be a large number of them stored in the database.

This presents quite a problem to the casual and non–specialist user of a database. It is possible to get the machine to tell the user what words it recognises. This is useful although it can be very tedious. A user seeing 'seaside' as an option will know that it is equivalent to 'by the sea'. Unfortunately the computer does not 'know' anything and cannot satisfy the request since 'by the sea' is not lexically equivalent to 'seaside'.

The book by Avison (8) explains the role of databases for this purpose in more detail.

5.4.2 The Browser

The above problem is exacerbated if the users are not sure what information they want to know. We all know how unhelpful people can be if they insist on answering literally the question which was asked and fail to offer additional information which they know you will need or suggest other places where you might find out what you want to know.

Conceptually Browsers are supposed to be able to solve these problems and allow more informal access to the data in the database. In reality current Browsers fall far short of providing the sort of assistance you would expect from a helpful person and provide little more than a facility for users to hunt around in the database to try to find what they are looking for. Browsers will not be able to be truly helpful until they can be provided with some degree of intelligence and intelligent behaviour in machines is still a long way off.

The four task structure advocated in Chapter 3 for supporting decisions has been designed to accommodate the limited facilities of Browsers. The first task is designed to formulate the decision. If the decision is well formulated the information required to make it should also be well specified and hence expressible in the query language. Situations will still arise, however, when a Browser will be required.

Consider the holiday example again and assume that you have decided what sort of generic holiday you would like. Let us assume that you would like a beach holiday in a hot, sunny climate staying in a five star hotel with its own swimming pool.

When you submit this to the database to get a list of holidays to choose from you discover that all of them are too expensive. You now have two alternatives: you can drop each of your requirements one at a time until you do have a selection of holidays which suit your budget, or you can browse. It is relatively easy to set up a Browser which would match any three of your five requirements and display them to you one at a time. It would be equally easy to allow you to short list ones you like so you can choose between them later.

5.4.3 Forecasting

The third module in the Information Gathering Task was a Forecaster. This is a very important facility in a Decision Support System because many decisions require an estimate of the future when they are being made.

Some people would argue that mathematical forecasting for making decisions is unreliable because it is so often wrong; but, how often is the human correct? What we must decide ourselves is whether or not the two of them together could do much better.

Consider an example from R, B & H. For many months the number of high quality worsted warping that they do has risen by 5% per month so their forecasting package forecasts that this will continue. Mr Keith, however, knows that the price for warping will have to increase due to a recent pay rise for their staff and Mr Philip knows that if the price for warping rises sales will drop temporarily. This could be considered to be a good reason for overriding the Forecaster. A better solution would be to refine the Forecaster so that it takes into account the asking price. The Forecaster would then balance the effect of steadily rising business against the counter effects of a price rise and will probably predict the sales more accurately than the brothers guess.

There are two problems related to forecasting. The first is caused by the natural random variations in data and the second is caused by the need to balance recent changes with longer term trends.

Random variation can mask a genuine trend but this can be easily overcome using mathematics to find a 'best fit' curve. The curve can then be extrapolated into the future to find a new average value. The average is of little value, however, unless there is some measure of how accurate it might be. The accuracy is determined by considering the variability once again in order to achieve a probability distribution for future values.

Balancing recent effects with longer term trends is a different problem which can be tackled by allowing the effect of information on a prediction to fade away as the information ages.

The following examples demonstrate these two points but they are only two of many statistical methods which could be provided as part of the Forecaster's facilities.

5.4.3.1 Regression Analysis

Regression analysis is the statistical term used to describe the 'best fit' calculations mentioned above. Sophisticated statistical packages are readily available for doing this sort of analysis. They will find the best curve for a given number of independent variables and will give a measure of how good the fit is. Only the principle is required for the purposes of this book so we will consider the simple case of one independent variable and try to fit a straight line to the data.

Suppose that Mr Keith and Mr Philip have a problem with absenteeism. The warpers, who are predominately women with families, are prone to be absent if their children are ill. The brothers do not mind this but it does make quoting delivery times difficult and they have been a little concerned recently that the absenteeism is on the increase. They would like to be able to measure trends in the absenteeism in some sort of objective way so that they can both try to improve quotes for delivery and so that they can try to counter absenteeism with incentives of some sort. When they plot abscntceism against time they get a scatter of points like those shown in Fig. 5.5 where the number of warpers absent is the dependent variable and time, in days, is the independent variable. Each dot represents the number of warpers away on a particular day.

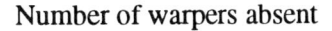

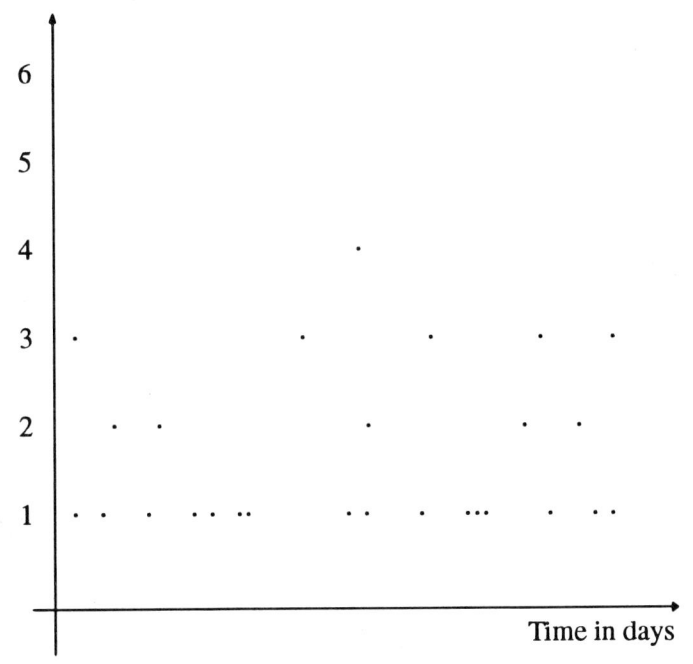

Fig. 5.5. Scatter diagram for absenteeism

We will use the method of 'least squares' for fitting a regression line to this data.

Suppose that y_i is the number of warpers absent on day x_i and that $y = ax + b$ is the equation of the 'best fit' line where a and b are constants. If the number of days in the time interval under consideration is n days then the average number of absentees/day is:

$$\bar{y} = (\sum_{i=1}^{n} y_i)/n \quad \text{and the 'average' day is} \quad \bar{x} = (\sum_{i=1}^{n} x_i)/n$$

So the 'average' point for all the dots in the scatter diagram is $(\bar{x}, \bar{y})$.

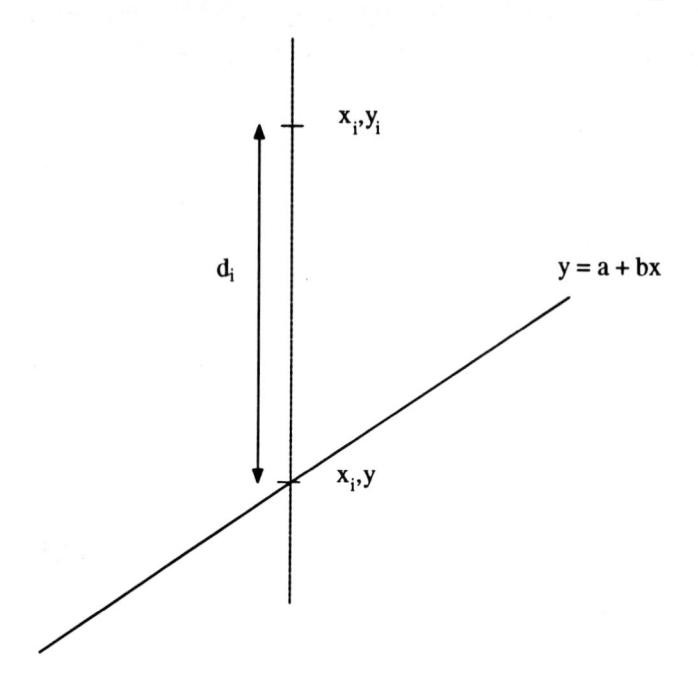

d_i = Distance from the ith point to the regression line

Fig. 5.6. Least squares curve fitting

As we will want the best fit line to pass through this average point:

$$\sum_{i=1}^{n} y_i = na + b \sum_{i=1}^{n} x_i \qquad (5.1)$$

In other words

$$a = (\sum_{i=1}^{n} y_i - b \sum_{i=1}^{n} x_i)/n \qquad (5.2)$$

Equation (5.2) is not sufficient to find the line, however, because there are two unknowns so a second criteria is required. The second criteria which is used in the least squares method is that the sum of the square of the vertical distances from all the points to the line is minimised.

Fig. 5.6 shows how to calculate the distance, d_i, from the ith point to the regression line, i.e.

$$d_i = y - y_i = a + bx_i - y_i \qquad (5.3)$$

If b is to be chosen so that the sum of the square of these distances is minimised then the first differential of d_i^2 with respect to b must be equal to zero, hence

$$\sum_{i=1}^{n} (a + bx_i - y_i) x_i = 0 \qquad (5.4)$$

i=1

whence

$$\sum_{i=1}^{n} x_i y_i = a \sum_{i=1}^{n} x_i + b \sum_{i=1}^{n} x_i^2 \qquad (5.5)$$

From (5.2) and (5.5)

$$b = \frac{n \sum_{i=1}^{n} x_i y_i - \sum_{i=1}^{n} x_i \sum_{i=1}^{n} y_i}{n \sum_{i=1}^{n} x_i^2 - \left(\sum_{i=1}^{n} x_i \right)^2} \qquad (5.6)$$

Equations (5.2) and (5.6) then determine the regression line uniquely.

Let us suppose that Mr Keith and Mr Philip discover that the regression line for their absenteeism is:

average absentees = 1/15 + (day number)/20,000

This means that on average one of the warpers will miss a day every three weeks and that this will double in the next five years. Mr Keith and Mr Philip can now allow for absenteeism and try policies to reduce it knowing that they will be able to measure whether or not their policies are working.

5.4.3.2 Exponential Smoothing

The least squares regression line will be excellent for detecting whether or not counter–absenteeism policy is working but something as variable as absenteeism may not be easy to forecast with the above technique.

A technique known as exponential smoothing may prove to be better for this purpose. This technique uses a very simple method which in effect decreases the value of information as it ages. The formula for exponential smoothing is:

$$Y_{t+1} = (1-a)Y_t + ay_t \qquad (5.7)$$

where:

Y_{t+1} is the forecast for the next period.

Y_t was the forecast for the most recent period.

y_t is the actual value for the most recent period.

a is a smoothing constant $0 < a < 1$

It is easy to see how this method works by simply expanding out the terms, e.g.

$$\begin{aligned} Y_{t+1} &= (1-a)Y_t + ay_t \\ &= (1-a)\{(1-a)Y_{t-1} + ay_{t-1}\} + ay_t \\ &= (1-a)^2 Y_{t-1} + a(1-a)y_{t-1} + ay_t \end{aligned} \qquad (5.8)$$

Successively substituting equations of the type (5.8) into equation (5.7) we can see that the following series develops:

$$Y_{t+1} = ay_t + a(1-a)y_{t-1} + a(1-a)^2 y_{t-2} + \\ + a(1-a)^3 y_{t-3} + \ldots \qquad (5.9)$$

Since $(1-a)$ is less than one, higher powers will become increasingly small so actual values from preceding periods contribute smaller and smaller amounts until they are essentially ignored.

Exponential smoothing assumes that the value being forecast has no upward or downward trend and does not display seasonal cycles. If this is not the case suitable allowances have to be made but the allowances themselves can be exponentially smoothed. For example a forecasted trend for time, $t + 1$, would be given by

$$T_{t+1} = (1-b)T_t + bt_t \qquad (5.10)$$

where:

T_{t+1} is the forecasted trend for the next period.

T_t was the forecasted trend in the most recent period.

t_t is the actual trend in the most recent period.

b is the smoothing constant $0 < b < 1$

The actual trend is given by the formula

$$t_t = y_t - y_{t-1} \tag{5.11}$$

The above assumes that the trend is inherently constant but things like seasonal cycles would violate this. But, seasonal cycles can also be exponentially smoothed as long as the components used for the smoothing are drawn from the same season. Hence, if a seasonal factor for the most recent period, f_t, is given by

$$f_t = \frac{y_t}{Z_t}$$

where Z_t is the non–seasonally adjusted forecast for the most recent period then

$$F_{t+N} = (1 - c)F_t + cf_t \tag{5.12}$$

is the formula for the forecast of the seasonal factor in N periods time when the season will again be the same as the current one.

The actual value including trends and seasonal factors is y_t so if z_t is the actual value excluding trends and seasonal factors then

$$y_t = (z_t + t_t)f_t \tag{5.13}$$

All of z_t, t_t and f_t can safely be assumed to be inherently constant and, consequently, each can be safely forecast using exponential smoothing. The forecast of the actual value, Y_{t+1}, will then be

$$Y_{t+1} = (Z_{t+1} + T_{t+1})F_{N+1} \tag{5.14}$$

where F_{N+1} is the forecasted factor for the appropriate season.

Mr Keith and Mr Philip could safely use the above technique to forecast absenteeism for 10–14 days ahead because seasonal disturbances, like the school holidays, will be catered for as will any general trend towards a higher level.

5.5 THE DEMANDS ON INFORMATION GATHERING SYSTEMS

Managers rely on information to make decisions and they have to make decisions to be effective at their job. Computers are good at manipulating information so managers naturally look towards computers to provide them with information.

But, providing information, especially on demand, i.e. in 'real time', will require particular types of computer systems. Users of information gathering systems should be aware of the enormous implications which these systems have for the hardware and software which will be required to support them. They should also be aware of the consequences of expecting a fast reply from a computer system. Consequently we must consider the demands that real time information gathering will place on the supporting technology.

The demands on computer technology imposed by users who wish to gather information more or less instantaneously arise, by and large, from five requirements:

(1) To be interactive.

(2) To respond within a short period of time.

(3) To permit managers to pose a large variety of queries, which in some cases might be 'one off' enquiries.

(4) To have access to data which may be stored in a remote location.

(5) The requirement for many managers to have access to the same data concurrently.

We will deal with each of these in turn.

5.5.1 The Requirement to be Interactive

This requirement immediately dictates that all managers must have a terminal on their desk which is connected by some means to the computer which stores the information that the managers are likely to require. This means providing at least a personal computer, or preferably a work station, for each manager.

The reasons for this are twofold. Firstly, many tasks are more conveniently undertaken with local processing power and these include the sorting and sifting of data and the preparation and/or presentation of documents. All of these are important tasks for most managers. The second reason is communication. Computer networks are very advanced and the source of information can be completely transparent to the user as long as the system can attach an address and a database name to every query which is made. It can even request this information from another computer on the network. Consequently, providing the power of a computer on the user's desk affords great flexibility to the system's designers, the computer manager and the user.

5.5.2 The Requirement of Short Response Times

Short response times can be achieved in a number of ways. Probably the most important of these is to provide desk top processing power. The speed of response is actually achieved by doing most of the processing locally but the processing can only be done locally if the programs and the data are available locally. However, if the programs are kept locally, they are very difficult to manage and maintain. It is much simpler to keep a single copy of a program so that the computer support staff can ensure that everybody has all the latest corrections and features. It is also much simpler to ensure that the company stays within the copyright laws if only a single copy is held. Consequently, on the one hand we would like a program and the data in every machine and on the other we would like a unique program and only one copy of the data.

This dilemma is solved by loading both the programs and the data over the network. In the case of data this sometimes means that the computer system will arrange for an entire portion of a database to be downloaded to a workstation in anticipation of the user's next request. This leads to slightly longer initial delays but provides very rapid responses after that.

5.5.3 To Facilitate a Large Variety of Queries

The problems that are posed for a computer system by a large variety of database queries are due to the fact that databases are constructed so that data can be retrieved by following predetermined paths. Any single query may cause a whole set of data items to be retrieved, each one satisfying the query. If all the required data lies on one path then it can be retrieved quickly. On the other hand, if each piece of data lies on a separate path then the time taken to retrieve it can be considerable. In the worst case every record in the database may have to be examined to decide whether or not it should be included in the prescribed set.

If a large variety of queries are to be facilitated then a large number of paths must be constructed. Every path has to be stored so a large database with a large number of paths requires a very large amount of storage. Consequently database designers like to limit the number of paths but in order to do this they must know in advance what queries the users are allowed to make. This is a very important point indeed because, in a Decision Support System, the nature of a query becomes difficult to predict. Consequently, Decision Support Systems are likely to throw up many such queries and answering them quickly is still a major problem.

5.5.4 Accessing Remote Data

It is generally advantageous to store locally any data which is generated and used locally and which is only infrequently accessed by remote users. But, wherever and by whomsoever data is used, it is nearly always desirable to keep only one copy, otherwise problems arise in keeping multiple copies consistent with each other. Consequently, if data is kept and maintained at a remote location it is nearly always better to access that data over a network than to attempt to keep a local copy.

The advent of modern computer networks has made this entirely feasible. Even small companies, who would be unable to afford a network of their own, can use commercial ones to link their sites. For example, it is now possible for a salesman to check the availability of an item before he sells it and to mark it as sold as soon as the customer buys it.

5.5.5 Concurrent Access to Data

Concurrent access to data is the source of some of computing's most intractable problems. The problem is as follows. If a user wishes to have access to any part of a database the request is granted and that part of the database which is affected is reserved. If a second user wishes to have access then there is a problem. The second user can be denied access and forced to wait but users do not like waiting. The second user can be allowed access and be warned that another user is also using that data. If the first user then updates one of the records the second user is viewing outdated information.

This problem is typified by an airline reservation system. Many offices, possibly from all over the world, are accessing one database. If a travel agent asks if a seat is available on a particular flight, the computer system will reply in the affirmative if, at the instant the request was made, a seat was available. If the agent tries to book the seat a few moments later, all the seats may have been sold. The customer will not be pleased but what the computer system must guard against is selling the same seat twice.

5.6 SUMMARY

The latest types of Real Time Management Information Systems provide the facilities required by the Information Gathering Task.

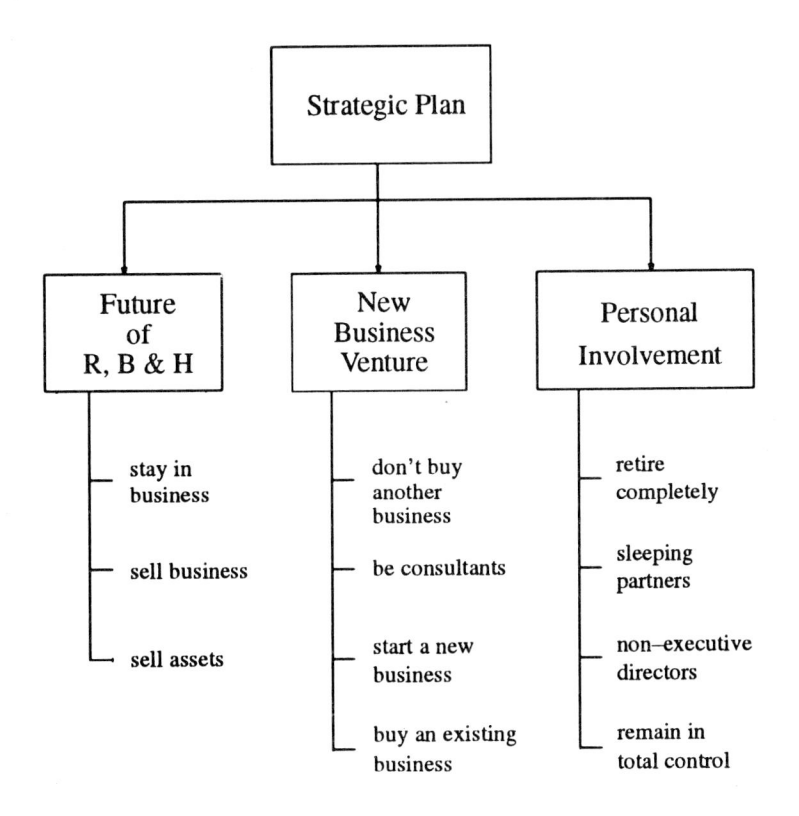

```
                          Strategic Plan
                                │
         ┌──────────────────────┼──────────────────────┐
    Future of              New Business            Personal
    R, B & H                  Venture             Involvement

  — stay in              — don't buy             — retire
    business               another                 completely
                           business
  — sell business        — be consultants        — sleeping
                                                   partners
  — sell assets          — start a new           — non-executive
                           business                 directors
                         — buy an existing       — remain in
                           business                 total control
```

Fig. 5.7. The uppermost level of R, B & H's strategic decisions

This does not mean to say that they are themselves Decision Support Systems, however. They are not designed to provide decision structuring and analysis nor facilities for allowing for risk and missing information. They also approach the collection of data with a fundamentally different philosophy. But, in spite of this, they can easily be made an integral part of a Decision Support System.

These new types of system will place heavy demands on the hardware and some computer science problems remain to be solved before all the facilities can be provided satisfactorily.

5.7 CASE STUDY: A MANAGEMENT INFORMATION SYSTEM FOR R, B & H

If we reappraise the R, B & H Business Plan represented by Fig. 2.9, we can see that Mr Keith and Mr Philip have not been completely general and that this plan presupposes that they are going to stay in business. If we ask Mr Keith and Mr Philip to try to be more general and to keep things simple for the moment, then Fig. 5.7 might be a better representation of the structure of the decisions which need to be made if R, B & H's future is to be thoroughly thought through.

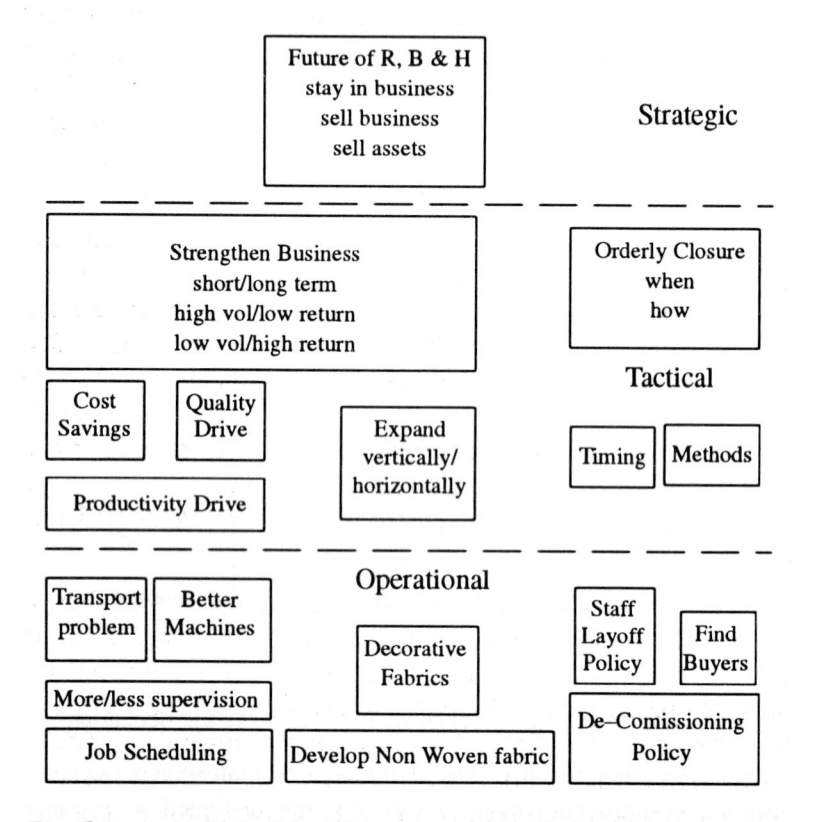

Fig. 5.8. A simplified decision structure for R, B & H

One of the decisions, which has been identified at the top of the hierarchy of decisions, is the 'Future of R, B & H' decision. It is very important, if not essential, that this decision is taken early in the decision process because it has a very significant impact on decisions lower down in the hierarchy. If the brothers are going to sell R, B & H, they have to find a buyer for either the business as a going concern or for the assets of the business once it has ceased trading. In the latter case, they must also decide what the timetable for closure should be. If they are to find a buyer for the business, it must be made to run as profitable as possible in the short term, even if this is not in the long term interests of the company. But, if they intend to stay in the business themselves, they will be looking for long term profitability and goodwill.

Fig. 5.8 attempts to depict these various decisions and to show their relationship to each other. The horizontal lines break the decisions into Strategic, Tactical and Operational decisions. Decisions at the same level should not affect each other. A decision at a particular level should only have to take into account the decisions above it. This enables decision makers to make decisions without worrying what their peers are doing. In Fig. 5.8 the decisions have also been placed into columns to indicate those decisions in higher echelons which are most likely to affect the ones beneath.

Our immediate concern is the provision of an Information Gathering Task to support these decisions. Having identified the decisions, we can now take a Decision Support System approach to deciding what information to gather. The information required is that which will assist in making the decision and that which will provide feedback for remaking the decision in future. The simplest approach is to take each decision in turn and identify the information required to assist with the making of that decision. It is also useful to categorise this data into internal information/external information and into primary information/feedback, i.e. into four categories.

If we proceed with this strategy and take the 'Future of R, B & H' decision the information required is something like that shown in Table 5.1. The information required, i.e. that shown in Table 5.1, must then be analysed to discover what data must be collected so that this information is available. For example, you cannot simply collect 'customer satisfaction'. It requires either a visit to the customer or a complaints procedure which is very easy for the customer to use or both. These procedures then glean individual facts, e.g. how many warps wove without difficulty, how many orders were delivered on time, whether urgent jobs were done quickly enough, whether did the company responded politely and promptly to enquiries, etc. It is these

Table 5.1. Information required for the 'Future of R, B & H' decision

Primary Information:

  External:

    State of the Textile Market in Europe/worldwide

    Present trends in Fashion

    Present trends in labour/running costs

    Common Market policy towards imported textiles

    Financial well–being of existing customers

    Customers' views on their continuing requirement for the services provided by R, B & H

    Forecasts of achievable prices for R, B & H's services

    Availability of suitable workforce

    The chances of selling the business/assets

  Internal:

    Financial/Technical strength of R, B & H

    The brothers' age and willingness to continue

    The existence of an internal successor

    Likely success of productivity/cost cutting exercises

Feedback:

  External:

    Customer Satisfaction

  Internal:

    Repeat orders

    Increasing/decreasing achievable prices

    New business

individual facts that the Information Gathering Task must collect, store and subsequently process into information to aid the decision maker.

In addition to the provision of the above, R, B & H's Information Gathering Task might be able to access information held on other machines. It would be worthwhile investigating whether the local Wool Exchange had a database which could be remotely accessed. Similarly, the textile trade association might offer a Management Information service which may be in the form of a remotely accessible database. If either of these provide useful information, it would be worth paying for access rights and extending the Information Gathering Task to include the ability to access this type of information.

We have only considered an extremely small part of the overall data gathering task but the reader may already be appreciating that the design and implementation of the Information Gathering Task will be a substantial and complex task. Other authors, e.g. Avison and Fitzgerald (9), have stated what the deficiencies of information gathering systems can be and the book by Avison and Wood–Harper (10) is clear evidence that the provision of management information is still problematical.

5.8 POINTS TO PONDER

(1) Justify the following statement:

The travel industry takes a Management Information System approach to helping its clients choose a holiday.

(2) Are there any instances when the travel industry takes a Decision Support System approach (i.e. puts the decision first and then selects the information required to make the decision)? Think carefully about your answer.

(3) Would a Decision Support System or a Management Information System be best for a holiday hunter?

5.8.1 Suggestions

(1) Almost every aspect of the travel industry takes a Management Information System approach to helping its clients choose a

holiday. The whole industry is based upon producing reports for the consumption of its clientele. These reports vary in form from books of timetables for rail, air and sea transport to the very glossy package holiday brochures. This is a clear example of taking the available data and representing it in the form of reports.

(2) Strictly speaking there is no aspect of the travel industry which takes a Decision Support System approach to helping its clients to choose a holiday. Some readers might feel that if a travel agent is asked to find a holiday which starts the next day then the travel agent would have to work in a Decision Support System mode. This idea is based on a misconception. It is true that the request is very specific. It is also true that the travel agent is going to have to do a search of remote databases, probably while the client waits, in order to answer the question, but this is no more than a Real Time Management Information System would do. The only help that will have been given is the production of a list of possible holidays. There will have been no assistance in deciding which possible holiday to choose. This is Management Information System help rather than Decision Support System help.

In practice, however, a travel agent probably does help a client to choose a holiday but it must be stressed that it is the agent, i.e. a person, who assists and not the computer system. Human beings have a knack of supplementing the technology and, because the agent wishes to make a booking, the agent provides the required assistance. How the agent helps with the client's decision may be worthy of further consideration. The reader is left to ponder this point.

(3) Whether or not a Decision Support System or a Management Information System approach is best for the holiday hunter raises many further issues. As the current systems are almost entirely Management Information Systems there must be some reason for their supremacy. Do the tour operators favour Management Information Systems? Do the public favour

Management Information Systems? Do the travel agents favour Management Information Systems? Does the current state of the art impose Management Information Systems?

The tour operators have good reason to favour a Management Information System approach. It is 'output oriented' and, whilst they would be quick to challenge an accusation of insensitivity to their customers' needs, they are in the business of persuading the public to buy what they have to sell.

Whether or not the public prefer Management Information System is less clear. Those who have difficulty in deciding on a holiday would almost certainly like some guidance and hence a Decision Support System. Others, who wish to be very independent, only want specific information. These people are, presumably, happy with the present system assuming that they are able to get the required information quickly and efficiently. Another section of the population selects a holiday on impulse and is quite happy to continue so to do.

In attempting to answer the questions about choosing a holiday we are raising many questions which have been addressed in earlier chapters. What are Decision Support Systems? Who requires them? Does everyone require the same things from them? These questions are central to the issues which surround Decision Support System and should also be considered.

5.9 FURTHER READING

- Ackoff, R.L. (1967) Management Misinformation Systems. *Management Science*, **14**, no. 4, December, pp. B140–B156.

- Avison, D.E. and Fitzgerald, G. (1988) *Information Systems Development: Methodologies, Techniques and Tools.* Blackwell Scientific Publications.

- Avison, D.E. and Wood-Harper, A.T. (1990) *Multiview: An Exploration in Information Systems Development.* Blackwell Scientific Publications.

- Checkland, P. (1981) *System Thinking, System Practice.* John Wiley & Sons.

- Davies, G.B. (1974) *Management Information systems: Conceptual Foundations, Structure and Development.* McGraw Hill.

- Dearden, J. (1972) MIS is a Mirage. *Harvard Business Review.* Jan–Feb, pp. 90–99.

- Murray, T.J. (1979) Data, Information and Intelligence in a Computer based Management Information System. *Journal of Applied Systems Analysis,* **6,** pp. 101–105.

- Naylor, T.H. (1982) Decision Support Systems, or Whatever Happened to MIS? *Interfaces,* **12,** no. 4, 1982, pp. 92–94.

- Sol, H.G. (1985) Aggregating Data for Decision Support. *Decision Support Systems,* pp. 111–121.

- Wright, D.J. et al (1986) Evaluation of Forecasting Methods for Decision Support. *International Journal of Forecasting* (Netherlands), **2,** no. 2, pp. 139–152.

5.10 REFERENCES

(1) Alter, S. (1977) A Taxonomy of Decision Support Systems. *Sloan Management Review,* no. 1, Fall, pp. 39–56.

(2) Finlay, P.N. and Forghani, M. (1987) The Concept of Management Intelligence Systems. *Journal of Applied Systems Analysis,* **14, October,** pp. 41–51.

(3) Hall, J.A. (1983) Management Information Systems. *Management Accounting,* **July,** pp. 10–23.

(4) Keen, P.G.W. (1981) Decision Support Systems: a research perspective. In *Decision Support Systems: Issues and Challenges,* Pergamon Press.

(5) Moore, J.H. and Chang, M.G. (1983) Meta–designs considerations in building DSS. In *Building Decision Support Systems,* Bennett J L (ed.), Addison–Wesley, pp. 173–204.

(6) Naylor, T.H. (1982) Decision Support Systems, or Whatever happened to MIS? *Interfaces,* **12,** no. 4, pp. 92–94.

(7) Sprague, R.H. and Watson, H.J. (1986) *Decision Support Systems: Putting Theory into Practice*. Prentice Hall.

(8) Avison, D.E. (1992) *Information Systems Development: A Database Approach.* 2nd ed., Blackwell Scientific Publications.

(9) Avison, D.E. and Fitzgerald, G. (1988) *Information Systems Development: Methodologies, Techniques and Tools.* Blackwell Scientific Publications.

(10) Avison, D.E. and Wood–Harper, A.T. (1990) *Multiview: An Exploration in Information Systems Development.* Blackwell Scientific Publications.

Chapter 6
Summary of the Probability Theory Required for Supporting Decisions

6.1 INTRODUCTION

The previous chapters have explained the role of Decision Support Systems and have prepared a framework for a working system. It is now necessary to explore techniques which will enable us to fill in the framework and produce a working system.

Surprisingly, although Decision Support Systems are a relatively new concept, many techniques exist which can contribute to the various parts of the overall system. This situation arises because the basic problems were known long ago and researchers developed mathematical methods of solving them. These methods have never been widely used because the technology required to deliver them to managers was not available even a decade ago. Consequently, mathematical disciplines such as Statistics and Decision Theory, which laid the foundations for supporting decisions several decades ago, have largely laid dormant since then.

Uncertainty is fundamentally inherent in decision making, so much so that making decisions in the absence of certainty is almost a routine exercise. Uncertainty, however, should not be confused with risk although the latter arises from the former. Two separate theories exist to address these topics: Probability Theory for addressing uncertainty and Utility Theory for addressing risk. This chapter restricts itself to those parts of Probability Theory which are required for handling uncertainty in the context of making decisions. Utility Theory as a formal method for handling risk is discussed later.

As uncertainty is so intertwined with decisions it is necessary to address it in its own right. The most appropriate mathematical formalism for addressing uncertainty is the theory of Probability (1) since this is a sound and well established theory. Furthermore, it need not be the daunting exercise posed by a rigorous mathematical exposition on the subject. In fact this chapter attempts to embrace the subject in a manner which should be comprehensible to anyone with a basic understanding of mathematics.

Probability Theory has stringent rules which must not be violated if the answers deduced by using it are to have any credibility. It is important to understand these rules and to appreciate that simple Probability Theory can only be applied in certain special cases. The simple cases are often applicable but it is nevertheless prudent to ensure that the correct conditions pertain before using them. Consequently this chapter devotes some time to a full explanation of these issues.

Having laid the foundation for a better understanding of the subject the chapter addresses other probabilistic concepts which will be required later in the book, in particular those of probability distributions, cumulative probability distributions and conditional probability.

6.2 INADEQUATE INFORMATION, UNCERTAINTY AND DECISION SUPPORT

Making decisions is only difficult when there is inadequate information and/or an element of uncertainty, i.e. when you cannot be certain that your chosen possible outcome will happen. If all the information is available, you can compute which possible outcome is best (whatever that might mean) and if you knew for certain that the possible outcome you had chosen would happen then the whole decision making process, although potentially tedious, would not be unduly difficult. However, if the information required to make a decision is incomplete, the best possible outcome may not be easy to identify and, even if it can be identified, as soon as uncertainty is involved you cannot be sure that it will happen. Consequently the combination of inadequate information and uncertainty increases the complexity of the problem to the extent that we might be unable to calculate the 'best' alternative. This is what makes decision making so difficult.

The most unfortunate consequence of lack of information and uncertainty is that a good decision may lead to a bad outcome, although it is also possible for a bad decision to lead to a good outcome. However, if there was no correlation between good decisions and good outcomes, decision support would be pointless. But, there are usually far more bad outcomes than good ones so formal methods of making decisions are likely to be more successful than ad–hoc ones.

Before we can explore this subject we must ensure that the terminology being used is well understood. Several different terms, which may well have specialist meanings, are used in this and other literature on uncertainty. Three of these will be discussed:

(1) Incomplete information.

(2) Uncertainty.

(3) Risk.

This chapter will then turn its attention to probability.

6.2.1 Incomplete Information

Few decision makers enjoy the luxury of knowing everything they need to know about the circumstances surrounding the decision they have to make. Given that the information available is incomplete we have two options:

(1) Proceed and make the decision using the information which is available.

(2) Estimate the missing information (on the basis of what is known) and then make the decision as if all the necessary information was available.

Both of these are valid ways to proceed.

6.2.2 Uncertainty

During the last decade there has been an increasing interest in uncertainty and particularly in Reasoning under Uncertainty. The interest in this has arisen from a desire to program computers so that they, like humans, can make deductions and come to conclusions using incomplete and uncertain information.

However, computer scientists, and those using the technology, wish to have the most reliable information possible given the incompleteness and the uncertainty. Users of Management Information Systems have long been aware that if bad data is collected and stored bad information is produced as a result. Decision Support Systems are more complex in this respect. If poor methods are used to handle the uncertainty, poor advice will be given even if the information which is available is good. Hence the interest in methods of Reasoning under Uncertainty.

Uncertainty affects all aspects of most decisions but we must ask ourselves whether or not these various types of uncertainty are different or whether they can always be described by a single theory. If they can all be described by a single theory the obvious candidate is Probability Theory (1) although alternative theories such as Possibility Theory (2), Fuzzy logic (3), modal logics (4) and non–monotonic logics (5) have been proposed.

Progress with the logics has been slow and they are unlikely to make a significant contribution to Decision Support Systems for some time. Consequently, they will not be discussed here. To some extent the same is true of Possibility Theory which is a measure of what could happen.

Suppose that Jane likes eggs for breakfast. Table 6.1 shows the probability and the possibility that Jane will eat a given number of eggs for breakfast. Notice that whilst Jane could easily eat three eggs for breakfast, and hence the possibility of Jane eating three eggs is unity, the probability that Jane eats three eggs is zero. Note also that the probabilities sum to unity, i.e. she always eats between zero and seven eggs for breakfast. This property is meaningless in possibility which simply measures the degree of feasibility for each alternative.

Table 6.1. Probability v possibility of Jane eating a given number of eggs for breakfast.

no. of eggs	0	1	2	3	4	5	6	7
probability	0.1	0.7	0.2	0.0	0.0	0.0	0.0	0.0
possibility	1.0	1.0	1.0	1.0	0.9	0.5	0.1	0.0

This example serves to highlight several things. Firstly there is no relationship between how possible something is and how probable it is except that nothing can be more probable than it is possible. This leads to the second point. Probability can be associated in a loose sense with some sort of expected frequency whilst possibility cannot. Arguably the uncertainty surrounding decisions is about expected frequency and not about whether or not something is possible.

Indeed, one way to visualise probability is to think of it as a type of frequency. For example, tossing a coin is an event which can have two possible outcomes, i.e. heads or tails. If a coin is tossed N times and the outcome was heads n times then an estimate of the probability of heads, Prob(heads), is given by

Prob(heads) = n/N

The value of n/N is only an estimate of the probability of heads but this value is a better estimate the larger the value of N.

The problem with accepting this definition is that some events only happen once but there can still be uncertainty about the outcome of the event, e.g. a horse race. In such cases the above definition of probability cannot be used because the occurrence cannot be repeated many times. You could say that if the race was repeated N times and you would expect a certain horse to win n times then the probability of that horse winning is n/N. This is usually referred to as subjective probability (6) and is common in decision making.

Other authors have debated both the applicability of probability and its precise meaning (7, 8). Cheeseman (1) argues that probability is a good measure for uncertainty in all its guises regardless of which way it is defined. Academics tend to prefer the subjective view of probability (9, 10) but the reader may wish to adopt the frequency approach. Either is acceptable.

6.2.3 Risk

If two people walk to work and one always carries either an umbrella or a raincoat but the other invariably carries neither then the latter is taking the greater risk of getting wet. The uncertainty about the weather does not change so risk is clearly not the same as uncertainty.

For the purposes of this book the word 'risk' will be given a specific meaning which is very close to the Concise Oxford Dictionary's definition 'chance of bad consequences, loss etc.'. In fact, the only difficulty with this definition is the word 'bad' which has to be interpreted relatively because a 'bad' outcome to one person may be no more than a minor inconvenience to another.

Consider the entrepreneur who is about to start a small business. Fifty per cent of small businesses do not survive five years and many entrepreneurs offer their houses as security against loans for their businesses. A fifty percent risk of losing your home is something you would not take lightly and the fact that the probability of success is 0.5 does not seem to completely convey the starkness of the situation.

Consider a further example which alludes to another aspect of risk and probability. Many people 'do' the pools. They pay a small stake in the hope of winning a fortune but the probability of success is miniscule and they realise this. The chances of a 'bad' outcome are very high. Why then is this not considered to be very risky? The answer is simple; they can afford to lose. In other words the outcome is not really 'bad' at all.

It should be clear by now that risk is more complex than probability. A one off decision is more risky than one which is one of many and a decision which could result in a severe loss is much more risky than one which could not. All this would be true even if the probability was equal for every case. However, we must now leave the discussion about risk for a later chapter.

6.3 PROBABILITY THEORY

As probability is the underlying measure of uncertainty it can be used to quantify uncertainty of all kinds. The ability to do this is useful in complex situations because Probability Theory can be used to combine uncertainty from all sources to produce a single quantitative measure of uncertainty. If probability is to have any quantitative meaning, however, the rules of probability must be strictly followed because invalid assumptions and/or improper manipulations of probabilities can quickly render any ensuing answer meaningless.

For this reason we will examine those theorems of Probability Theory which will be required later in the book. The theory will be developed by example rather than in a rigorous manner. This is because an understanding of the issues is required for decision support rather than a precise mathematical derivation. The rigorous mathematical proofs can easily be found in any textbook on Probability Theory.

6.3.1 Definition of Probability

For convenience we will adopt the definition of probability which is based on a frequency interpretation. This gave the probability for an outcome of an event, i.e. heads or tails, in terms of a number of repeated occurrences of that event.

If an event, e, has only two possible outcomes, i.e. true and false, we shall assume that in any occurrence of e, e will either take the value

E, i.e. the outcome was true, or e will take the value ~E, i.e. the outcome was false. A Venn diagram will be used to represent many occurrences of e and the proportion of those occurrences when e=E and when e=~E is represented by their relative areas in the diagram. Fig. 6.1 is one such diagram.

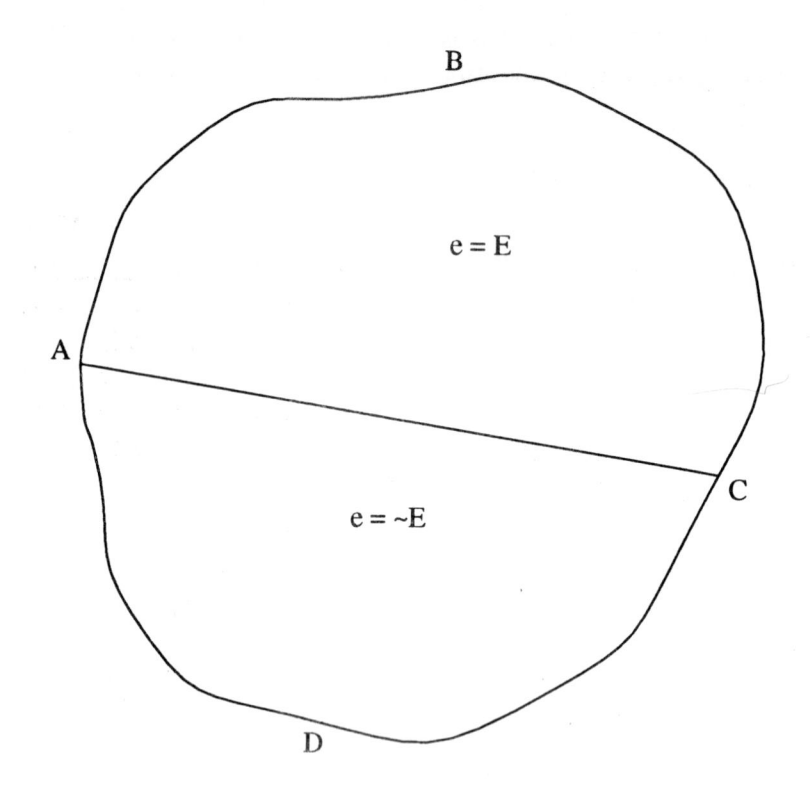

Fig. 6.1. Venn diagram of probability for an event

In Fig. 6.1 the area within the closed curve ABCD is assumed to represent the number of occurrences of e. Let us assume that this is N. The line AC divides the area within ABCD into two areas ABC and CDA. The area enclosed within ABC represents the number of occurrences when e was true, i.e. e=E. Let this be $n_{e=E}$. The area enclosed within CDA represents the number of occurrences when e was false, i.e. e=~E. Let this be $n_{e=\sim E}$. The occurrences when e=E are then separated from those when e=~E by the line AC. The probability of e=E, which should be written P(e=E) but is usually shortened to P(E), is then defined to be:

Summary of Probability Theory for Supporting Decisions 137

$$P(E) = \lim_{N \to \infty} \left(\frac{n_{e=E}}{N} \right) \tag{6.1}$$

Note that N, the total number of occurrences, must be very large (i.e. approaching infinity) for the r.h.s of equation (6.1) to be an accurate measure of P(E) and not just an estimate. Now, since

$$n_{e=E} + n_{e=\sim E} = N \tag{6.2}$$

equations (6.1) and (6.2) give

$$P(E) + P(\sim E) = 1 \tag{6.3}$$

which is usually written

$$P(\sim E) = 1 - P(E) \tag{6.4}$$

Events do not have to be two valued, however. Consider a normal die. Throwing a die is an occurrence of a six valued event, d, and $d = f_i$ for $i = 1...6$ are the six possible outcomes where f_i refers to an outcome where the face which shows the number i is uppermost. If the die is unbiased each face will be uppermost equally often and the Venn diagram which depicts this situation is shown in Fig. 6.2.

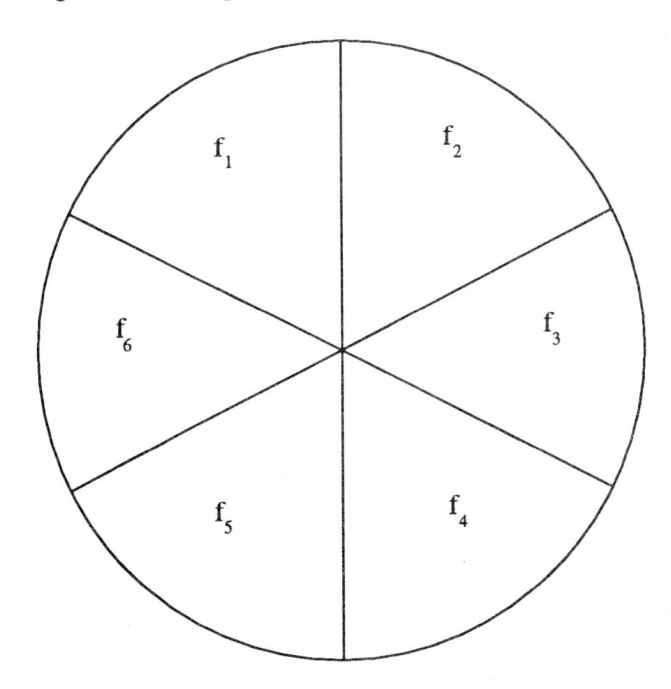

Fig. 6.2. Venn diagram for an unbiased die

Notice now that

$$P(f_1) + P(f_2) + P(f_3) + P(f_4) + P(f_5) + P(f_6) = 1 \qquad (6.5)$$

Equations (6.3) and (6.5) express a property known as exclusivity.

6.3.2 Exclusivity

If the possible outcomes of an event are such that one occurs to the mutual exclusion of the others and this is true for every occurrence of the event then the possible outcomes are said to be mutually exclusive. A die is the classical example. If the face with six dots is uppermost it is physically impossible for any of the other faces to be uppermost.

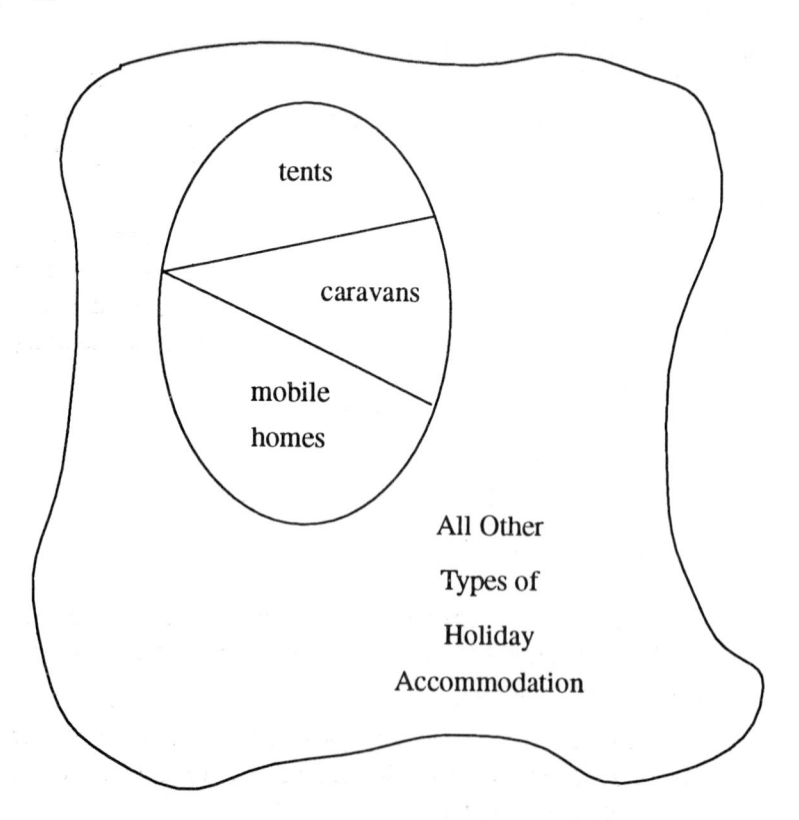

Fig. 6.3. Exclusive types of holiday accommodation

Exclusivity is an important property in probabilistic theory because the probability of several possible outcomes occurring is the sum of the probabilities of the individual possible outcomes. For example, the probability that the uppermost face of a die is either 1,2

Summary of Probability Theory for Supporting Decisions 139

or 3 is a half. This is a very useful property but it must be used with care.

Consider the holiday example again. Suppose that 2% of people who go on holiday use tents for accommodation, 3% take a caravan and 1% use a mobile home. If camping is defined to be any one of these then 6% of the population go camping for their holidays. Expressing this in probabilistic terms we would say:

P(tent) = 0.02

P(caravan) = 0.03

P(mobile home) = 0.01

P(camping) = 0.06

Note that this computation is only correct if a tent cannot be a caravan and a caravan cannot be a mobile home, etc.. A Venn diagram to depict this is given in Fig. 6.3.

Let us now suppose that 'under canvas' describes the use of either a tent or a caravan awning. In this case, i.e. 'under canvas', tents and caravans are no longer exclusive. Suppose that the percentages of the population undertaking holidays with the various types of camping accommodation are now as follows

caravan 3.0%

mobile home 1.0%

under canvas 3.5%

The percentage of the population who go camping could still be 6% even though the column total is 7.5%. This should become clear by examining the Venn diagram in Fig. 6.4.

In order to avoid caravan awnings being counted twice, the number of caravan awnings must be deducted from the total. Hence the number of campers is given by

$$\text{campers} = \text{no. under canvas} + \text{caravan} + \text{mobile home} - \text{awnings} \quad (6.6)$$

and if 50% of caravans have awnings, i.e. number of holiday makers using awnings is 1.5%, then the number of campers is still 6%.

When the above is expressed in probabilistic terms, the formula for calculating the probability of a person taking a camping holiday is:

P(campers) = P(under canvas) + P(caravan) + P(mobile home)
– P(under canvas and caravan)
– P(under canvas and mobile home)
– P(caravan and mobile home)
– P(under canvas and caravan and mobile home) (6.7)

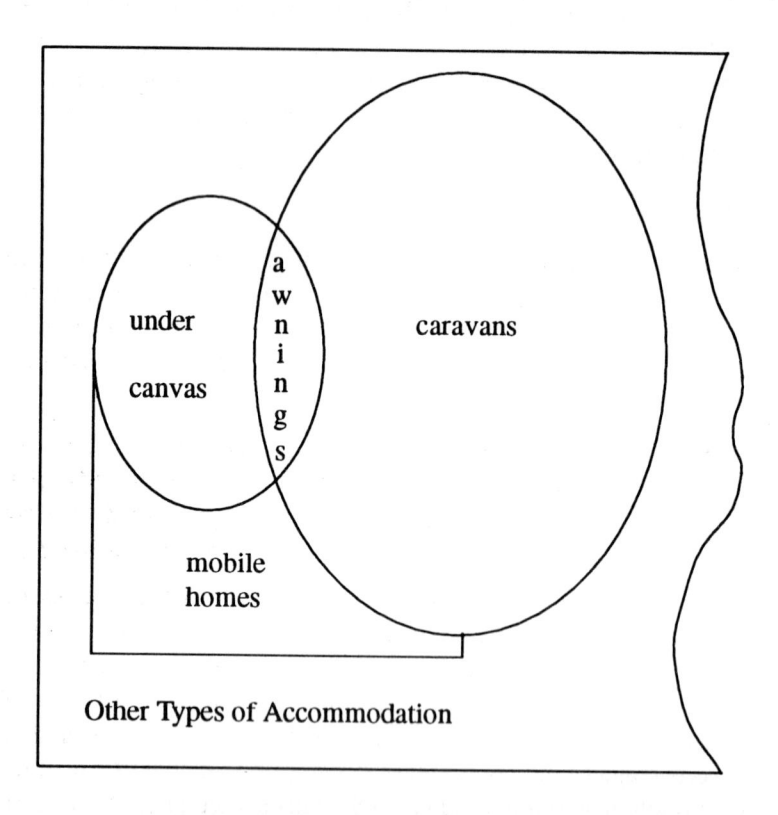

Fig. 6.4. Non–exclusive types of holiday accommodation

All the negative terms are combinations of possible outcomes which may have been counted twice in the first line of the expression. From Fig. 6.4 it can be seen that the last three terms in this expression are zero, i.e. no caravan is also a mobile home and consequently 'caravan and mobile home' cannot exist; equally no mobile home has an awning so 'under canvas and mobile home' cannot exist either. 'Under canvas and caravan' is precisely those caravans which have awnings and hence the full probabilistic expression given by equation

(6.7) reduces to the common sense one given by equation (6.6). Equation (6.7) is, however, the correct way to compute combined probabilities if the possible outcomes are not exclusive.

This example demonstrates the care which must be exercised when expressing the real world in probabilistic terms. If mistakes are made the final results will be worthless.

Problems with exclusivity are reasonably easily rectified, however. If all the separate areas in the Venn diagram are individually specified, they are mutually exclusive. For example if we considered the possible outcomes: tents, caravans without awnings, caravans with awnings and mobile homes, then we would have overcome the above problems.

6.3.3 Exhaustivity

A set of mutually exclusive possible outcomes for an event are exhaustive if, given any occurrence of the event, one of the mutually exclusive possible outcomes must occur. In other words an exclusive and exhaustive set of possible outcomes is one in which one, and only one, of the possible outcomes occurs.

This is a useful property from a probabilistic point of view because the sum of the probabilities of all the possible outcomes is unity. It is also an important property from a decision support point of view because it ensures that all possible outcomes are being considered.

Consider the die example again. Since we are assuming that one of the sides must be uppermost when the die comes to rest, equation (6.5) expresses the fact that the $f_1 \ldots f_2$ outcomes are exclusive and exhaustive. If we thought that there was a significant probability of something else happening, e.g. the die becoming lost, the die landing in a place where the uppermost face could not be seen, the die landing propped onto one edge, etc. then we would have to make allowances for this in equation (6.5). One way to achieve this is by adding all the additional possible outcomes to a general category such as 'other' which by definition excludes those already stated. Some degree of probability could then be apportioned to this possible outcome.

For example, if the die has a 0.04 probability of being lost, unseen or on edge, then each face can be allocated a probability of 0.16. We would then have a fairly good probabilistic model of reality.

In decision support situations the 'other' possible outcome may never need to be explored because its overall probability should remain low and the decision maker has presumably grouped things of little interest into the 'other' category. If during the decision making process it became clear that the 'other' possible outcome was accruing a significant probability of occurring then it would have to be investigated in greater detail.

6.3.4 Independence

Another important property in Probability Theory is that of independence because, if a situation possesses this property, the computation of the probabilities is very significantly simplified. If two or more events occur then they are said to be independent of each

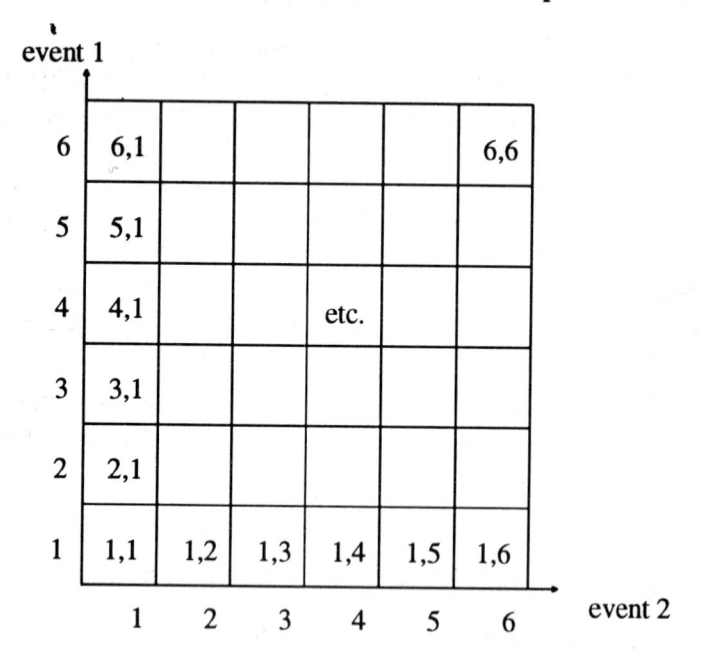

Fig. 6.5. Possible outcomes from two independent dice

other if the outcome of one cannot influence the outcome of the other. Notice that independence relates to joint possible outcomes of two or more events whilst exclusivity and exhaustivity refer to the possible outcomes of a single event.

One of the simplest cases to consider is that of throwing two dice. Each die can produce any outcome from 1 to 6 and the outcome of one does not affect that of the other. This can be represented by the diagram in Fig. 6.5.

As the probability of each joint possible outcome is equally likely and there are 36 of them, each has a probability of 1/36 of occurring. But this is conveniently the product of each occurring individually. So, for example:

P (6,6) = P(6) * P(6)
= 1/6 * 1/6
= 1/36

This is the reason for saying that independence greatly simplifies the computation of probabilities because, if joint probabilities (e.g. the probability of double six) can be computed from the product of the individual ones, far less information is required.

Consider the situation where three dice are thrown but they are known to be biased dice. We would require a knowledge of the probabilities for each face for each die, i.e. 18 pieces of information. With this information we could compute the probability of each of the 216 possible outcomes. If the dice were not independent of each other, e.g. connected by a string, then we would require 216 pieces of information before we knew the probability of all the possible outcomes. The impact of this on Decision Support Systems is quite dramatic because all that extra information has to be gathered from somewhere.

If events are not independent of each other, there is no simple trick which renders them so. Consider a compound event where a six sided die is thrown and then :

(1)   If the result is 5 or 6 another six sided die is thrown.

(2)   If the result is 3 or 4 a four sided die is thrown.

(3)   If the result is 1 or 2 a disc is thrown.

The four sided die can have outcomes from 1 to 4 and the disc can be either 1 or 2. The two events, (a) the throwing of a six sided die and (b) the throwing of an appropriate second die, are not now independent of each other. The possible outcomes are depicted in Fig. 6.6.

It is instructive at this stage to try to compute the probability distribution for both cases. It introduces the idea of a probability distribution and serves as an example of both exhaustive possible outcomes for a single event and indepenence between two or more events.

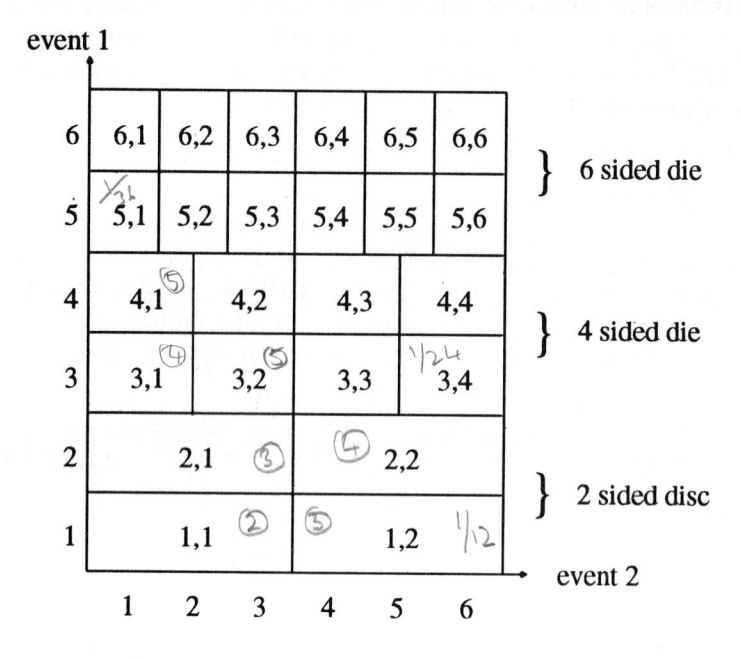

Fig. 6.6. Outcomes for two dependent events

6.3.5 Probability Distributions

A probability distribution is a mechanism for attaching a probability to each member of a set of mutually exclusive and exhaustive possible outcomes. In both of the above cases the set of all possible outcomes is {2,3,4,5,6,7,8,9,10,11,12} and a probability distribution would allocate a probability to each of these. We will denote the probability P(i) to be the probability that the sum of the numbers on the uppermost faces of the two dice is i.

Consider the possible outcomes with a total value of 5. In the first example, i.e. two independent dice, this can be achieved by the following combinations:

    1,4   2,3   3,2   4,1

None of these can occur together so they are exclusive, whence

    P(5) = P(1,4) + P(2,3) + P(3,2) + P(4,1)

But, the two events are independent so

    P(i,j) = P(i)*P(j)   for   i = 1 ... 6 ;   j = 1 ... 6

and if we assume both dice are unbiased,

$P(k) = 1/6$ for $k = i$ or j.

Consequently

$P(i,j) = 1/36$ for $i = 1 ... 6$; $j = 1 .. 6$

and

$P(5) = 4/36$

If the probabilities for all the values 1 ... 12 are calculated then the probability distribution for the independent case can be seen to be those shown in Table 6.2.

Table 6.2. Probability distribution for two independent dice

Total	2	3	4	5	6
Probability	1/36	2/36	3/36	4/36	5/36

Total	7	8	9	10	11	12
Probability	6/36	5/36	4/36	3/36	2/36	1/36

In the second case, when the dice are not independent, the calculations are not quite so easy but even the second case is not completely devoid of some element of independence so we can proceed as follows. The set of all possible outcomes is {2 ... 12} again. These totals can be acquired in various ways but the different ways are still exclusive hence,

$P(5) = P(3,2) + P(4,1)$

but the P(1,4) and P(2,3) terms are missing because they cannot occur since, if a 1 or 2 is thrown for the first die, the second die can only produce a 1 or 2. However, once we know that the first die was either a 3 or a 4 we know that the second die is four sided and the first die cannot influence the outcome any further. Consequently

$P(3, 2) = P_6(3) * P_4(2)$

where $P_6(3)$ is used to denote the probability of getting a three from a six sided die and $P_4(2)$ is used to denote the probability of getting a 2 from a 4 sided die. Hence

$$P(5) = P_6(3) * P_4(2) + P_6(4) * P_4(1)$$
$$= 1/6 * 1/4 + 1/6 * 1/4$$
$$= 2/24$$

The complete probability distribution for the second case is given in Table 6.3.

Table 6.3. Probability distribution for two dependent dice

Total	2	3	4	5	6
Probability	6/72	12/72	9/72	6/72	8/72
Total	7	8	9	10	11	12
Probability	10/72	7/72	4/72	4/72	4/72	2/72

It is easy to see that the two events are not independent, i.e. the probability of double six is not the product of the probability of a six for both events. The second event now has a rather skew distribution.

It is worth computing the probability distribution for the second event. All three types of dice should be thrown equally often because there is no bias in the die used in the first event. The probability that a particular type of die is thrown is, therefore, 1/3. Consequently

$$P_6(1) = P_6(2) = P_6(3) = P_6(4) = P_6(5) = P_6(6) = 1/3 * 1/6 = 1/18$$

$$P_4(1) = P_4(2) = P_4(3) = P_4(4) = 1/3 * 1/4 = 1/12$$

$$P_2(1) = P_2(2) = 1/3 * 1/2 = 1/6$$

because the three dice used in the second event are exclusive, i.e. only one of them is used in one event, the appropriate probabilities can be added together. So, the probability distribution for the second event is given in Table 6.4.

Now the probability of getting a six from the first event is 1/6 and the probability of getting a six from the second event is 1/18 so, if the two events were independent, the probability of a double six would be 1/6 * 1/18 = 1/108. But this is not the case. The probability of a double six, given by Table 6.3 is 1/36. Clearly the two events in this second example are not independent of each other.

Table 6.4. Probability distribution for the second event

P(1) = 1/18 + 1/12 + 1/6 = 11/36

P(2) = 1/18 + 1/12 + 1/6 = 11/36

P(3) = 1/18 + 1/12 = 5/36

P(4) = 1/18 + 1/12 = 5/36

P(5) = 1/18 = 2/36

P(6) = 1/18 = 2/36

The difference between 1/108 and 1/36 is rather marked and indicates the degree of error which is possible if due care is not taken.

6.4 CONDITIONAL PROBABILITY

Conditional Probability is an important concept which is particularly pertinent to Decision Support Systems. Consider again case B above. Table 6.4 gives the probability distribution for each possible outcome of the second event assuming that the first event has not happened. But, the probabilities in Table 6.4 can be revised as long as the outcome of the first event is known.

For example, suppose that the first event has produced a two, the probability of the second event producing a 3, 4, 5 or 6 is now zero and the probability of the second event producing a 1 or a 2 is 1/2. In cases like this we talk about the probability of the second event, E2, given the first event, E1, and write it as P(E2|E1). Venn diagrams are again useful for visualising what is happening.

Fig. 6.7 depicts two valued events a and b. Event a has possible outcomes A or ~A and similarly event b has possible outcomes B or ~B. In both cases these can be interpreted to mean that the event is either true or false. The closed curve VWXY in Fig. 6.7 depicts all occurrences of A and B and is usually referred to as the Universe of Discourse.

The area above the line VX is that part of the universe of discourse in which a is true, i.e. a = A. Event a is false, i.e. a = ~A, in the area beneath it. Similarly to the left of WY the event b is false, i.e. b = ~B, and to the right of the line WY b is true, i.e. b = B. These two lines split the domain into four portions one in which both a and b are true, i.e. AB, one in which a is true and b is false, i.e. A~B, one in which a is false and b is true, i.e. ~AB, and one in which both a and b are false, i.e. ~A~B. Let us presume that both VX and WY bisect the domain, then:

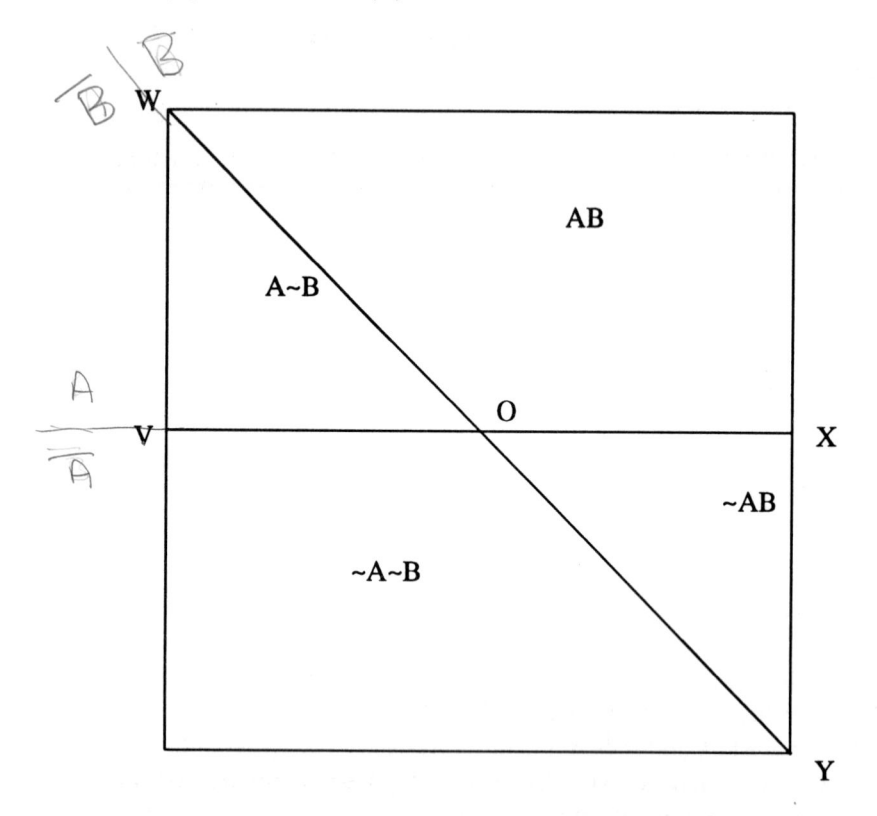

$$P(A) = 0.5 \text{ and } P(B) = 0.5$$

Fig. 6.7. Venn diagram for conditional probabilities

Let us now assume that we know the value of event a to be true, i.e. a = A. The domain of discourse is now restricted to that part of VWXY above the line VX because we know that a = A. The probability that b = B, is now the proportion of the area VWX in which b = B,

i.e. P (B|A) = Area WXO/Area VWXO (6.8)

which is about 0.75 in the diagram. P(AB) can be represented by the formula

P(AB) = Area WXO/Area VWXY (6.9)

and the probability of a = A can be represented by

P(A) = Area VWXO/Area VWXY (6.10)

so we can intuitively deduce that

P(B|A) = P(AB)/P(A) (6.11)

Furthermore, we can extend this to produce Bayes' theorem which states that

P(B|A) = P(A|B)*P(B)/P(A) (6.12)

Conditional probability extends some of the properties described in section 6.3 above. The ones which are worthy of note at this stage are:

(1) Independence.

(2) The probability of multiple events.

(3) Conditional independence.

6.4.1 Independence

Two events a and b are independent if

P(A|B) = P(A)

and/or

P(B|A) = P(B) (6.13)

for outcome A of a and B of b. In other words a is independent of b if knowing the outcome of event a does not alter the probabilities of the possible outcomes of event b.

This can be seen graphically by referring back to Fig. 6.5. Notice that the lines separating the possible outcomes of event 1 from those of event 2 are drawn at right angles to each other and are continuous so, whatever the outcome of event 1, event 2 still has exactly the same probability distribution for its possible outcomes. Note that this is not true for Fig. 6.6.

6.4.2 Probability of Multiple Events

The probability distribution for the multiple event represented by Fig. 6.6 was computed and presented in Table 6.3. The argument that was used can now be formalised.

Table 6.3 was computed by taking each possible outcome of event 1 in turn and examining the probability of the possible outcomes of event 2 given the specified outcome of event 1. For example if we know that event 1 produced a 2 then:

P(e2 = 1|e1 = 2) = 0.5

and

P(e2 = 2|e1 = 2) = 0.5

because event 2 in this case would be the flipping of a disc. But, we know that

P(e2 = 1, e1 = 2) = P (e2 = 1|e1 = 2) * P (e1 = 2)

whence, in the shorthand notation used previously

P(1, 2) = $P_2(1) * P_6(2)$

This is a particular case of a general result which says that

P (ABCD ...) = P(A).P(B|A)*P(C|AB)*P(D|ABC)...   (6.14)

Note that this rule is true whether or not A, B, C and D are independent of each other. If A, B, C and D are independent, however,

P(B|A) = P(B), P(C|AB) = P(C), P(D|ABC) = P(D), etc.

so

P(ABCD) = P(A)*P(B)*P(C)*P(D)

as we would expect.

One further property of multiple events which is referred to as marginal values will be required later. Marginal values occur when one of the events is eliminated by summing over all its possible outcomes. With two valued events this can be expressed as:

P(ABC) = P(ABCD) + P(ABC~D)

6.4.3 Conditional Independence

In decision making another type of independence can also be useful, namely conditional independence. This type of independence occurs when two events are not independent of each other in the whole domain of discourse but they are independent of each other in a limited part of the domain. They are then independent of each other

Summary of Probability Theory for Supporting Decisions 151

on the condition that we are interested in only the limited part of the domain of discourse, i.e. they are conditionally independent.

Consider our dice example again and suppose that after the initial throw of an unbiased six sided die, two dice of the appropriate type are thrown. Once the first die has been thrown the two dice which are thrown next are independent of each other whether they be both six sided dice, both four sided dice or both two sided dice. This can be quantified as follows. The joint probability of a particular outcome from three separate events is given by:

P(ABC) = P(A)*P(B|A)*P(C|AB)

In the case which we are considering the outcome of the second event cannot affect the third, hence

P(C|AB) = P(C|A)

so

P(ABC) = P(A)*P(B|A)*P(C|A) (6.15)

but

P(ABC) <> P(A)*P(B)*P(C)

i.e. B and C are conditionally independent of each other given A but not mutually independent of each other.

For example, if we use equation (6.15) to compute the probability distribution of the triple event above we have:

P(1, 1, 1) = $P_6(1) * P_2(1) * P_2(1)$ P(3, 1, 1) = $P_6(3) * P_4(1) * P_4(1)$

P(1, 1, 2) = $P_6(1) * P_2(1) * P_2(2)$ ...

P(1, 2, 1) = $P_6(1) * P_2(2) * P_2(1)$ P(5, 1, 1) = $P_6(5) * P_6(1) * P_6(1)$

P(1, 2, 2) = $P_6(1) * P_2(2) * P_2(2)$ ...

P(2, 1, 1) = $P_6(2) * P_2(1) * P_2(1)$ P(6, 6, 6) = $P_6(6) * P_6(6) * P_6(6)$

...   .

...   .

and the probability distribution for this case will be that shown in Table 6.5.

Table 6.5. Probability distribution for outcome of three dice

P(3) = 1/24	P(7) = 49/864	P(11) = 63/864	P(15) = 7/216
P(4) = 3/24	P(8) = 75/864	P(12) = 53/864	P(16) = 5/216
P(5) = 13/96	P(9) = 83/864	P(13) = 11/216	P(17) = 3/216
P(6) = 7/96	P(10) = 73/864	P(14) = 9/216	P(18) = 1/216

Now the probability distribution for the first die is the uniform distribution $P(1) = P(2) = P(3) = P(4) = P(5) = P(6) = 1/6$ and the probability distribution for the second and third event is that given by Table 6.4. So, the probability of throwing a total of 18 if the three events are assumed to be independent of each other is

$$P_6(6) * P_{table6.4}(6) * P_{table6.4}(6) = 1/6 * 1/18 * 1/18 = 1/1944 \qquad (6.16)$$

This does not equal the true value given in Table 6.5 which is 1/216 and so demonstrates that the multiple events are not independent of each other.

Note that it is the value given by equation (6.16) which is surprising but this is because, in this case, you instinctively use conditional probability, i.e. you know the first outcome was a six, so you know that the second and third dice are six sided so you compute the probability $1/6 * 1/6 * 1/6 = 1/216$; but the second two values are conditional probabilities based on the knowledge that the first outcome was a six. This demonstrates yet again how very careful you have to be.

Note also that, whilst the above example demonstrates that conditional independence does not necessarily result in mutual independence, the opposite is also true, i.e. mutual independence does not necessarily result in conditional independence. Figures 6.8 and 6.9 demonstrate this graphically.

In Fig. 6.8 event a is true, i.e. a = A, above the line VW and event a is false, i.e. a = ~A, below this line. Event b is true to the left of line XY and false to the right of this line. Event c is true to the top/right of line PQ and false to the bottom/left of this line. From the geometry of the diagram it is clear that:

$P(A) = 0.5, \quad P(B) = 0.5, \quad P(C) = 0.5$

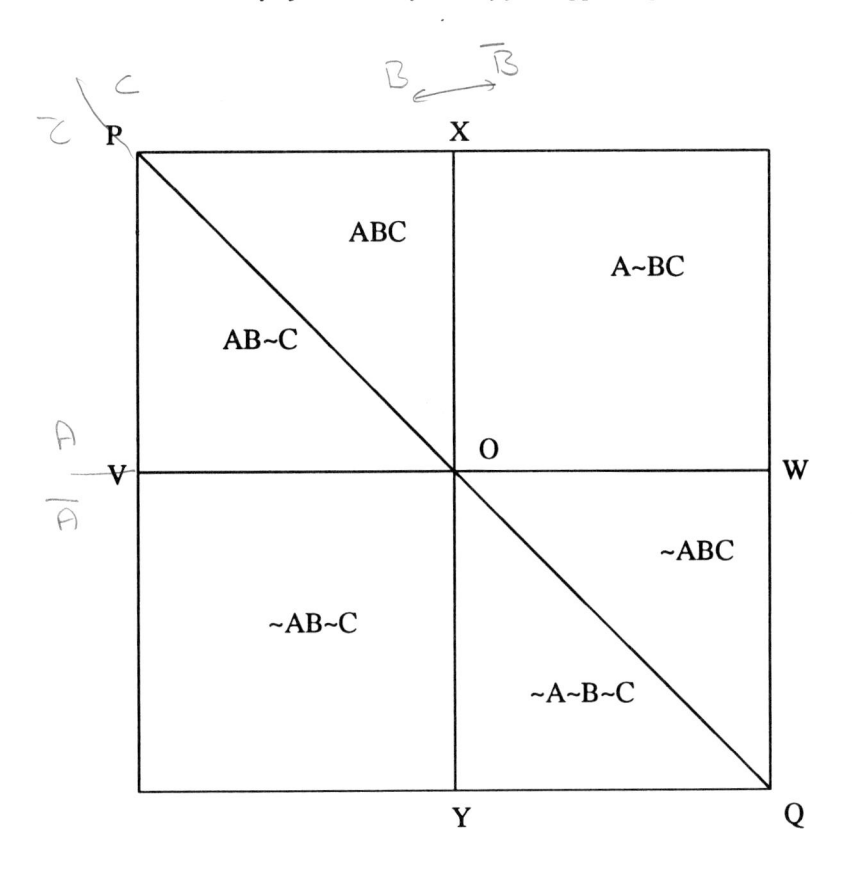

Summary of Probability Theory for Supporting Decisions 153

Fig. 6.8. Mutual but not conditional independence

It is also clear that event a and b are independent, i.e.

$P(AB) = P(A) * P(B) = 0.25$

But,

$P(A|C) = 0.75$ and $P(B|C) = 0.5$

So,

$P(A|C) * P(B|C) = 0.375$ which does not equal $P(AB|C) = 0.25$

In other words, events a and b are not conditionally independent.

If we now consider Fig. 6.9, we can see that event a is true above and to the right of line PQRS and false below and to the left of it. Event b is true above the line XY and false below it. Event c is true within the inner box and false outside it.

If the diagram is studied further, it should be clear that events a and b are conditionally independent given event c = C but that they are not mutually independent, i.e.

$P(AB|C) = P(A|C) * P(B|C)$ but $P(AB) <> P(A) * P(B)$

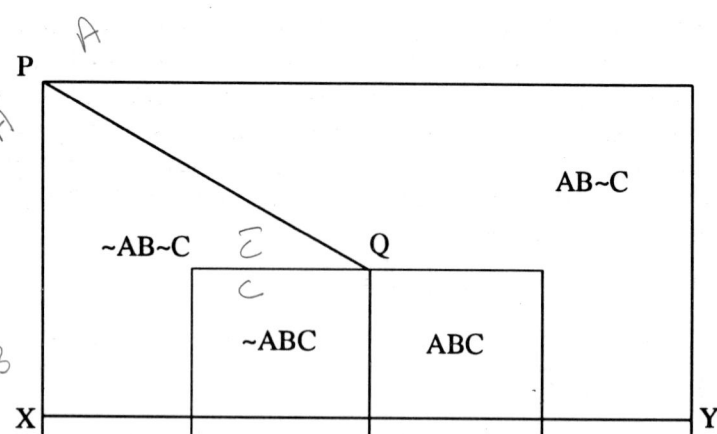

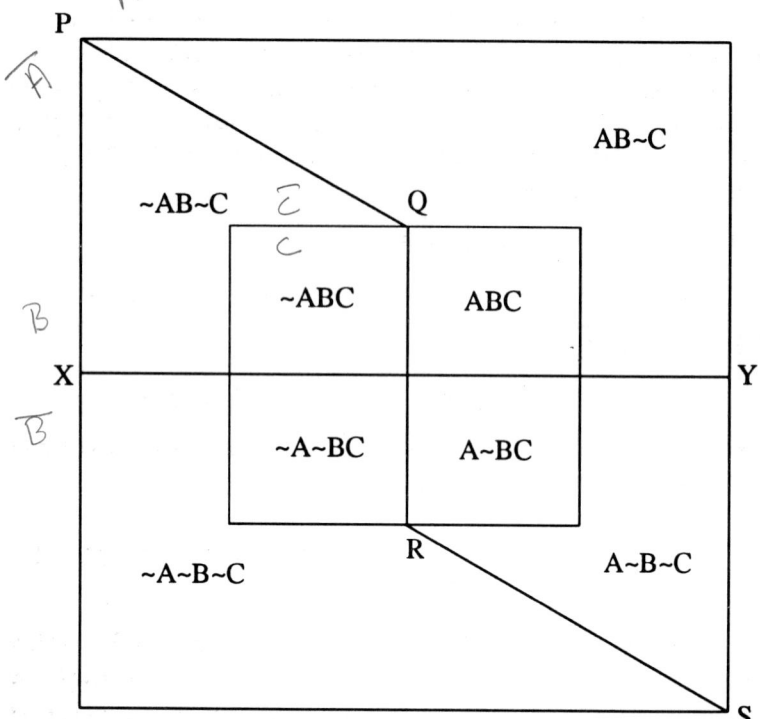

Fig. 6.9. Conditional but not mutual independence

6.5 PROBABILITY AND LOGIC

In the previous discussions we have always talked about probabilities of events which occur together in terms of the outcome A of event a 'and' the outcome B of event b happening together. We denoted this as P(AB) but sometimes it is convenient to separate the occurrences with a comma, i.e. P(A,B), so the comma denotes the 'and', hence

$P(e3 = 1 | e1 = 1$ and $e2 = 1)$

is usually written

$P(e3 = 1 | e1 = 1, e2 = 1)$

or if the order of e3 e2 and e1 is clearly understood this can be abbreviated to P(1 | 1,1).

When possible outcomes are mutually exclusive, we will talk about

P(e2 = 1 | e1 = 1 or e1 = 2).

This apparent use of logic within probabilistic terms must be treated very cautiously. Firstly the 'and' is associated with the outcomes of separate events which are occurring together whereas the 'or' is used to compute the joint probability of a set of possible outcomes which are mutually exclusive. The similarity to logical 'and' and logical 'or' is deceptive. For example, De Morgan's theorem in logic states:

A and (B or C) = (A and B) or (A and C)

Much more care is required, however, when trying to compute

P(A and (B or C))

if only because 'A and B' is not independent of 'A and C'.

For the sake of simplicity, this book will avoid such uses except where they are handled explicitly.

6.6 CUMULATIVE PROBABILITY DISTRIBUTIONS

Now that the concept of 'or'ing exclusive possible outcomes is established, we can consider a form of probability distribution which is very useful in some decision support methods. For example, it would allow us to tell a manager what the probability of making 'at least' 80% profit might be. In order to do this we would have to sum the probability of making 80%–90% profit with the probability of making 90%–100%, for example. This is precisely what cumulative probability distributions do.

Consider the throwing of two unbiased six sided dice. This would normally be considered as two independent events. The probability distribution for the combined total was given in Table 6.2 and is given again in the 'Probability' row of Table 6.6. The cumulative probabilities are given by the 'Cumulative A' and 'Cumulative B' rows. The 'Cumulative A' row gives the probability that the outcome will be at most the value shown at the head of the column and the 'Cumulative B' row gives the probability that the outcome will be at least the value at the head of the column.

For example, the probability of throwing 5 from two dice is 4/36, the probability of throwing at most 5 is 10/36 and the probability of throwing at least 5 is 28/36. Both of these are relevant for decision support.

Table 6.6. Cumulative probability distributions for two independent dice

Total	2	3	4	5	6
Probability	1/36	2/36	3/36	4/36	5/36
Cumulative A	1/36	3/36	6/36	10/36	15/36
Cumulative B	36/36	35/36	32/36	28/36	23/36

Total	7	8	9	10	11	12
Probability	6/36	5/36	4/36	3/36	2/36	1/36
Cumulative A	21/36	26/36	30/36	33/36	35/36	36/36
Cumulative B	17/36	12/36	8/36	5/36	3/36	1/36

6.7 EXPECTED VALUES

One further concept is required for supporting decisions, namely the Expected Value of an event. We have already alluded to this when we discussed racehorse owners.

The Expected Value, EV, of an event which has N possible outcomes is defined as:

$$EV = \sum_{i=1}^{N} \{P(\text{possible outcome}_i) * \text{payoff}_i\}$$

and is a type of weighted mean where the weights are the probabilities that the possible outcomes will occur.

If we assume that the probability distribution given by Table 6.7 represents the probability of a race horse winning the amount shown in any year, then the Expected Value of the winnings from one horse per year is:

0.4 * 0 + 0.3 * 10000 + 0.2 * 20000 + 0.1 * 30000 = 10000

We can now understand risk a little better. The more racehorses you have the better your chances of making the Expected Value on average. If you only have one racehorse you must be able to afford the bad years in between the good ones but in the long run you should still achieve the Expected Value. Expected Values are the essence of decision making.

Table 6.7. Probability distribution for annual winnings

Winnings/year	00000	10000	20000	30000
Probability	0.4	0.3	0.2	0.1

6.8 RELEVANCE OF PROBABILITY THEORY TO DECISION SUPPORT SYSTEMS

All the above results are pertinent to Decision Support Systems because, in the appropriate circumstances, they can assist in making decisions.

Suppose for a moment that event b represent some form of feedback and event a is a decision which uses the feedback, the probability P(A|B) would then represent the probability that positive action should be taken given positive feedback. It may be P(A|~B) which is of more interest, i.e. the probability that positive action should be taken given negative feedback. Alternatively we may be interested in P(B|A) and P(~B|A), i.e. if we act positively, what is the probability that the feedback will be positive. This is a formal way of asking how reliable the feedback is.

Diagnostic procedures and Expert Systems are other examples of the use of conditional probabilities (11). These systems use conditional probabilities as a means of computing the probability that a particular fault has occurred or that a particular action should be taken.

Identifying a complete set of possible outcomes is important in decision making. A complete set of possible outcomes is an exclusive and exhaustive set in probabilistic terms. Each possible outcome can be given a probability and the sum of the probabilities must be unity. The probabilities can represent either the probability that the possible outcome will occur or the probability that the possible outcome will be the best one. One or other of these is always appropriate depending on the circumstances.

If a large decision has been broken up into smaller decisions and the smaller decisions are independent of each other then the product rule can be invoked to calculate the probability of the compound possible outcomes for the main decision. If the decisions are not independent, more care is required.

6.9 ESTIMATING PROBABILITIES IN THE PRESENCE OF DEPENDENCIES

The problem of choosing a holiday has already been mentioned in Chapter 3. It involved making several sub–decisions such as the type of accommodation which is preferred, the type of location, the type of weather, the distance away, the mode of transport, the cost, etc.. These were listed in Fig. 3.3 and some of the possible outcomes were given in Fig. 3.4.

If we examine the list of sub–decisions they are all reasonably independent with the exception of cost and some of the modes of travel. Clearly all holidays are not available across the entire price range, e.g. far away places which are not tourist destinations are bound to be expensive.

There are several ways of tackling dependencies such as these. We will discuss three:

(1) Ignore the dependencies.

(2) Re–express the sub–decisions.

(3) Use conditional probabilities.

6.9.1 Ignoring the Dependencies

Sometimes it is safe to ignore the dependencies. Consider for example cost and far away places. If we assume that these are independent some probability will accrue to this combination which should have been apportioned elsewhere. But, since holidays in far away places will have a low probability anyway, the proportion of wrongly allocated probability will be small and can probably be ignored. In fact, since choosing between possible outcomes is relative in nature, we can afford to wrongly assume independence as long as we are sure that this does not alter the relative probabilities of the other possible outcomes. Unfortunately dependencies usually do exactly that so ignoring them must be treated with great caution.

6.9.2 Re–Expressing Sub–Decisions

Sub–decisions need to be chosen with care and their exact purpose scrutinised. For example, consider walking as a mode of transport. The question which must be posed is whether walking is genuinely considered to be a mode of transport or whether it is really an activity. You can fly to a destination which is ideal for a walking holiday or you can set out from home with a pack on your back. Walking as an activity is independent of location and cost; walking as a mode of transport is not independent of location and cost because it must be related to cheap holidays near home.

Another factor to consider at this stage is the nature of the probabilities which are being assigned. If we are trying to assign probabilities which represent the likelihood that we would enjoy a holiday, then cost and mode of transport are independent of each other. Our enjoyment of a holiday may well depend on whether or not we feel we can afford it. That part of our enjoyment which depends on the cost will not be influenced by how far away our destination is. Whether or not we like to go to far away places is a separate issue. Consequently the frame of reference can be very important when assessing independence.

It is for precisely this reason that some people (12) argue that there is no such thing as an absolute probability. They argue that every probability is conditioned by something and that it is important to state what the conditioning circumstances are. The above paragraph is then easily expressed by saying that cost and distance to destination are conditionally independent of each other given that the holiday maker can afford the holiday or, alternatively, given that the holiday maker will enjoy the holiday.

6.9.3 Using Conditional Probabilities

If the sub–decisions cannot be expressed so that they are more or less independent of each other then equation (6.14) must be invoked. In other words if we assumes that the sub–decision about cost is not independent of the others, we can allocate probabilities to the possible outcomes of the other decisions given the cost. In our example, this would mean allocating three probabilities to every alternative of every other sub–decision which is dependent on cost, e.g. P(far away place | cheap), P(far away place | affordable), P(far away place | expensive). This requires a lot of information but in cases of severe dependencies there is no other option. To assume independence would be to simplify recklessly and to jeopardise the whole purpose of the exercise.

6.10 SUMMARY

Uncertainty nearly always accompanies decision making and, despite attempts to formulate alternative theories, probability is still the most appropriate theory for formalising the inherent uncertainty in decisions. Consequently, this chapter discussed probability and considered some of its fundamental properties.

The discussion was extended to simplifying assumptions, i.e. independence, exclusivity and exhaustivity, which may be used in appropriate circumstances. Some cautionary examples were also provided to demonstrate that these simplifying assumptions must be used with care because, if the assumptions are not valid, the decision maker can be misled by grossly inaccurate results.

Conditional probabilities were then discussed as a means of avoiding the use of invalid assumptions. Unfortunately, if no simplifying assumptions are made, the amount of information required to describe the system becomes excessive. The weaker assumption of conditional independence may be appropriate in some circumstances so conditional independence was discussed and compared with mutual independence.

After providing some cautionary comments about trying to mix probability and logic and briefly discussing cumulative probability distributions, the discussion was concluded with a brief look at the relevance of Probability Theory to decision making.

6.11 R, B & H CASE STUDY

As an example of probabilistic methods applied to decision making, consider the top level strategic decision for R, B & H which was briefly mentioned in the last chapter. This is shown again in Fig. 6.10.

Mr Philip has been thinking about the future and has identified the three sub–decisions shown in Fig. 6.10 as being critical for a successful strategic plan. He considers each of these sub–decisions to be more or less independent of each other because the future of R, B & H must be settled regardless of what he and Mr Keith decide to do personally and they can consider starting a new venture whether or not they continue to run R, B & H.

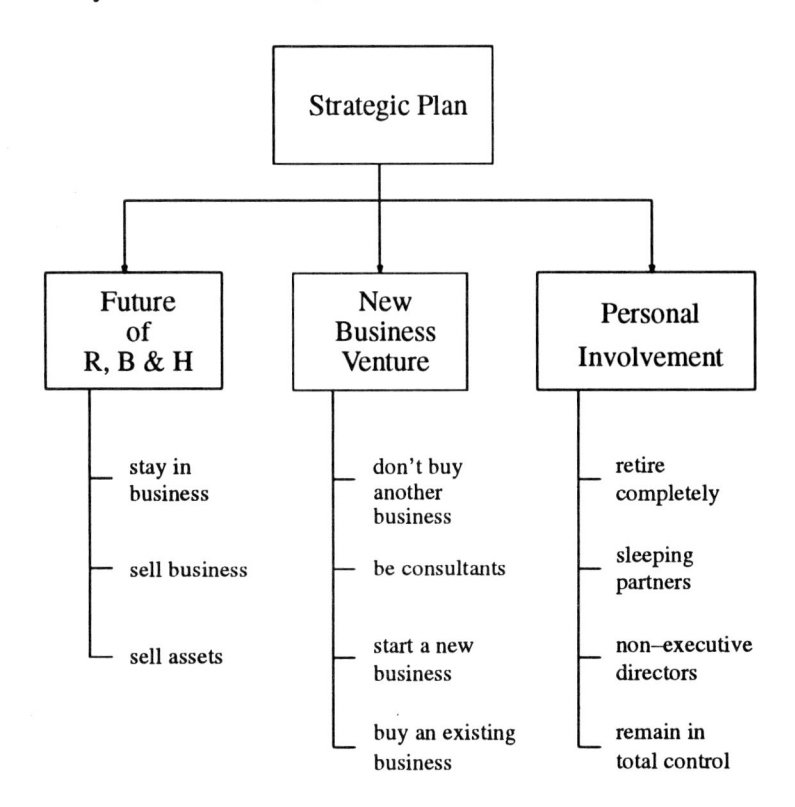

```
                        ┌─────────────────┐
                        │  Strategic Plan │
                        └─────────────────┘
                                │
        ┌───────────────────────┼───────────────────────┐
┌───────────────┐      ┌─────────────────┐      ┌───────────────┐
│    Future     │      │      New        │      │   Personal    │
│      of       │      │    Business     │      │  Involvement  │
│   R, B & H    │      │    Venture      │      │               │
└───────────────┘      └─────────────────┘      └───────────────┘
        │                       │                       │
   ─ stay in                ─ don't buy             ─ retire
     business                 another                 completely
                              business
   ─ sell business         ─ be consultants        ─ sleeping
                                                     partners
   ─ sell assets           ─ start a new           ─ non–executive
                             business                directors

                          ─ buy an existing        ─ remain in
                            business                 total control
```

Fig. 6.10. Top level strategic decision for R, B & H

Mr Philip has identified a set of exclusive and exhaustive possible outcomes for each of the sub–decisions. He considers the possible outcomes for the 'New Business Venture' sub–decision to be exclusive because he and Mr Keith would have neither the energy nor the resources to undertake more than one. He now wishes to allocate to each of the possible outcomes a probability which represents his assessment of the chances of that particular course of action being the best one to chose, i.e. will prove to be the most satisfactory in the long term for Mr Keith and himself. His probabilities are given in Table 6.8. Notice that these are simple probabilities and, at present, Mr Philip has not considered the payoff associated with each possible outcome.

Consider now one of the forty eight possible outcomes of the combined sub–decisions namely, 'stay in business', 'don't buy another business' and 'retire completely'. The probability that this will be successful is 0.001, i.e. 0.1 * 0.1 * 0.1. This may seem rather small but as yet we have no quantitative way of knowing how good or bad it is.

Table 6.8. Simple probabilistic analysis of the R, B & H strategic decision

Strategic Sub–Decisions

Future of R < B & H		New Business Venture		Personal Involvement	
Pos–Outcomes	Prob	Pos–Outcomes	Prob	Pos–Outcomes	Prob
stay in business	0.1	don't buy another	0.1	retire completely	0.1
sell business	0.3	become consultants	0.3	be sleeping partners	0.1
sell assets	0.6	start a new business	0.1	non–executive directors	0.2
		buy existing business	0.5	remain in total control	0.6

We can ascertain this by considering the 'don't know' situation, i.e. by assuming that all the possible outcomes have been allocated equal probabilities. The probability distribution of the 'don't know' scenario is that every possible outcome has a probability of 1/48, i.e. 0.020833. The probability of each possible outcome can now be viewed in terms of this 'don't know' scenario. It is then apparent that the possible outcome 'stay in business', 'don't buy another business' and 'retire' is approximately twenty times less likely to succeed than the 'don't know' scenario which can be considered as a sort of average. Compare this with the best strategy, namely 'sell assets', 'buy a traditional business' and 'remain in total charge' which has a probability of 0.18 of being the best one to choose. This has a probability nine times better than the average.

Summary of Probability Theory for Supporting Decisions 163

Consider now what we would have to do if we did not think that the sub–decisions were independent of each other. Let us assume that the 'New Business Venture' sub–decision is dependent on the 'Future of R, B & H' sub–decision because more money will be available for the new venture if R, B & H is sold. In this case we need two conditional probabilities for each of the possible outcomes of the 'New Venture' sub–decision, one for the 'stay in business' outcome of the 'Future of R, B & H' sub–decision and one for the other two outcomes. Table 6.9 gives Mr Philip's values for these probabilities.

Table 6.9. Conditional probabilistic analysis of the R, B & H strategic decision

Strategic Sub–Decisions

Future of R < B & H		New Business Venture		Personal Involvement	
Pos–Outcomes	Prob	Pos–Outcomes	Prob	Pos–Outcomes	Prob
stay in business	0.1	don't buy another	0.1|S 0.3|~S	retire completely	0.1|aopo 0.8|s&db
sell business	0.3	become consultants	0.3 0.3|~S	be sleeping partners	0.1|aopo 0.1|s&db
sell assets	0.6	start a new business	0.1|S 0.1|~S	non–executive directors	0.2|aopo 0.1|s&db
		buy existing business	0.5|S 0.3|~S	remain in total control	0.6|aopo 0.0|s&db

S	=	'stay in business'
~S	=	'sell business' or 'sell assets'
s&db	=	'sell business' or 'sell assets' and 'don't buy another business'
aopo	=	all other possible outcomes

If we further assume that the dependence of the 'Personal Involvement' sub–decision on the previous two is restricted to one case when the brothers intend to sell R, B & H and do not intend to buy another business and a second case which includes all other possible outcomes of the first two sub–decisions, the 'Personal Involvement' sub-decision will then also need two conditional probabilities for each of its possible outcomes. These are also shown in Table 6.9.

We can now compute the probability that a particular outcome would be the best one to chose. In order to do this we must return to equation (6.14) whereupon the probability of the possible outcome 'sell assets','don't buy another business' and 'retire completely' becomes

P(sell assets)*P(don't buy another business|sell assets)*

P(retire completely|sell assets 'and' don't buy another business)

= 0.6 * 0.3 * 0.8

= 0.144

The 'don't know' probability is still 0.0208 because all possible outcomes are given equal probability, so this is seven times better than 'average'. It can only be challenged by the probability associated with the best possible outcome in the independent case, i.e. 'sell assets', 'buy a traditional business' and 'remain in total control' which is now 0.108, i.e. only five times better than average. Note that considering the dependencies has resulted in a different outcome being chosen.

This analysis has made the possible outcomes for Mr Keith and Mr Philip much clearer and easier to assess. By using the decision support method advocated earlier, the brothers have managed to structure their decision and identify all the possible outcomes. The only tricky step is allocating the probabilities to the possible outcomes of the sub-decisions. Mr Philip could have done this by collecting information about the various outcomes and then using his judgement to assign the probabilities. If this were so, the decision would have been made qualitatively.

There are three points to note about the above procedure:

(1) Its simplicity.

(2) Its qualitative nature.

(3) Its compatibility with the Decision Support System Architecture.

6.12 POINTS TO PONDER

(1) Write a list for both the internal and external data which Mr Philip would need in order to provide his assessment of the

probability of the various possible outcomes being 'the most satisfactory long term outcome for Mr Keith and Mr Philip'.

(2) What would be likely sources of this information and how could it be incorporated into Management Information Systems?

(3) Assuming Mr Philip did not sell the business, what sort of data could he use as feedback to measure the success of his strategy? Could Mr Philip be certain that his feedback is correct or might this also have an element of uncertainty about it?

(4) Try allocating probabilities (of enjoyment) to the possible outcomes of the holiday decision's sub–decisions and then try to be much more quantitative about why you allocated your particular probabilities.

(5) Are there any possible outcomes for which you are unable to give probabilities?

(6) Should a Decision Support System try to assist with the allocation of probabilities to possible outcomes?

6.13 FURTHER READING

- Alter, S. and Ginzberg, M. (1978) Managing Uncertainty in MIS Implementations. *Sloan Management Review*, Autumn, pp. 23–31.

- Drake, A.W. (1967) *Fundamentals of Applied Probability Theory.* McGraw–Hill.

- Fine, T. (1973) *Theories of Probability.* Academic Press.

- Holloway, C.A. (1979) *Decision Making Under Uncertainty: Models and Choices.* Prentice Hall.

- Holzman, S. and Breeze, J. (1986) Exact Reasoning about Uncertainty: On the Design of Expert Systems for Decision Support. In *Uncertainty in Artificial Intelligence,* Lemmer, J.F. and Kanal, L.N. (eds), North Holland, pp. 339–345.

- Shannon, C.E. and Weaver, W. (1949) *A Mathematical Theory of Communication.* University of Illinois Press.

Tversky, A. and Kahnemann, D. (1974) Judgement under Uncertainty: Heuristics and Biases. *Science*, **185**, pp. 1124–1131.

6.14 REFERENCES

(1) Cheeseman, P. (1985) In Defence of Probability. In *Proceedings of the 8th International Joint Conference on AI (IJCAI)*, Los Angeles, pp. 1002–1009.

(2) Zadeh, L.A. (1978) Fuzzy Sets as a Basis for a Theory of Possibility. *Fuzzy Sets and Systems*, **1**, 1978, pp. 3–28.

(3) Zadeh, L.A. (1983) The Role of Fuzzy Logic in the Management of Uncertainty in Expert Systems. *Fuzzy Sets and Systems*, **11**, 1983, pp. 199–227.

(4) Chellas, B.F. (1980) *Modal Logic: An Introduction.*, Cambridge University Press.

(5) McDermott, D. and Doyle, J. (1980) Non–monotonic logic I. *Artificial Intelligence*, **13**, 1980, pp. 41–72.

(6) Holloway, C.A. (1979) *Decision Making Under Uncertainty: Models and Choices.* Prentice Hall, p. 82.

(7) de Finetti, B. (1968) Probability Interpretations. *International Encyclopedia of the Social Sciences*, Macmillan.

(8) de Finetti, B. (1974) *Theory of Probability, vol. 1.* Wiley.

(9) Savage, L.J. (1972) *The Foundations of Statistics.* 2nd rev. ed., Rover Publications.

(10) Tribus, M. (1969) *Rational Descriptions, Decisions and Designs.* Pergamon, pp. 30,81.

(11) Neapolitan, R.E. (1990) *Probabilistic Reasoning Expert Systems: Theory and Algorithms.* John Wiley & Sons, Inc..

(12) Tribus, M. (1969) *Rational Descriptions, Decisions and Designs.* Pergamon, pp. 24–26.

Chapter 7
Structuring the Decision

7.1 INTRODUCTION

The notion of structuring a decision was introduced in section 3.2. In that section the simple approach of decomposing the decision into a tree of sub-decisions was suggested as one way in which the decision could be structured. This is a powerful, if simplistic, way to proceed but it has its limitations.

As decisions become more complex, e.g. have temporal properties, more formal methods are required to structure them. The more formal methods will enhance rather than replace decomposition, however, because decomposing complex decisions into simpler sub-decisions is often a necessary precursor to using formal analysis. The decision maker will, therefore, need a suite of structuring methods each of which can be applied in the appropriate circumstances.

Although most decisions involve uncertainty some do not and some which do, do so at such a simple level that the uncertainty can be assessed intuitively by the individual. As decision situations become more complex more sophisticated methods are required for representing them and intuition must give way to more structured methods of assessing the uncertainty and evaluating the decision.

This chapter pursues these issues, establishes a formal representation for decisions and discusses methods of evaluating them.

7.2 PAYOFF TABLES

Few decisions are devoid of uncertainty but certain types of simple decision depend only on well understood uncertainties. With these types of decision the value of all the possible outcomes can be calculated ignoring the risks. An adjustment for risk can be added as a further step.

The simplest type of decision to treat in this way is one which:

(1)   Involves only one uncertain event.

(2) The same uncertain event will occur whatever the outcome of the decision.

In these cases the possible actions which could be taken by the decision maker can be tabulated against the set of possible outcomes for the uncertain event to give a matrix showing every eventuality.

7.2.1 Example: The Baker's Dilemma

A baker must decide how many loaves of bread to bake for the next day. He bakes at 4am and must make enough for the whole day. His oven bakes 20 loaves at a time so he always produces multiples of 20 loaves. In a normal day he sells between 100 and 200 loaves. It costs him 40 pence to make a loaf which he sells for 90 pence. If a loaf is not sold the day it is made, it is sold for 10 pence for cattle food.

The baker is clearly in a dilemma when deciding how many to bake. He loses 30 pence on every loaf he makes and does not sell but he loses 50 pence potential profit for every loaf he could have sold when he has no bread to sell.

The set of possible actions for the baker is to bake multiples of 20 loaves. The uncertain event is the number that he will sell. As he only bakes 20 at a time a sensible set of possible actions is to bake:

100, 120, 140, 160, 180 or 200

loaves. A payoff tables shows the profit/loss for each of these possible actions against each of the possible outcomes. In this case we will consider the possible outcomes shown in Table 7.1.

With a simple structure like the Payoff Table, the baker still has to make the decision. The advantage is merely that he now has all the possible outcomes presented to him in a digestible form. If we want the system to provide further assistance we require a more advanced method.

7.2.2 Evaluating Payoff Tables using Expected Values

The above table, whilst it shows all the practical possibilities, does not help to assess the risk associated with them. The baker may do this for himself, e.g. tomorrow is Tuesday, there is no reason to believe it will be any different from any other Tuesday and we usually bake 160 loaves on a Tuesday morning.

He could, however, be much more systematic in pursuing the line of thought outlined above. In order to do this he would have to understand the concept of Expected Values as described in the previous chapter.

Let us assume that the probability distribution of the demand for bread for a normal midweek day is given by Table 7.2. Note that the probabilities of the possible outcomes sum to unity and, by definition, only one outcome can actually occur on any given day, i.e. they are an exclusive and exhaustive set.

Table 7.1. A Payoff Table

	Number of loaves sold	\multicolumn{6}{c}{Number of loaves made}
		100	120	140	160	180	200
0.0	100	50	44	38	32	26	20
0.1	120	50	60	54	48	42	36
0.2	140	50	60	70	64	58	52
0.5	160	50	60	70	80	74	68
0.2	180	50	60	70	80	90	84
0.0	200	50	60	70	80	90	100

(annotations: "certain event" beside left column)

Table 7.2. The probability distribution for the sale of bread on a 'normal' day

Number of loaves sold	90–109	110–129	130–149	150–169	170–189	190–210
Prob	0.0	0.1	0.2	0.5	0.2	0.0

Assume now that the baker always bakes 160 loaves on a 'normal' day and wishes to know what his average daily profit will be. This is computed by calculating the Expected Value, i.e. summing, for all possible outcomes, the product obtained by multiplying the probability of selling a given number of loaves by the payoff (i.e. the profit) associated with that number. The result of doing this is shown in Table 7.3.

Table 7.3. Expected Value for a normal day if 160 loaves are made

Demand for loaves	100	120	140	160	180	200
Prob	0.00	0.10	0.20	0.50	0.20	0.00
Payoff	32.00	48.00	64.00	80.00	80.00	80.00
Expected Value	0.00 +	4.80 +	12.80 +	40.00 +	16.00 +	0.00
	= 73.60					

The values for the payoffs in Table 7.3 are taken from the appropriate column in Table 7.1.

We can now resolve the Baker's Dilemma. An Expected Value can be computed for every possible action. The one which gives the best Expected Value is the one to choose as long as the baker can afford any short term losses. The results of these calculations are shown in Table 7.4 and making 160 loaves for a normal day is clearly optimal. The baker had discovered from experience the best number to make.

Table 7.4. Expected values for all the baker's possible actions

Loaves made	100	120	140	160	180	200
Expected Value	50.00	60.00	68.40	73.60	70.80	64.80

7.2.3 Supporting the Baker's Decision

Payoff Tables are extremely easy to compute using a spreadsheet. If a probability distribution is provided for the number of loaves which might be sold on a normal day, another one is provided for quiet days and yet another for busy days, then the baker could enter the type of day and be advised about how many loaves to bake.

The advantages of formalising the decision like this lie in our ability to tie it in with the surrounding business activities. The right sort of till will automatically record the number of loaves sold on a given day and a correctly prepared calendar utility would provide the type of day automatically. With this sort of feedback the probability distributions can be continuously revised and seasonal elements could also be included. When this information is in place the baker can be provided with daily and seasonal adjusted sales figures. These figures provide feedback for him to make other decisions. If he bakes exceedingly good loaves he will know this because his sales figures will rise. If people are moving away from brown bread to white bread he will know about that too.

This example emphasises two points made previously. Firstly that many decisions can be supported with existing techniques and secondly that the true strength of a Decision Support System does not lie in the support it can provide for a single decision but rather in the integrated support which can be provided to a whole operation.

7.3 DECISION DIAGRAMS

If the baker is trying to decide whether to bake another 20 loaves or bake 40 teacakes instead the decision changes radically. The reason for this change is that the probability distribution for the demand for teacakes is likely to be very significantly different from that for bread. Consequently, a matrix structure is no longer appropriate and a different way of representing the decision is required.

Decision Diagrams were designed for this purpose. They are built in the form of a tree with either square or round boxes at the branching points. The square boxes represent decisions and the round boxes represent uncertain events. These boxes form nodes of the tree-like structure whilst the branches, depicted by lines, represent the possible outcomes of uncertain events and the possible actions of decisions. Fig. 7.1 shows a decision diagram for the baker who is trying to decide whether to bake bread or teacakes.

Node A, is a square box representing the decision which has only two possible actions, namely to bake bread or teacakes. Nodes B and C are nodes representing the uncertainty surrounding the number of loaves or teacakes which will eventually be sold.

Chapter 7

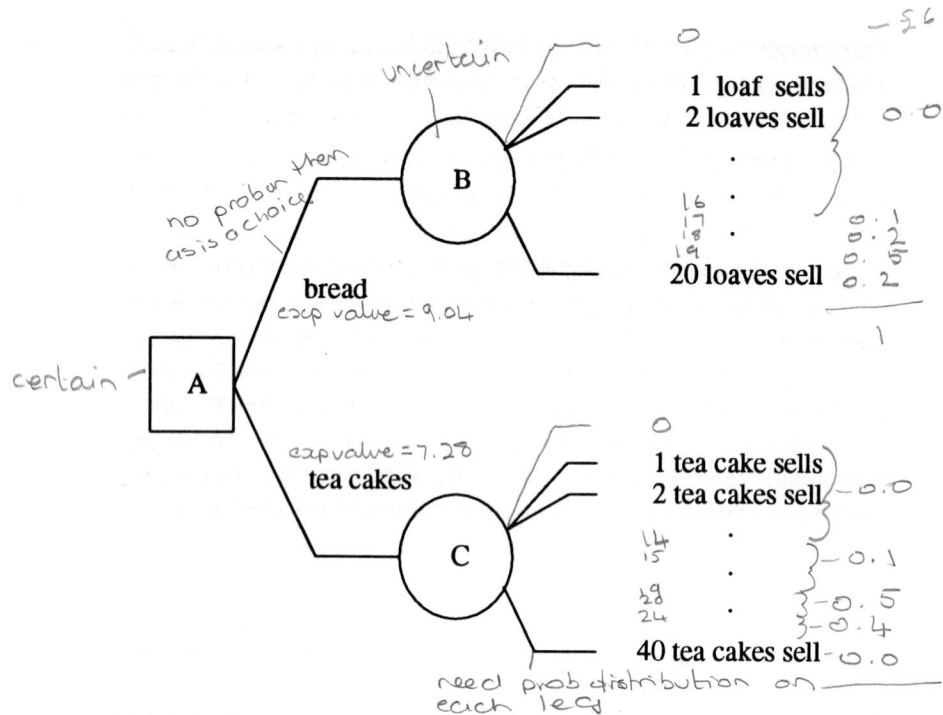

Fig. 7.1. Decision diagram for making bread or teacakes

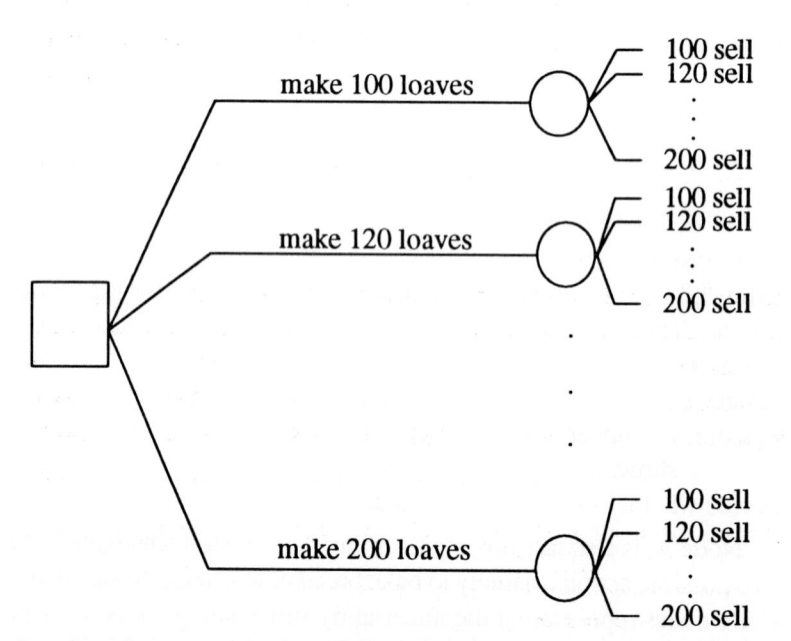

Fig. 7.2. Repetition in decision diagrams

Structuring the Decision

Note that there would be needless repetition if the previous baker's decision were to be modelled using decision diagrams. This is shown in Fig. 7.2. Figures 7.1 and 7.2 between them demonstrate that Decision Diagrams are more flexible than Payoff Tables but are over elaborate if the same uncertain event occurs for each possible action associated with a decision.

The decision represented by Fig. 7.1 can be evaluated using expected values in much the same way as the decision was finally made for the Payoff Table. Assume that the probability distribution for selling a given number of loaves from the next batch of twenty is that shown in Table 7.5. The Expected Value of node B will then be 9.04. Table 7.6 shows the equivalent table for the teacakes and the expected value of this option is 7.28. The decision A is then simply a case of choosing the highest Expected Value, i.e. to bake bread.

Table 7.5. Expected Value of the next batch of 20 loaves

Number sold	1 – 16	17	18	19	20
Probability	0.00	0.10	0.20	0.50	0.20
Payoff	6.80	7.60	8.40	9.20	10.00
Expected Value =	0.00 +	0.76 +	1.68 +	4.60 +	2.00
=	9.04				

best is bread – so that is decision

Table 7.6. Expected Value of a batch of 40 teacakes

Number sold	1 – 14	15 – 19	20 – 24	25 – 29	30 – 40
Probability	0.00	0.10	0.50	0.40	0.00
Payoff	– 6.00	2.80	6.00	10.00	16.00
Expected Value =	0.00 +	0.28 +	3.00 +	4.00 +	0.00
	= 7.28				

7.3.1 The Use of Decision Diagrams

The beauty of Decision Diagrams is that they can handle complex decisions and ones which involve developing a strategy over a period of time. This is because the outcome of an uncertain event may lead to another decision whose outcomes may lead to further uncertain events or even another decision. This process continues until the decision is fully specified. This can result in a very complex tree.

Consider an example from R, B & H. Mr Philip has received an enquiry from a weaver who is trying to win a contract for providing fabric for some very expensive suits. The weaver will only want either two or four warps depending on whether the suits sell well and a second batch is made. The probability of an order for the second batch is about 2/5. There will only ever be two batches made to ensure that the suits are exclusive. The price on offer would produce a profit of £1,000 per warp, were it not for the rather unusual mixture of yarn which none of the machines at R, B & H can process without modification.

Mr Philip consults Mr Keith and Donald and between them they decide that the job could be done in one of three ways. They could modify a machine to do it, they could use two machines to do it or they could subcontract it to another contract warper who has a suitable machine for the purpose. Alternatively, they could simply refuse the job.

Their cheapest option would be to modify one of their machines so that it would do the job. Donald estimates that their chances of this succeeding are 50:50. The modifications would cost £200 and, if they failed, they would have to pay for wasted materials which would cost about £3,000. The modifications would have to be removed when the job was finished.

As an alternative they could do the job in stages by making two warps on two separate machines each suited to one type of yarn and then combine both warps together to make a single one. This would overcome the problems but the extra processing would cut the profit to £500 per warp.

The weaver is prepared to let them make all four warps at the same time if they wish but will only pay for two if the repeat order is not forthcoming. R, B & H will lose £500 if a warp is made and not paid for.

Structuring the Decision

The most they can expect to make by subcontracting is £200 per warp.

The decision diagram which represents this problem is shown in Fig. 7.3.

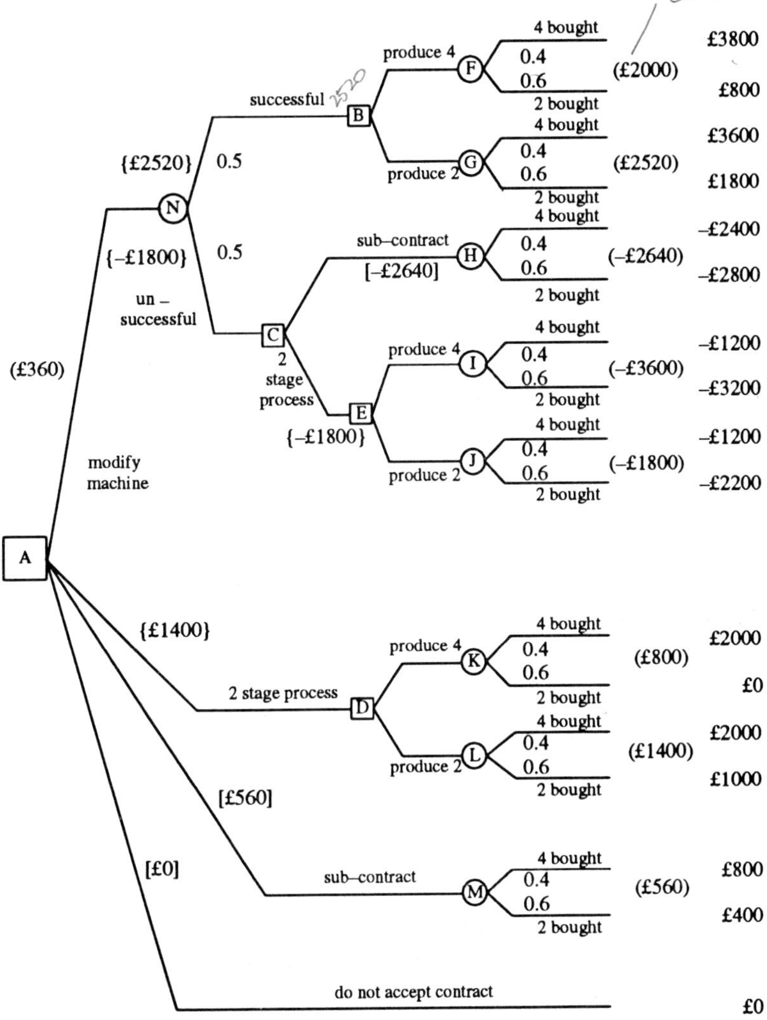

1520
480
expected values

1440
1080

```
                                                    4 bought
                                       produce 4    0.4          £3800
                                            F              (£2000)
                              successful  1520    0.6          £800
                                 B              2 bought
                                                    4 bought
                                                    0.4          £3600
            {£2520}   0.5                   G              (£2520)
                                       produce 2    0.6          £1800
                  N                             2 bought
                                                    4 bought
            {−£1800}  0.5    sub-contract   H       0.4          −£2400
                             [−£2640]              (−£2640)
                  un−                               0.6          −£2800
                  successful                    2 bought
                             C                      4 bought
  (£360)                     2       produce 4   I   0.4         −£1200
                             stage                         (−£3600)
                             process             0.6          −£3200
                                E               2 bought
                             {−£1800}               4 bought
           modify                                   0.4          −£1200
           machine                   produce 2  J          (−£1800)
                                                    0.6          −£2200
                                                 2 bought

    A
                                                    4 bought
           {£1400}                   produce 4   K   0.4          £2000
                                                            (£800)
                  2 stage process                   0.6          £0
                              D                  2 bought
                                                    4 bought
                                                    0.4          £2000
                                     produce 2  L          (£1400)
                  [£560]                            0.6          £1000
                                                 2 bought

           [£0]                                     4 bought
                       sub−contract     M           0.4          £800
                                                            (£560)
                                                    0.6          £400
                                                 2 bought

                       do not accept contract                    £0
```

Fig. 7.3 Diagram for the warping decision

These diagrams are constructed by deciding which decision must be made first, for either temporal or logical reasons. All the possible actions for the first decision are then identified and represented by radiating lines on the diagram. Each possible action is then considered individually and the next logical or temporal event is determined. This can either be a decision node or an uncertain event. A node of the appropriate type is drawn on the end of the possible action line and the whole process is repeated until the entire decision is formulated.

7.3.2 Evaluating Decision Diagrams

If a decision diagram is to be used to advice a decision maker to take a particular set of possible actions, it must first be evaluated. Evaluating a decision diagram involves substituting a value for each uncertain event node and removing decision nodes by choosing one of the possible actions.

Multistage decision diagrams, like that shown in Fig. 7.3, must be evaluated using a technique known as Rollback. Each stage of the Rollback procedure can use Expected Values as a method of providing a value to substitute for an uncertain event but other methods such as Outcome Dominance, Probabilistic Dominance, Direct Choice or Certainty Equivalence can also be used.

Expected Values, Outcome Dominance and Probabilistic Dominance are quantitative methods which are suitable for direct computer support. The other two are qualitative but this does not preclude them from being computer assisted.

7.3.2.1 Rollback

Representing decisions using decision diagrams and using rollback to evaluate them is one of the most structured approaches to making decisions. Any of the above four methods for providing a value to substitute for an uncertain event can be used in conjunction with rollback to add versatility to simplifying the decision.

Rollback starts by looking at those nodes which are immediately prior to the final outcome, e.g. the leaf nodes F, G, H, I, J, K, L and M in Fig. 7.3. The payoff versus the risk is then assessed for these nodes.

For the moment we will do this by computing the expected values. The expected values for the outcomes F, G ... M in Fig. 7.3 are shown inside round brackets, e.g. the expected value for F is (£2000). These nodes, e.g. nodes F ... M, are removed and replaced by their expected value. A simpler diagram can then be drawn for the tree which is now one layer shallower. This process continues until the root node is all that is left.

All the leaf nodes in Fig. 7.3 were uncertain events. This is often the case and once the initial uncertain event nodes are replaced by their expected value the next set of leaf nodes are likely to be decision nodes. These are treated differently in that the preferred possible action, which presumably is the one with the best payoff, is chosen and this replaces the decision node. Values derived in this manner are shown contained within curly brackets in Fig. 7.3, e.g. the chosen outcome for decision C is {–£1800}.

Those numbers which are enclosed in square brackets in Fig. 7.3 have simply been copied further back up the tree for convenience, e.g. [–£2920] in decision C.

If this process is continued backwards up the tree, the root decision is eventually the only one left, e.g. A in Fig 7.3. This is then a straight choice between the expected values which represent the payoffs. In our example, the brothers would choose the possible action '2 stage process' followed by the possible action 'produce 2' as this strategy has the highest expected value, i.e. £1400.

7.4 NODE SUBSTITUTION METHODS

Five node substitution methods which can be used with rollback were listed above. The first of these, Expected Values, was described in the previous chapter since it is a standard probabilistic measure. The remaining four require further explanation:

(1) Outcome Dominance.

(2) Probabilistic Dominance.

(3) Direct Choice.

(4) Certainty Equivalence.

7.4.1 Outcome Dominance

Sometimes one stage of a decision can be made purely by inspection because the payoffs associated with one of the possible actions are better than those of the other possible actions for every possible outcome. This is known as outcome dominance.

Consider decision D in Fig. 7.3. If four warps are eventually bought the payoff is the same whether one produces two batches of two warps or makes all four warps in one run. If only two warps are bought it is far better to have only made two warps. There is, therefore, no point in making four warps in one batch. Contrast this with decision B where there is no such outcome dominance.

Note also that Outcome Dominance has to be dealing with a decision where the possible outcomes are the same for all possible actions. This is essential as it makes it possible to directly compare the alternatives.

7.4.2 Probabilistic Dominance

In slightly more complex cases it can become apparent that, even if a decision does not exhibit outright dominance, one set of outcomes dominates all the others when uncertainty is taken into account. This is referred to as Probabilistic Dominance.

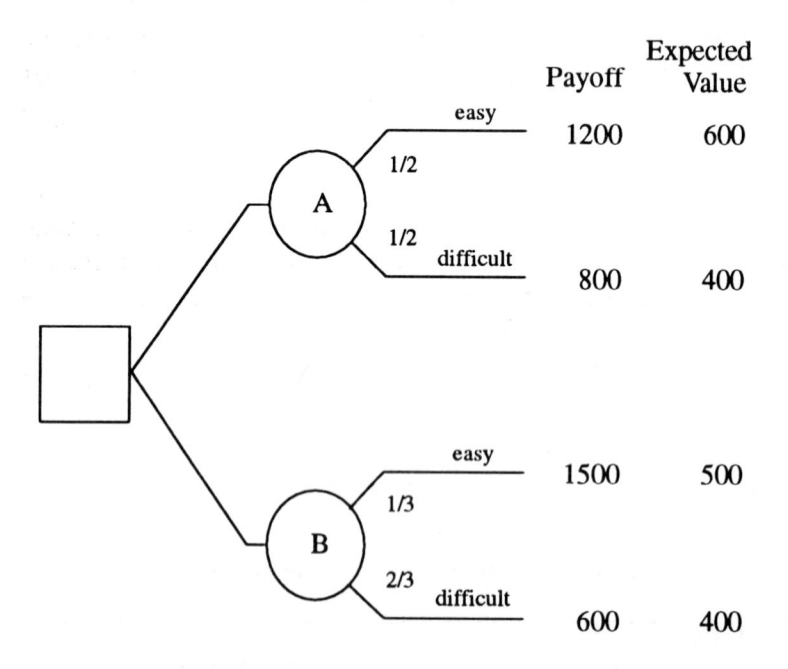

		Payoff	Expected Value
A easy (1/2)		1200	600
A difficult (1/2)		800	400
B easy (1/3)		1500	500
B difficult (2/3)		600	400

Fig. 7.4. Probabilistic Dominance

Consider a slightly different example. One of R, B & H's customers has asked Mr Keith for advice about which of two types of fabric to make. The customer can get a higher price for fabric B but fabric A would be easier to make. This is because fabric B contains a yarn which is attractive but difficult to process. Mr Keith thinks that the chances of type A processing easily are 50:50, whereas those of type B are only 1/3 : 2/3. Consequently, Mr Keith's assessment of the situation is shown in Fig. 7.4.

Although this situation does not exhibit outcome dominance, probability dominance dictates that outcome A is preferred to outcome B. This is because the Expected Value of outcome A dominates that of outcome B. Note that the Expected Value of each outcome is computed in this example as opposed to computing the Expected Value of the uncertain event. Both methods would draw the same conclusion.

Sometimes it is not quite so simple to determine probabilistic dominance and graphical methods have to be used instead. This is not necessarily a bad thing because a pictorial representation of information can often lead to a better understanding by the user of the situation. Consider the following example.

Mr Philip is trying to decide whether or not to buy a new warping machine. One possibility, Machine A, will do plain jobs and is faster than the others but plain work only contributes £200 per warp to profits.

If they try to move into new specialist markets there is a possibility that they will get no orders at all but work for these markets is more lucrative than the work they currently do. Machine B could serve one such market and contribute £400 per warp whilst machine C would serve another and contribute £300 per warp.

Machine A will make about 250 warps per year and they have a good chance of finding enough work to keep it fully occupied. The chances of finding enough work to keep the others fully occupied are worse even though these machines are slower.

Table 7.7. Probability distributions for available work

| Warping machine | Contribution per warp | \multicolumn{6}{c}{Probability v Work available} |
		0	50	100	150	200	250
A	200	0.0	0.0	0.1	0.1	0.1	0.7
B	400	0.1	0.2	0.2	0.4	0.1	0.0
C	300	0.2	0.2	0.3	0.2	0.1	0.0

180   Chapter 7

The brothers have decided that the chances of getting work for the three machines are those shown in Table 7.7 which also summarises the rest of the available information.

The analysis of this decision is simple and results in the decision diagram which is shown in Fig. 7.5. This diagram could be evaluated using Expected Values in exactly the same way as Fig. 7.3 but, in order to portray the decision in a manner which aids understanding, a different style of evaluation can be adopted. This is depicted by Fig. 7.6 which plots the cumulative probability of each machine contributing a given amount.

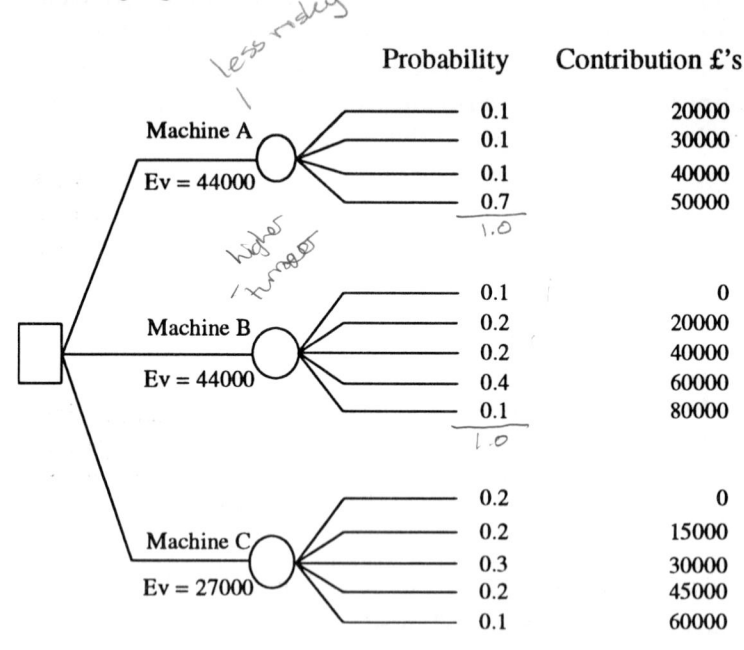

```
                                    Probability      Contribution £'s
           less risky
                                       0.1              20000
        Machine A                      0.1              30000
                                       0.1              40000
        Ev = 44000                     0.7              50000
                                       1.0

           higher                      0.1                  0
           turnover                    0.2              20000
        Machine B                      0.2              40000
                                       0.4              60000
        Ev = 44000                     0.1              80000
                                       1.0

                                       0.2                  0
        Machine C                      0.2              15000
                                       0.3              30000
        Ev = 27000                     0.2              45000
                                       0.1              60000
```

Fig. 7.5. Decision diagram for choosing a new warping machine

The advantage of using cumulative probability distributions is that, since they give the probability of a contribution which is less than or equal to that shown on the x–axis, any curve to the left and above another is less desirable than one to the right and below.

7.4.3 Direct Choice

This is the most intuitive method of making a decision as it involves assessing a decision directly without any formalism to assist. As a consequence it is rarely applied to a complex decision but is still a useful technique especially in clear cut cases. It is quick and easy to

Structuring the Decision 181

apply but it requires the decision maker to simultaneously assess the chances of success and the size of the potential payoff.

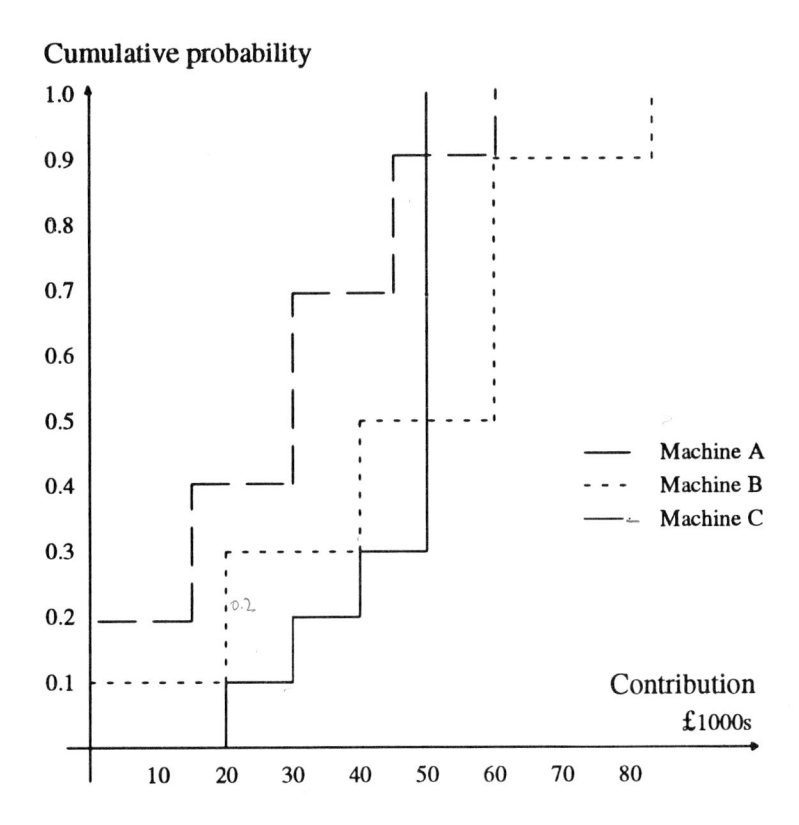

Fig. 7.6. Cumulative probability distribution showing probabilistic dominance

Consider the decision represented by Fig. 7.3 again. A whole block of outcomes involving the uncertain events H, I and J incur losses which are larger than the potential gains offered by F and G. If these are compared with the generally favourable results from D and M, the possible action 'modify machine' will be rejected as too risky with too little payoff. If declining to accept the contract is also rejected, a straight choice between '2 stage process' and 'subcontract' is all that is left. In decision D, i.e. 'two stage process', the outcomes of L, i.e. 'produce 2', dominate the outcomes of K, i.e. 'produce 4', whereupon the outcomes of L dominate those of M, i.e. 'subcontract', and the possible action 'produce 2 by a 2 stage process' has been chosen by more or less intuitive means.

In this example, machine B dominates machine C which is always a worse option. Of more interest, however, is the relationship between machine A and machine B. Machine A dominates machine B below £50,000 contribution but machine B dominates machine A above that figure. It is clear from Fig. 7.6 that machine A is less risky but does not have the potential of machine B. But, machine A cannot be used to try to break into new markets. The precise relationship between the two choices is made clear with this approach whereas it would be hidden if only expected values were used.

7.4.4 Certainty Equivalents

The advantage of the direct choice method above is that decision makers incorporate their own attitude to risk because, in assessing the rewards, the payoff is intuitively balanced by the risk. This balancing of payoff and risk can be formalised by using Certainty Equivalents.

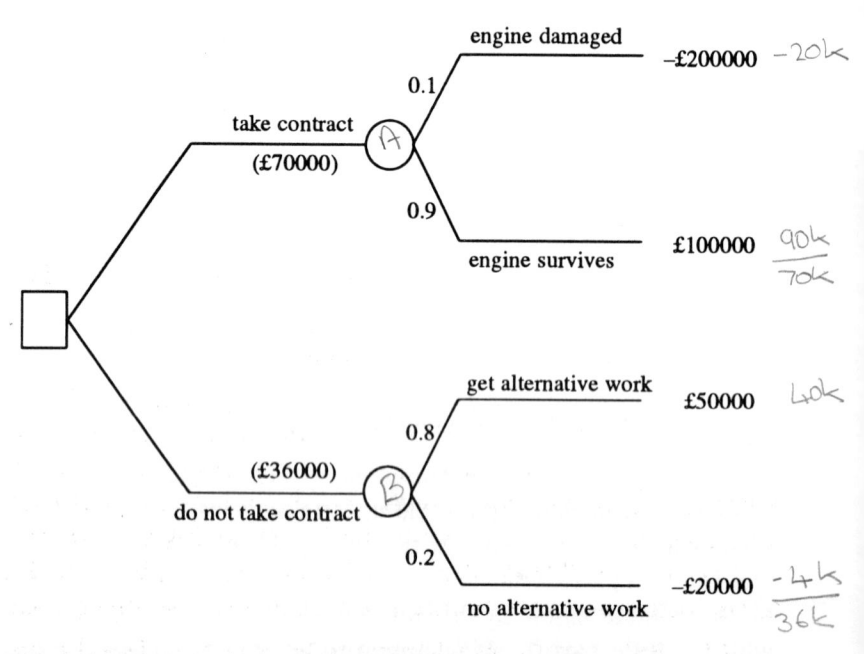

Fig. 7.7. The helicopter owner/pilot's alternative/decisions

Consider a different example. A helicopter owner/pilot has only one helicopter and makes his living by flying spare parts and people to oil platforms in the North Sea. He is offered a lucrative contract to fly to the most northerly rig on a regular basis but his mechanic warns him that severe weather could cause irreparable damage to the engine

Structuring the Decision

of his helicopter. After analysing the alternatives the pilot is faced with the decision depicted by Fig. 7.7.

The helicopter pilot may well have difficulty in trying to make a direct choice between the uncertain events A and B because both involve risk. It may not be as difficult to choose between an uncertain event and a certain one, however.

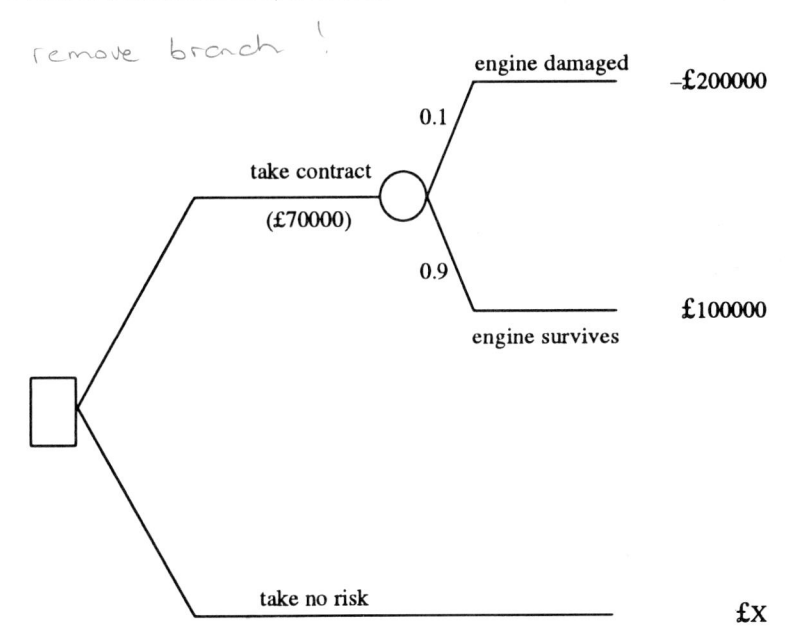

remove branch

```
                        engine damaged
                    0.1 ─────────────── -£200000
        take contract ○
          (£70000)
                    0.9 ─────────────── £100000
                        engine survives

□

        take no risk
        ─────────────────────────────── £X
```

Fig. 7.8. Finding the certainty equivalent

Consider the decision shown in Fig. 7.8. If the variable payoff X was assigned a value of −£200,000 then the pilot would never choose this outcome. If the variable payoff X was assigned a value of £100,000 then the pilot would always chose this outcome. Consequently X can be assigned a value somewhere between −£200,000 and £100,000 which would cause the pilot to be undecided about whether to choose the uncertain event A or choose X for certain.

When the value of X is such that the pilot cannot decide whether to take the risk or accept a known return, it is known as the Certainty Equivalent. If the pilot will just accept £50,000 rather than take the risk of engine failure, the Certainty Equivalent of the 'take contract' option is £50,000. A similar approach could be used on the second uncertain event. We could assume, for example, that the pilot may be prepared to accept work for £30,000 rather than take the risk of no work. The value of £30,000 would then be the certainty equivalent for the uncertain event B in Fig. 7.7. If this were the case the pilot should accept the contract because, even when his attitude to risk is taken into account, he values the contract higher than the alternative.

If the pilot's certainty values are examined more closely, his attitude to risk can be quantified. The Expected Value associated with taking the contract is £70,000. The pilot only valued it at £50,000. The difference, £20,000 is what the pilot would pay to avoid the risk. This is known as the Risk Premium. Considered in another light, it is the amount that the pilot would be prepared to pay for an insurance policy to cover him against damage to his engine.

7.4.5 The Relevance of the Different Node Substitution Methods

Given that there is such a wide diversity of methods, we will have to consider when one should be used rather than another. Some of them, e.g. Certainty Equivalent, have a specific purpose, i.e. to allow for risk, but others, e.g. Expected Values and Probabilistic Dominance can be used for the same decisions. Why then do we need so many? This is because the more operational a decision is, the more mechanical the decision support can be; the more strategic a decision is, the more the support must aid understanding.

This is not purely coincidence. It reflects the nature of the senior management role as opposed to the more junior one. It does have an impact on our choice of evaluation technique, however, because it suggests that it would be desirable to encourage lower levels of management to use the more mechanical ways of evaluating decisions whilst encouraging the senior management to use methods which provide more insight. Senior managers may even be well advised to use more than one of the methods and compare the results.

7.5 DECISION DIAGRAMS WITHIN DECISION SUPPORT SYSTEMS

Decision Diagrams are a powerful tool for use with Decision Support Systems and they match the decision making process outlined in Fig. 3.5 particularly well, especially when they are developed and evaluated in the appropriate order.

Consider again the warping decision depicted by Fig. 7.3. The decision making process described in Chapter 2 advocated that the sub-decisions of the main decision be identified first by using the

Decision Formulation Stage on node A. The sub–decisions at this stage are 'modify machine', '2 stage process', 'subcontract' and 'decline contract'. The decision making process then advocated that one of these be pursued individually. If 'modify machine' is chosen, a new Decision Formulation Stage is started to pursue this sub–decision. When this is done, two outcomes are possible, 'successful' and 'unsuccessful', one of which must be pursued. If the 'successful' outcome is chosen then yet another Decision Formulation Stage is required to pursue the sub–decisions 'produce 4' or 'produce 2'. If 'produce 4' is pursued then two outcomes are possible. The customer buys all four or only buys two of them.

At this stage there are no more sub–decisions so a value has to be assigned to each of these possible outcomes and an estimate given for the likelihood that they will occur. This is the role of the Ordering/Choosing Stage in Fig. 3.5. The values in Fig. 7.3 are presumed to be the ones provided by the decision maker so an Equivalent Value or some other suitable measure, e.g. Certainty Equivalents, can be computed for those outcomes.

It is then necessary to return to the previous decision, i.e. the Decision Formulation Stage for node B. Backtracking like this is not a natural way to reason for most people because it requires the line of reasoning to be remembered and unwound. However, with computer support (or a little training) this is not at all difficult. Consequently, the procedure would be to simply backtrack to node B, assign the expected value, (£2,000), to the 'produce 4' outcome and pursue the 'produce 2' outcome with the Decision Formulation Stage for node B.

This would be pursued in exactly the same way as the possible action 'produce 4' and eventually the decision maker would backtrack to the Decision Formulation Stage for node B with the expected value (£2520) for the possible action 'produce 2'. The decision maker would now invoke the Ordering/Choosing Stage for node B and choose one of these expected values, there being some presumption that the higher one will be chosen, i.e. (£2520).

The decision maker would then backtrack to the Decision Formulation Stage for node N and allocate the chosen value, i.e. (£2520), to the branch which leads to the sub–tree which has been explored. This whole process will continue until eventually all the alternatives have been explored and the topmost level, the decision at Node A, will move through to the Choosing/Ordering Stage where the original decision will finally be made.

7.6 STRATEGIES

A strategy is a route from the root node of a decision diagram to one of its leaves, usually the most desirable outcome. A Complete Strategy is a collection of Strategies which make provision for the chance nodes not turning out favourably.

For example consider Fig. 7.3 again. The best outcome taking into account the risk that the customer will only buy 2 warps is that represented by node G. The strategy {A, N, B, G} may, therefore, be a good one to pursue. A Complete Strategy would have to provide a Strategy for the situation which would arise if the modifications to the machinery were unsuccessful. Consequently, a complete strategy would be {A, N, B, G} or {A, N, C, E, J}. In rather less formal terms, the complete strategy would be to try modifying the machine but if that did not work to revert to the two stage process.

Strategies are a very useful technique for pruning a decision tree and enabling the decision maker to concentrate on a few promising possibilities. The only difficulty with strategies is that organisations and occasionally individuals can get locked into one strategy and fail to realise that changing circumstances have made another more attractive.

7.6.1 Example: The Hardakers' Holiday

As an example consider a man and wife who are contemplating mixing holidays with family duties. Mr and Mrs Hardaker live in the North of England and have a son at Southampton University who is graduating in the summer. Mrs Hardaker's father lives in Plymouth and, as she has not visited him for some time, a trip to Plymouth is overdue. Both Plymouth and Southampton are about 350 miles away from the Hardakers' home but only about 150 miles apart so a round trip would 'kill two birds with one stone'. The date and time of the degree congregation is fixed so a few days in the New Forest (countryside close to Southampton) which incorporated the degree day could be preceded by, or could precede, a few days in Plymouth. Taking the holiday cannot be guaranteed because Mr Hardaker has not been well recently and may be unable to travel and there is a very remote possibility that their son might fail his final exams.

The Hardakers have a caravan but it is only a two berth caravan and either their son or daughter or both may wish to join them for some of the time. Consequently, the Hardakers have considered several

Structuring the Decision

possible actions including hiring self-catering accommodation, buying an awning for the caravan, staying in hotels or staying in bed and breakfast accommodation.

The Hardakers decide to reject hotel and bed and breakfast accommodation as possible strategies because they are expensive and inflexible. The two strategies they continue to consider, shown in Fig. 7.9, are buying an awning for the caravan (so they can sleep four) and renting self-catering accommodation.

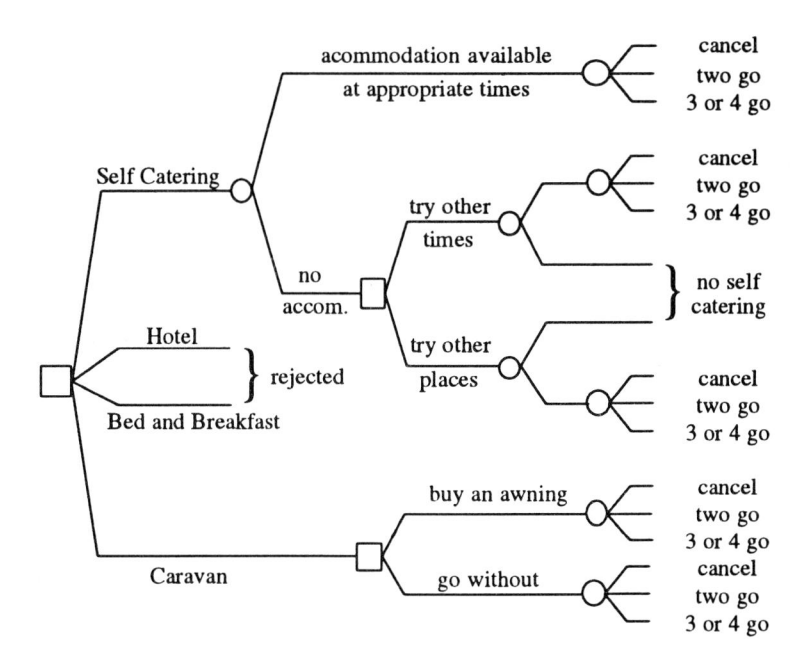

Fig. 7.9. Strategies for the Hardakers' holiday

If they take the caravan they can travel any day of the week and would not need to book a site in advance. If they hire self-catering accommodation they would have to book and arrange a common changeover day between the two locations.

Initially they decide to pursue a strategy of purchasing an awning for the caravan because this provides the maximum flexibility. But, after gathering information about the price of awnings, they realise that this will not be a cheap option.

With the 'awning' strategy more expensive than they thought the Hardakers turned their attention to the 'self-catering' strategy and duly collected information about self-catering properties for rent.

After many phone calls requesting availability and prices the Hardakers found themselves trying to juggle dates, size of properties and locations to try to meet their requirements.

The Hardakers were so immersed in pursuing this strategy that they nearly failed to realise that this strategy exceeded the cost of buying an awning for the caravan by a considerable margin. Upon re–evaluation of the two strategies the 'awning' strategy was clearly the best so they revised this strategy as shown in Fig. 7.10.

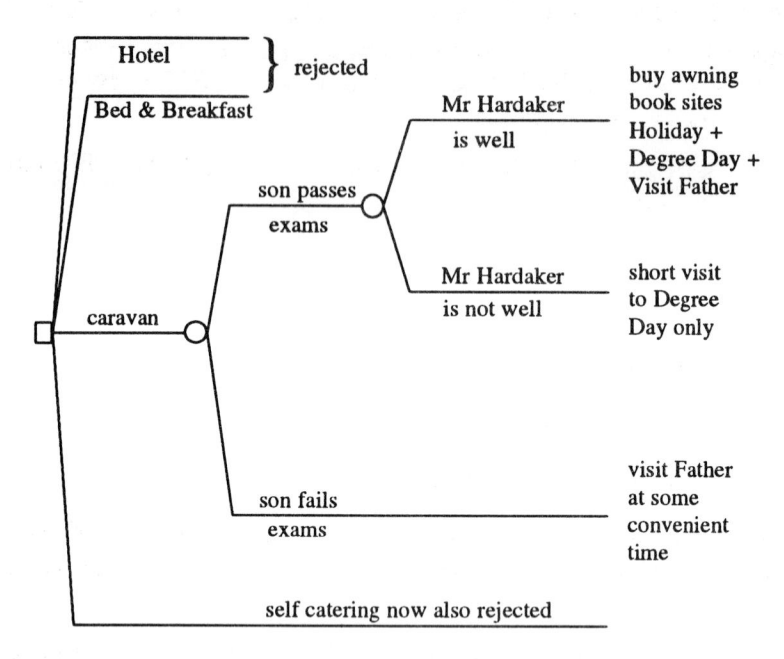

Fig. 7.10. Revised strategy for the Hardakers' holiday

7.6.2 Notes on the Hardakers' Holiday example

(1) The Hardakers considered all the possible actions but rejected two as soon as it became apparent that they were not as desirable as the other two.

(2) The Hardakers nearly became so engrossed in one strategy that they forgot to check that others had not become more desirable.

The latter is a particularly easy trap for industrialists to fall into because the person who decides upon the strategy is not necessarily the same person who executes the strategy. In such cases it is essential that feedback concerning the execution of the strategy is available to the person who chose it so that alternative strategies can be initiated if this becomes necessary.

7.7 INFLUENCE DIAGRAMS

Influence Diagrams were developed in the early 1980s by Howard and Matheson (1) as a much more compact way to represent decisions in comparison to Decision Diagrams. Decisions Diagrams are capable of growing exponentially whereas Influence Diagrams only grow linearly. However, Influence Diagrams have a wider field of application and are particularly interesting when events are not independent of each other and hence cannot be accurately portrayed by a Decision Diagram.

An Influence Diagram is a singly connected, acyclic directed graph with two types of nodes :

(1) Decision Nodes, denoted by squares;

(2) Chance Nodes, denoted by circles;

and two types of arrows :

(3) Conditioning Arrows;

(4) Information Arrows;

and typically, though not necessarily, a single sink node of type 'chance' denoted by an octagon. Fig. 7.11(a) shows a Decision Diagram with two uncertain events.

Fig. 7.11(b) shows the same decision represented by an influence diagram. The octagon V is the sink node with seven possible outcomes. The arrow from A to V is an information arrow which determines whether V takes one of its outcomes for certain or is a chance node with the remaining six possible outcomes. The circles B and C represent the uncertain events and these influence V directly since if the uncertainties are resolved the outcome of V is known. The influence of B on V and C on V is represented by the influence arrows from A and C to V. Border Nodes are Chance Nodes which have no Chance Nodes as predecessors so B and C are Border Nodes.

It has been argued by Samuel Haltzman (2) that a goal directed, i.e. backwards, approach to formulating a decision strategy is optimal because the information actually required to solve the problem is the only information which is sought.

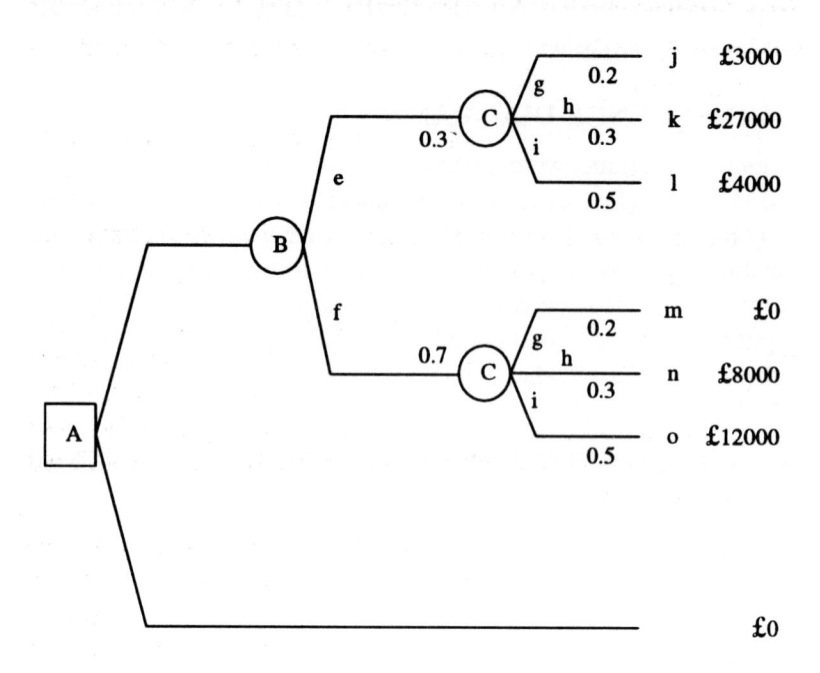

Fig. 7.11(a). Decision diagram for comparison with Fig. 7.11(b)

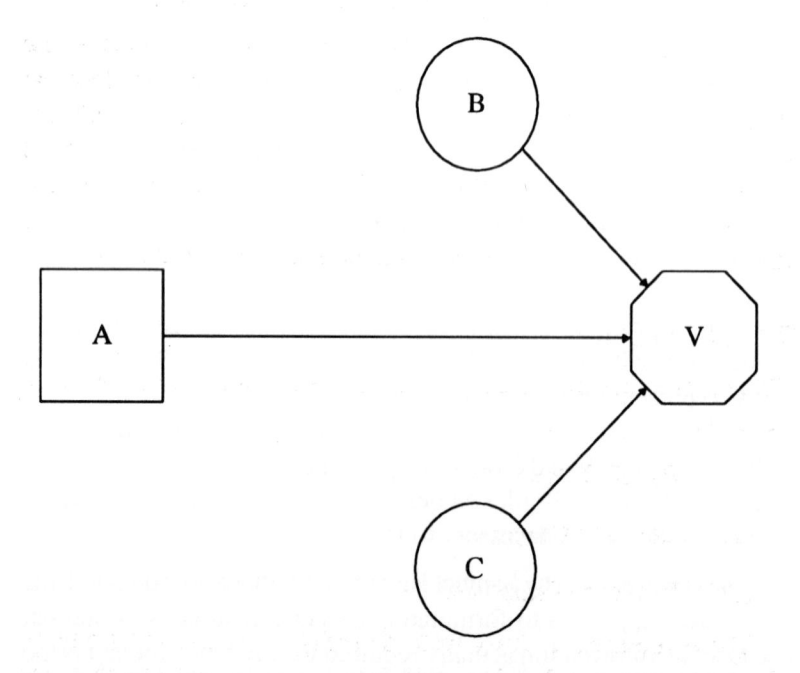

Fig. 7.11(b). Influence diagram for comparison with Fig. 7.11(a)

7.7.1 Comparison of Influence Diagrams and Decision Diagrams

Influence Diagrams do have certain advantages over Decision Diagrams, mainly:

(1) They focus the attention of the user onto a solution to the problem.

(2) They identify the type of information which is required to make a decision.

The second of these has additional associated beneficial effects. Because the type of information that is required is clearly highlighted and its relationship with the rest of the decision is well defined, whole sub-decisions can be passed to people who are well qualified to make them. The results of their deliberations can then be easily recombined with the rest of the model.

In addition, the cost of these deliberations can probably also be estimated as can the likely impact of the results. If the degree of certainty with which the decision can be made does not increase in proportion to the cost of gathering the extra information required to achieve that increase, the information is not worth gathering. Consequently the value of information can be determined.

The disadvantage of Influence Diagrams is, however, that they are complex and expensive to evaluate. This, together with the fact that they perform better than decision diagrams on unstructured problems, means that they are only likely to be used for the most critical of decisions such as strategic planning decisions. Furthermore their use is likely to be left to the professionals in the field unless future developments make them easier and more obvious to use.

7.8 SUMMARY

This chapter has discussed three different methods of structuring a decision:

(1) Payoff Tables.

(2) Decision Diagrams.

(3) Influence Diagrams.

These represent a fairly wide diversity of structuring methods. The first is suited to decisions with minimal, or easily assessable, risk but is restricted to decisions which can be represented in matrix form. The second has no such restrictions and has a further advantage that any risk assessing method can be used in conjunction with it. The third method was introduced to demonstrate that formalisms do exist for representing decisions which are not well structured or which are not easy to structure rigidly.

A collection of methods, such as these, should provide decision makers with a very powerful tool for expressing their decisions. This is demonstrated by the following case study.

7.9 CASE STUDY: THE R, B & H STRATEGIC PLAN

Consider again the R, B & H Strategic Plan which Mr Philip was working on in Chapter 6. This is shown again in Table 7.8.

Table 7.8. The R, B & H strategic sub–decisions

Strategic Sub–Decisions

Future of R < B & H		New Business Venture		Personal Involvement	
Pos–Outcomes	Prob	Pos–Outcomes	Prob	Pos–Outcomes	Prob
stay in business	0.1	don't buy another	0.1|S 0.3|~S	retire completely	0.1|aopo 0.8|s&db
sell business	0.3	become consultants	0.3 0.3|~S	be sleeping partners	0.1|aopo 0.1|s&db
sell assets	0.6	start a new business	0.1|S 0.1|~S	non–executive directors	0.2|aopo 0.1|s&db
		buy existing business	0.5|S 0.3|~S	remain in total control	0.6|aopo 0.0|s&db

S	=	'stay in business'
~S	=	'sell business' or 'sell assets'
s&db	=	'sell business' or 'sell assets' and 'don't buy another business'
aopo	=	all other possible outcomes

Structuring the Decision   193

When Mr Philip was evaluating this decision, he provided probabilities which represented his assessment of the chances that a particular course of action would be the best one to chose, i.e. would prove to be the most satisfactory in the long term for Mr Keith and himself, but he did not consider the payoff associated with the possible outcomes at that stage. We can now structure the sub–decisions more formally and start adding some of the payoffs.

7.9.1 The 'Future of R, B & H' Sub–decision

Mr Philip decided to structure the 'Future of R,B & H' sub–decision using a Decision Diagram. This can be seen in Fig. 7.12. However, this diagram must be refined before we can use it to support the decision.

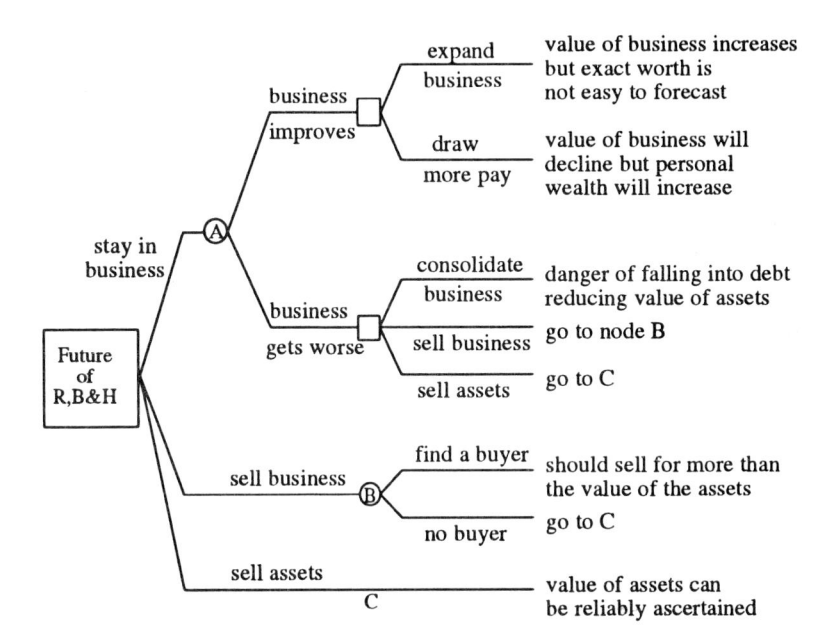

Fig 7.12. Structuring the 'future of R, B & H' sub–decision

The first refinement was to develop every possible outcome until a payoff could be attached to it. In order to do this, Mr Philip estimated a value for the business in five years' time and used Discounted Cash Flow to convert the estimate into today's equivalent values. By doing this, he could compare payoffs which would be available in five years time if they kept the business and sold it then, with those that they could have if they sold the business now. In addition, he pretended that they would sell the business in five years' time in order to achieve a complete Decision Diagram, including payoffs, like the one shown in Fig. 7.13.

The only remaining task was to add probabilities to the chance nodes and then the diagram could be evaluated.

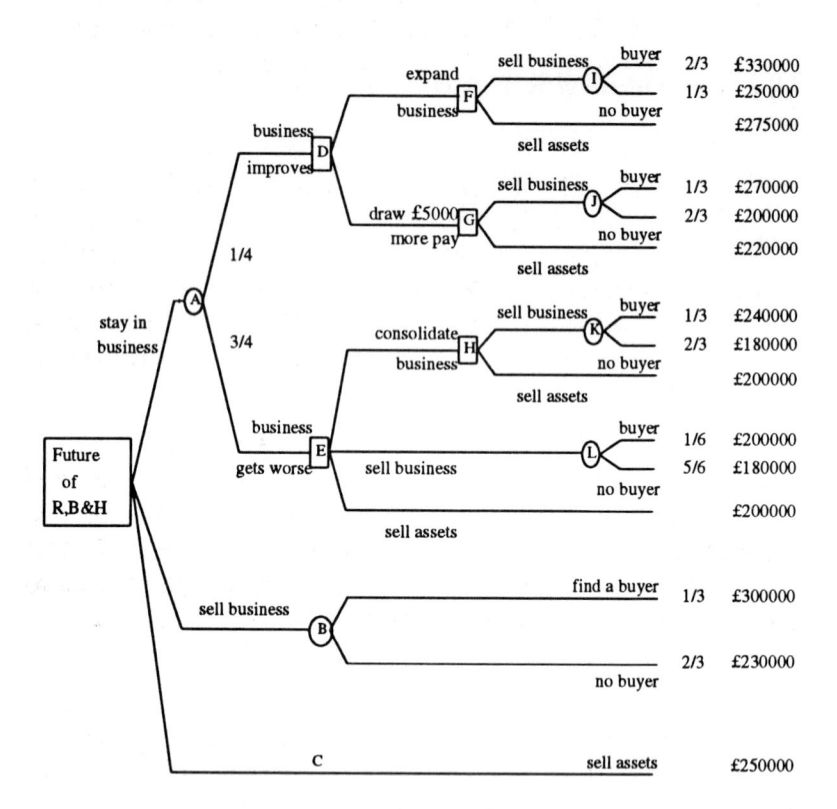

Fig. 7.13. The refined 'future of R, B & H' sub–decision

Mr Philip's next job was to decide the chances of improving the business, i.e. chance node A in Fig. 7.13. After searching through literature published by the Textile Trade Association, Mr Philip decided that the probability of business improving was about 0.25 so he added this to his diagram. The probabilities for the chance nodes I, J, K and L in Fig. 7.13 must now be estimated. He estimated that the chances of finding a buyer for the business at that time were about 1/3, i.e. P(B) = 1/3, but, if they decided to stay in business and the business declined, he thought that this would halve, i.e. P(L) = 1/6. However, if the textile trade declined but they managed to consolidate R, B & H,

Mr Philip thought that they would still have the same chance of selling the business, i.e. P(K) = 1/3.

If business improved but they took the improvement as extra wages, Mr Philip estimated that the business would be as easy/difficult to sell as for case B, i.e. P(J) = 1/3. On the other hand if they ploughed back the returns from the improvement in business, Mr Philip estimated that the chances of selling the business could double, i.e. P(I) = 2/3. All these estimated probabilities are shown in Fig. 7.13.

Mr Philip evaluated his Decision Diagram as follows. Node I has an Expected Value of £303,000 which is better than selling the assets so decision F passes back an Expected Value of £303,000 to decision D. Node J has an Expected Value of £223,333 which is just better than selling the assets. But, £50,000 has been taken out in extra wages so decision G passes back an Expected Value of £273,333 to decision D. The best value at decision D is the £303,000 from F so the latter is chosen for passing back to chance node A.

Chance node K has an Expected Value of £200,000 which is exactly the same as selling the assets so H passes back an Expected Value of £200,000 to decision E. Chance node L has an Expected Value of £183,333 which is passed back to decision E. Hence, the best Expected Value that E can attain is £200,000 which is passed back to chance node A. The Expected Value of A is, therefore, £225,750 which is passed back to the 'Future of R, B & H' sub–decision.

The Expected Value of chance node B is £253,000 and this is also passed back to the 'Future of R, B & H' sub–decision. Consequently, the choice for the 'Future of R, B & H' sub–decision is between 'stay in business' which has an Expected Value of £225,750, 'sell business' which has an Expected Value of £253,000 and 'sell assets' which is expected to realise £250,000. Mr Philip had to choose between these possible outcomes.

7.9.2 The 'New Business Venture' Sub–Decision

The next sub–decision he tackled was the 'New Business Venture'. He did this by using a Payoff Table, as shown in Table 7.16. He used the Information Gathering Task to find a probability distribution for the likely state of the economy in the next five years. This is shown in the columns labelled 'State of the Economy' and 'Probs' in Table 7.9.

Table 7.9. Structuring the 'New Business Venture' sub-decision

State of the economy	Probs	New Business Venture			
		become consultants	start a new business	buy existing business	don't buy business
Very buoyant	0.05	£100,000	£100,000	£60,000	–
Buoyant	0.20	£50,000	£50,000	£50,000	–
Static	0.35	£30,000	£0,000	£40,000	–
Depressed	0.30	£0,000	–£10,000	£35,000	–
Very depressed	0.10	–£15,000	–£40,000	£25,000	–
Expected Value		£24,000	£8,000	£40,000	–

He then estimated the likely payoffs for each of the possible actions of the 'New Business Venture' decision together with each of the possible outcomes of the uncertain event, 'State of the Economy'. These are shown in the body of Table 7.16 together with the Expected Values. The column for the possible action 'don't' (buy another business) has been left blank because Mr Philip's views about this depend on whether or not they decide to keep R, B & H. He rated the possible action, 'don't' (buy another business), as being equivalent to the 'start a new business' if they were going to keep R, B & H. So his Expected Values were £24,000, £8,000, £40,000 and £8,000 respectively. At this stage he would have decided to buy an existing business as this has the highest Expected Value.

Alternatively, he could use these results to estimate the probabilities to associate with the possible outcomes quoted in Table 7.15. To do this, he would have noted that the Expected Values are in the ratio 3:1:5:1 respectively. These sum to ten so, if they are multiplied by 0.1, they could be adopted as his assessment of the chances that the possible action concerned would be the best one to chose.

However, if they were not going to continue with R, B & H, Mr Philip considered the 'don't' (buy another business) possible action

Structuring the Decision 197

to be at least as desirable as buying an existing business. Again he could have chosen one of the possible outcomes by studying the Expected Value or he could use the ratios, i.e. 3:1:5:5, to compute probabilities for Table 7.15. These need to be scaled to convert them into probabilities. Mr Philip had done this rather roughly; his 0.3, 0.3, 0.1, 0.3 should really have been 0.36, 0.21, 0.07 and 0.36.

7.9.3 The 'Personal Involvement' Sub–Decision

The final sub–decision, 'Personal Involvement', was a particularly unpromising sub–decision to structure so Mr Philip decided to use Influence Diagrams to formalise this sub–decision. The results of his efforts are shown in Fig. 7.14 but the evaluation of this must wait until later.

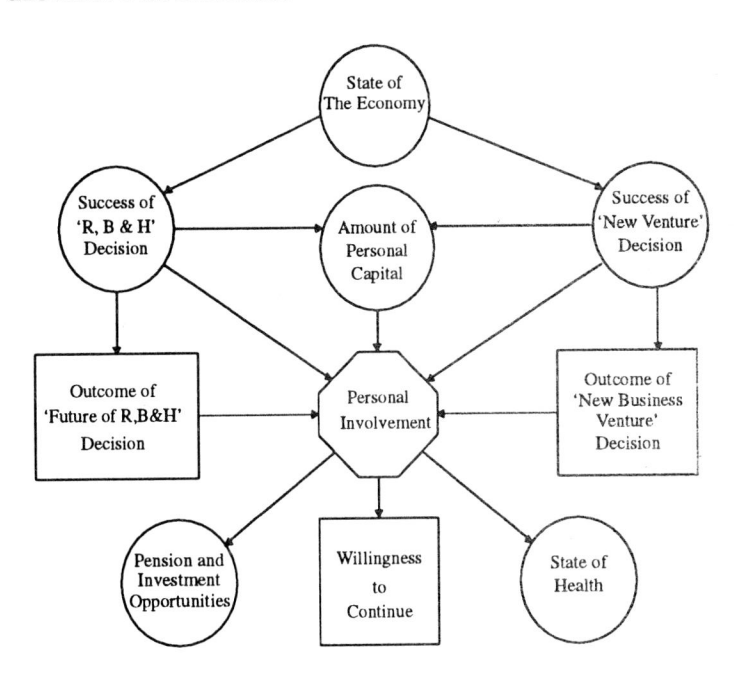

Fig. 7.14. Structuring the 'personal involvement' sub–decision

7.9.4 Points to Note

Notice that Mr Philip has used the full range of structuring methods available to him. He has used decomposition to split the main decision into smaller, more manageable sub–decisions. He has then applied different structuring methods to each of these sub–decisions. When all the sub–decisions have been taken, they will have returned the information required for Mr Philip to be able to proceed and make the main decision.

7.10 POINTS TO PONDER

(1) In the Hardakers' Holiday example the most desirable outcome changed as more information was gathered. Would you expect this to be true in real life? If so what consequences would it have for a Decision Support System?

(2) Decision Diagrams frequently have repeating sub–trees, e.g. the number of people who eventually go on the Hardakers' holiday and the entire two stage process in the warping example. This is tedious repetition for the user. Do you think it would be possible to devise a system which maintained the integrity of the Decision Diagram but allowed the user to invoke an existing part of the tree?

(3) Try to do the Strategic Plan for R, B & H without subdividing the decision first, e.g. try to draw a single Decision Diagram for the 'Strategic Plan', the 'Future of R, B & H', the 'New Business Venture' and the 'Personal Involvement'.

7.11 FURTHER READING

- Holloway, C.A. (1979) *Decision Making Under Uncertainty: Models and Choices.* Prentice Hall.

- Holtzman, S. (1989) *Intelligent Decision Systems.* Addison–Wesley.

- Howard, R.A. and Matheson, J.E. (eds.) (1984) *Readings on the Principles and Applications of Decision Analysis.* Menlo Park California: Strategic Decisions Group, **2**.

- Raiffa, H. (1970) *Decision Analysis: Introductory Lectures on Choices Under Uncertainty.* Addison–Wesley.

- Schachter, R.D. (1986) Evaluating Influence Diagrams. *Operational Research*, **34**, no. 6, pp. 871–882.

7.12 REFERENCES

(1) Howard, R.A. and Matheson, J.E. (1984) Influence Diagrams (1981). In *Readings on the Principles and Applications of Decision Analysis*, Howard, R.A. and Matheson, J.E. (eds.), Menlo Park California: Strategic Decisions Group, **2**, pp. 719–762.

(2) Holtzman, S. (1989) *Intelligent Decision Systems*. Addison–Wesley, pp. 65–71.

Chapter 8
Allowing for Risk

8.1 INTRODUCTION

Risk is uncertainty with a price tag attached. Our attitude to risk is dependent on our circumstances and our attitude of mind but most of us avoid it as far as possible.

Utility Theory was developed, arguably as early as 1738 **(1)**, to quantify this aversion to risk and, later **(2, 3, 4, 5)**, to establish a more theoretical footing for the generally held corporate wisdom which is often prepared to pay quite a high premium to avoid risk. For example, even the insurance companies whose business is risk, minimise risks rather than taking them.

This chapter develops a form of Utility Theory which is comparable to Probability and is ideal for use in supporting decisions. The comparability of the two theories enables decision makers to use probability to assess a risk neutral attitude to a decision whilst simultaneously evaluating the decision according to their own attitude to risk. This results in an ability to quantify the risk premium, i.e. the cost incurred in reducing or eliminating the risk.

Some Economics and Business Studies books call Utility Theory 'Preference Theory' because 'utility' already has a specialist and different meaning in their context. This book will use the word 'Utility' only in the context of the theory described in the following pages and hence there is no clash of meaning.

8.2 RISK AND CORPORATE MANAGERS

In any business, large or small, the managers of that business have to make decisions every day which involve risk. Since their attitude to risk will vary from individual to individual and even within a single individual on different occasions, the company has no ability to develop, or control, a corporate attitude to risk.

It is highly desirable for a company to have a corporate policy towards risk, i.e. be able to adjust its attitude to risk as a strategic reaction to market and business forces. But, if a company is going to be able to do this, it must be capable of both developing an attitude to risk and then persuading managers to heed the corporate policy and not simply use their own judgement.

If the company is going to use a Decision Support System, this is entirely practical. As part of the support provided for the decision makers, they can be shown a set of payoffs which have been modified to take account of risk in accordance with the corporate policy. The decision makers can then decide whether or not to accept the advice given by the system.

This chapter will develop this theme, describe the theory which is required to implement it and show how it can be incorporated into the overall system.

8.3 ORDERING PREFERENCES

The two previous chapters of this book have mentioned the difference between risk and chance, a difference which is encapsulated by Certainty Equivalence and Expected Value respectively. It should, however, be noted that the Certainty Equivalence is a quantification of a qualitative process. It is a formal or quantified method of making decisions involving risk and is a replacement for direct choice which is entirely qualitative.

There are essentially only three stages to making an atomic decision :

(1) Identify the possible outcomes/possible actions.

(2) Estimate the consequences of each possible outcome/possible action.

(3) Choose the most preferable possible outcome/possible action.

In decisions involving risk the problem is to quantify the preferences required for the choice step numbered 3 above.

There are fundamentally only two types of decision which can be considered in step 3 above:

(1) Direct Decisions

I prefer outcome A to outcome B

(2) Risky Decisions

I prefer outcome C for certain rather than adopting a course of action with a 30% chance of achieving A and a 70% chance of achieving B.

Although some business decisions are of type (1) most decisions have an element of (2) and the most difficult decisions are a mixture of both. Consequently a theory of choice is required which can cope with both types of decisions.

Certainty Equivalents, as used so far, are capable of providing an assessment of a particular risk for a given individual. Consequently, if we computed a Certainty Equivalent for a whole range of risks, we might have an appropriate one to hand when a given risky decision had to be made. This idea embodies the mathematical concept of a function, i.e. when the function is told what the particular risk is, it will return an appropriate Certainty Equivalent.

Consequently we need a preference ordering function which we will call u, the utility function. This function will modify the payoff of a possible outcome to take into account the risks associated with that outcome. In other words, the utility function will take the chances and associated payoff for a possible outcome and return a number which will rank the acceptability of this outcome as compared to others.

If this function is to behave sensibly for decision making, it will have to have the following properties:

(1) u is defined for all possible outcomes.

(2)   if outcome A is preferred to outcome B then $u(A) > u(B)$.

(3)   if the chances p_i of achieving outcomes A_i are preferred to the chances q_j of achieving B_j then

$$\sum_{i=1}^{n} p_i * u(A_i) > \sum_{j=1}^{m} q_j * u(B_j)$$

where n and m are the number of outcomes in A and B respectively, and $\sum_{i=1}^{n} p_i = 1, \sum_{j=1}^{m} q_j = 1$.

The above definitions may require some explanation to overcome the formality of the mathematics but first we must understand exactly what a function is and that we can prescribe properties for a function without ever specifying precisely what the function is.

A function is a mathematical operator which accepts any number of parameters as arguments and returns a single value. As an example, consider $y = x^2$. In this expression, y is a function because if a value for the argument, x, is provided, 2 say, the value of y is returned by the expression, i.e. 4. Similarly, in the expression $v = x + y + z$, v is a function because if values are provided for x, y, and z the expression returns a single value for v. The only difference between the previous examples and the definition of the utility function, *u*, is that, for the moment, we do not want to provide an expression for *u* because we do not know what it should be and it will vary from person to person. For the time being the best that we can achieve is to specify what properties *u* must have. The items (1) to (3) above do this precisely.

The first property, '*u* is defined for all possible outcomes', is essential if you are going to be able to rank a set of alternative possible outcomes. It is not possible to use *u* as a mechanism for ranking alternative possible outcomes if *u* does not provide a value for all the alternatives under consideration.

The second property is obvious. The function, *u*, would not be an ordering function if it did not reliably return a higher value for a more preferred outcome. This property also takes care of the direct decisions and can easily be extended to prove that *u* will order any number of outcomes, i.e. if A is preferred to B, B is preferred to C, C is preferred to ... etc., then $u(A) > u(B) > u(C)$ etc.

The third and final property deals with 'risky' decisions and asserts that something which looks very like the Expected Value in probabilistic terms will be greatest for the preferred possible outcome. If we compare the expression

$$\sum_{i=1}^{n} p_i * u(A_i)$$

with the expression for the Expected Value which is

$$\sum_{i=1}^{n} p_i * v(A_i)$$

where $v(A_i)$ is the payoff for the outcome A then we can see the very great similarity between the two. The payoff $v(A_i)$ is a matter of fact, probably the cash return which is expected from the outcome A. The utility function, *u*, may well not order the As in the same order as their Expected Values, *v*. Clearly, if *u* does not order the possible outcomes in the same sequence as *v*, then *u* is taking something into account which *v* did not. The phenomenon which *u* measures and *v* does not measure is the user's attitude to risk.

We have already considered one function which measures a user's attitude to risk, namely the Certainty Equivalent. The Certainty Equivalent should, therefore, be a suitable candidate for specifying u when risk is the 'extra ingredient'. We can define a utility function using Certainty Equivalents but before we do so we will make a couple of observations.

8.3.1 Quantifying Qualitative Decisions

Risk does not have to be the 'extra ingredient' and Utility Theory can be used to quantify other qualitative factors which occur in decisions.

For example, the utility function could be used to weigh the impact on the environment against the cost of a civil engineering scheme. It could also be used to weigh the importance of family life against the highest paid job. But, in both of these cases, the Certainty Equivalent would not be an appropriate function to use for the utility function.

8.3.2 Defining Rational Decisions

It is also possible to use utility to define a rational decision. This is done as follows:

> A rational decision is one which maximises utility.

This makes it clear that, since utility is a personal thing, two people may each make a very rational decision, in exactly the same circumstances, which differ one from the other.

If you observe the world around you, very few decisions appear irrational under the above definition. It is much more usual to find that different people have markedly different utility functions and hence markedly different values. It is quite an interesting exercise to try to deduce the utility function of a person who is making decisions which would be irrational under your utility values.

8.4 EVALUATING A UTILITY FUNCTION

In order to evaluate a utility function we must first define how to measure utility and then measure it across the entire range of possible outcomes. We will consider each of these steps separately.

8.4.1 Methods of Measuring Utility

There are only two fundamentally different approaches to measuring utility:

(1) Analyse past decisions.

(2) Experiment with simple hypothetical decisions.

But within each of these there are many variants. The first method, analyse past decisions, is frequently impossible because the circumstances surrounding the decisions are not known in sufficient detail to make analysis possible.

The second method, 'experiment with simple hypothetical decisions', is more satisfactory in many ways because the utility function can be derived under controlled and repeatable conditions. Furthermore, in business we might not be trying to ascertain a particular person's attitude to risk; we may be trying to ascertain the attitude to risk which the company wishes its employees to take.

If we are going to ascertain utility using a simple hypothetical decision, the easiest one to choose is known as the standard gamble.

8.4.2 The Standard Gamble

The standard gamble is a minimal assumption method of determining a unidimensional utility function, i.e. one which only takes one parameter (note: a 2 dimensional graph defines a unidimensional function). The method works by establishing the Certainty Equivalents of a series of simple gambles and plotting these on a graph. The simple decision in question, i.e. the standard gamble, is expressed as follows:

Assume you are investing £100,000 and you have the option of putting it in a Building Society and getting X interest for certain or buying Premium Bonds and taking a chance P of receiving £10,000 if your Bond wins or nothing if not.

The equivalent decision diagram is shown in Fig. 8.1

A value is chosen for X, e.g. X = £2000, and you provide a value for P which renders you indifferent to the two possible outcomes, e.g. P = 0.5 say. The value of X is then changed and the process repeated. If you continue repeating this process you will eventually have a whole series of values for X and associated values for P. These can be plotted on a graph.

The text book way to plot a standard gamble is to fix the value of X and then ask the recipient to specify the value of P. Some people prefer to give the values the other way round, i.e. they prefer to fix P and give X. This is quite acceptable and should lead to the same curve.

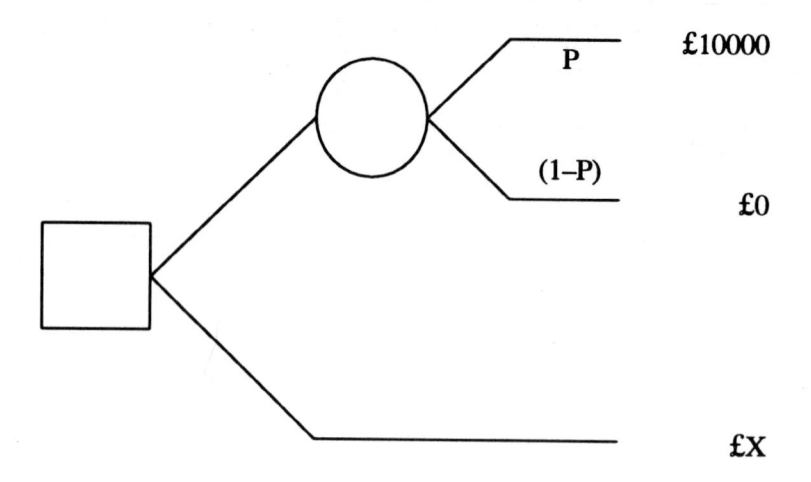

Fig. 8.1. The standard gamble

Notice that the £100,000 is really irrelevant (it does not appear in the decision diagram) and that the range 0 – £10,000 was chosen here purely as an example. In reality the range of the utility function must encompass all possible outcomes and the lower limit may well be negative, e.g. –£200,000 to £1,500,000.

In the second of the two ways of plotting P versus X, X is clearly the Certainty Equivalent. Hence, the resulting graph is a plot of probability against the Certainty Equivalent for the gamble in question. But, if the utility function is to be used to allow for risk, the X,P graph is precisely what we require for the utility function. The reader can check that this curve satisfies the requirements for the utility function given in section 8.3 above.

Notice that we can calculate a value of P which would make X equal to the Expected Value, e.g. if X = £2,000 and was equal to the Expected Value, then:

P * £10,000 + (1–P) * £0 = £2000,   i.e. P = 1/5.

Fig. 8.2 shows the straight line which results from plotting X against P for Expected Values.

If a person is prepared to accept the value of P which has been computed using Expected Values then that person is not placing any premium on the risk involved and is said to be risk neutral. Most people would want a premium for taking the risk or, in other words, most people would accept the £2,000 rather than risk getting nothing. This is known as being risk averse. Risk aversion varies from person to person. It even varies within an individual depending on mood and changing circumstances.

Probability

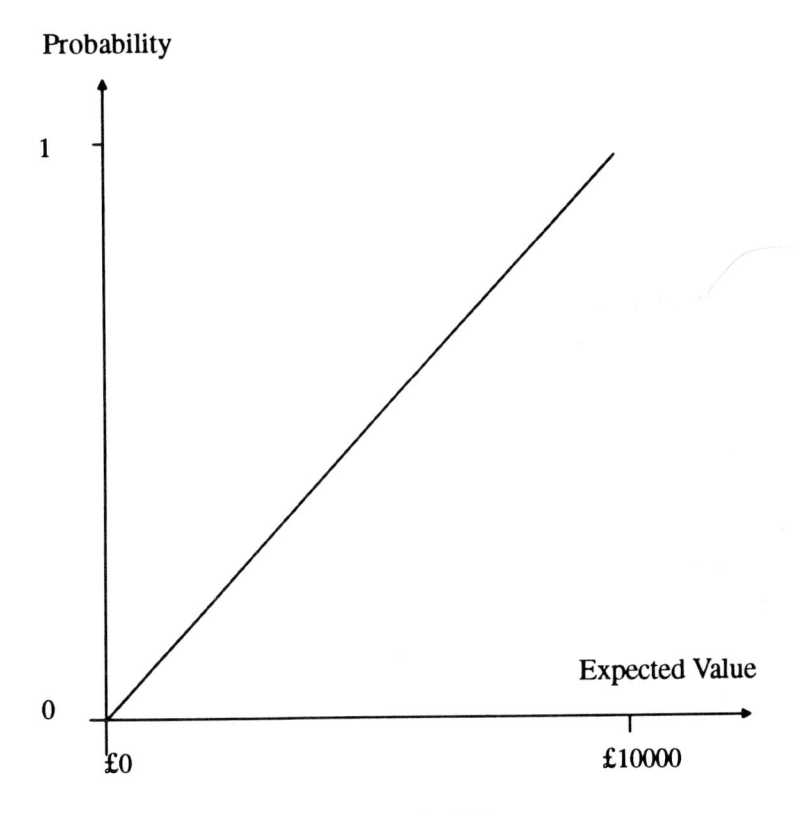

Fig. 8.2. Expected Value versus probability

The utility value is a measure of this aversion. For example, if X = £2000 and the probability of winning £10000 was 1/4 would you accept the gamble? The Expected Value with P = 1/4 is £2,500 but would you still prefer the £2,000 for certain? What would your attitude be if the probability was increased to 1/3, or to 1/2? When you find a value of P for which you would just be prepared to gamble then the point (£2000,P) is a point on your utility curve. The risk neutral value for P is 1/5. The difference between (£2000,P) and the point (£2000,1/5) is a measure of your risk aversion. If many such points are plotted it usually results in a curve such as the one shown in Fig. 8.3.

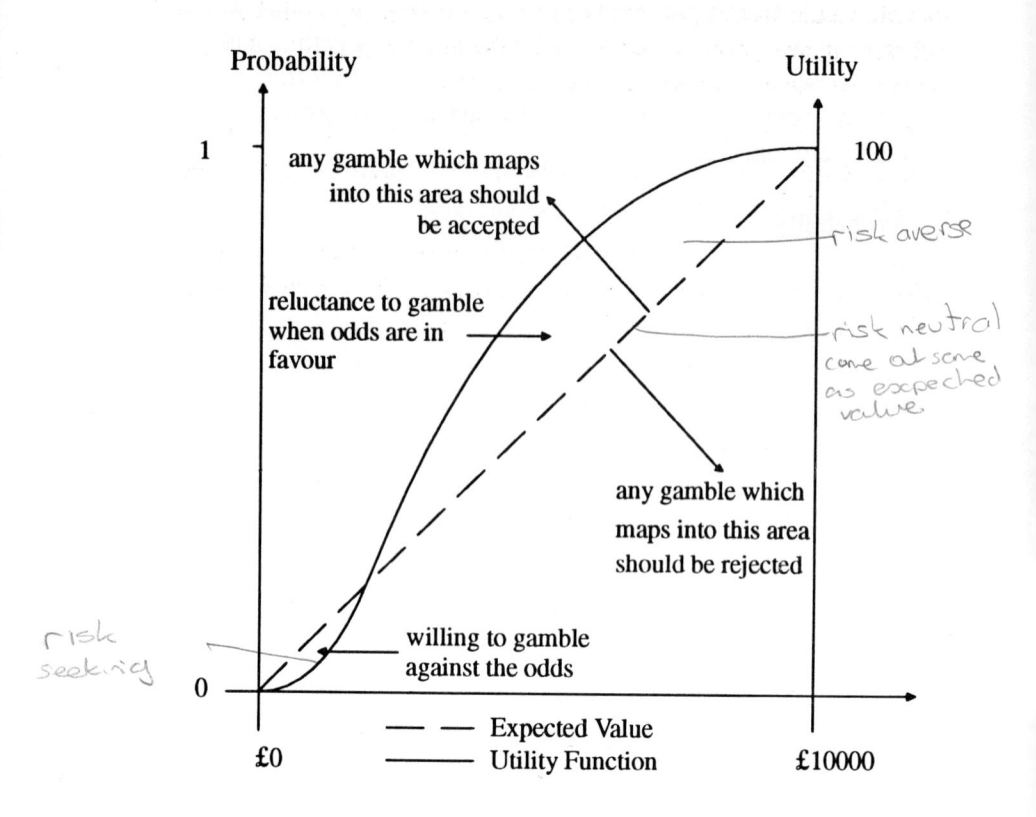

Fig. 8.3. A typical utility function

The scale on the utility axis can be arbitrarily chosen since its absolute value is immaterial. For the moment we will designate u(£0) = 0 and u(£10,000) = 100 to make a distinction between utility and probability.

8.5 INTERPRETATION OF THE UTILITY FUNCTION

The utility curve shown in Fig. 8.3 can now be studied to try to understand a person's attitude to risk.

Assume that the amount which is offered for certain is fixed at £5000 and the gamble is either £10000 or nothing. We can then establish, by looking at the utility curve shown in Fig. 8.3, the probability that the gambler would require in order to take the gamble. It is clearly very much larger than the 0.5 value obtained from the Expected Value and yet, for all probabilities greater than 0.5, i.e. above the line, the odds are in favour of winning. Consequently the area above the diagonal dotted line and below the solid line in Fig. 8.3 indicates a reluctance to take a gamble even when the odds are favourable. This is known as risk aversion.

For very much lower Certainty Equivalents, e.g. £10, the curves have reversed. This indicates a willingness to gamble against the odds which is known as risk seeking.

Since Fig. 8.3 was a typical utility curve it depicts a single individual who is at one point risk seeking and at another risk averse and we might justifiably wonder why this should be.

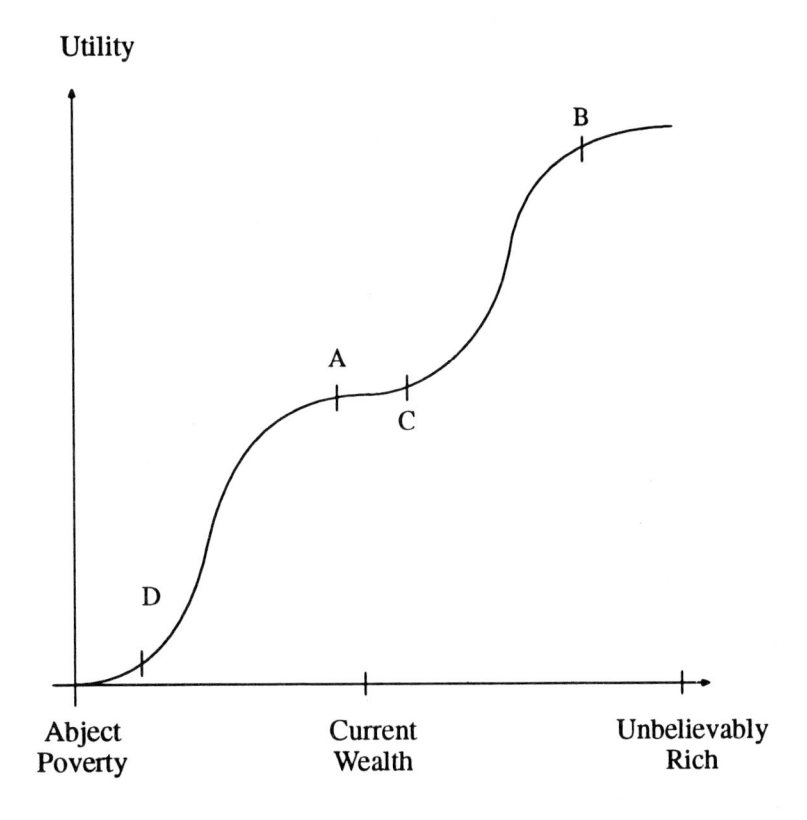

Fig. 8.4. The utility function over the whole range of wealth

The answer is believed to lie in our perception of wealth. Those people who are involved with decisions which could increase their wealth by £10,000 do not consider a gain of £10 for certain to be very significant. They are, therefore, prepared to gamble the £10 against the odds in an attempt to gain a significant increase in wealth. The same people may not be able to lose say £2000 in an attempt to gain

£10000. This would be seen as a significant reduction in wealth and highly undesirable. Hence the reluctance to gamble even with odds in favour of the gamble.

Fig. 8.3 is in fact only part of the full utility curve for a person. Consider Fig. 8.4 which shows the utility curve over the whole range of wealth. The curve is almost horizontal in three areas and only rises significantly twice. The curve shows that people do not mind being slightly less wealthy or slightly more wealthy than their current level of wealth, probably because it would not significantly change their life style. Outside this area people react quite strongly and being significantly richer is seen as having a decidedly higher utility, whilst being significantly poorer is seen as having a decidedly lower utility. This effect tails off as the extremes of wealth and poverty are reached, e.g. only a millionaire perceives being a multi-millionaire as having a significantly increased attraction.

The position of the middle plateau is always at the current level of wealth. Its height with respect to the utility axis, however, will change. A poor person will not perceive being slightly poorer as significantly different in utility value; neither will a rich person. The poor person would, however, almost certainly give a very much lower utility value to their current state of wealth when compared to that of a rich person.

8.5.1 Utility, Insurance and Gambling

The above interpretation of utility functions helps to explain what would otherwise appear to be the irrational behaviour of gambling against very heavy odds, e.g. football pools, whilst insuring against unlikely loss, e.g. house fires. The former is risk seeking and the latter is risk averse so this sort of behaviour would seem to be contradictory. It is, however, quite common.

If we accept the definition of rationality given earlier in this chapter, i.e. a rational decision maximises utility, and we accept the curve given in Fig. 8.4 as representing a typical utility function, we can see that the above behaviour is entirely rational.

Consider the points A, C and B on the curve in Fig. 8.4. These represent respectively 'wealth having taken a gamble and lost', 'current level of wealth' and 'level of wealth having taken a gamble and won'. Now if $u(A) = u(C)$, as it may well do for small premiums such as those for the football pools, then even the most infinitesimal

Allowing for Risk

probability of achieving B maximises utility and the decision to gamble is rational.

The same argument holds if the points A and D represent the possible outcomes of insuring against loss. In this case it is aversion to risk which dictates the outcome. If the cost of insuring is relatively cheap, the loss of utility due to taking out insurance is perceived to be very small. Consequently people will insure against what they see as a major loss of utility, however unlikely it might be. Conversely, when the insurance premiums become significant, people do question the value of insurance.

8.6 MULTIDIMENSIONAL UTILITY FUNCTIONS

A unidimensional utility function measures utility for only one parameter. They are used on decisions where the outcomes are described in terms of a single variable, e.g. money. In business many decisions are reduced to this form since the underlying philosophy is the creation of wealth and this is usually measured in monetary terms. All the utility functions considered so far have been unidimensional.

A multidimensional utility function is one which takes two or more arguments. They are used for decisions where the outcomes cannot be specified in single terms and must be quantified using more than one measure, e.g. cost, convenience, time and comfort, as measures for ranking different forms of transport.

The vast majority of decisions fall into the multidimensional class but utility functions for these are difficult to formulate. One way to formulate them is to try to map all the parameters onto one parameter, usually money. For example

cost ⟶ money
time ⟶ money
comfort ⟶ money

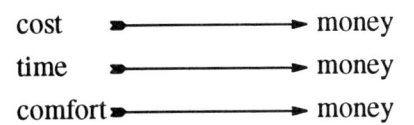

But, convenience is rather more difficult to convert in this way. However, if convenience is measured by the difference in time between when a traveller is ready to start a journey and when the traveller can actually start the journey, e.g. the time of the next train, then convenience can be converted as

convenience ⟶ time ⟶ money

When all the parameters have been converted to money equivalents they can be combined using a weighted mean. The mean value is then acceptable to a unidimensional (money) utility function.

Such conversions are easy and expedient as long as the conversions are linear, e.g. delay = £20 per hour, but some parameters, such as delays, are not perceived by people to be linear. For example, a person may well feel that every additional hour is twice as long as the preceding hour, whence their cost of delays would be:

1 hour £20, 2 hours £60, 3 hours £140, 4 hours £300, etc.

In such cases multidimensional utility functions have to be used even if the internal operation of the function is to undertake the non–linear conversion in order to produce a utility value.

8.7 UTILITY FUNCTIONS AND BUSINESS DECISIONS

Statisticians have shown that a risk seeker will always eventually lose. Consequently, for a business to stay in being for a long time they, i.e. the managers and other decision makers, must be risk averse. It can be argued, therefore, that the choice of a utility curve for a business should not represent the attitude of a person; it should be chosen in order to make the business prosper. Clearly the attitude to risk of people who do well in a business and/or the attitude to risk of the board of directors, will influence the choice of the utility function but the function is more likely to be chosen for its empirical properties rather than because it represents some person's actual utility function.

Consider aversion to risk. It has already been noted that companies must behave in a risk averse manner if they are to stay in business so they require a risk averse utility function. Fig. 8.5 demonstrates this property in a utility function. It is assumed that the manager who will be using the curve will not normally undertake a course of action which will expose the company to losses of more than £10,000 and equally would not normally expect to have possible actions which would make more than £50,000 for the company. The utility for –£10,000 is, therefore, arbitrarily set at 0 and that for £50,000 is arbitrarily set at 100. A suitable utility curve for this manager's use is one which is always risk averse, i.e. one which either crosses the line BC twice or not at all, assuming that the line BC is always parallel to the line OA but may be any distance away from it.

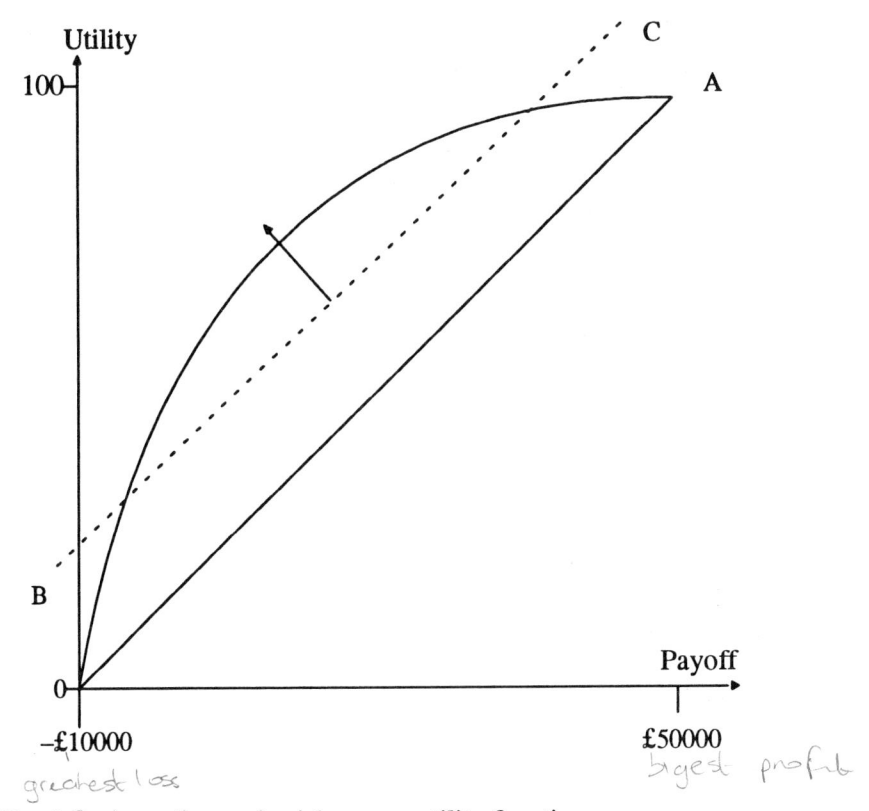

Fig. 8.5. A continuously risk averse utility function

It is much easier to propose a function which has the desired properties and approximates to the wishes of the management of a company than it is to generate a function by experimentation. It is also unlikely that this degree of approximation will make a significant difference to the outcome of decisions. For example, consider the following function:

$$u(x) = 100 * \{(x + £10000)/£60000\}^{1/2} \qquad (8.1)$$

where u is the utility function and x is the value of a payoff. This function has been chosen because it is easily evaluated, has the right sort of properties and represents a level of risk aversion.

In pursuit of the latter point, i.e. the level of risk aversion, consider a board of directors who are trying to make a decision which could make the company £50 million or lose £10 million and the loss of £10 million would close the company. Now ask yourself if the curve given in equation (8.1) would suffice with a simple rescaling of the constants. The answer is not likely to be in the affirmative. It is much more likely that the directors, and those who rely on their judgement, would like to see a larger degree of risk aversion. This can easily be achieved by changing the power of the root, e.g.

$$u'(x) = 100 * \{(x + £10000)/£60000\}^{1/8} \quad (8.2)$$

where u' is a utility function which has been modified to be far more averse to risk than u. Fig. 8.6 shows what this would look like.

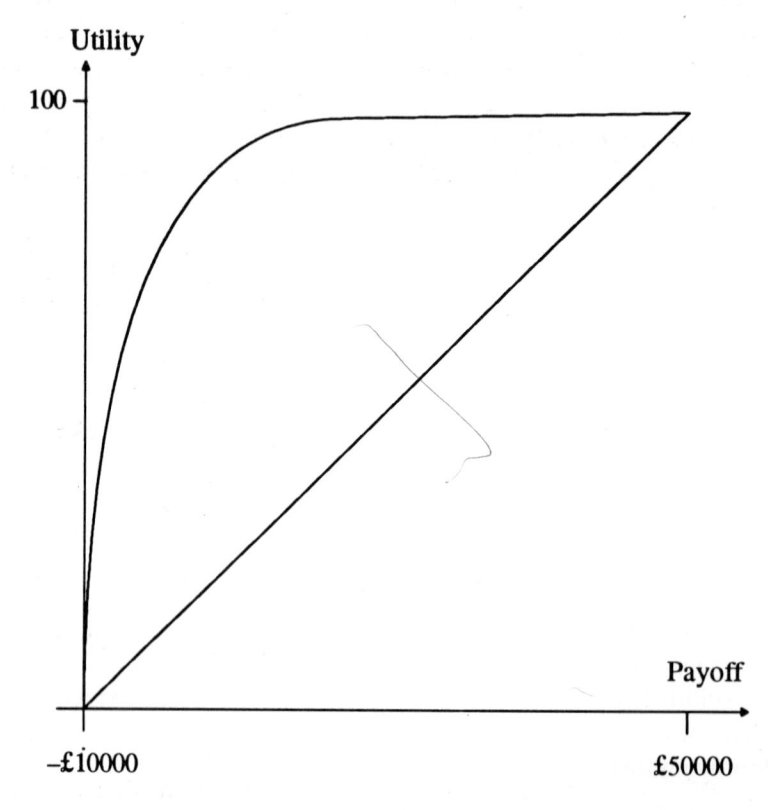

Fig. 8.6. A very risk averse utility function

It is possible, therefore, to assume that the utility function has a specific algebraic form and to choose certain parameters to mould the algebraic form into an approximation of the true utility curve. For example the general form of the function used above is

$$u(x) = 100 * \{(x - a)/(b - a)\}^{1/n} \quad (8.3)$$

where n is the degree of the root, a is the lower payoff in the standard gamble and b is the highest.

8.8 UTILITY THEORY AND DECISION DIAGRAMS

It is now possible to evaluate decision diagrams paying due regard to the risks. This is done by calculating the Expected Preference for each risk node. The Expected Preference, EP, is defined as:

$$EP = \sum_{i=1}^{n} p_i * u(x_i) \qquad (8.4)$$

where an event has n possible outcomes, p_i is the probability of the ith outcome which has a payoff of x_i and u is the utility function. Notice the similarity between the structure of the Expected Preference and that of the Expected Value. The difference lies in the function u which has replaced the actual value of the outcome by some measure which incorporates the risk. Hence Expected Preference is a measure which is cognisant of the risks involved in an option.

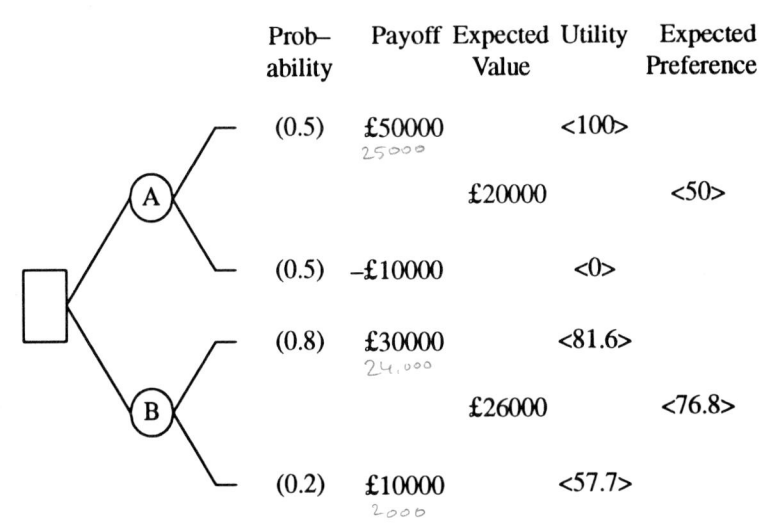

	Prob-ability	Payoff	Expected Value	Utility	Expected Preference
A	(0.5)	£50000 25000		<100>	
			£20000		<50>
	(0.5)	−£10000		<0>	
B	(0.8)	£30000 24,000		<81.6>	
			£26000		<76.8>
	(0.2)	£10000 2000		<57.7>	

Fig. 8.7. Decision diagram evaluated using utility functions

Assume that the utility function shown by Fig. 8.5 is expressed algebraically by equation (8.1). The simple decision shown in Fig. 8.7 could then be evaluated using equation (8.4) and the results would be those shown in Fig. 8.7. Values in angled braces, i.e. <>, are derived using the utility function given by equation (8.1). Probabilities are shown in normal brackets, i.e.( ).

There is no need to convert utility values back into Certainty Equivalents in order to make the decision because the Expected Preference for event A will be larger than that for event B if outcome

A is preferred to B. Consequently, the outcome with the highest Expected Preference can be chosen. However, if we wish to know the Certainty Equivalent, equation 8.1 can be rearranged in order to find it:

$$CE(x) = \{(EP(x)/100)^2 * £60000\} - £10000 \qquad (8.5)$$

where $CE(x)$ is the Certainty Equivalent and $EP(x)$ is the Expected Preference for the outcome. In this case the Certainty Equivalent for outcome A is £5,000 and that for outcome B is £25,389. Notice that the Certainty Equivalent for outcome A is much smaller than the Expected Value, i.e. £5,000 << £20,000. This reflects the risks associated with this possible outcome. The difference between the Certainty Equivalent and the Expected Value for node B is far less, i.e. £25,389 c.f. £26,000. This reflects the far smaller risks for node B. Notice also that the utility function should be defined for the most extreme cases so that all outcomes can be given utility values.

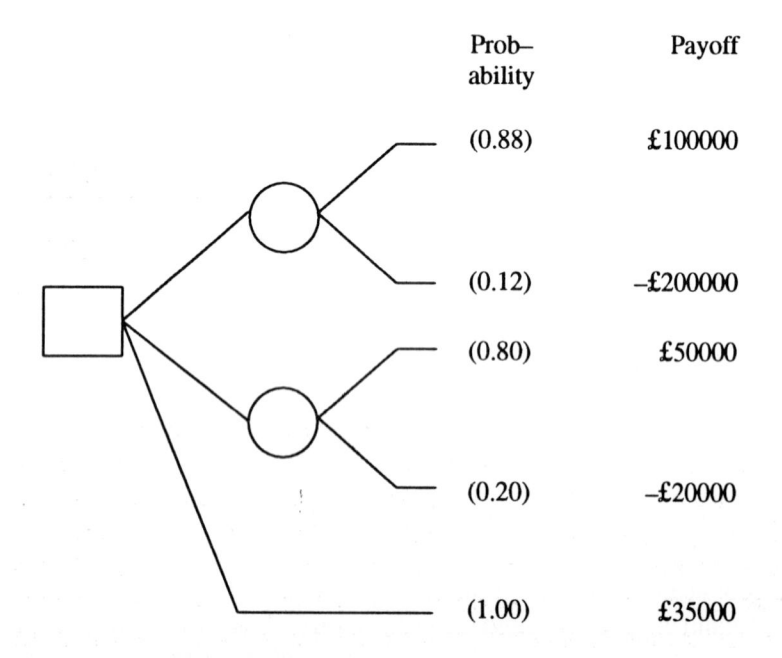

	Probability	Payoff
	(0.88)	£100000
	(0.12)	–£200000
	(0.80)	£50000
	(0.20)	–£20000
	(1.00)	£35000

Fig. 8.8. The helicopter pilot's decision

8.8.1 Example: The North Sea Helicopter Owner/Pilot's Decision

We can now look again at the helicopter owner/pilot's decision which was described in the previous chapter and we can see what would happen if the pilot was risk averse, risk neutral or risk seeking.

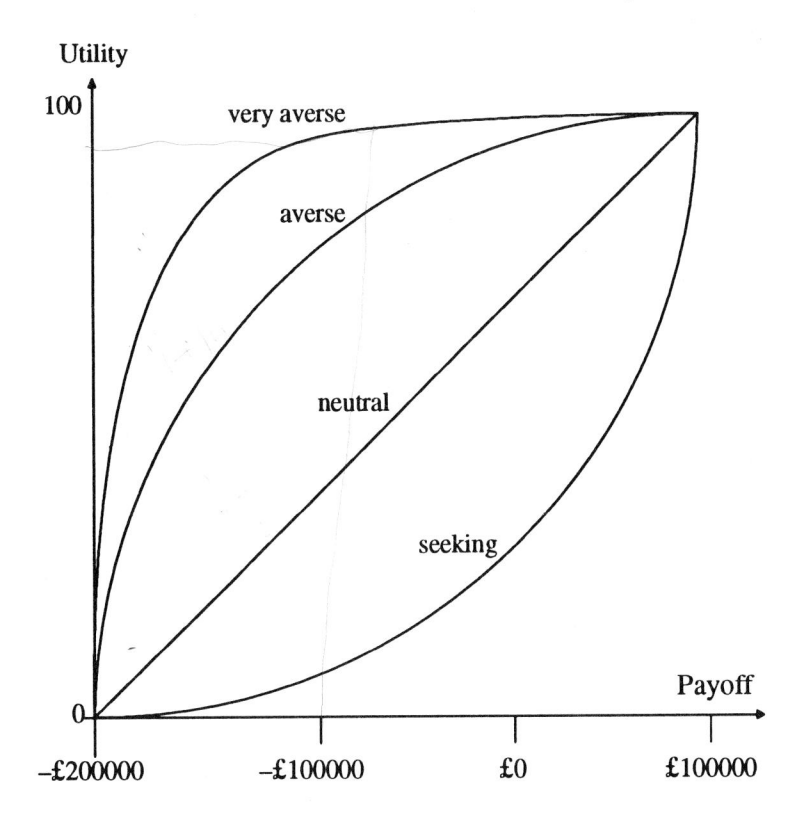

Fig. 8.9. The helicopter pilot's utility curves

The earlier helicopter pilot's decision is now extended by the addition of a third option, namely selling up and working for an established operator. This is shown in Fig. 8.8. We will assume that we are going to examine the attitude of four pilots to this decision. The first is very risk averse, the second is only risk averse, the third is risk neutral and the fourth is risk seeking. The utility curves corresponding to these four pilots are shown in Fig. 8.9 and the functions which have been used to represent these attitudes are given as part of Tables 8.1(a) to 8.1(d) respectively.

An examination of Tables 8.1(a) to 8.1(d) shows that the Certainty Equivalent of any decision involving risk reduces as the person becomes more risk averse.

Table 8.1(a). A very risk averse pilot

	Outcome A succeeds	Outcome A fails	Outcome B succeeds	Outcome B fails	Outcome C
Payoff	100000	−200000	50000	−20000	35000
Utility	100	0	95.54	88.01	
Probability	0.88	0.12	0.8	0.2	
	88.00	0.0	76.43	17.60	
Expected Preference		88.00		94.03	
Certainty Equivalents		20091		34524	35000

Utility function = $100 \cdot \{(payoff + 200000)/300000\}^{1/4}$

Cert. Equivalent = $\{(Expected\ Preference/100)^4 * 300000\} - 200000$

Table 8.1(b). A risk averse pilot

	Outcome A succeeds	Outcome A fails	Outcome B succeeds	Outcome B fails	Outcome C
Payoff	100000	−200000	50000	−20000	35000
Utility	100	0	91.29	77.46	
Probability	0.88	0.12	0.8	0.2	
	88.00	0.0	73.03	15.49	
Expected Preference		88.00		88.52	
Certainty Equivalents		32320		35074	35000

Utility function = $100 \cdot \{(payoff + 200000)/300000\}^{1/2}$

Cert. Equivalent = $\{(Expected\ Preference/100)^2 * 300000\} - 200000$

Allowing for Risk 219

Table 8.1(c). A risk neutral pilot

	Outcome A		Outcome B		Outcome C
	succeeds	fails	succeeds	fails	
Payoff	100000	−200000	50000	−20000	35000
Utility	100	0	83.33	60.00	
Probability	0.88	0.12	0.8	0.2	
	88.00	0.0	66.67	12.00	
Expected Preference	88.00		78.67		
Certainty Equivalents	64000		36000		35000

Utility function = $100 \cdot \{(\text{payoff} + 200000)/300000\}$

Cert. Equivalent = $\{(\text{Expected Preference}/100) * 300000\} - 200000$

Table 8.1(d). A risk seeking pilot

	Outcome A		Outcome B		Outcome C
	succeeds	fails	succeeds	fails	
Payoff	100000	−200000	50000	−20000	35000
Utility	100	0	69.44	36.00	
Probability	0.88	0.12	0.8	0.2	
	88.00	0.0	55.55	7.20	
Expected Preference	88.00		62.75		
Certainty Equivalents	81425		37645		35000

Utility function = $100 \cdot \{(\text{payoff} + 200000)/300000\}^2$

Cert. Equivalent = $\{(\text{Expected Preference}/100)^{1/2} * 300000\} - 200000$

The remainder of Tables 8.1(a) to 8.1(d) show the calculation for evaluating the decision in each case.

Note that the Expected Preferences cannot be compared between tables. This is because the utility functions are different so the Expected Preferences are on different scales. The Certainty Equivalents can be compared, however, because they have been converted back into a common measure. Notice also that the Certainty Equivalent for the risk neutral pilot is exactly the same as the Expected Value.

The tables show that the very risk averse pilot would sell up and go to work for someone else, the risk averse pilot would seek alternative work, the risk neutral pilot would accept the contract as would the risk seeking pilot.

8.9 ASSUMPTIONS USED BY DECISION AND UTILITY THEORY

It is often the case that simplifying assumptions are made in order to keep a problem within the realms of known mathematical theories.

Whenever this is the case it is important to review the simplifying assumptions and try to ensure that they are sensible and that the errors introduced by them are bounded. The above is equally true of decision theory and the supporting Utility Theory so we will look again at the five assumptions which have to be made in order to derive Utility Theory (3, 5, 6):

Assumption 1

A decision maker can order any two possible outcomes and the ordering is transitive, i.e. if O_1 is preferred to O_2 and O_2 is preferred to O_3 then O_1 is preferred to O_3.

Assumption 2

The decision maker is indifferent between a compound uncertain event and a simple uncertain event if the two are equivalent according to standard Probability and Utility Theory.

Assumption 3

A probability p can always be found such that a decision maker is indifferent between a certain event A and the compound event B which has a probability p of outcome B and (1–p) of outcome B.

Assumption 4

If a decision maker is indifferent between an uncertain event A and an uncertain event B when considered in isolation then the same decision maker will accept substitution of one for the other in a more complex situation.

Assumption 5

A decision maker would prefer the uncertain event E which has a probability P_1 of outcome O_1 and $(1 - P_1)$ of outcome O_2 to the uncertain event E which has a probability P_2 of the outcome O_1 and $(1 - P_2)$ of the outcome O_2 if and only if P_1 is greater than P_2 and O_1 is preferred to O_2. See Fig. 8.10.

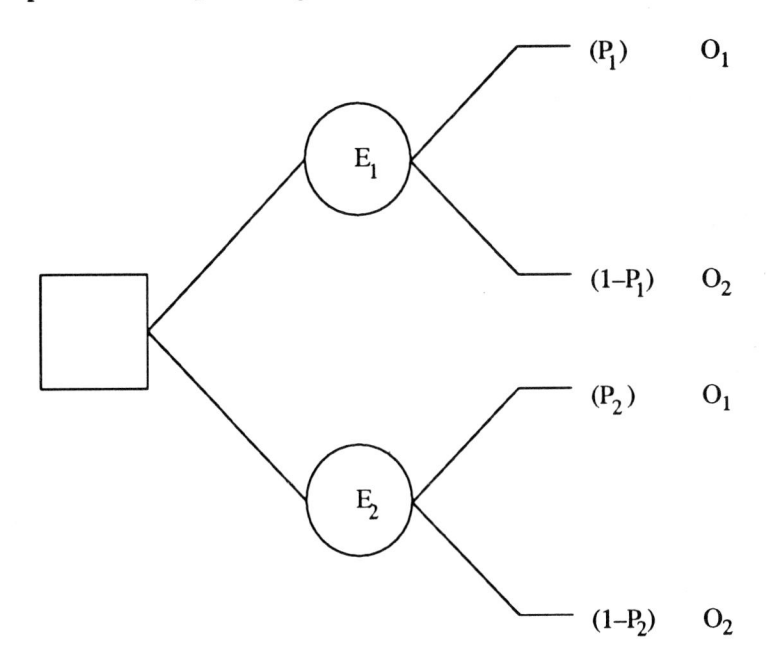

Fig. 8.10. E_1 is preferred to E_2 if and only if $P_1 > P_2$ and O_1 is preferred to O_2.

8.9.1 The Utility Postulate

If the above assumptions are accepted, it is possible to postulate the existence of the utility function. This postulate underpins the whole of Utility Theory and can be expressed as follows :

If assumptions 1 to 5 hold, then there exists a set of numbers

$u_{1i}, u_{2i}, ..., u_{n_i i}$

which can be associated with the outcomes

$O_{1i}, O_{2i}, ..., O_{n_i i}$

having probabilities

$p_{1i}, p_{2i}, ..., p_{n_i i}$

of any uncertain event, E_i. Whereupon if E_h is preferred to another uncertain event, E_j, then $u_h > u_j$ where

$$u_x = \sum_{k=1}^{n_x} P_{kx} * u_{kx} \quad \text{and} \quad \sum_{k=1}^{n_x} P_{kx} = 1 \quad \text{for } x = h, j$$

8.9.2 The Validity of the Assumptions

The above assumptions must not be simply taken for granted. It is important to examine what they mean and to ensure that Utility Theory is only used for cases where we are satisfied that they hold true. Consequently, each assumption will be examined by looking at a counter example where possible.

8.9.2.1 Assumption 1

Consider the following example :

> Fred prefers Steak to Dover Sole and he prefers Dover Sole to Chicken Kiev but in a restaurant offering Steak and Chicken Kiev Fred chooses the Chicken Kiev.

On the face of it Fred is violating assumption 1 and making it impossible to give an ordered utility value to the three options. In reality, however, it is more likely that the utility function is multi-valued and some other significant value has not been taken into account. For example, Fred considers the Steak far too expensive in comparison to the Chicken Kiev. Consequently, Assumption 1 is well worth checking because, if it does not hold, the factors affecting the utility value should be re-examined.

8.9.2.2 Assumption 2

Assumption 2 says that there is nothing about the actual complexity of a decision which affects the decision maker's preference. For

Allowing for Risk 223

example, the decision shown in Fig. 8.11 should leave a risk neutral person undecided. For a given individual this might not be the case but for business use it is a sound basis on which to proceed.

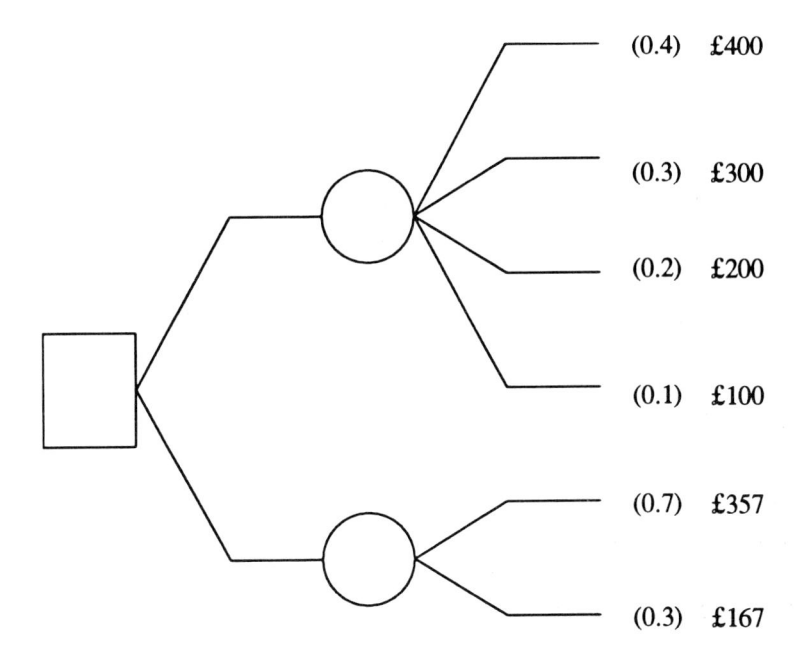

```
                    (0.4)  £400
                    (0.3)  £300
                    (0.2)  £200

                    (0.1)  £100

                    (0.7)  £357
                    (0.3)  £167
```

Fig 8.11. Equally risky uncertain events of different complexity

8.9.2.3 Assumption 3

Consider the gamble depicted by Fig. 8.12. It can be argued that, in a case like this, no value of P, except unity, can be found for which an individual would accept the gamble. It is, therefore, impossible to establish a Certainty Equivalent and hence a utility function for such decisions. If the above argument held and particularly if it was also true when 'death' was replaced by 'liquidation' in a business sense then there would be very serious doubts about the use of Utility Theory in business.

However, consider the following scenario:

> Friends have booked a holiday in the Bahamas. They have rented a colonial mansion for a fortnight with butler, cook, a full complement of servants, the use of a sailing boat moored by the private jetty and the use of a luxurious chauffeur driven car. At the last minute they cannot go and they are prepared to

give you the plane tickets and the booking vouchers so you can go instead. The only problem is that you live in Cornwall and the plane leaves Heathrow in 5 hours' time. You can get the time off work and you reckon you can drive to Heathrow in four hours. Would you try to catch the plane?

You would probably accept the tickets without wasting your time trying to work out a Certainty Equivalent but in doing so you have demonstrated that the gamble is acceptable to most people. A four hour drive, particularly in the circumstances described, involves a slight risk of death. In addition, success is not guaranteed. Nevertheless, many people would try to catch the plane. If people are prepared to gamble with death, we can probably accept that a utility function can cope with business decisions.

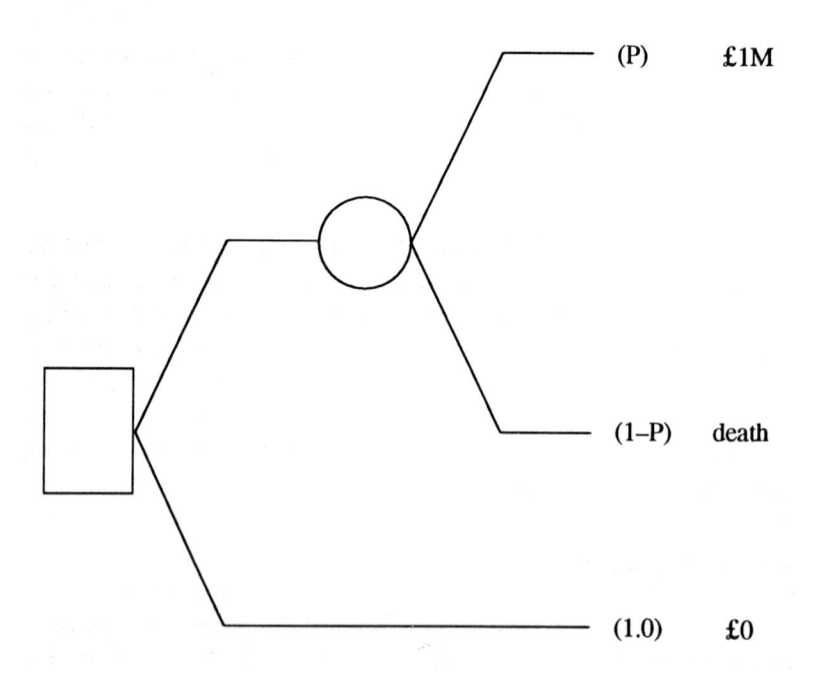

Fig 8.12. The 'do or die' gamble

8.9.2.4 Assumption 4 and 5

Both of these assumptions lay down conditions which facilitate mathematical manipulation of a decision in order to evaluate it. Most quantitative decision makers will accept these without difficulty.

8.10 CORPORATE ATTITUDES TO RISK

We can now see how a company might use a Decision Support System to try to guide its decision makers in their attitudes to the risks which are being taken.

If a Decision Support System incorporates a utility function within it, it would be possible for every decision maker to have a decision's payoffs and associated risks converted into Expected Preferences or Certainty Equivalents. This removes the risk element from the decision and makes the Ordering/Choosing Task much simpler.

A Company may not wish to adopt a single utility function across the whole of its business. Some areas, e.g. when the risks are taken repeatedly, may be able to use a risk neutral curve whilst others, e.g. strategic decisions involving the future of many people, should be taken using a very risk averse curve. Initially, this allocation might seem strange because decisions which are taken frequently have the lower safeguards. However, if the true meaning of Expected Value is considered, it becomes clear that this allocation is precisely as it should be.

It would not be difficult to organise a Decision Support System so that a decision maker was given the appropriate utility function for the decision in hand; nor would it be difficult to change the utility functions used if this became necessary. Consequently, a Decision Support System would be an ideal way for the managers of a corporate body to introduce a quantifiable level of control to corporate risk taking. In fact, this facility could become an important part of any Decision Support System.

8.11 SUMMARY

This chapter has introduced the idea of modifying the payoffs associated with a decision to allow for the risks involved. This idea was formalised by the introduction of an ordering function which we chose to call the utility function.

Some properties which would be required of this function were proposed and this was followed by a discussion of what these functions might be and how they can be determined. It was noted that they are personal things and disclose a person's attitude to risk, insurance and gambling.

Some standard functions were then studies for possible use as utility functions. This was followed by a few examples which showed how utility functions are used in decision making and how they can significantly alter the possible action which is chosen.

Most formalisms require assumptions to be made in order to limit the complexity of real life to that which can be accommodated by the formalism. Utility Theory is no exception. Assumptions should not go unchallenged nor unheeded, so those surrounding Utility Theory were duly aired.

The chapter concluded by discussing the possibility of using Utility Theory within a Decision Support System to help a company adopt and implement a corporate strategy to risk taking.

8.12 CASE STUDY: A UTILITY FUNCTION FOR R, B & H'S STRATEGIC DECISIONS

Consider again the 'New Business Venture' sub–decision which was depicted in Table 7.16 and is represented again by Table 8.2.

Table 8.2. Decreasing Risk Averse Utility Function Applied to the R, B & H 'New Business Venture' Decision.

State of the economy	Probs	become consultants	start a new business	buy existing business	don't buy business
Very buoyant	0.05	£100,000	£100,000	£60,000	–
Buoyant	0.20	£50,000	£50,000	£50,000	–
Static	0.35	£30,000	£0,000	£40,000	–
Depressed	0.30	£0,000	–£10,000	£35,000	–
Very depressed	0.10	–£15,000	–£40,000	£25,000	–
Expected Value		£24,000	£8,000	£40,000	–
Certainty Equivalent		£19,659	£343	£39,654	–

Allowing for Risk

When we considered it before, Mr Philip had calculated the Expected Value. If we can find a suitable utility function we could now provide a mechanism for making this decision whilst allowing for Mr Keith's and Mr Philip's attitude to risk.

At present, Mr Keith and Mr Philip could afford to retire. They will jeopardise this situation if they lose money whilst trying to continue with R, B & H or whilst trying a new venture. Consequently, they need to be exceedingly risk averse to possible losses but can afford to be less averse as the magnitude of the losses decreases. In other words they need a utility function which has decreasing risk aversion. Rubenstein (7) supported the use of such a utility function because it modelled the behaviour of investors. In their present circumstances, Mr Keith and Mr Philip may well be behaving like investors. Consequently, a more suitable utility function may well be:

$$u(x) = \ln(x + A) \text{ where } x + A \qquad (8.6)$$

In equation (8.6), x is again the payoff and A fixes the degree of risk aversion but the risk aversion decreases as A increases.

Any chance node with n outcomes having payoffs $x_1, x_2, ..., x_n$ with probabilities $p_1, p_2, ..., p_n$ respectively and a utility function given by equation (8.6) will have a Certainty Equivalent given by the formula:

$$CE = (x_1 + A)^{p_1} (x_2 + A)^{p_2} ... (x_n + A)^{p_n} - A \qquad (8.7)$$

Whilst this is a complex equation to evaluate, it is a suitable function for R, B & H. All that remains is to find a suitable value for A. The worst payoff in the table is –£40,000. A has to be larger than this because of the condition that $x_i + A > 0$ for all i possible outcomes. If we try this value, we discover that it is slightly too averse. If we continue to experiment we will find that A = £60,000 gives the Certainty Equivalents shown in Table 8.2 and these are near enough to the those used by Mr Philip for 60,000 to be a good value for A.

Notice how the Risk Premium, i.e. the difference between the Certainty Equivalent and the Expected Value, decreases as the possible action becomes less risky. For example, the possible action 'start a new business' has a risk premium of £7,657 whilst the risk premium for 'buy an existing business' is £346. Notice also that the Decision Support System will not need to store, or use, the utility function. The function for the Certainty Equivalent, which is deduced from the utility function, is all that is required. For any uncertain event, this function will convert the set of payoffs and associated probabilities into a Certainty Equivalent.

8.13 POINTS TO PONDER

Rework the 'Future of R, B & H' sub-decision in section 7.6.1 using the newly adopted utility function which results in a Certainty Equivalent given by equation 8.7 with A = 60000.

8.13.1 Suggestion

Write a small computer program or use a spreadsheet to evaluate the function.

8.14 FURTHER READING

- Arrow, K.J. (1963) *Social Choice and Individual values.* 2nd ed., Yale University Press.

- Bodily, S.E. (1979) A Delegation Process for Combining Individual Utility Functions. *Management Science,* **25,** no. 10.

- Bodily, S.E. (1985) *Modern Decision Making.* McGraw Hill, Chapters 7 & 8.

- Brock, H.W. (1980) The Problem of Utility Weights in Group Preference Aggregation. *Operations Research,* **28,** no. 1, pp. 176–187.

- Dyer, J.S. and Rakesh, K.S. (1979) Measurable Multi–Attribute Value Functions. *Operations Research,* **27,** no. 4, pp. 810–822.

- Hammond, J.S. (1967) Better Decisions with Preference Theory. *Harvard Business Review,* Nov–Dec.

- Holtzman, S. (1989) *Intelligent Decision Systems.* Addison–Wesley, Chapter 3.

- Keeney, R.L. and Raiffa, H. (1957) *Decisions with Multiple Objectives: Preferences and Value Tradeoffs.* John Wiley.

- North, D.W. (1968) A Tutorial Introduction to Decision Theory. *IEEE Transactions on Systems Science and Cybernetics SSC4,* no. 3, pp. 200–210.

- Raiffa, H. (1970) *Decision Analysis: Introductory Lectures on Choices Under Uncertainty.* Addison–Wesley.

8.15 REFERENCES

(1) Bernoulli, D. (1738) Specimen Theriae Novea de Mensora Sortis. *Papers of the Imperial Academy of Science in Petersburg,* **5**, 1738, pp. 175–192.

(2) de Finetti, B. (1937) La Prevision: Ses Lois Logiques, ses Sources Subjectives. *Annales de l'Institut Henri Poincare,* **7**, pp. 1–68.

(3) von Neumann, J. and Morgenstern, O. (1947) *Theory of Games and Economic Behavior.* Princeton University Press.

(4) de Finetti, B. (1983) Probability: Interpretations. In *International Encyclopedia of the Social Sciences,* Macmillan, pp. 496–505.

(5) Savage, L.J. (1972) *The Foundations of Statistics,* Dover.

(6) Howard, R.A. (1984) Risk Preference. In *Readings on the Principles and Applications of Decision Analysis,* Howard, R.A. and Matheson, J.E. (eds.), Menlo Park California: Strategic Decisions Group, **2**, pp. 626–663.

(7) Rubenstein, M. (1976) The Strong Case for the Generalised Logarithmic Utility Model as the Premier Model of Financial markets. *Journal of Finance,* May, pp. 551–571.

Chapter 9
Making Decisions with Incomplete Information

9.1 INTRODUCTION

One criticism of the methods outlined in the preceding chapters is that they need complete information. This arises from such things as the requirement to associate a probability with each branch of a decision diagram. Critics would argue that complete information of this sort is not available in a practical situation. Since, for example, a decision diagram cannot be evaluated unless the branches have associated probabilities, incomplete information renders the method useless.

The counter argument proceeds as follows. Whilst it is very true that there will never be enough information to completely specify all the uncertainty surrounding a real problem, it cannot possibly make sense to dispense with the information which is available just because it is incomplete. Furthermore, if the best decision possible is to be made, all the information available must be used and not just part of it.

One possible approach would be to use the information which is available to estimate the information which is missing. The estimation process can be impartial and hence not prejudice the decision. When the information is complete, albeit partly estimated, formal decision procedures can be used. In a business setting, decisions based on formal methods using all the information which is available with estimates of that which is missing should be the best available. At least, with this approach, if the decisions turn out to be bad, they can be analysed to see where things went wrong.

We are, therefore, going to have to accept a few basic realities about decision making. These can be informally expressed as:

(1) If the information is incomplete, the uncertainty and risk increase.

(2) All the available information must be used to make the decision.

(3) A decision which was made using all the information which was available at the time could not have improved even if it turns out to have been a bad decision in retrospect.

The final point is in response to those who criticise with hindsight. Most things become clearer as time progresses but you cannot use hindsight to criticise a decision unless it becomes apparent that information which was available at the time was not used or that the information was used badly.

In business decisions the missing information is usually the payoff for some, or all, of the possible outcomes and/or the uncertainty, i.e. probability, which should be associated with the possible outcomes. The former has much to do with accountancy practice and most companies are used to estimating the payoff for the various possible outcomes. Estimating the uncertainty is, however, a different matter and few companies have established procedures for doing this. The situation is exacerbated by the fact that estimating probabilities is by no means a trivial exercise and is fraught with consistency problems if done by guesswork. This chapter will, therefore, concentrate on estimating the missing probabilities.

Nowhere in this book are the desiderata given in Chapter 1 more relevant than they are now. They can be used formally as an axiomatic starting point for a theory (1) but that is not the purpose of this chapter. Our aim is to understand the principles behind the theory so we only develop an informal rationale for it.

9.2 THE PRINCIPLE OF INSUFFICIENT REASON

The rationale behind the theory described here started with Hume (1) when he proposed his theory of insufficient reason in 1740. In everyday language the Principle of Insufficient Reason states that, if an event is capable of many outcomes and there is insufficient reason for doing otherwise, equal values must be assigned to the probability of each outcome. For example, if you were given a die which was apparently a perfect cube and equally balanced then you would rightly assign a value of 1/6 to the probability of any given face being uppermost after the die was thrown.

If, however, you conducted some experiments and discovered that in twenty out of one hundred throws the six face was uppermost then you would quite correctly revise your estimate of the probabilities for each possible outcome. Your estimate for the six face should now be 1/5 but, since you have at this stage no information to distinguish between the other faces, each of these would be assigned its share of the remaining probability, i.e. 1/5 of 4/5 = 4/25. However, if a 'dice expert' told you that when one face appears too often the opposite face appears proportionately too infrequently, the assignments to the probabilities should be:

$P(6) = 1/5$, $P(1) = 2/15$

$P(2) = P(3) = P(4) = P(5) = 1/6$

where P(1) indicates the probability that face 1 will land uppermost and opposite faces sum to seven.

9.3 MAXIMUM ENTROPY

The above calculations are easy and reasonably intuitive but unfortunately information is not always available in such a convenient form. For example, frequently the only information which is available is in the form of means or some other measure of average. The situation is then no longer quite so simple.

Consider an experiment where a die is thrown, the value of the uppermost face is recorded and the mean calculated after a considerable number of throws. If the die is unbiased, the result should be 3.5, i.e. the Expected Value, give or take a little. If the result was 2.5 what could we deduce? It certainly is not an unbiased die but could we deduce the value for the probability of each face being uppermost, i.e. a probability distribution for the die?

We could postulate that the die had a probability distribution as follows:

$P(1) = P(4) = 1/2$, $P(2) = P(3) = P(5) = P(6) = 0$

but both common sense and the Principle of Insufficient Reason would reject this distribution on the grounds that it is most unlikely and we have no evidence to suggest that it might be correct. Unfortunately neither common sense nor the Principle of Insufficient Reason suggest what a suitable distribution might be.

This is precisely what the theory of Maximum Entropy was designed to do. The full mathematical treatment of this theory is fairly complex so the explanation which follows is offered as a digestible explanation of why Maximum Entropy is plausible. A sound mathematical derivation can be found in Tribus (2).

In order to understand the ideas behind Maximum Entropy, consider first an experiment involving the throwing of a coin. The coin can only land with the 'head' face up or with the 'tail' face up. We will denote these as H and T respectively. The probability of either a 'head' or a 'tail' must be unity, hence P(H or T) = 1. If we throw the coin many times, either a 'head' or a 'tail' must occur at each attempt so the possible outcomes are:

(H or T) and (H or T) and (H or T) and etc.

If we restrict ourselves to three throws the possible outcomes are:

HHH or HHT or HTH or THH or HTT or THT or TTH or TTT   (9.1)

The 'and' has been taken as understood. Since the order is immaterial, i.e. HHT is the same as HTH, expression (9.1) can be written

HHH or 3HHT or 3HTT or TTT

Such trials are known as Bernoulli trials and, if the separate throws are independent of each other, the probability of getting two 'heads' and a 'tail', but not necessarily in that order, can be seen to be $3*P(H)*P(H)*P(T)$. In general this result is written as:

$$P(H^r T^{n-r}) = \left\{\frac{n!}{r!(n-r)!}\right\} * P(H)^r * P(T)^{n-r} \qquad (9.2)$$

where $H^r T^{n-r}$ means that in n repeats there have been r 'heads' and (n − r) 'tails' whereas $P(H)^r$ is the the probability of 'heads' raised to the power r.

If equation (9.2) is generalised for an event with m possible outcomes it becomes:

$$P(O_1^{n_1} O_2^{n_2} ... O_m^{n_m}) = \left\{\frac{n!}{n_1! n_2! ... n_m!}\right\} P(O_1)^{n_1} P(O_2)^{n_2} ... P(O_m)^{n_m}$$

$$= \left\{\frac{n!}{n_1! n_2! ... n_m!}\right\} \prod_{i=1}^{m} P(O_i)^{n_i} \qquad (9.3)$$

where $n = n_1 + n_2 + ... + n_m$ and n_i is the number of times outcome O_i occurred.

Now, if we repeated the above experiment a very large number of times, we would expect outcome O_i to occur on $n*P(O_i)$ occasions. So, in equation (9.3) we can replace n_i by $n*P(O_i)$, whence:

$$P(O_1^{n_1} O_2^{n_2} ... O_m^{n_m}) = \left\{\frac{n!}{n_1! n_2! ... n_m!}\right\} \prod_{i=1}^{m} P(O_i)^{n.P(O_i)} \qquad (9.4)$$

Now, if we did a second experiment which had the same possible outcomes we could test to see if we were actually only doing a second run of the same experiment by measuring the difference between the distribution for the first trial with that for the second trial by using the expression:

$$\text{Diff} = \left\{\frac{n!}{n_1!n_2!\ldots n_m!}\right\} \prod_{i=1}^{m} P(O_i)^{n.P(O_i)} \quad (9.5)$$

$$- \left\{\frac{n'!}{n'_1!n'_2!\ldots n'_m!}\right\} \prod_{i=1}^{m} P'(O_i)^{n'.P'(O_i)}$$

where ' has been used to indicate the values associated with the second experiment.

Now, it can be shown that the value of $P(O_1^{n_1} O_2^{n_2} \ldots O_m^{n_m})$ is a maximum when every outcome occurs equally often, i.e. $n_1 = n_2 = \ldots = n_m$. This happens to be the least prejudiced distribution, i.e. the one which is derived from the Principle of Insufficient Reason. Consequently, if the first experiment was one in which every outcome occurs equally often, the first term in equation (9.5) is always going to be larger than the second. If the information about the second experiment is incomplete and we want the distribution for the second experiment to be as close as possible to the first, i.e. minimally prejudiced, it can be shown that we must maximise

$$- \prod_{i=1}^{m} P'(O_i)^{P'(O_i)} \quad (9.6)$$

From a purely mathematical point of view, equation (9.6) can be simplified by taking logs and this gives us the property known as Entropy. Hence,

$$\text{Entropy} = - \sum_{i=1}^{m} P'(O_i) . \ln P'(O_i) \quad (9.7)$$

We may not have a free hand in maximising the entropy, however, because the solution which maximises Entropy must conform with the existing knowledge about the probability distribution. In this situation we say that the existing knowledge constrains the probability distribution and that Entropy must be maximised within these constraints.

9.4 MAXIMISING ENTROPY

It can be shown that Entropy is maximised if the constraints are linear and,

$$P(O_i) = e^{-\lambda_0} e^{-\lambda_1 s_{i1}} e^{-\lambda_2 s_{i2}} \ldots e^{-\lambda_N s_{iN}} \tag{9.8}$$

where   N is the number of constraints

λ_j $j = 0 .. N$ are constants known as Lagrange multipliers

s_{ij} are selection functions

e is the natural antilogarithm

The selection functions s_{ij} have the following properties:

s_{ij} = the coefficient of $P(O_i)$ if $P(O_i)$ is present in the jth constraint

$s_{ij} = 0$ otherwise.

In any probabilistic system there is always the constraint that:

$$\sum_{i=1}^{m} P(O_i) = 1 \tag{9.9}$$

This is the zeroth constraint and determines the value of λ_0. Every $P(O_i)$ is present in this constraint and so λ_0 does not require a selection function.

9.5 MAXIMUM ENTROPY IN PRACTICE

The mathematics given in sections 9.3 and 9.4 conceals the ease with which Maximum Entropy can be used in practice. Simple examples can be solved algebraically and numerical methods exist which can solve most Maximum Entropy problems. Here are a few simple examples.

9.5.1 Regular Six Sided Die – No Additional Knowledge

In this case there is only one constraint, namely

$$P(1) + P(2) + P(3) + P(4) + P(5) + P(6) = 1 \tag{9.10}$$

The general solution is, therefore,

$$P(i) = e^{-\lambda_0} \tag{9.11}$$

Substituting equation (9.11) into equation (9.10) we find that

$$6e^{-\lambda_0} = 1 \quad \text{i.e.} \quad e^{-\lambda_0} = 1/6$$

whereupon

$$P(1) = P(2) = P(3) = P(4) = P(5) = P(6) = 1/6$$

which, not surprisingly, is the same solution as that achieved by using the Principle of Insufficient Reason.

9.5.2 Six Sided Die with P(6) = 1/5

In this case there are two constraints

zeroth:
$$P(1) + P(2) + P(3) + P(4) + P(5) + P(6) = 1 \quad (9.12a)$$

first:
$$P(6) = 1/5 \quad (9.12b)$$

The general solution is, therefore,

$$P(i) = e^{-\lambda_1 s_{1i}} \quad (9.13)$$

where $s_{1i} = 1$ if $i = 6$; $s_{1i} = 0$ otherwise, whereupon

$$P(1) = P(2) = P(3) = P(4) = P(5) = e^{-\lambda_0} \quad (9.14a)$$

$$P(6) = e^{-\lambda_0} e^{-\lambda_1} = 1/5 \quad (9.14b)$$

Substituting equation (9.14a) and equation (9.14b) into equation (9.12a) gives:

$$5e^{-\lambda_0} + 1/5 = 1$$

whence

$$e^{\lambda_0} = 4/25$$

Hence,

$$P(1) = P(2) = P(3) = P(4) = P(5) = 4/25$$

$$P(6) = 1/5$$

Making Decisions with Incomplete Information 237

which is again the solution derived earlier using the principle of insufficient Reason.

9.5.3 Six Sided Die with P(6) = 1/5 and P(1) + P(6) = 1/3

There are now three constraints

zeroth:
$$P(1) + P(2) + P(3) + P(4) + P(5) + P(6) = 1 \quad (9.15a)$$

first:
$$P(6) = 1/5 \quad (9.12b)$$

second:
$$P(1) + P(6) = 1/3 \quad (9.15c)$$

The general solution is, therefore,
$$P(i) = e^{-\lambda_0} e^{-\lambda_1 s_{1i}} e^{-\lambda_2 s_{2i}} \quad (9.16)$$

where $s_{1i} = 1$ if $i = 6$ and $s_{1i} = 0$ otherwise
$s_{2i} = 1$ if $i = 1$ or 6 and $s_{2i} = 0$ otherwise

Substituting equation (9.16) into the three equations (9.15) gives:

$$e^{-\lambda_0}\{e^{-\lambda_2} + 4 + e^{-\lambda_1} e^{-\lambda_2 s_{2i}}\} = 1 \quad (9.17a)$$

$$e^{-\lambda_0} e^{-\lambda_1} e^{-\lambda_2} = 1/5 \quad (9.17b)$$

$$e^{-\lambda_0}\{e^{-\lambda_2} + e^{-\lambda_1} e^{-\lambda_2}\} = 1/3 \quad (9.17c)$$

Using equation (9.17a) and equation (9.17c),
$$4e^{-\lambda_0} + 1/3 = 1 \quad \text{i.e.} \quad e^{-\lambda_0} = 1/6$$

Using equation (9.17b) and equation (9.17c),
$$e^{-\lambda_0} e^{-\lambda_2} + 1/5 = 1/3 \quad \text{i.e.} \quad e^{-\lambda_0} e^{-\lambda_2} = 2/15$$

whence
$$P(1) = 2/15, P(2) = P(3) = P(4) = P(5) = 1/6, P(6) = 1/5$$

This is again the same as the answer derived earlier using the Principle of Insufficient Reason. This demonstrates that Maximum Entropy is

9.5.4 Six Sided Die with Expected Value of 2.5

There are only two constraints,

zeroth:
$$P(1) + P(2) + P(3) + P(4) + P(5) + P(6) = 1 \qquad (9.18a)$$

first:
$$P(1) + 2.P(2) + 3.P(3) + 4.P(4) + 5.P(5) + 6.P(6) = 2.5 \qquad (9.18b)$$

The general solution is,
$$P(i) = e^{-\lambda_0} e^{-\lambda_1 s_{1i}} \qquad (9.19)$$

But, $s_{1i} = i$ for $i = 1$ to 6 and is never zero.

When equation (9.13) is substituted into equation (9.18a) and equation (9.18b)

$$e^{-\lambda_0} \sum_{i=1}^{6} e^{-i\lambda_1} = 1$$

$$e^{-\lambda_0} \sum_{i=1}^{6} i.e^{-i\lambda_1} = 2.5$$

Eliminating $e^{-\lambda_0}$ gives,

$$2.5 \sum_{i=1}^{6} e^{-i\lambda_1} = \sum_{i=1}^{6} i.e^{-i\lambda_1}$$

and if we let $v = e^{-\lambda_1}$ this results in the equation

$$1.5 + 0.5v - 0.5v^2 - 1.5v^3 - 2.5v^4 - 3.5v^5 = 0$$

which must be solved for a suitable value of v. Solving numerically gives,

$$v = 0.690010173$$

whence

$$e^{\lambda_0} = 0.503607$$

and

$$\begin{aligned} P(1) &= 0.347494 \\ P(2) &= 0.239774 \\ P(3) &= 0.165447 \\ P(4) &= 0.114160 \\ P(5) &= 0.078772 \\ P(6) &= 0.054353 \end{aligned} \quad (9.20)$$

This solution could not be derived using the Principle of Insufficient Reason and it is difficult to see what other rationalisation could have been used to solve the problem.

9.6 MINIMALLY PREJUDICED DISTRIBUTIONS

The probability distribution given by equation (9.20) would almost certainly turn out to be wrong if further trials were done and more information gathered. Why then do we get so excited by the Maximum Entropy solution? The reason is that it 'hedges its bets'. The Maximum Entropy solution does not commit itself to any possible outcome more than is absolutely necessary. In so doing it is an excellent distribution on which to base business decisions.

The Maximum Entropy distribution maximises vagueness whilst conforming with the current knowledge. As such it is maximally influenced by new information. In other words, new information will be given due credence. Jaynes (3) gave this the name Minimally Prejudiced which he defined as follows:

> 'The minimally prejudiced probability distribution is that which maximises the entropy subject to constraints supplied by the given information.'

We can view it as a way of getting started. It is not possible to proceed with many of the decision strategies unless complete probability distributions are available. Maximum Entropy will provide the 'safest' distribution to use whilst ensuring that it conforms with the constraints set by the available knowledge.

9.7 MAXIMUM ENTROPY ON A MANAGER'S DESK

The theory outlined in the previous sections is too complex to be used manually on every day problems. Its use in Decision Support

Systems would be very limited were it not for computers. If a manager is provided with such assistance, however, there is no reason whatsoever why it should not be simply used as a tool. As long as the manager can express the constraints, the rest is perfectly capable of being automated. In most cases the constraints will be no more and no less than the available knowledge. Consequently, this process should appear to the manager as one which simply estimates the unknown information when all the available information has been given.

For example, earlier chapters in this book have outlined methods of analysing and formalising decisions. During this process the decision maker will have identified decisions and sub-decisions and the various possible outcomes for them. Once this has been done, as much probabilistic information as possible can be supplied and the computer used to fill in the rest in a minimally prejudiced manner.

If the values provided by the computer surprise the decision maker then the computer may not have been given all the available information. The fact that the decision maker was surprised suggests an expectation which was not fulfilled. This could either be because information was available which was not declared or because the decision maker has preconceived ideas which are not based on available information. Either way, the decision and the decision maker will benefit from having to resolve the discrepancy.

9.8 SUMMARY

This chapter noted that the preceding theories require full information if they are to be used to support decisions. Whilst most companies have established techniques for estimating the payoffs associated with the possible outcomes of an uncertain event, few have established techniques for estimating the probabilities associated with these possible outcomes.

This chapter discussed two theories appropriate to this problem. The first, the Principle of Insufficient Reason, attributes equal probability to all possible outcomes unless it has reason to do otherwise. The second, the Theory of Maximum Entropy, used rather more elaborate methods to estimate missing probabilities whilst taking into account those that are known. These two theories were shown to be equivalent if the Maximum Entropy Theory took the uniform probability distribution to be the default distribution.

9.9 CASE STUDY: R, B & H PERSONAL INVOLVEMENT SUB–DECISION

In the preceding sections of this chapter we have seen how Maximum Entropy can be used to estimate missing values of a probability distribution. It is easy to see how this could be applied to the estimation of missing probabilities for the possible outcomes of a chance node in a Decision Diagram but these probabilities can often be estimated by the decision maker. Other situations arise, however, in which the decision maker could not possibly estimate safe values to use for the missing probabilities. This is because the probabilities are inter related and the values used for the 'don't know' probabilities, i.e. the missing ones, must not inadvertently influence the outcome. In other words, we wish the estimates to be minimally prejudiced. One such situation is the 'Personal Involvement' sub–decision in Chapter 7. This was left unresolved so we will return to it now and see whether or not we can make progress using Maximum Entropy.

For the sake of simplicity, and so that the brothers can have access to existing software, we will convert this decision into a slightly different style. The style we will use is that of Laurentzen and Spiegelhalter (4). In order to specify the sub–decision in the above form we have to express every node as a chance node. When this is done, the Influence Diagram shown in Fig 7.14 becomes the Directed Acyclic Graph shown in Fig. 9.1. In these graphs, the direction of the arrows indicates the direction of influence, e.g. node A influences node B.

The nodes have been lettered for convenience and we are now going to simplify things even further by assuming that the chance nodes can only take the two values. The values we shall use are as follows:–

A = State of the Economy	buoyant	not buoyant
B = Profitability of R, B & H	profitable	not profitable
C = Capital for Retirement	enough	not enough
D = ROI of New Business	good	not good
E = Future of R, B & H	buyer	no buyer
F = Personal Involvement	retire	do not retire
G = Pension Arrangements	adequate	not adequate
H = Good Health	continues	does not continue

Notice that the 'decision' nodes have been removed. This has been done by considering only one of the possible cases. The sub–decision concerns the brothers' involvement in R, B & H so Fig. 9.1 has been drawn assuming that R, B & H will remain in business otherwise there is nothing for the brothers to retire from. It has also been assumed that the brothers are going to try a new business venture. Directed Acyclic Graphs can be drawn for the other cases which are much simpler, e.g. node D disappears if the brothers do not try a new business venture.

A
P(A) = 0.25
State of the Economy

P(B|A) = 0.4
P(B|~A) = 0.2

P(D|A) = 0.6
P(D|~A) = 0.5

B
Profitability of 'R, B & H'

P(C|B) = 0.5
P(C|~B) = 0.1

C
Capital for Retirement

P(C|D) = ?
P(C|~D) = 0.02

D
ROI of 'New Venture'

P(E|B) = 0.333
P(E|~B) = 0.001

P(F|B) = ?
P(F|~B) = ?

P(F|C) = 0.9   P(F|~C) = 0.1

P(F|D) = ?
P(F|~D) = ?

E
future of R, B & H

P(F|E) = 0.9
P(F|~E) = ?

F
Personal Involvement

G
Pension Arrangements

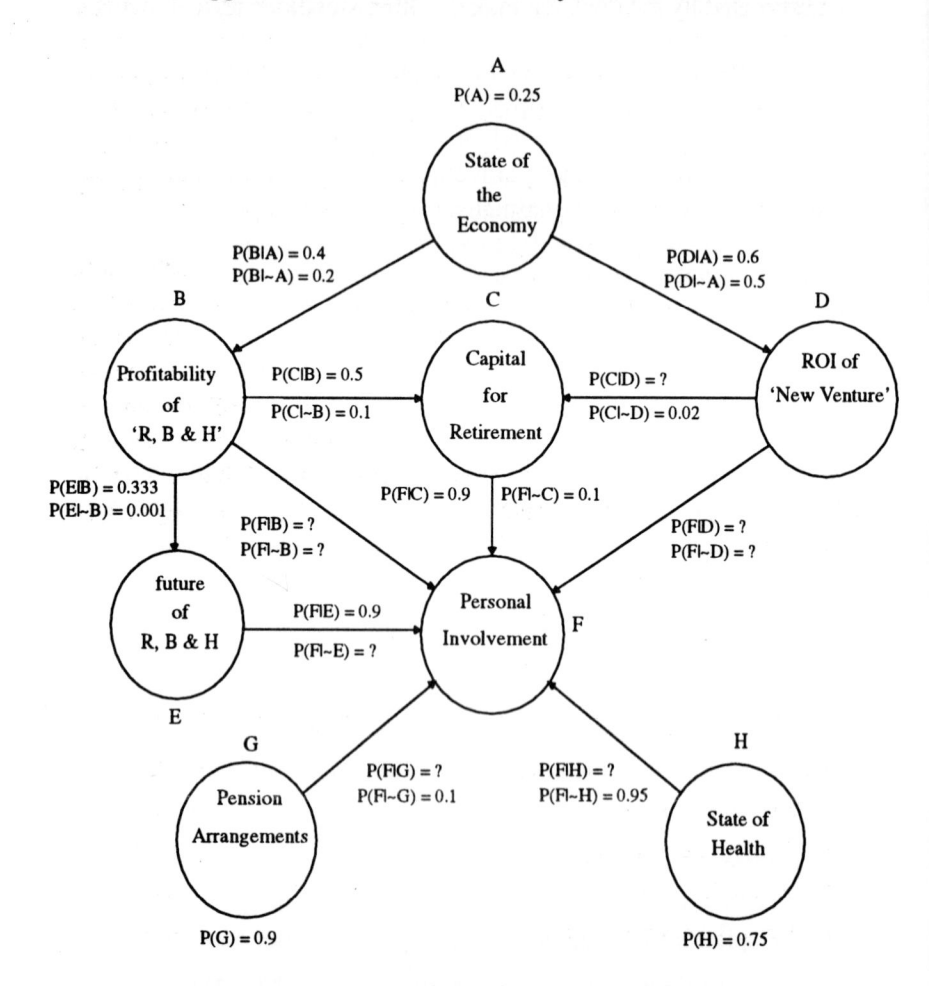

P(F|G) = ?
P(F|~G) = 0.1

P(F|H) = ?
P(F|~H) = 0.95

H
State of Health

P(G) = 0.9

P(H) = 0.75

Fig. 9.1. The 'personal involvement' sub–decision

In order to evaluate this diagram using Laurentzen and Spiegelhalter's method (4), we need to provide conditional probabilities for all the influences. In particular, the brothers would have to provide probabilities for 'Personal Involvement' given all combinations of the six chance nodes labelled B, C, D, E, G and H in Fig. 9.1. There are 64 of these and the brothers would be overwhelmed if they were asked to provide this information.

What we shall do instead is ask them to try to provide two pieces of information for each arrow, namely the probability of the influenced node given that the influencing node is true and the probability of the influenced node given that the influencing node is false. We will also ask them to try to provide the probability of source nodes, i.e. all nodes which are not influenced by another node. Mr Keith's and Mr Philip's attempt at doing this is shown in Fig. 9.1. The probabilities which they cannot provide are shown equated to a query, i.e. P(C|D) = ?. The challenge for Maximum Entropy is to estimate the missing probabilities and hence the probabilities for the nodes.

This can be done using a method developed by Garside and Rhodes (6) and the results of interest to the brothers are shown in Table 9.1. Knowing the missing probabilities is immaterial to the brothers except for checking that none of them are clearly nonsense. The important probability for the brothers is the probability of node F, i.e. the probability that they should stay personally involved with R, B & H. Maximum Entropy predicts the probability of this node to be 0.26 and hence they should stay personally involved, i.e. they should not retire.

Table 9.1. Missing information estimated using Maximum Entropy

P(State of R, B & H = profitable)	= 0.25
P(Capital for Retirement = enough)	= 0.2
P(ROI of New Business = good)	= 0.575
P(Future of R, B & H = buyer)	= 0.084
P(Personal Involvement = retire)	= 0.26

The strength of this type of decision making, however, lies in its ability to easily remake the decision given new information. Suppose, for example, that business confidence suddenly rose and the probability of the economy becoming buoyant dramatically increased to 0.8, i.e. $P(A) = 0.8$. All the information estimated using Maximum Entropy could be used to recalculate the probability of staying personally involved given this change in the economic outlook. When this is done, the revised probability of node F becomes $P(F|A=0.8) = 0.33$ and the brothers should review their previous decision in this new light.

However, if the brothers can find a buyer for R, B & H and arrange good pensions then the probability that they should retire is $P(F|EG) = 0.9$. If they want to retire, this suggests a strategy for doing so.

9.10 POINTS TO PONDER

(1) Is the 'Personal Involvement' sub–decision over complex because Mr Keith and Mr Philip have failed to break it down into atomic decisions? If so, how would you break it down further?

(2) The average person has no feel for conditional probabilities (6). Is there a sensible alternative? If there is, how could it be used to support the decision?

9.11 FURTHER READING

- Griffeath, D.S. (1972) Computer Solutions of the Discrete Maximum Entropy Problem. *Technometrics*, **14**, no. 4, pp. 891–897.

- Hunter, D. (1980) Uncertain Reasoning Using Maximum Entropy Inference. In *Uncertainty in Artificial Intelligence*. Kanal, L.N. and Lemmer, F.J. (eds.), Elsevier Science Publishers B V (North Holland), pp. 203–209.

- Levine, R.D. and Tribus, M. (eds.) (1979) *The Maximum Entropy Formalism*. MIT Press.

- Maung, I. and Paris, J.B. (1900) A Note on the Infeasibility of some Inference Processes. *International Journal of Intelligent Systems*, **5**, no. 5, pp. 595–603.

- Shore, J.E. and Johnson, R.W. (1980) Axiomatic Derivation of the Principle of Maximum Entropy and the Principle of

Minimum Cross–Entropy. *IEEE Transactions on Information Theory*, **IT-26**, pp. 26–37.

- Tribus, M. (1969) *Rational Descriptions Decisions and Designs*. Pergamon.

- Wise, B.P. and Henrion, M. (1986) A Framework for Comparing Uncertain Inference Systems to Probability. In *Uncertainty in Artificial Intelligence*, Kanal, L.N. and Lemer, J.F. (eds.), Elsevier Science Publishers B V (North Holland).

9.12 REFERENCES

(1) Hume, D. (1740) *Treatise of Human Nature*.

(2) Tribus, M. (1969) *Rational Descriptions Decisions and Designs*. Pergamon.

(3) Jaynes, E.T. (1969) *Course Notes on Probability Theory in Science and Engineering*. Physics Department, Washington University, St Louis.

(4) Lauritzen, S.L. and Spiegelhalter, D.J. (1988) Local Computations with Probabilities on Graphical Structures and their Application to Expert Systems, *Journal of the Royal Statistical Society Series B*, **50**, no. 2, pp. 157–224.

(5) Anderson, S.K., Olesen, K.G., Jensen, F.V. and Jensen, F. (1990) Hugin – a Shell for Building Bayesian Belief Universes for Expert Systems. In *Readings in Uncertain Reasoning*, Shafer, W. and Pearl, J. (eds.), Morgan Kaufmann.

(6) Garside, G.R. and Rhodes, P.C. (1991) *Maximum Entropy for Expert Systems: the Horns of a Dilemma*. Department of Computing, University of Bradford, technical report no. CS–13–91.

(7) Hink, R.F. and Woods, D.L. (1987) How Humans Process Uncertain Knowledge: An Introduction for Knowledge Engineers. *The AI Magazine*, **8**, Fall, pp. 41–53.

Chapter 10
Choosing the Best Possible Outcome

10.1 INTRODUCTION

Choosing the best possible outcome is the job of the Ordering/Choosing Task. In its simplest form the Ordering/Choosing Task only has to order a set of possible outcomes according to some measure of their desirability but the measure of their desirability is that part of the decision making process which is most influenced by the decisions further up the hierarchy. If a decision is being made in isolation, the value associated with each outcome is not constrained in any way, i.e. the decision maker is free to allocate any value to an outcome. The effect of a hierarchy of decisions is to change this.

In hierarchical decision structures, the decisions at the top of the hierarchy provide strong guidance about the value which should be placed on the possible outcomes of the decisions lower down. In fact, the higher decisions may severly restrict the number of outcomes which can be considered by the lower decisions. That is precisely why the hierarchy of decisions exists. It simplifies each layer of decisions as follows.

The higher decisions determine what the general strategy should be whilst generality keeps the number of possible outcomes small. Then, by the time that the detail of the decision would have caused the number of possible outcomes to be very large, the higher decisions have severely restricted the number of outcomes to be considered. This keeps the lower decisions bounded. It is also an important mechanism which enables the senior managers to direct and keep control of a company.

The decision maker can use the Information Gathering Task to retrieve the outcome of the higher decisions and hence determine what constraints should be imposed on the lower level decision. The decision maker must then provide the lower level Ordering/Choosing Task with some guidance in the form of values which should be allocated to each possible outcome at that level. The Ordering/Choosing Task can then order the possible outcomes of the lower level decision.

For the purposes of this section, we will assume that the decision maker has removed possible outcomes which are unacceptable because of directives from above and has provided a set of values for the remaining possible outcomes. We can then examine how the Ordering/Choosing Task should order the remaining possible outcomes.

10.2 THE TYPE OF CHOICES

We have already noted that in its simplest form the Ordering/Choosing Task only has to order a set of possible outcomes according to some measure of their desirability. It is clearly not as simple as this in all cases so we need to examine the types of possible outcomes which will need ordering, analyse their complexity and find suitable ways of sorting them.

Since compound decisions break down into collections of atomic decisions, it makes sense to start by looking at the various ways of ordering a set of possible outcomes for an atomic decision. We can then look at the various ways of combining the ordered outcomes from atomic decisions to provide an ordered set of outcomes for a compound one. The ordering of the possible outcomes for any decision must be some combination of these two.

10.3 ORDERING THE POSSIBLE OUTCOMES FOR ATOMIC DECISIONS

The possible outcomes of any atomic decision can be represented in several different ways but the processing which has been done at the end of the Decision Structuring Task reduces the number of representations to two or possibly four. This arises because the elements of risk and uncertainty have already been accounted for. So, for example, each possible outcome associated with an uncertain event will already have been replaced by a Certainty Equivalent. The Ordering/Choosing Task will be working on these values because they measure the decision maker's preferences. Consequently there are two categories which can be identified:

(1) A Discrete Set of possible outcomes.

(2) A Continuous Set of possible outcomes.

However, both of these can be in either multiparameter or single parameter form.

Consider the route for a new road example used in Chapter 3 Section 3.6.3. This could have as parameters price, usage, number of people displaced, number of people subjected to increased noise and impact on the environment.

Using the method advocated in this book, each of these would be best considered as a sub-decision of their own. The sub-decisions will have the same possible outcomes, i.e. the various routes proposed, but each sub-decision will submit the various routes to its own Ordering/Choosing Task and have them ranked. At the sub-decision level this presents no problem whatsoever. The problems only arise when the ordered possible outcomes from each sub-decision have to be recombined. We will address this problem later, so we can assume that any multiparameter decision is actually a compound decision which should be split into various sub-decisions each dealing with one parameter at a time. Atomic decisions can then only be of the types 1 and 2 above.

10.3.1 Ordering Discrete Possible Outcomes

Discrete possible outcomes can easily be ordered once they have been reduced to a single parameter measure. They are simply ordered in decreasing values of that measure.

Simply keeping the order may not be desirable, however. Suppose that a person really liked one possible outcome and did not like any of the others at all. This should be apparent from the Certainty Equivalents which have been assigned to them. If the only information which is kept is the relative order of the possible outcomes, the fact that one is vastly preferred over all the others will be lost. Consequently it will be necessary to keep some form of weight with each possible outcome so that the relative merits of the possible outcomes are conserved.

10.3.2 Ordering Continuous Possible Outcomes

Some decisions have so many possible outcomes that they become easier to think of in terms of a continuous variable.

Consider the toy maker's dilemma again. He does not know how many bears to stockpile for Christmas. Now, whilst he could express the number of bears he wishes to stockpile as a whole number or maybe even round to the nearest ten, there is every reason why he should formulate his decision as a continuous problem. There will be a probability distribution for the sales of bears next Christmas so, for every number of bears which could be made, there is a probability distribution for profit/loss. Using Utility theory these distributions can be allocated a certainty equivalent. The result is a curve giving the Utility value of making a given number of bears. This curve will have a maximum value which can be found using calculus. The only complication is that, although the optimum number of bears to make will have only one Utility value, i.e. the highest one, there will be two 'number of bears to make' figures for every Utility value less than the best, i.e. one less than the optimum and another more than the optimum. The decision maker will have to choose whether the Ordering/Choosing task should retain that part of the curve between 0 and the optimum 'number of bears to make' as the value to associate with each possible outcome, or that part from the optimum to the maximum.

10.4 ORDERING POSSIBLE OUTCOMES FOR COMPOUND DECISIONS

The ease with which the possible outcomes for compound decisions can be ordered is entirely dependent upon the degree of independence between the sub–decisions. If the sub–decisions are independent, ordering the possible outcomes is relatively easy but, if they are not, the problem can become quite complex.

10.4.1 Independent Sub–Decisions

Consider the holiday decision again and pretend that a rich uncle has said that he will pay for a two week holiday for you regardless of cost. The sub–decisions, i.e. the location, the accommodation, the climate, the means of travel, etc. are now essentially independent of each other.

Each of the sub–decisions would return an ordered list of possible outcomes. The Ordering/Choosing Task for the compound decision would then have to decide how to combine all these lists. The top of the list is simply a combined possible outcome which consists of the top possible outcome off each individual list, e.g. 5 star hotel at a quiet seaside resort in a hot sunny place with easy access by air.

If no holiday can be found to suit the first choice a second choice has to be made. This will consist of the first choice from all sub–decisions except one and the second choice from that one. It is now that we need to know the Certainty Equivalent associated with second choices because there are several second choices to choose from. The sub–decision whose second choice is taken needs to be the one which has the next highest total Certainty Equivalent. It will probably be one where the difference between the value of the first choice and the second choice is not great. It certainly should not be one where everything except the first choice was not really acceptable. In this case all the other sub–decisions could be adopting the third or fourth possible outcome before the first possible outcome of the critical sub–decision was relinquished.

The above procedure assumes that a common Utility function is used for each sub–decision, i.e. it assumes that all sub–decisions are equally important. This might not be the case and it might be better to specify the relative importance of the decisions. This is again a time for considering Critical Success Factors. If good accommodation is critical and the actual location far less so, alternative locations should be explored before accommodation of a lower standard is considered.

10.4.2 Dependent Sub–Decisions

As soon as the sub–decisions become dependent upon each other the task of ordering the compound possible outcomes becomes appreciably more difficult. The simplest form of dependency is when all the possible outcomes have to be resourced from a single finite source. In other words the sub–decisions are independent of each other except that they are competing for a single resource which is usually monetary.

Consider the holiday decision again. Accommodation costs money, travelling costs money, the times of the year when the weather is guaranteed to be good are more expensive than those when it is not, etc.. If there is a maximum amount of money which can be spent on the holiday then, not only is there an outright restriction on the cost of the holiday, there is also competition between the various sub–decisions for their share of the money which is available.

This problem can be solved using Cost Benefit Analysis which simply converts the outcomes of every sub–decision into a notional equivalent of money known as the cost benefit.

Consider the routes for the new road again. Each route has been ranked by separate sub–decisions which considered each of the various aspects. The cost of the road is already in monetary terms and stands as a negative cost benefit. The number of people using the road can be turned into a cost benefit by putting a value on the time which will be saved for each driver. The number of people displaced can be turned into a negative cost benefit by taking the compensation costs and a similar process can be used for noise nuisance to those who are affected by it. The process is somewhat less quantifiable, however, when a negative cost benefit for harm to the environment is required.

However, if all these positive and negative cost benefits are aggregated for each route, the routes can be ordered in terms of decreasing positive cost benefit.

10.5 SEARCH TREES FOR ORDERING POSSIBLE OUTCOMES

In the above example all the sub-decisions had the same set of possible outcomes to put into an order, namely the various routes which had been proposed. This is a rather atypical situation and it is far more common for each sub-decision to have its own set of possible outcomes, as is the case in the holiday example. In such cases every combination of possible outcomes has to be considered and the combinations are most easily expressed as a tree structure such as that shown in Fig. 10.1. These trees are called search trees because each leaf defines one of the combinations of possible outcomes.

In order to use this tree the relative desirability of the various combinations of possible outcomes must be established, e.g. do you prefer a five star hotel and the risk of poor weather or good weather and a four star hotel? When this has been established every combination of possible outcomes can have two values associated with it, one being its price and the other its desirability. Every leaf in the tree can then have a total cost and a total desirability computed for it. Those which are too expensive are discarded and the remaining ones are ranked in order of desirability.

Unfortunately the amount of searching and computation which is required to do this can be daunting, even for computers, so solving a problem like this requires specialist techniques which minimise the amount of searching which has to be done. Algorithms for doing this are known as tree pruning algorithms because the search can be considerably reduced if it can be shown that some branches do not need searching because an optimum combination cannot exist down that branch.

252   Chapter 10

```
sub-decision 1

possible outcomes        1           2           3           etc

sub-decision 2

possible outcomes    1  2  3 etc  1  2  3 etc  1  2  3  etc

sub-decision 3

possible outcomes                 1  2  3 etc

sub-decision 4

possible outcomes                 1  2  3  etc

        etc              etc              etc
```

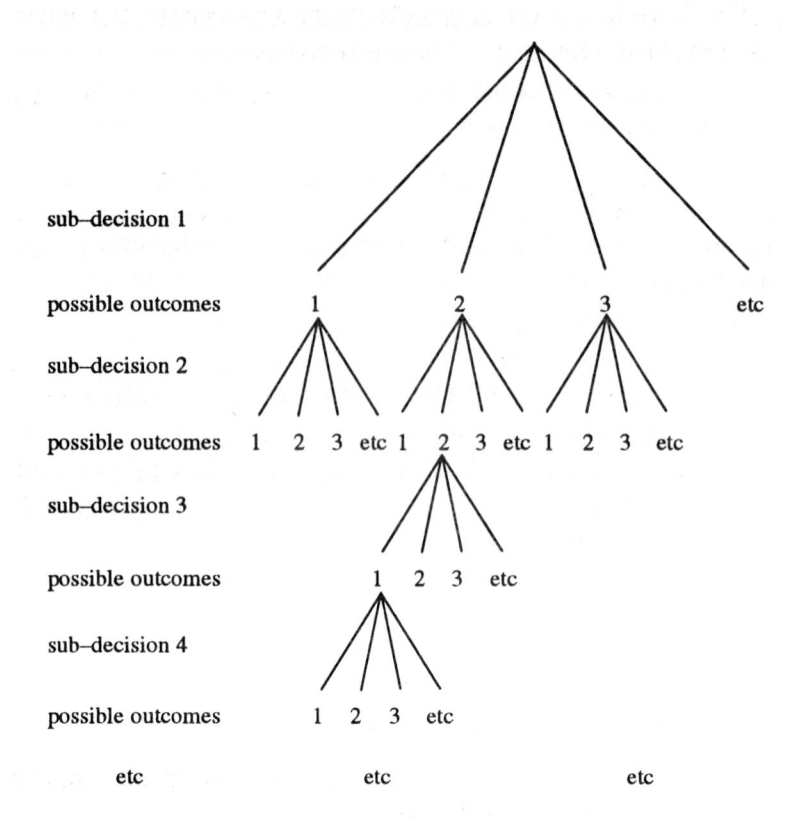

Fig. 10.1. Search tree for combinations of possible outcomes

In the above holiday problem there are several lists of items, i.e. one list for the possible outcomes of each sub–decision, and only one item can be chosen from each list. If each item in each list is allocated a cost and each list is ordered in increasing cost, the search for a solution can be pruned because a given total cost must not be exceeded.

A more interesting case, which also demonstrates the same principle, occurs when the possible outcomes are not exclusive and you can have more than one possible outcome as long as you can afford to pay for them. Consider the following example.

A company wishes to set up warehouses in various parts of the country so that it can supply its customers faster. It has a fixed amount of money to build as many warehouses as it can but it would like to open far more than it can afford. It knows the cost of setting up each warehouse and the amount each warehouse will contribute to its profits. What it has to do is to find out which warehouses to build to maximise its profits using the money available.

This problem is entirely analogous to the Knapsack Problem which is posed as follows:

A scout is going camping with his pack. The scout master has put an absolute limit on the total weight of his knapsack but he wishes to take more items than the weight limit permits. How should he decide what to take?

He has to start by assigning a value to every item which depicts its usefulness at camp. He then needs to find the most valuable combination which lies within his weight limit. If he tried to compute the value and the weight of every possible combination of items he would miss his holiday and still be computing so he must prune the search somehow. He does this by putting the items in ascending order of weight as follows:

Object	1	2	3	...	n
Weight	w_1	< w_2	< w_3	< ...	< w_n
Value	v_1	v_2	v_3	...	v_n

The maximum weight allowable is W.

Once the information is presented as shown above, the problem can be stated in more formal terms:

An optimal solution is a subset, S, of the objects such that

$$\sum_{i \in S} v_i \text{ is maximised subject to } \sum_{i \in S} w_i \leq W$$

The search proceeds by deciding whether or not to include the next item in the set and this is governed by two conditions. The first relates to the weight. The ith object can only be included if:

weight of set + w_i < W (10.1)

If the ith object cannot be included no other items can be included because the items are in order of increasing weight. Consequently if the ith object cannot be included the search terminates for that branch of the tree.

The second criteria relates to the value of the ith item and whether or not it can be left out of the set. Assume that several sets have been identified which have a weight less than W and that the one with the highest value has a value, V, then the ith object cannot be excluded if:

$$\text{achievable value} - v_i < V \qquad (10.2)$$

The achievable value is the total possible value minus the value of those items which have already been left out. Equation (10.2) says, if the achievable value after the ith object has been left out is less than the value of the best set so far, there is no point in pursuing a set with v_i missing and hence equation (10.2) is a second criteria for pruning the tree.

The method is best explained by using a trivial example. Assume that actual values for the scout's problem are those given below:

Item	1	2	3	4	5
Weight	4	6	9	11	12
Value	5	4	2	3	2

W = 25

Note that the total value of the objects, i.e. the initial achievable value, is 16. Referring to Fig. 10.2, the process starts by deciding whether or not to include item 1. Initially this is included because its weight is less than 25 and the criterion for value cannot be used yet. With item 1 included the present set of items, $S_1 = \{1\}$, has a weight, $W_1 = 4$, and an achievable value $AV_1 = 16$. The next decision is whether or not to include item 2. If item 2 is included then $S_1 = \{1,2\}$, $W_1 = 10$ and $AV_1 = 16$. This process can continue until $S_1 = \{1,2,3\}$, $W_1 = 19$ and $AV_1 = 16$ and we have to decide whether or not to include item 4. Item 4 cannot be included because W would be greater than 25. If item 4 cannot be included no item whose number is greater than 4 can be included so the search terminates here with

$$S_1 = \{1,2,3\}, \ W_1 = 19 \text{ and } V_1 = 11$$

being the first possible solution, where W is the weight of the first possible set and V is the value of the first set. We must now backtrack and decide whether or not we can afford to leave out item 3. After backtracking the set has been reduced to.

$$S_2 = \{1,2\}, \ W_2 = 10, \ AV_2 = 16$$

if item 3 is omitted then equation (10.2) gives

$$AV_2 = 16 - 2 = 14 > V_1$$

so item 3 can be omitted and we can still achieve a value greater than V_1. We therefore consider whether or not to include item 4 whence

Choosing the Best Possible Outcome 255

$S_2 = \{1,2,4\}$, $W_2 = 21$ and $AV_2 = 14$

Trying to include item 5 violates the weight restriction so S cannot be improved and

$S_2 = \{1,2,4\}$, $W_2 = 21$ and $V_2 = 12$

This set is more desirable than the first so S_2 is adopted as optimum.

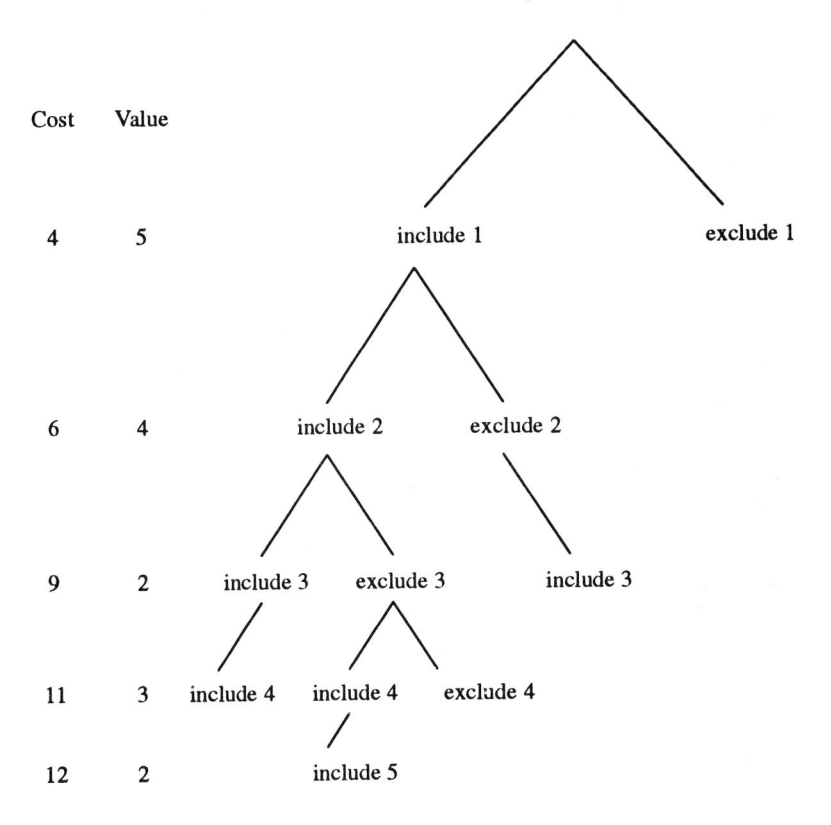

```
Cost   Value

 4       5                      include 1              exclude 1

 6       4              include 2    exclude 2

 9       2         include 3  exclude 3    include 3

11       3       include 4  include 4  exclude 4

12       2                  include 5
```

Fig. 10.2. Pruned search tree

Backtracking again, we have to decide whether or not we can afford to leave out item 2 so

$S_3 = \{1\}$, $W_3 = 4$ and $AV_3 = 16$

If item 2 is omitted equation (10.2) gives

$AV_3 = 16 - 4 = 12 = V_2$

so omitting item 2 might provide a solution which is as good as S_2 but cannot better it, however

$S_3 = \{1,3,4\}$, $W_3 = 24$, $V_3 = 10$

cannot be extended to include any more items and is not as valuable as S_2 so this terminates the search with item 2 omitted.

Backtracking again leaves us asking whether or not we can afford to omit item 1. However, if we omit item 1, from equation (10.2)

$$AV_4 = 16 - 5 = 11 < V_2$$

so no set which omits item 1 can better set S_2 and the search terminates. The reader can confirm for themselves that there are thirty one sets and we have only examined nine of them in order to find the optimum one.

10.6 COMPOUND DECISIONS WITH DEPENDENT CONTINUOUS SUB–DECISIONS

Compound decisions whose sub–decisions are highly dependent on each other and have continuous possible outcomes to maximise are amongst the most complex types of decision to make. Operational Research researchers have already found methods which can be used to make many of these decisions. The only problem is that the methods are mathematical and not easily appreciated by an untrained user.

In this section we will use one of these methods, look at it as a piece of mathematics, look at it again from a decision maker's viewpoint and finally look at it all again in the context of the Ordering/Choosing task. This will demonstrate the advantages of adopting a structured approach to making decisions.

Consider the following situation. Mr Philip has the opportunity to accept a job to make two types of warps which we will refer to as type A and type B. The yarn for the warps was salvaged from a mill fire, is wet and in poor condition. R,B & H is the preferred supplier and the customer is prepared to give them as much of the work as they can do but the warps must be delivered in 3 weeks time. The customer will pay £2.20 per Kg for type A warps and £3.00 per Kg for type B warps.

Mr Keith estimates that it will cost 6 pence per Kg to dry the yarn which will then have to be rewound prior to warping. The drying process will take 5 working days which will leave 10 working days for the winding and warping operations. Mr Keith has established that the yarn for type A warps will have to be wound on one type of winding machine, winding machine 1 say, which can be made available for a maximum of 5 hours per day. The yarn for type B warps will have to be wound on another winding machine, winding machine 2 say, which can be made available for 6 hours per day. During the winding process, Mr Keith expects a 10% wastage of yarn for type A warps and a 20% wastage of yarn for type B warps.

Once dried and rewound both types of yarn can be made into warps on the same machine and wastage will be negligible. Mr Keith is prepared to make one warping machine, which could be run for 10 hours per day, available for this job. The warping cannot start until enough dry, rewound yarn is available to make one complete warp. A type A warp weighs 3 tonnes and a type B warp weighs 4 tonnes. Because of the wastage in winding, a type A warp requires 3300Kg of yarn to be wound. Winding machine 1 processes yarn at 660 Kg per hour so it will take 5 hours to wind enough yarn to start warping. Similarly it will take 12 hours to wind enough yarn to start a type B warp. Mr Keith estimates that, since the warper is available 10 hours a day and it can start on a type A warp, there will only be a half day delay before the warping machine can start. The warping machine can then work for 9.5 days. Winding machine 1 must finish at least 5 hours before the deadline so it is only available for 9 days at most. Similarly the winding machine 2 is only available for 8 days at most.

The cost of running the three machines is as follows:

winder 1 costs £280 per hour

winder 2 costs £330 per hour

the warping machine costs £360 per hour.

The processing speeds are:

winder 1 rewinds at 660 Kg per hour

winder 2 rewinds at 400 Kg per hour

the warping machine warps at 300 Kg per hour.

How many type A and type B warps should the brothers agree to do if they are to maximise the profitability of the job?

This type of decision can be resolved using a technique known as linear programming (but it is possible to solve this one by trial and error). This example is expressed in business terms. If it is to be solved by conventional mathematical methods, it will have to be expressed in mathematical terms. This is not a trivial task and the reader should attempt to formalise the above decision before reading further. This will provide some insight into how difficult it is to be specific and will highlight the difficulties faced by decision makers in business.

10.6.1 Linear Programming

The type of decision quoted above can be resolved using an Operational Research technique known as Linear Programming. This technique will be used here to demonstrate the problems of bringing mathematical methods into every day use. For this reason we will restrict ourselves to decisions which only involve two variables. These can be resolved using graphical methods which help to make the appropriate points simply and clearly.

10.6.1.1 General Linear Programming Problems

Linear programming problems are a class of problems in which there exists a linear function

$$z = c_1 X_1 + c_2 X_2 + ... + c_n X_n$$

where c_i for $i = 1...n$ are constants and X_i for $i = 1...n$ are variables and z is to be maximised (or sometimes minimised) subject to m linear constraints:

$$a_{11} X_1 + a_{12} X_2 + ... + a_{1n} X_n <=> b_1$$
$$a_{21} X_1 + a_{22} X_2 + ... + a_{2n} X_n <=> b_2$$
$$...$$
$$a_{m1} X_1 + a_{m2} X_2 + ... + a_{mn} X_n <=> b_m$$

where a_{ij} and b_i for $i = 1...m$ and $j = 1...n$ are constants and $<=>$ is a conditional which must be either 'less than' or 'equality' or 'greater than'.

The general principle for finding a solution is to define a feasible region, which is a portion of the multidimensional space $X_1 \times X_2 \times ... \times X_n$, in which all the constraints are satisfied. The position, within the feasible region, of the maximum value of the optimising function, z, must then be found. With linear problems it can be shown that the maximum must occur at one of the vertices of the feasible region.

10.6.1.2 Two Dimensional Linear Programming

The general statement of a linear programming problem is much simpler when it is reduced to two dimensions. This is quite adequate for our purposes so consider the following example.

A model aeroplane manufacturer requires 0.005 cubic metres of balsa wood to produce a 48" model and 0.006 cubic metres to produce a 54" model. They have difficulty acquiring balsa wood of the required quality and can only get 3.0 cubic metres per week. Their machine can make five 48" models per hour and two 54" models per hour and is available for 160 hours per week. The profit on the 48" model is £2 per model and the profit on the 54" model is £4 per model. How many 48" models and how many 54" models should they make to maximise profit?

The problem can be expressed in mathematical terms by first considering the constraints. They cannot make less than no models per week so, if x is the number of 48" models and x is the number of 54" models made in a week then:

$$x_1 \geq 0 \quad (10.3)$$

$$x_2 \geq 0 \quad (10.4)$$

The limit on the amount of balsa wood available also constrains the number of models which can be made, i.e.

$$0.005x_1 + 0.006x_2 \leq 3.0 \quad (10.5)$$

Their machine also limits their production, i.e.

$$0.2x_1 + 0.5x_2 \leq 160 \quad (10.6)$$

The function which must be maximised is profit which is given by the expression:

$$p = 2x_1 + 4x_2 \quad (10.7)$$

The first step in finding a solution is to determine the feasible region. This can easily be done by drawing a graph. This is shown in Fig. 10.3.

The next step is to maximise the profit. Fig. 10.4 shows several possible profit lines and demonstrates that the profit increases as the line moves away from the origin into the positive quadrant. Clearly if nothing restrains x_1 and x_2, the profit can be increased without limit but the feasible region constrains x_1 and x_2.

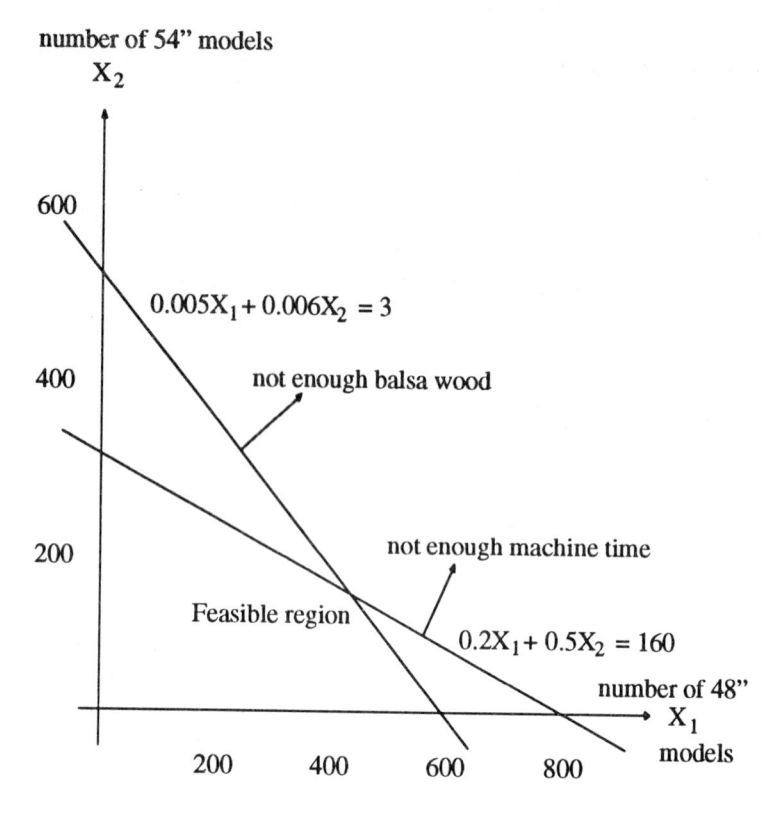

Fig. 10.3. Linear programming: the feasible region

In order to find the maximum profit which can be made subject to the constraints, Fig. 10.4 must be superimposed onto Fig. 10.3. This is shown in Fig. 10.5. The line which represents the maximum profit is now obviously the line which passes through the top left vertex of the feasible region. The maximum will always occur at a vertex which is where two constraint lines cross. Moreover we can calculate how many models to make of each type. If X_1, X_2 is the point at which the profit is maximised then

$$0.2X_1 + 0.5X_2 = 160 \text{ and } 0.005X_1 + 0.006X_2 = 3 \tag{10.8}$$

Solving equations (10.8) for X_1 and X_2 gives

$$X_1 = 415.5 \text{ and } X_2 = 153.8$$

but as whole numbers of models must be made they will have to make either 415 of the 48" models and 154 of the 54" models or 416 of the 48" models and 153 of the 54" models. The profit for the former is £1446 and for the latter £1444 so the former would be chosen.

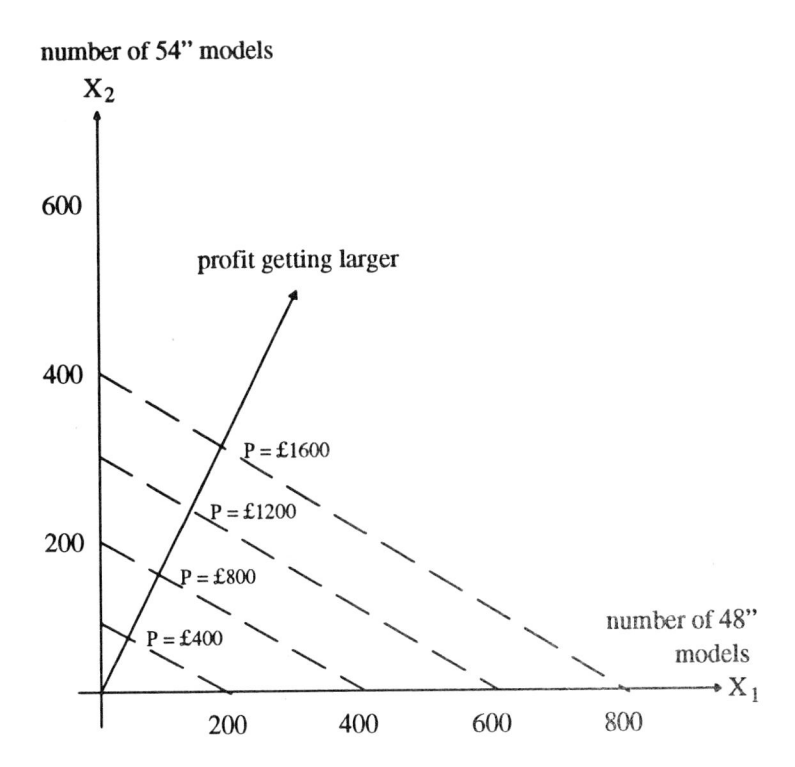

Fig. 10.4. Linear programming: maximising profit

10.6.2 Problems Which Can Arise With Linear Programming

Several problems can arise when Linear Programming is used to solve problems like the above. Specialist users of this technique know what the problems are and how to overcome them. If the method is to be provided for decision makers, additional assistance will have to be provided to overcome these problems.

10.6.2.1 No Unique Solution

The first problem to consider is when no unique solution exists. Fig. 10.6 shows what happens if the company manages to increase the profit on 54" models to £5 per model. The line for profit is now parallel to the constraint line which was derived from the time available on the machine which made the models.

This means that the profit is at its maximum value anywhere along the line from (320,0) to (415,154). In order to decide how many models to make, the constraint line and the profit line must be considered to decide which is more likely to be correct. For example, if the £1 per kit price rise on the 54" model is not acceptable to customers, the price may have to be reduced again. In this eventuality the previous solution would still be optimal.

number of 54" models

X_2

maximum profit

600

$P_1 = 2X_2 + 4X = £1446.20$

not enough balsa wood

400

200

Feasible region

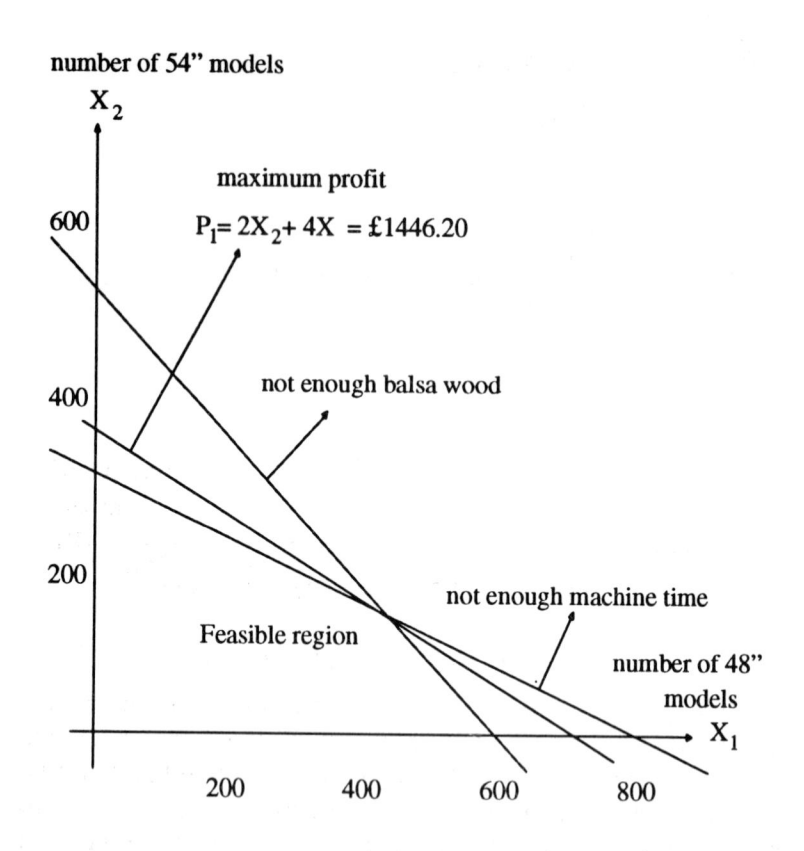

not enough machine time

number of 48" models

X_1

200   400   600   800

Fig. 10.5. Linear programming: deciding how many models to make

The problem faced by Decision Support System designers is how to provide sufficient interaction between the decision maker and the system to allow this extra information to influence the decision. The decision to keep making 48" models until the profit on 54" models was assured, is an intelligent reasoning process which did not require any computation. It would, therefore, be better left to the decision maker. Consequently, in this case, it would be better to convey to the decision maker that a whole series of options was possible and request that the preferred option is chosen. This may not always be the case, however.

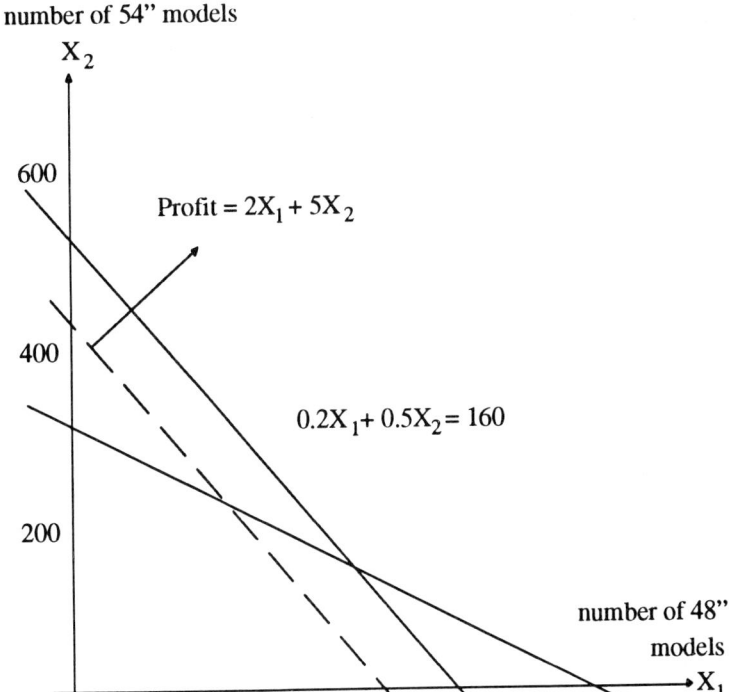

Fig. 10.6. Linear programming: no unique solution

An alternative would be to do sensitivity analysis on the constraints. Does it really take half an hour to make a 54" model and only 12 minutes to make a 48" one? Both of these times will be averages and we could check the sensitivity of the profit to perturbations in each. The computations required make this task more suitable for the machine. In this case, the decision maker would request that sensitivity analysis be used to resolve the decision and allow the machine to make a recommendation.

10.6.2.2 No Feasible Region

Assume that the model plane manufacturer has to make at least 350 models of one type in one production run in order to make the profit figures stated above. They may then be tempted to set as constraints:

$$X_1 \geq 350 \tag{10.9}$$
$$X_2 \geq 350 \tag{10.10}$$

instead of equations (10.3) and (10.4). The graph for the feasible region would then be that shown in Fig. 10.7 and no feasible region exists.

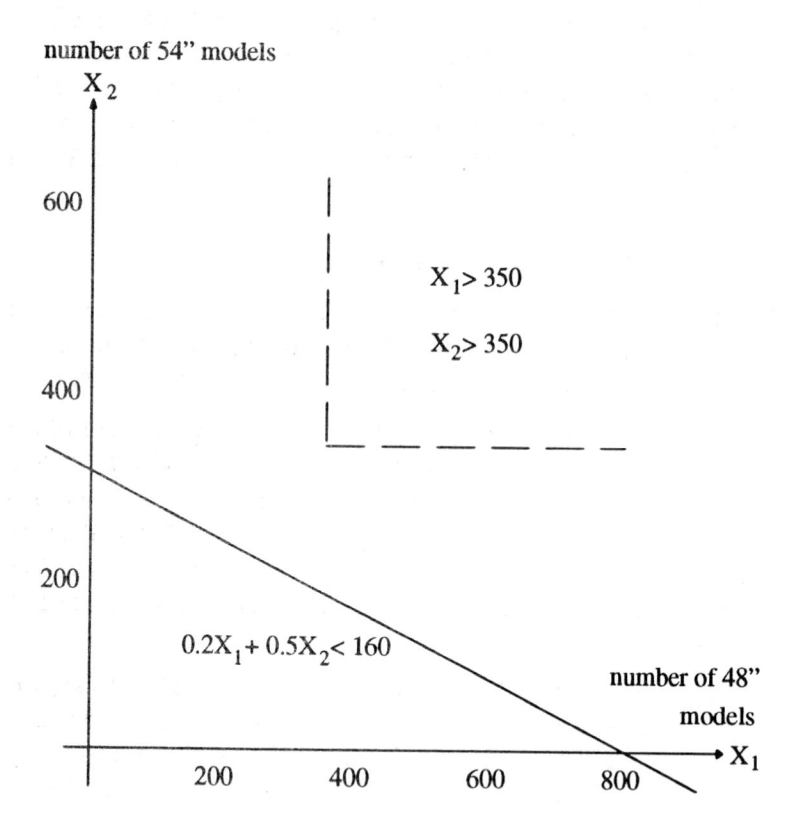

Fig. 10.7. Linear programming: no feasible region

On the face of it, this would not seem to be difficult to report to the decision maker but you would have to be careful. The decision maker may not know anything about feasible regions in which case reporting that the feasible region does not exist would be a meaningless message. Even reporting that there is no solution to the problem or that there are no possible outcomes for the decision is unhelpful because the decision maker would need to know what to do about it.

The error message would have to convey that the problem was over–constrained and, in order to be helpful, would also probably have to give the constraints which are in conflict. This is not easy to do because it is often groups of constraints which are in conflict and not individual ones. For example, neither constraint (10.9) nor constraint (10.10) is in conflict with constraint (10.6) but when taken together they are. This is not easy to convey to a person who does not understand the method.

The above problem demonstrates a point which has already been made. The technology exists to support these decisions but we still have to discover how to deliver the technology in a generally acceptable form for the decision maker. This is a problem for the Human Computer Interface and much work has still to be done in this area.

10.6.2.3 Ill–Defined Feasible Region

This problem is almost the opposite to the previous one. It is most likely to arise due to omission of a constraint. Such an omission becomes increasingly easy as the number of variables increases.

Two dimensional problems are rather trivial but suppose that the model plane manufacturers have got minimum production runs fixed in their minds, have found an almost infinite supply of balsa wood and forget to declare their production capacity. The result would be the graph shown in Fig. 10.8 in which the feasible region is unbounded. X_1 and X_2 are then unbounded and they can make as many models as they like.

This problem should not be so difficult to report. In fact, the Decision Support System designer may choose not to report it as a fault. The decision maker could be invited to say why an arbitrarily large number of models cannot be made. This should prompt for the missing constraints.

10.6.3 The Use of Operational Research Methods in Real Situations

Consider again the above R, B & H example. All the information required to resolve the decision was given in section 10.6. At the time, the reader was invited to try formalising the problem and this invitation is now repeated. Formalising the above problem even with a full understanding of Linear Programming is still not a trivial task. What is required is a structured method for formalising the decision and converting it into a form which is amenable to mathematical processing.

In Decision Support Systems we would like to be even more subtle than this. We would like the decision makers to formulate the decision in their own terms but to formulate it precisely enough for the machine to be able to use mathematical methods to order the possible outcomes. The case study later in this chapter uses the above example to demonstrate how this might be achieved.

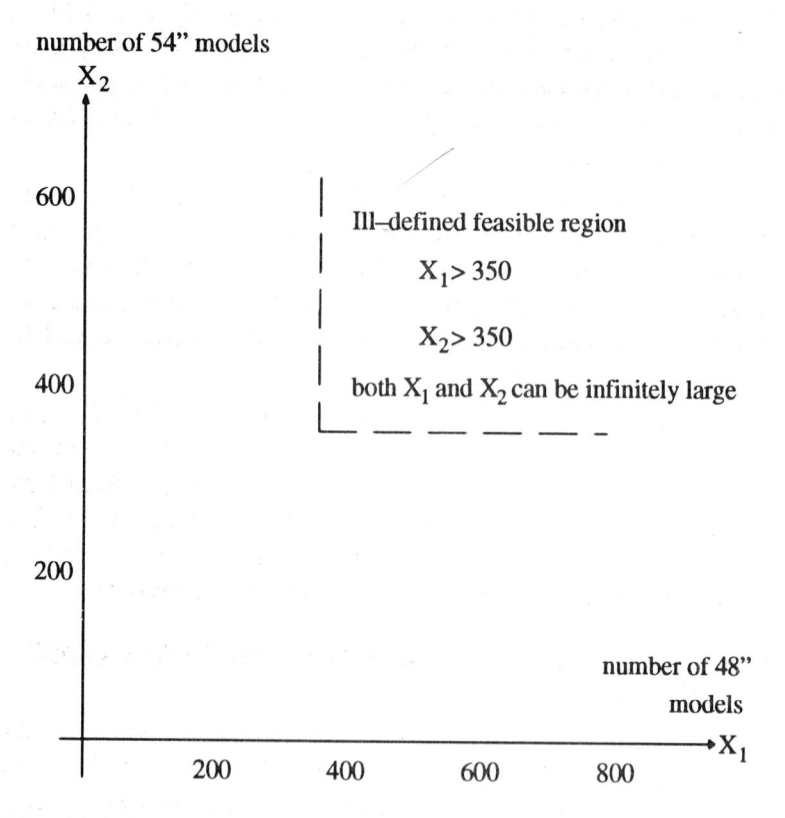

Fig. 10.8. Linear programming: Ill-defined feasible region

10.7 OTHER ALGORITHMS FOR ORDERING/ CHOOSING POSSIBLE OUTCOMES

This chapter has concentrated, by way of example, on the use of Linear Programming for the Ordering/Choosing Task. This could give a totally wrong impression of reality. The Ordering/Choosing Task may well have to optimise to rank the possible outcomes but equally it may only have to order them. There is a plethora of ordering and optimising algorithms available, most of which would be useful within the Ordering/Choosing Task at some time or other. Most, if not all, of these algorithms have been optimised for use on computers and are readily available to the Decision Support System designer.

Yet again, the technology exists and only has to be used in an appropriate fashion.

10.8 SUMMARY

The Ordering/Choosing Task's role for an atomic decision with an exclusive set of possible outcomes can be as trivial as ordering those outcomes in descending order of value to the decision maker. As the decisions become more complex so does the role of the Ordering/Choosing Task.

When compound decisions are being made, the Ordering/Choosing Task must be capable of ordering or maximising a set of possible outcomes bearing in mind the dependencies between the sub–decisions which are being recombined. If the sub–decisions are not independent of each other, fairly sophisticated techniques will be required to assist the decision maker.

These techniques do exist, however, and are well tried. The only problem is the interface between the decision maker and the techniques. The techniques usually involve methods which have invariably been designed by specialists for the use of specialists. The problems at this interface are becoming better understood, however, but it will still be some time before they are fully overcome.

10.9 CASE STUDY: R, B & H WARPING SALVAGED YARN

In this chapter we will look at two R, B & H decisions as part of our case study. The first will be the Warping Salvaged Yarn Decision from section 10.6 above. The second will be the R, B & H Strategic Plan which has been the subject of the Case Study for the last three chapters.

This book has consistently advocated breaking decisions down into sub–decisions and continuing this process until atomic (single variable) decisions have been achieved. More recently, the book has advocated that this process is followed even if the sub–decisions are not independent of each other. The problem of recombining the sub–decisions can then be tackled after the sub–decisions have been made. This procedure will now be used on the above examples.

10.9.1 The Warping Salvaged Yarn Decision

In the example given in section 10.6, the brothers have to decide how many warps of type A and how many warps of type B to make in order to maximise profits. We will assume that penalty clauses exist which make it essential to get the decision right and not be recklessly over ambitious. We are also looking for a structured approach to formalise the decision so that a computer can assist in the decision making.

The compound decision in question is:

To maximise profit by deciding how many warps of type A and how many warps of type B to make.

This can be split into two sub–decisions:

(a)   How many warps of type A and type B to make.

(b)   How to maximise profit.

Note that the two decisions are by no means independent of each other but we will ignore this fact for the moment. Sub–decision (a) conceals some of the processing because the warps cannot be made until yarn is wound for them. Consequently sub–decision (a) splits further into:

(a.1)   How many warps of type A and type B to make.

(a.2)   How much yarn to wind for type A warps

(a.3)   How much yarn to wind for type B warps

The sub–decisions (b) and (a.3) have been separated because there are two different machines involved. Sub–decision (a.1) can be further sub–divided into:

(a.1.i)   How many warps of type A to make

(a.1.ii)   How many warps of type B to make

These are now atomic decisions which must be made but there are no constraints at all to restrict the values we choose so instead of providing an actual value we will opt for an expedient way out of the problem and decide to make:

(a.1.i) N_A warps of type A.

(a.1.ii) N_B warps of type B.

Having made the atomic decisions we return to sub–decision (a.1). Mr Keith is only prepared to make one warping machine available for both types of warp and this can be run for 10 hours per day for 9.5 days, i.e. a total of 95 hours. The warping machines processes yarn at 300 Kg per hour so it can warp 28.5 tonnes of yarn in the time available. Warps of type A weigh 3 tonnes and warps of type B weigh 4 tonnes, so the outcome of this decision is that:

$$3N_A + 4N_B \leq 28.5 \tag{10.11}$$

We now need to turn our attention to decisions (b) and (a.3). Consider (b) first. If we wish to make N_A type A warps which each need 3 tonnes of yarn then we need $3N_A$ tonnes of yarn. If 10% of the yarn is wasted in the winding process, we will need to wind $3.3N_A$ tonnes of yarn. Winding machine 1 is available for 5 hours per day, for at most 9 days and can rewind yarn at a rate of 660 Kg per hour. Consequently, winding machine 1 constrains the number of warps of type A which can be made to:

$$N_A < 9 \tag{10.12}$$

The calculations for sub-decision (b) are similar. Type B warps weigh 4 tonnes, 20% of the yarn is wasted, the winding machine is available for 6 hours per day for a maximum of 8 days, hence winding machine 2 places the following restriction on the number of type B warps which can be produced:

$$N_B < 4 \tag{10.13}$$

Sub-decision (a) is a combination of sub-sub-decisions (a1), (a2) and (a3) and the relationship between them dictates that the sub-sub-decision's outcomes, i.e. expressions (10.11), (10.12) and (10.13), must hold simultaneously. Notice that the Ordering/Choosing Task for these atomic and sub-decisions has not had to do anything because only one outcome has been available.

Our attention must now turn to sub-decision (b). This can be split into sub-decisions:

(b.1) Maximise profit for type A warps.

(b.2) Maximise profit for type B warps.

These decisions are again not independent of each other nor are they independent of the sub-decision (a). At this stage the only dependency that matters is that we have decided to make N_A type A warps and N_B type B warps. Sub-decisions (b.1) and (b.2) are not atomic because profit is calculated from selling price minus cost so:

(b.1.i)   Decide cost of type A warps.

(b.1.ii)   Decide selling price of type A warps.

(b.2.i)   Decide cost of type B warps.

(b.2.ii)   Decide selling price of type B warps.

These may or may not be considered to be atomic decisions but, not surprisingly, most managers would have no difficulty with this type of calculation which proceeds as follows:

(b.1.i)   Cost of making type A warps
    Drying Costs: 3300 Kg @ 6 pence per Kg   198
    Winding Costs: 3300 Kg @ 660 Kg/hour = 5 hours
        5 hours at £280 per hour   1400
    Warping Costs: 3300 Kg @ 300 Kg/hour = 11 hours
        11 hours at £360 per hour   3960

    Total Cost   5558

(b.1.ii)   Selling Price for type A warps
    3000 Kg @ £2.20 per Kg   6600

(b.1)   Profit for type A warps is (b.1.ii) − (b.1.i) = $1042 * N_A$

(b.2.i)   Cost of making type B warps
    Drying Costs: 4800 Kg @ 6 pence per Kg   288
    Winding Costs: 4800 Kg @ 400 Kg/hour = 12 hours
        12 hours at £330 per hour   3960
    Warping Costs: 4800 Kg @ 300 Kg/hour = 16 hours
        16 hours at £360 per hour   5760

    Total Cost   10008

(b.2.ii)   Selling Price for type B warps
    4000 Kg @ £3.00 per Kg   12000

(b.2)   Profit for type B warps is (b.2.ii) − (b.2.i) = $1992 * N_B$

Combining the (b) sub–decisions together we discover that the only outcome is to maximise the profit, P, which is given by:

$$P = 1042 * N_A + 1992 * N_B \qquad (10.14)$$

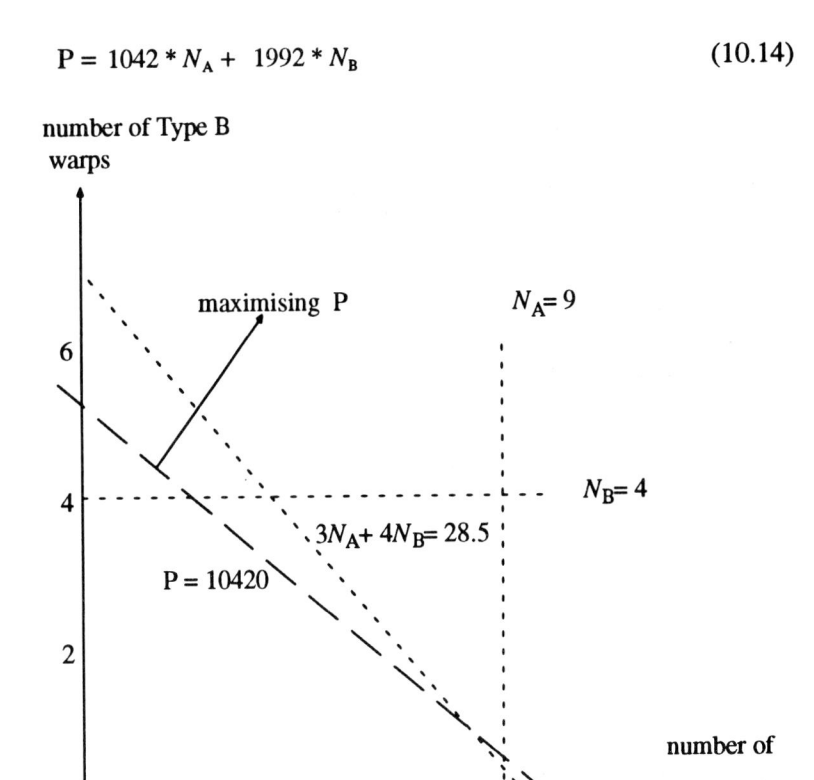

Fig. 10.9. Solution to the reclaimed yarn warping problem

The Ordering/Choosing Task for sub–decision (b) cannot produce an ordered set of outcomes so it passes expression (10.14) back to the top level decision. The top level decision combines the (a) and (b) sub–decisions and is left with a set of possible outcomes which are described simultaneously by expressions (10.11) to (10.14). The top level decision's Ordering/Choosing task can maximise this set of expressions and it would invoke a Linear Programming algorithm to do it.

Using Linear Programming to solve this problem produces a graph like the one shown in Fig. 10.9.

The optimum number of warps of type B is clearly four, i.e. $N_B = 4$. The number of warps of type A is calculated by substituting $N_B = 4$ into equation (10.11) whence $N_A = 4.1$ but fractions of warps are not possible so $N_A = 4$. The maximum profit that can be made, which is computed from equation (10.14), is £12136 and the decision making process is complete.

This example demonstrates that breaking the decision down into sub– and atomic decisions and ordering/optimising the possible outcomes of each sub–decision during the reassembly process is both a natural and very practical way to proceed, even when the sub–decisions are not independent of each other, It also has the very real advantage that it can be supported by computers in a manner which leaves the intelligence with the decision maker and places the computational load on the machine.

10.9.2 The R, B & H Strategic Plan

The R, B & H Strategic Plan was broken down into three sub–decisions namely, the 'Future of R, B & H', the 'New Business Venture' and the 'Personal Involvement' sub–decisions. The way in which these sub–decisions could be made has been the topic of previous Case Studies.

We know that these sub–decisions are not independent of each other but we also know that if we consider one first, then consider a second given the outcome of the first and finally consider the third given the outcome of the first two then Probability Theory will allow us to compute the joint probabilities by multiplying the individual ones.

We can apply this same approach to ordering the possible outcomes. This is, in effect, putting the sub–decisions into a hierarchy and consequently the technique used here will also demonstrate how higher decisions in the hierarchy affect lower ones. We will assume that the 'Future of R, B & H' is the dominant sub–decision, The 'New Business Venture' sub–decision is next and the 'Personal Involvement' sub–decision is last. We will further assume that the brothers have ordered the possible outcomes for the 'Future of R, B & H' sub–decision as 'sell business (as a going concern)', 'sell assets' and 'stay in business' respectively.

The brothers now have to consider the 'New Business Venture' sub–decision in the knowledge that they intend to sell R, B & H as a going concern. This will mean that they do not intend to be involved with R, B & H indefinitely and that they will need to expend some considerable effort to both get the business running profitably and attract a potential buyer.

The 'New Business Venture' sub–decision has now become a multiparameter decision. The first parameter, the monetary payoff was properly assessed in Table 7.16. The second parameter is the amount of time and effort that this venture would need, as this would detract them from the strategic aim of selling R, B & H. A possible third parameter is their desire to still be in business and hence have the new venture to turn to.

The brothers would like to retire, i.e. choose the 'don't buy another business' outcome for the 'New Business Venture' sub–decision but they can only do this if they can raise sufficient capital for that to be possible. This is clearly a decision which needs to be made prior to the 'New Business Venture' sub–decision. In fact, it is a previously unidentified sub–decision of the 'Strategic Plan' and it lies second in the hierarchy of sub–decisions. However, this need not cause concern. It is simple enough to backtrack, add this decision to the list of sub–decisions and place it in the correct position in the hierarchy.

Suppose that, given that the brothers intend to sell R, B & H, they can afford to retire. They can then return to the 'New Business Venture' decision and order the possible outcomes on the basis that they are going to sell R, B & H and will then have enough money to retire. They may then decide that the best monetary outcome, i.e. 'buy an existing business', is still not lucrative enough to override the prospect of retirement, i.e. 'don't buy another business' is the preferred possible outcome of the 'New Business Venture' sub–decision.

The brothers can then decide whether or not to stay personally involved, i.e make the 'Personal Involvement' sub–decision. For completeness sake, let us assume that they do decide to 'remain in total control' until such time as the business is sold and their involvement terminates.

The brothers have now decided what they would like to do but the chosen possible outcome for the first decision, on which all the others rest, is not a certainty. Consequently, the brothers do not have, as yet, a complete strategy (see section 7.9). In order to achieve a complete strategy they need to remake the decision assuming that the outcome of the first decision is 'Sell Assets' because, if they cannot find a buyer, that is what they will have to do.

It is easy to see how pursuing this could make the decision more complex again and may even lead to a change in the original decision.

However, it is important to have a complete strategy so that every consequence of the proposed action has been considered. We will assume that the brothers can afford to retire even if they have to resort to selling the assets, so the original decision stands.

10.9.3 Points to Note

The above two examples show a marked contrast in the way the decision was supported. The first decision was supported using some fairly complex mathematics. The second decision was supported only to the extent that the system imposed an orderly structuring of the decision and kept track of the various sub-decisions and the way in which they should be defined. The brothers took most of the decision without asking the system to undertake formal analysis.

These are good examples of the extremes at which a Decision Support System should be capable of providing support. On the one hand it should keep the decision making process orderly and do the 'housekeeping' but when necessary it should be capable of providing mathematical support in the least obtrusive way possible.

10.10 POINTS TO PONDER

(1) The method used for the 'Warping Salvaged Yarn' Case Study, although very 'manager' oriented, does work more smoothly if you realise that the constraints are imposed by the availability of machines. The decisions can then be subdivided along these lines and the decision falls naturally into a Linear Programming problem.

Decision makers will quickly learn which approach works best for their problems. But the method does not rely on breaking the decisions into sub-decisions in a particular order. Try breaking the decisions down differently and see what happens. You will find that as long as you follow the method carefully and patiently, the decision will become a well formulated Linear Programming problem.

(2) Earlier chapters discussed uncertainty and risk. The 'Warping Salvaged Yarn' example is clearly a case of taking risks. The yarn is salvaged from a fire. Nobody can be sure what state it is

in. Mr Keith has estimated that 10% of type A yarn and 20% of type B yarn will be wasted. These figures will actually be some form of estimates which will only have a given probability of being correct. Try to formalise the problem with the uncertainty and attitudes to risk explicitly stated.

(3) The 'Strategic Plan' is a strategic decision and consequently difficult to structure. In the above Case Study we have made the decision largely qualitatively. Try to formalise this decision more quantitatively and see if you can devise a way to order the possible outcomes rather than choose a complete strategy.

10.11 FURTHER READING

- Bundy, B.D. and Garside, G.R. (1987) *Linear Programming in Pascal*. Edward Arnold.

- Hiller, F.S. and Lieberman, G.J. (1967) *Introduction to Operations Research*. Holden–Day.

- Rivett, P. and Ackoff, R.L. (1963) *A Manager's Guide to Operational Research*. John Wiley and Sons.

Chapter 11
Validating the Decision

11.1 INTRODUCTION

Validation is the last step in the decision making process but the job of making a decision is not complete until it is done. The validation stage can, however, be used in several different ways according to the style and temperament of the decision maker.

A methodic, quantitative decision maker will have structured the problem, allowed for risk and uncertainty, ordered the possible outcomes and chosen the one which seemed best when everything was taken into account. For this type of decision maker the validation stage is exactly what its name implies. Its purpose is to double check to ensure that nothing unforeseen will render the choice less desirable in practice.

At the other extreme is the impulsive decision maker who instantly decides what should be done and may have skipped the decision structuring and ordering stages. This person is relying on the validation stage to ensure that the outcome of the decision is acceptable. They may even try to use this stage, on a trial and error basis, to find some sort of optimum outcome.

These two extremes are by no means the only ones possible. For example it would be perfectly acceptable for a person to structure a decision carefully and then make some sub-decisions impulsively and others formally. This would not matter. The Validation Task associated with the various sub-decisions would be used in a very different manner but this would not prevent the top level decision being made successfully.

The Validation Task has to cope with the above extremes in decision making and the wide diversity in between. This is not a problem because there is a universally acceptable form that the Validation Task can take. This universally acceptable form is that of models. Models can be simple and cheap or complex and expensive, they can be highly mathematical or highly practical and both are ideally suited for use with computers. But, most importantly of all, they are highly acceptable to their human users.

One very important point must be made before the Validation Task is discussed in detail. The validation process must not use a substantially similar technique to that used by the Ordering/Choosing Task. If this were done it would only check that the process had been correctly executed both times. What is required is an entirely different approach so that the decision itself is thoroughly exercised and the consequences of adopting it made apparent.

In this context it becomes clear that we need two independent techniques for the validation process and the ordering/choosing process. One way to achieve this is to make the Ordering/Choosing Task an optimising process because that is its purpose in life. The Validation Task can then use a model of the world to which the current decision relates. The consequences of pursuing the chosen 'optimum outcome' in the real world should then become apparent in the validation process. It is entirely possible that some of the consequences, particularly side affects, are unacceptable. This is because the optimising process was not considering side effects.

For example, a decision has been made to extend a harbour at the entrance to a river so that it can accept larger vessels. The decision has been made on financial and environmental grounds but a model of the proposed scheme shows that the extension will cause a sand bar across the river rendering it unnavigable to the small boats which use it. The decision to extend the harbour was a sound business decision but the consequences for neighbouring activities are such that it must be reconsidered.

This chapter will consider models and their role as a validation tool. We will start by looking at the various ways of using them and then examine the various types of model which are available and the circumstances in which they prove useful.

11.2 THE USE OF MODELS

When the BBC Computer was first introduced, a free game 'The Game of Life' was provided with it. In this game the player was the chief of a village and had to organise the villagers to tend the fields, to repair the river banks and to defend the village against bandits.

It was a game where you could not win. If you did not defend the village well enough either against the river or against the bandits, disaster struck and the village was wiped out. But, if you defended the village vigorously against the bandits, they died out freeing effort to reinforce the river defences. The village then prospered until there were too many villagers for the land to support and again disaster struck. You had to callously use the bandits to control the population and let the river flood every few years in order to maintain the village in a prosperous state.

This game demonstrates many things which are fundamental to the use of models in everyday life. The first is that incredibly simple models can be quite realistic in use. The reason for this is bound up with a second point. We can often determine a whole series of cause/effect relationships, e.g. the river floods, the crops are lost, the villagers starve, but we find it very difficult to work out what will happen when there are many interrelated causes and effects. But, even when there are many of these relationships, it can be a relatively simple job to get a computer to simulate what the compound effects are going to be.

The example also demonstrates the way people use models to learn and gain experience. For example, in the above game you soon discover that you can extinguish the bandits. You can also easily discover that the river usually floods at certain times of the year. Both of these occurrences involve a fair degree of uncertainty. The river does not always flood and does not always flood at the same time of year. The bandits raid at unpredictable times and in unpredictable numbers. But, in spite of the uncertainty, you soon get to be quite a good village chief, albeit at the expense of a few extinct imaginary villages.

This principle is now used quite extensively. Most managers who have had formal training will have 'played' business games. In other professions it is imperative to learn using models. Pilots now learn to fly aircraft and handle dangerous situations using simulators. Astronauts have to learn their trade using simulators. These are very extreme cases of the same principle. These people must learn to make correct decisions very quickly and the simulator validates their decisions by providing instantaneous feedback very like that of the real world.

The latter are examples of using the model to find the optimum outcome. In these cases it is the only way to proceed but, in general, this is a very inefficient way to make decisions. Simulation is expensive and time consuming so it is usually much better to optimise first and then simulate as a means of checking the supposed optimum outcome. This is not to say that making decisions by trial and error should not be allowed but it is saying that it should not be encouraged.

11.3 NUMERICAL MODELS

Models do not have to be expensive and complicated to be useful. Far from it. Spreadsheets are a fine example of a simple tool which is frequently used to make simple models. The Baker's Dilemma could have been formulated in model form, in which case the formulae and the probability distributions would have been used to provide the baker with the number of loaves sold and the profit made once the baker had said how many loaves he was going to bake and how busy he expected the day to be.

Modern spreadsheets also have what is known as 'what if' and 'goal seeking' options. These facilities allow the model to be used in a trial and error mode. For example, the baker could say 'what if' I bake 190 loaves or, in the 'goal seeking' mode he could ask 'how many loaves would I have to bake on a good day to make £50 profit'. It is interesting to note that these packages do not usually allow the baker to ask 'how many loaves do I need to make to MAXIMISE profit'. It is also interesting to see how these packages handle the Human Computer Interface problems, e.g. when the user has given the goal seeking option an unobtainable goal.

Financial modelling packages are available which offer modelling facilities at a rather more sophisticated level. These packages follow roughly the same approach as that proposed in this book. First of all the problem must be formally stated, e.g.

10 SALES = 6000 THEN PLUS 12 PER CENT PER YEAR
20 PROFIT = SALES_VALUE – VARIABLE_COSTS – FIXED_COSTS
30 VARIABLE_COSTS = 0.40*SALES
40 SALES_VALUE = 0.60*SALES
50 FIXED_COSTS = 1000 THEN PLUS 15 PER CENT PER YEAR

etc.

SOLVE FOR NEXT 4 YEARS

They then solve the problem in tabular form, e.g.

	YEAR 1	YEAR 2	YEAR 3	YEAR 4
SALES	6000	6720	7526	8430
PROFIT	200	194	183	165
SALES_VALUE	3600	4032	4516	5058
VARIABLE_COSTS	2400	2688	3010	3372
FIXED_COSTS	1000	1150	1323	1521

They then allow the user to try 'what if' and 'goal seeking' exercises to help them understand and solve the problem, e.g.

WHAT IF
10 SALES = 6000 THEN PLUS 15 PER CENT PER YEAR

or

GOAL
PROFIT = 200 THEN PLUS 10 PER CENT PER YEAR
CHANGE SALES
SEEK

Notice that these packages do not require the statements to be in sequence as would a programming language. They also automatically provide values for all the variables mentioned over a period of time specified.

They are exceedingly useful packages, particularly for financial and other monetary problems, but note that they do not really support the decision making function. They do allow the user to formulate the problem but they do not provide adequate techniques for handling uncertainty nor for assessing risk and, if they are to be used to make the decision, they must not be used to validate it. For this reason, they are probably best used as validating packages, i.e. used to make financial models which can validate decisions made by other means.

11.4 PROBABILISTIC MODELS

Earlier in this book we discussed methods of making decisions which handled the uncertain nature of the outcomes. In many cases, the outcomes were assigned a pseudo probabilistic value which represented either an Expected Value or some form of Certainty Equivalent. The Ordering/Choosing task was then used to rank the various possible combinations of outcomes using the values associated with the individual outcomes and the relationship between the sub-decisions.

A decision which is made in this manner is probably sound but it lacks an expression of its inherent probabilistic nature. Even if probability distributions are used instead of point values, it is unlikely to impart to the user an understanding of what could happen.

The Validation Task can be used to overcome this deficiency because it is not difficult to make probabilistic models which if run repeatedly build up a much fuller picture of the likely eventualities. This can highlight short term problems due to 'bad luck' or show the benefits to be gained from a 'lucky run'.

Many techniques exist which could be used for this purpose but we will discuss just two: Monte Carlo Simulation and Markov Analysis.

11.4.1 Monte Carlo Simulation

Monte Carlo Simulation addresses the problem of uncertainty in a very simple but effective manner. It simulates a probabilistic event by using a random number generator and the probability distribution for the event. By doing this repeatedly and determining the outcome each time, an overall picture of the distribution of the possible outcomes is achieved.

Consider the statement:

PROFIT = SALES * PROFIT_PER_ITEM - FIXED_COSTS

This is easily computed if:

SALES = 6000

PROFIT_PER_ITEM = 0.6

FIXED_COSTS = 1000

But, if sales, profit per item and fixed costs are uncertain values which can only be described using probability distributions, then computing the profit is no longer a trivial task and it too will be an uncertain value described by a probability distribution.

Consider the 'New Warping Machine' example which was used earlier in the book. Mr Philip was trying to decide whether or not to buy a new warping machine. Two warping machines were of interest. One, machine A, was a fairly safe bet but restricted them to their current markets. Machine B was more risky but was suitable for opening up new markets. Could they afford to choose machine B?

A simple financial model for running any machine might well be:

$$\text{CONTRIBUTION} = \text{NUMBER\_OF\_WARPS\_PROCESSED} * \text{CONTRIBUTION\_PER\_WARP} - \text{MAINTENANCE\_COSTS} - \text{FINANCE\_COSTS} \quad (11.1)$$

but all the variables on the right hand side of the expression are probabilistic. When Mr Philip took the decision he made some simplifying assumptions. He assumed that the maintenance costs and the financial costs were insignificant and assumed that the contribution per warp was a fixed amount. Better assumptions for all these values are given in Tables 11.1 to 11.4.

Table 11.1. Probability distribution for the number of warps processed

Number	0	50	100	150	200
Probability	0.15	0.20	0.20	0.40	0.05
Cum. prob.	0.15	0.35	0.55	0.95	1.00

Table 11.2. Probability distribution for the profit per warp

Profit/warp	400	600	800
Probability	0.25	0.50	0.25
Cum. prob.	0.25	0.75	1.00

Table 11.3. Probability distributions for maintenance costs

No. of Warps		Cost of Maintenance per Year		
		1000	5000	10000
0 – 50	probability	0.85	0.15	0.00
	cum. prob	0.85	1.00	1.00
51 – 100	probability	0.35	0.60	0.05
	cum. prob	0.35	0.95	1.00
101 – 250	probability	0.15	0.70	0.15
	cum. prob	0.15	0.85	1.00

Table 11.4. Probability distribution for the financial costs

Finance costs	12000	16000	20000	24000
Probability	0.25	0.40	0.30	0.05
Cum. prob.	0.25	0.65	0.95	1.00

Monte Carlo simulation proceeds by taking a number from a random number stream and using that number to obtain an actual value using the cumulative probability distribution. This process transforms the uniform distribution on [0,1], i.e. the random numbers, into the desired probability distribution. The results of 25 trials are shown in Table 11.5. Each row in the table is an evaluation of equation (11.1) and the values used are those derived from the cumulative probability distributions given the respective random number. Note that the mean contribution per warp, shown in Table 11.5, is exceedingly close to that used by Mr Philip to make the decision.

Table 11.5. Monte Carlo simulation

Random number	No. of warps	Random number	Contribution per warp	Random number	Maintenance costs	Random number	Finance costs	Net contribution
5	100	1	400	1	1000	5	16000	23000
3	50	9	800	9	5000	1	12000	23000
2	50	8	800	1	1000	7	20000	19000
8	150	4	600	8	5000	8	20000	65000
4	100	3	600	1	1000	3	16000	43000
4	100	8	800	3	1000	10	24000	55000
9	150	1	400	1	1000	4	16000	43000
7	150	7	600	3	5000	3	16000	69000
1	0	6	600	5	1000	3	16000	−17000
7	150	1	400	10	10000	6	16000	34000
9	150	3	600	2	5000	4	16000	69000
9	150	2	400	7	5000	6	16000	59000
6	150	9	800	8	5000	8	20000	95000
9	150	2	400	1	1000	2	12000	47000
7	150	9	800	9	10000	6	16000	94000
5	100	10	800	3	1000	10	24000	55000
4	100	5	600	3	1000	7	20000	39000
2	50	3	600	3	1000	3	16000	13000
6	150	4	600	5	5000	9	20000	65000
5	100	6	600	1	1000	8	20000	39000
7	150	1	400	1	1000	3	16000	43000
6	150	3	800	4	5000	1	12000	73000
6	150	3	600	2	5000	1	12000	73000
8	150	8	600	9	10000	1	12000	98000
6	150	4	600	2	5000	2	12000	73000

Total contribution   1292000
Mean contribution   51680
Mean contribution/warp   423.6

Table 11.6 shows the frequency, probability and cumulative probability distributions for the contribution expected from machine B.

Validating the Decision

Table 11.6. The probability distributions for the contribution

Contri-bution	–19K : 0K	1K : 20K	21K : 40K	41K : 60K	61K : 80K	81K : 100K
Frequency	1	2	5	7	7	3
Probability	0.04	0.08	0.20	0.28	0.28	0.12
Cumulative probability	0.04	0.12	0.32	0.60	0.88	1.00

Fig. 11.1 compares the cumulative probability distribution resulting from the Monte Carlo Simulation with that derived from the Expected Values in Chapter 7. None of the results given by this validation exercise would give cause for concern and Mr Philip could stand by his original decision.

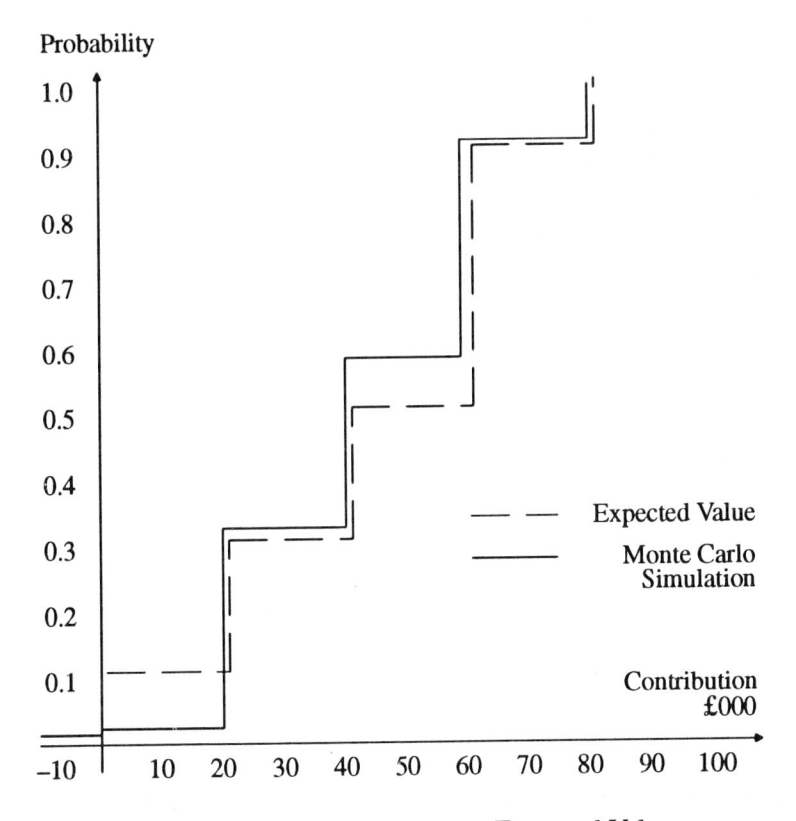

Fig. 11.1. Monte Carlo simulation versus Expected Value

11.4.2 Markov Analysis

Sometimes decisions are policy decisions and the policy will then be applied over and over again until it requires to be changed for some reason. In such cases, the validation of the decision needs to ascertain what the steady state will be after the policy has been in existence for some considerable time. Markov Analysis will model this situation.

R,B & H are situated in a town with several ethnic groups which are a significant minority of the population. The brothers wish to pursue a rigidly non–racist policy. They would like the distribution of races amongst their employees to be the same as the distribution of the races in the surrounding area. Consequently, when somebody leaves, the replacement is chosen carefully to ensure that they not only have the necessary skill but that they comply with the non–racist policy.

Staff do not leave often and their present distribution of staff is reminiscent of the distribution of races some time ago. However, they wish to confirm that their present policies will rectify the situation in the fullness of time, i.e. they wish to validate the non–racist policy.

In order to do this they have noted the ethnic group of those leaving the company and the ethnic group of the people who are recruited to replace them. The results have yielded the information shown in Table 11.7.

Table 11.7. Ethnic groups of leavers and new recruits

Ethnic group	No. in group at beginning	No. leaving per year	Replacement drawn from A	B	C
A	85%	9.0%	4.0%	3.0%	2.0%
B	12%	0.6%	0.2%	0.4%	0.0%
C	3%	1.0%	0.3%	0.0%	0.7%

The proportion of the ethnic groups in the recruitment area is 60:30:10 for A:B:C respectively.

We can determine whether or not the policy is going to achieve its aims in the following manner. We must first calculate the number of people in each of the groups at the end of the year and then construct the matrix shown in Table 11.8.

Table 11.8 assumes that if a person who belongs to ethnic group A leaves and is replaced by a person from ethnic group B, that is equivalent to a person moving from group A to group B. The values across the diagonal show the proportion of employees who did not change group, i.e. 80% of people in group A stayed in group A or were replaced by another person from group A. The other entries show the number of people who did move. The columns show where they were at the beginning of the year and the rows show where they were at the end.

Table 11.8. Movement between ethnic groups

	A	B	C	Number at end
A	80.0%	0.2%	0.3%	80.5%
B	3.0%	11.8%	0.0%	14.8%
C	2.0%	0.0%	2.7%	4.7%
Number at beginning	85.0%	12.0%	3.0%	100.0%

The probability that a person in group A stays in group A is 80/85. Similarly, the probability that a person in group A moves to group B is 3/85 and the probability that a person in group A moves to group C is 2/85. So, Table 11.8 can be re-expressed in terms of the probability that people stay or move. This is shown in Table 11.9.

Table 11.9. Probability that people move between ethnic groups

	A	B	C
A	0.941	0.017	0.100
B	0.035	0.983	0.000
C	0.024	0.000	0.900

Now if the system has reached equilibrium, the number at the beginning must be the same as the number at the end. Furthermore, the number of people expected to move from one group to another must be the product of the probability of that move and the number of people in the group. Consequently, if N_A, N_B and N_C are the proportions of people in the groups when equilibrium has been reached,

$$0.941 N_A + 0.017 N_B + 0.100 N_C = N_A$$
$$0.035 N_A + 0.983 N_B = N_B \qquad (11.2a)$$
$$0.024 N_A + 0.900 N_C = N_C$$

but, the proportion of people in each group must sum to unity, hence

$$N_A + N_B + N_C = 1 \qquad (11.2b)$$

Solving equations (11.2a) and (11.2b) we discover that:

$$N_A = 0.303 \quad N_B = 0.624 \quad N_C = 0.073$$

These are in the ratio 30.3 : 62.4 : 7.3 and it is clear that in their efforts to be fair to the minorities, the brothers are inadvertently favouring the B group.

11.5 SIMULATION

Simulating the real world using computer models is a well developed and very specialised field in its own right. It is, yet again, an example of a well developed technology which can be incorporated into Decision Support Systems to good effect.

Producing computer simulations can be an expensive exercise even though the tools for doing so are now very sophisticated. Consequently, simulation is usually only worthwhile if the decision is a major one or if the model is going to be of general use to several decision makers over a period of time. Simulation does have its advantages, however, because the user actually 'sees' what is likely to happen in real life. As a result, if a decision is a poor one, the decision maker can often see why and hence the chances of making a better decision the next time round are enhanced.

There are two approaches to computer simulation: continuous simulation and discrete event simulation. Both have their place. Continuous simulation is based on the solution of simultaneous partial differential equations and, as its name implies, is ideal for modelling continuous systems, e.g. the vibrations in a spring. Discrete event simulation is a 'physical' approach and is good for discontinuous systems such as the queues at supermarkets.

Both methods adopt the same overall strategy for building models. This is:

(1) Clearly define what is to be modelled.

(2) Decide what must be included in the model and what can be omitted. Start with a simple model and be driven to increased complexity only if accurate modelling makes it necessary.

(3) Collect data for the model (which may take years).

(4) Implement the model and check that it accurately models the data collected in (3) above.

(5) Compare the model with real life using fresh information.

(6) If the results are bad, return to (2) and reassess what should be included in the model.

(7) If the results are good, the model can be used to:

    (a)   predict the future

    (b)   test ideas

    (c)   optimise.

Step (7) states succinctly the potential which simulation offers the decision maker but steps (1) to (6) hint at the large amount of detailed work which may be required to produce a good model.

11.5.1 Continuous Simulation

One technique for modelling using continuous simulation is to imagine the system to be a set of compartments each with an input and an output. If the relationship between the inputs and the outputs is expressed as differential equations with time as the independent variable, the computer can solve the differential equations simultaneously, taking into account the interactions between the compartments, and can plot what happens to the system as time passes.

The idea of several compartments can be depicted as a cascade of waterfalls as shown in Fig. 11.2. The level in each tank is varying with time. The top tank is emptying, the bottom tank is filling and the ones in between fill initially and then empty again. Trying to think of this as a complete system is difficult but the solution for each tank is relatively easy. The level of the water in the tank at a given instant is the level at the immediately preceding instant plus the increase in level due to water running in from the tank above minus the reduction in level due to water running out into the next tank. As no water runs into the top tank and no water runs out of the bottom tank we can solve the equations for successive instances in time.

In order to see how this is applicable to Decision Support Systems, we will consider a type of model known as a Pharmokinetic model. These models try to determine the concentration of drug within the body using continuous simulation techniques.

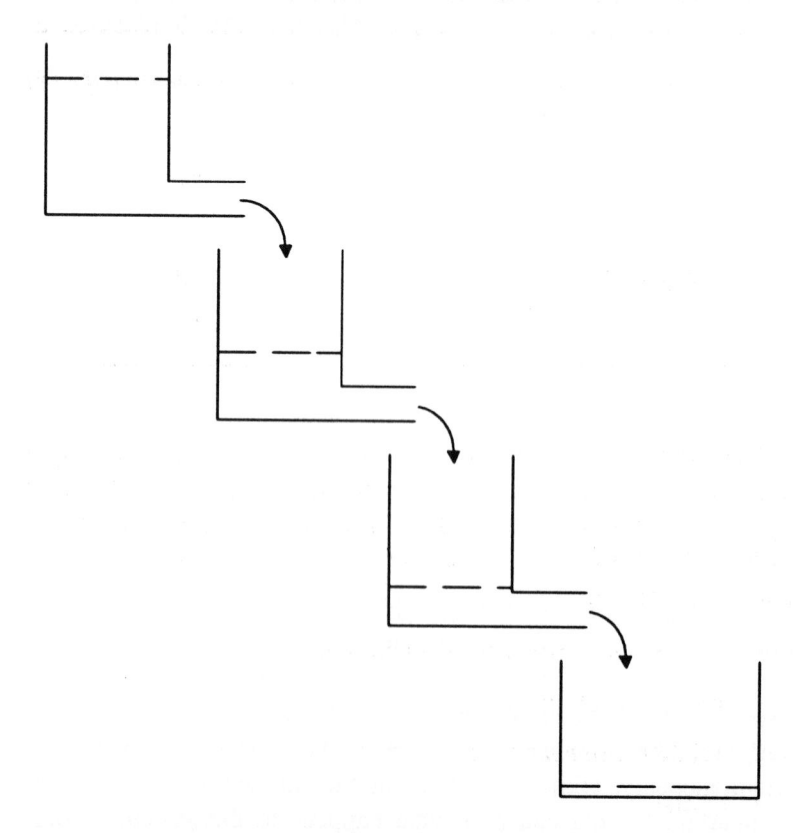

Fig. 11.2. A four compartment model

Initially, we will consider the body to be a single compartment, i.e. the blood stream, which is capable of eliminating drugs from within

Validating the Decision

itself, i.e. metabolism and excretion. We will also assume that the drug is injected directly into the blood stream so that it appears at an instant in time. This is a fair representation for intravenous injection of drugs. We then wish to consider how fast the concentration of drug decays.

Assume that in a clinical trial when 100mg of drug was injected at time 0 the concentration at later times was as shown in Table 11.10. The graph of Concentration versus Time is shown in Fig. 11.3 but in the form shown it is not particularly useful. The curve is more useful expressed by plotting log(Concentration) versus Time as shown in Fig. 11.4.

Table 11.10. Concentration decaying with time

Time (hours)	Concentration (micro grams/ml)
4	10.5
7.5	6.5
12.0	4.7
16.0	2.5
20.0	1.7

The points now almost lie on a straight line and the best straight line to use can be computed using regression analysis, e.g. the least squares line described earlier. Having achieved a straight line graph we know that the rate of change of log(Concentration) with respect to Time is a constant.

If, for convenience, we adopt the notation

C = Concentration

C_0 = Initial Concentration

t = Time

then

$$\frac{d(\log C)}{dt} = -k \tag{11.3}$$

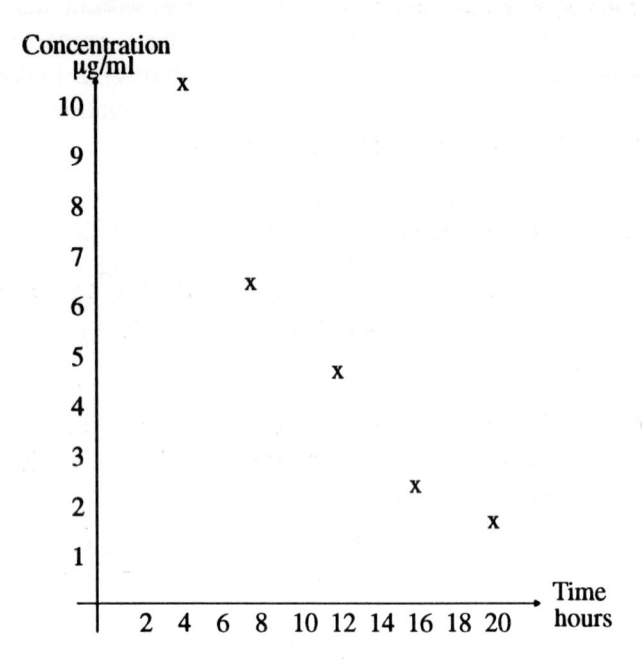

Fig. 11.3. Drug concentration versus time

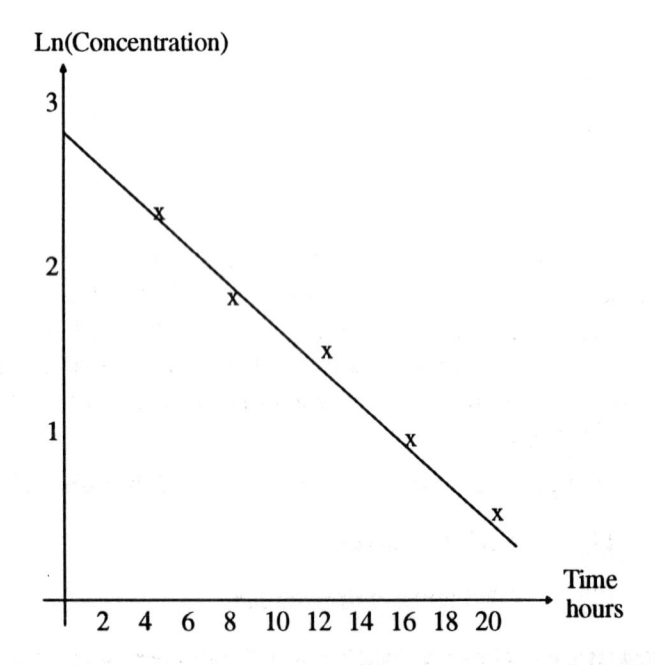

Fig. 11.4. Regression line for log(concentration) versus time

Validating the Decision

which, differentiating the log, gives

$$\frac{d(C)}{dt} = -kC \tag{11.4}$$

Let us assume that either the regression analysis or the graph shows that

$C_0 = 16.7$ micro grams/ml

then the effective blood volume is 6 litres. This means that in general we can assume that the initial concentration is given by:

$C_0 = $ dose(mg)/6 litres

It is now possible to build our complete model. If sophisticated languages, such as the Bradford University BEDSOCS (1), are available, this is as easy as writing:

```
10  PRINT "SINGLE COMPARTMENT MODEL: RAPID IV"
20  INPUT "HOW MUCH DRUG (mg) WAS INJECTED ? "; D
30  C = D/6
40  INPUT "ELIMINATION CONSTANT IS ? "; K
200 DYNAMIC
300 EQUATIONS
310 INDVAR T
320 DER C = -K*C
330 DISPLAY C
400 EQUEND
500 DYNEND
999 END
```

Lines 10 – 40 are BASIC–like statements. Lines 200 – 500 are BEDSOCS statements and that is all the user is required to write. Note that the user does not need to know how to solve the equations or even, when many equations are involved, how to order them. BEDSOCS will sort that out and plot whatever variables have been requested for display, i.e. line 330.

The above program could then be used to find the effect of :

    (1)   Different doses.

    (2)   Different elimination rates.

But great care must be exercised because the above program assumes that the elimination rate is independent of:

(1)   Dose.

(2)   Drug.

(3)   The patient.

The model also would need careful checking to ensure that these simplifying assumptions are realistic.

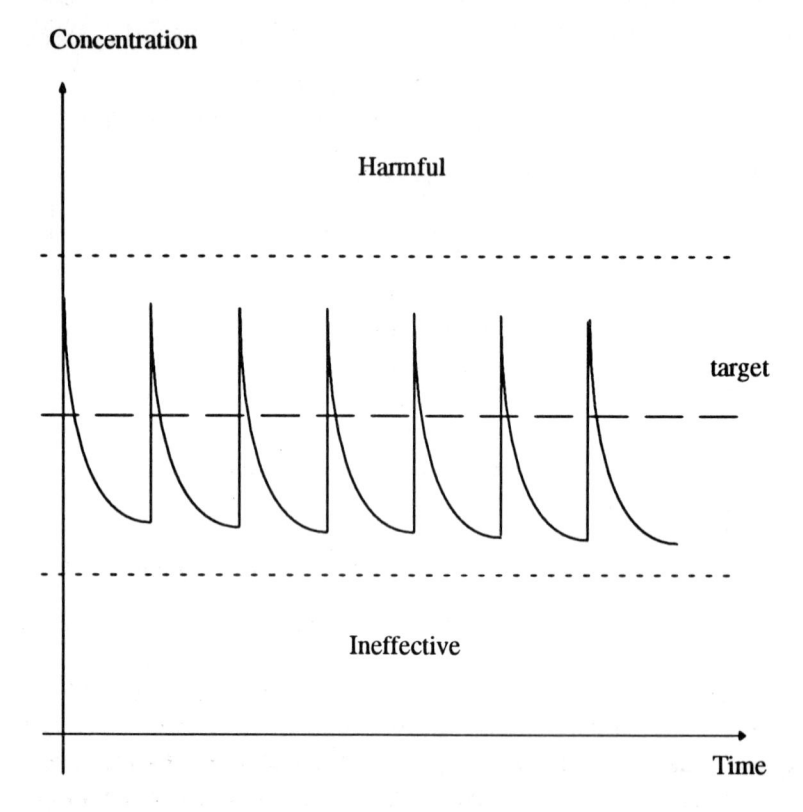

Fig 11.5. Simulating repeated doses

If the model proved successful it could be used in its decision support role. Assume that a patient needs a very toxic drug which is ineffective when the concentration is too low but harmful if it is too high. The pharmacist has to decide on a dose and a repetition interval which will keep the concentration half way between these two limits. The decision will probably be based on experience but the values which are chosen can be supplied to the simulation program to see what the effect would be. If the results were as shown in Fig. 11.5 there should be no problems and the decision is validated.

11.5.2 Discrete Event Simulation

Discrete Event Simulation takes a different view of the world. It views the world as a set of events which happen at discrete points in time. It then simulates the passage of time, causing the events to happen and keeping track of their side effects.

An event is defined as a point in time at which a change of state occurs. Many processes in life can be described in these terms, e.g. an aircraft flight from an airport's point of view would look like this:

event	change of state
1	aircraft enters airport's air traffic control
2	gets a landing slot
3	starts descent
4	gets permission to land
5	lands
6	clears runway
7	arrives at gate
8	gets a take off slot
9	leaves gate
10	arrives at end of runway
11	gets permission to take off
12	takes off
13	achieves cruising flight
14	leaves airport's traffic control zone

Now, a busy airport will have many planes using its facilities and, at any one time, there could be several planes within its jurisdiction. It is imperative, however, that only one plane uses a given runway at any point in time and a gate can only provide facilities for one aircraft at a time. This brings us to a very important feature of discrete event simulation. The runway and the gates are resources which all the aircraft have to use. These resources have to be reserved when in use and freed when no longer required. A request for a resource cannot be granted if the resource is being used. The requester must wait in turn and hence a queue can form. It is the automatic handling of these queues which gives the discrete event simulation packages their power.

The other feature which is required of a discrete event simulation package is a model of uncertainty. For example, not every aircraft will take the same length of time at a gate. The time will vary with the size of the aircraft but it could also vary due to unforeseen circumstances, late passengers, baggage delays, etc.. The latter causes are probabilistic and have to be simulated in a manner similar to that used by Monte Carlo Simulation.

Modern simulation languages are so powerful that the user does not need to know much about how the simulation is achieved. In fact, they are so expressive that the easiest way to explain how to use them is simply to provide an example.

Let us suppose that we want to simulate a warping job at R,B & H. This could be as simple as writing the following:

a WARPING_JOB is

    delay prob_dist(getting_started)   %wait for yarn etc.%

    request 1 WINDING_MACHINE   %must wait until one is available%

    delay prob_dist(WINDING_TIME)   %time taken to rewind yarn%

    free WINDING_MACHINE   %somebody else might want it%

    request WARPING_MACHINE   %must wait until one is available%

    delay prob_dist(WARPING_TIME)   %not sure how long it will take%

    request STORAGE_SPACE   %to keep warp until collected%

    free WARPING_MACHINE   %may be needed for other jobs%

    delay prob_dist(TRANSPORT)   %wait for carrier to collect%

    free STORAGE_SPACE   %not required any more%

end WARPING_JOB

Now that the warping job is described, albeit in terms of requests, delays, frees and probability distributions, we have to tell the system that there are many of them and a new one occurs every so often. We can do this by introducing a new job at intervals which have the correct probability distribution. Hence,

for DURATION_OF_JOB do

    start 1 WARPING_JOB now

    delay prob_dist(INTERVAL_BETWEEN_WARPING_JOBS)

repeat

The only thing that the simulation program still needs to specify is how many WARPING_MACHINEs and WINDING_MACHINEs R,B, & H have and how long the simulation should run for so, the simulation has

    2 WINDING_MACHINE%s%

    17 WARPING_MACHINE%s%

run for

    2 years

end

All that is left to do is to compile and run the program.

The brothers could use the above model to see the effect of accepting the job using salvaged yarn. They could also use it to find out what the effects of buying a new machine might be. They might discover that the bottleneck is actually the winding machines.

11.6 EXPERT SYSTEMS

In the context of this book, Expert Systems are best thought of as a type of simulation and consequently as a validation tool. The simulation methods described above simulate very tangible things such as financial dealings, systems governed by the laws of physics and stochastic systems. None of these methods are suitable for modelling thought processes or knowledge. This is the role of the Expert System.

The role of Experts Systems is clear but how well they achieve this role is clouded with controversy. This is because they are almost impossible to test and even the test standards are disputed. For example, is an Expert System which gives the same answer as a human expert correct when the answer given by the human expert was wrong?

Obviously there are researchers who are interested in how human beings think and who are trying to make computers emulate human thought. For applications like the one proposed here, it is now generally accepted that it is more important to get the correct answer than to emulate human thought. Consequently, researchers in the field have turned their attention back towards the classical theories, such as probability, and moved away from the ad hoc methods used in early systems.

It is important to appreciate this point. If you want to build an expert system which can handle uncertainty you need to choose the method very carefully. The early simple methods are now known to be highly inaccurate at best (2) and even the most recent systems make potentially dangerous assumptions and require the user to present information in a precisely specified form (3).

There are several different approaches to building Expert Systems but perhaps the best, if uncertainty features in the model, are the probabilistic type which are based on influence diagrams (4). We will briefly look at these systems because they give some insight into the potential uses of Expert Systems in decision support.

Consider again the example about making warps from salvaged yarn. Mr Keith knows that yarn which is on damaged bobbins will probably not wind well and that yarn which does not wind well usually does not warp well either. This knowledge can be encoded in diagrammatical form as shown in Fig. 11.6.

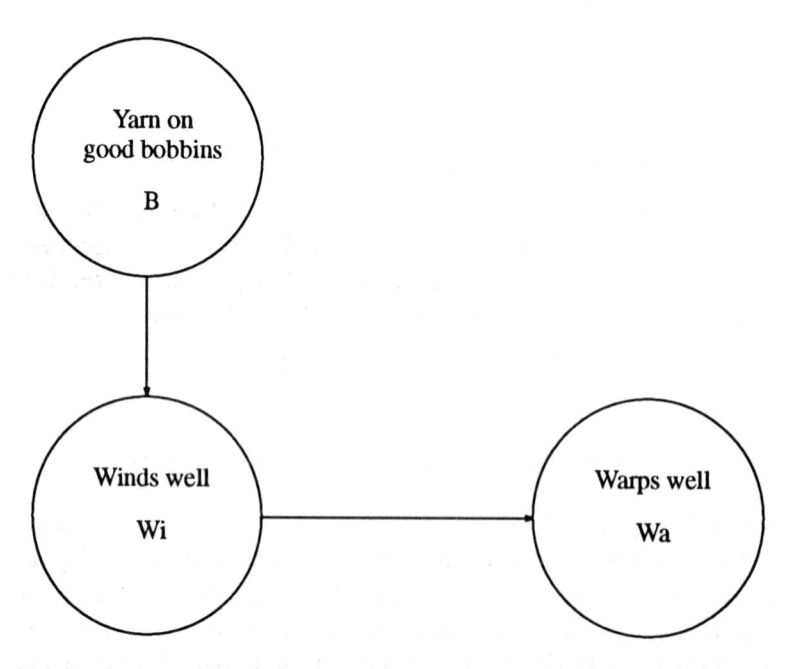

Fig. 11.6. A simple influence diagram for ease of warping

If the diagram is going to be useful, Mr Keith will have to be more specific about the strengths of the influences. The knowledge which we will need from Mr Keith is:

(1) The probability that the yarn will wind well given that it is on good bobbins, i.e. P(Wi|B).

Validating the Decision

(2) The probability that the yarn will wind well given that it is not on good bobbins, i.e. P(Wi|~B).

(3) The probability that the yarn will warp well given that it wound well, i.e. P(Wa|Wi).

(4) The probability that the yarn will warp well given that it did not wind well, i.e. P(Wa|~Wi).

(5) The probability that the yarn will arrive on good bobbins, i.e. P(B).

If we are given this information we can calculate the prior probability that the yarn will wind well and that it will warp well, i.e. P(Wi) and P(Wa), since

P(Wi) = P(WiB) + P(Wi~B)

= P(Wi|B)*P(B) + P(Wi|~B)*{1–P(B)}

and similarly

P(Wa) = P(Wa|Wi)*P(Wi) + P(Wa|~Wi)*{1–P(Wi)}

If information is available about the condition of the bobbins for a particular job, e.g. suppose that the probability that the salvaged yarn is on good bobbins is P(B'), then the probability that it will wind and warp well, P(Wi') and P(Wa') respectively, is given by

P(Wi') = P(Wi|B)*P(B') + P(Wi|~B)*{1–P(B')}

and

P(Wa') = P(Wa|Wi)*P(Wi') + P(Wa|~Wi)*{1–P(Wi')}

So, from a general knowledge of the way in which yarn processes given the state of the bobbins and particular knowledge about the state of the salvaged yarn's bobbins, Mr Keith can estimate the probability that the salvaged yarn will process well. This would enable Mr Philip to estimate the profit on the job more accurately and hence decide whether or not to accept it.

The influence diagram is unlikely to be quite as simple as that shown in Fig. 11.6. A more complex diagram such as that shown in Fig. 11.7 may well be required.

Fig. 11.7 depicts Mr Keith's knowledge that good bobbins influence how well yarn winds as does the length of yarn on a bobbin.

300   *Chapter 11*

How well the yarn wound influences how well it will warp. But, short length packages also influence directly the chances that the yarn on them will warp well. This is because there will be many more knots in the yarn and knots tend to slip, causing problems. The diagram also shows that whether or not the yarn is worsted yarn affects both the ease of winding and of warping. This is because worsted yarn is high quality yarn which is very strong.

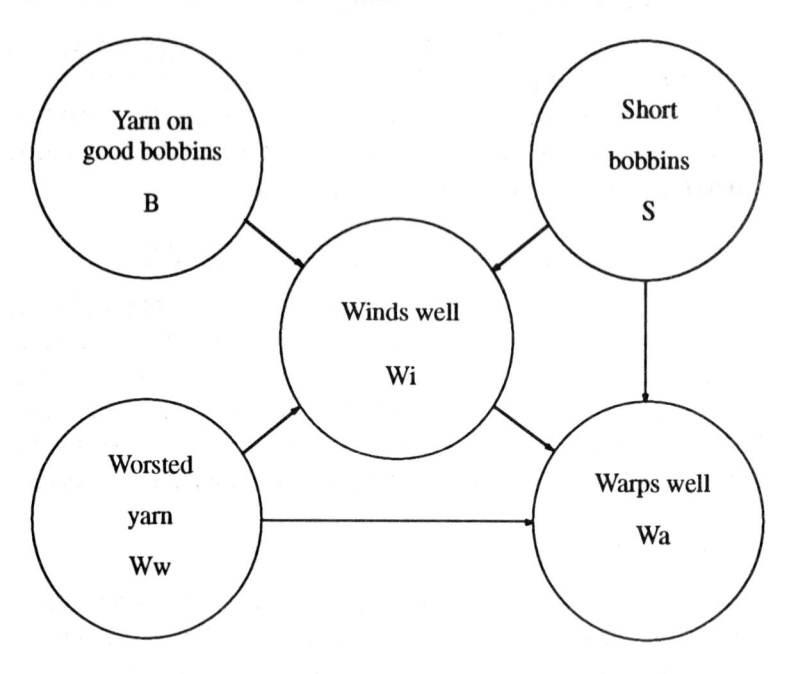

Fig. 11.7. Influence diagram for ease of processing

The strengths of the influences would have to be depicted by providing probabilities but this is one of the main difficulties with this approach. At the time this book was written, the best method for evaluating the above influence diagram (5) would require the following information.

P(B)	P(S)	P(Ww)	
P(Wi|BSWw)	P(Wi|BS~Ww)	P(Wi|B~SWw)	P(Wi|~BSWw)
P(Wi|B~S~Ww)	P(Wi|~BS~Ww)	P(Wi|~B~SWw)	P(Wi|~B~S~Ww)
P(Wa|SWiWw)	P(Wa|SWi~Ww)	P(Wa|S~WiWw)	P(Wa|~SWiWw)
P(Wa|S~Wi~Ww)	P(Wa|~SWi~Ww)	P(Wa|~S~WiWw)	P(Wa|~S~Wi~Ww)

This information might not be available because Mr Keith might not know all the complex probabilities. However, Mr Keith might well be able to provide estimates for some of the simpler conditionals, e.g.

P(Wi|B) P(Wi|~B) P(Wi|S) P(Wi|~S) etc.

One way to overcome this problem is to use Maximum Entropy to estimate the missing information. However, if Maximum Entropy is to be used to estimate the missing information, it can also be used to provide sufficient information to evaluate the influence diagram from first principles. A method for doing this has already been proposed by Garside and Rhodes (6).

A full discussion of the methods used to evaluate influence diagrams is beyond the scope of this book. What is important here is that these methods do exist and it is possible to model a person's knowledge and not just the physical world. These models can then be used to help with the decision making process.

11.7 THE HUMAN COMPUTER INTERFACE

This book has not stressed the problems which exist at the Human Computer interface but this should not give the reader the impression that they are simple or non-existent. The problems associated with trying to provide non-specialist interfaces to simulation packages are like those of providing non-specialist interfaces to the Operational Research packages and both will take time and ingenuity to solve.

11.8 SUMMARY

Validation is the last but essential step in decision making. It is analogous to the old adage 'the job is not done until the paper work is done'. Because of the complexities of many variables, uncertainty, risk and the lack of information, decision making methods have to be approximate. Validating them is, therefore, a wise precaution.

It would, however, be pointless to use the same method for validation as for making the decision. This could only ever guard against careless mistakes along the way. Consequently, we require one type of method to assist with the decision making and another to validate the decision. In business, decision makers should be searching for as many possible outcomes as they can identify and then subjecting these to an optimising process because the 'best' decision is sought and 'best' usually refers to some quantifiable measure such as return on investment. The decision making process is, in so doing, using searching and optimising methods. This leaves modelling as an obvious candidate for the validation method because modelling does not use searching or optimising techniques.

Fortunately modelling is a well developed discipline and many types of useful modelling tools are available. Models fall into several categories of which the most interesting ones are:

(1)   Financial models.

(2)   Probabilistic models.

(3)   Simulation techniques.

(4)   Expert systems.

Any company should be able to find several models, from within these broad categories, which will serve their validation needs.

11.9 CASE STUDY: THE USE OF MODELS BY R, B & H

Individual examples of the various types of models have been given above but it would be beneficial to have an overview of two types of models which R,B & H could use to support their decision making processes.

It would clearly be advantageous to have a financial model of the company and one which took into account the business universe as well as the internal state of R,B & H. Trade associations are beginning to offer access to financial models especially where many small or medium sized companies form the association, e.g. in the engineering sector. These models relate to the particular business area. A participating company can find out how well they are doing compared with others in the same business as well as how their business area is doing compared with other business areas. An individual business can sometimes also get a prediction of how well they might do if they pursue their current strategic aims.

These models are excellent but pose a potential problem. If everybody uses the same model, everybody gets the same advice. The model assumes that everyone else is going to proceed as normal when it advises one 'user' to pursue a particular strategy. The spectre of everybody using the same, or very similar, model to advice them raises the possibility that everyone might suddenly take the same, or similar, action. This might have contributed to the stock market crash in 1989 because the same model was widely used to offer advice about when to buy and sell shares.

A second model which would be of use to R,B & H would be a discrete event simulation of their production facilities. A model of this sort would be very useful to them in deciding what type of machinery to buy and what mix of jobs to do, etc.

Notice that models readily support the strategic type of decision. This is particularly fortunate because these decisions are not readily supportable by other methods. This is not to say that strategic decisions should not be broken down and made at the simplest level possible but it is a fact that, even at the simplest level, strategic decisions are hard to quantify and consequently rely more on the validation stage.

11.10 POINTS TO PONDER

Try to outline a discrete event simulation of a holiday. Then consider how you might use it to validate your choice of holiday. Consider also what you might do to find out what your holiday would be like if everything went wrong.

11.10.1 Some Suggestions

Think first about simulating a single day. You might want several types of day, for example a beach day, a touring day, etc.. You will also need a travelling out day and a returning home day.

The holiday itself would then consist of a combination of these days and might be simulated as follows:

for 14 days do

    TODAYS_WEATHER is prob_dist(CLIMATE)

    if TODAYS_WEATHER is HOT then BEACH_DAY

    if TODAYS_WEATHER is COLD then TOURING_DAY

    if TODAYS_WEATHER is WET then SHOPPING_DAY

etc.

and you add this to your simulated journey out and your journey back.

The simulation would have probability distributions for all the uncertain aspects of your holiday. For example, you could have probability distributions for:

(1)   Delays in travelling.

(2) Bad weather.

(3) Poor accommodation.

(4) Illness whilst away.

(5) Property being stolen.

etc.

In order to find out what a thoroughly bad holiday might be like, you would load the probability distributions in favour of all the things which could go wrong. This might be worth doing for something like the weather if you were going somewhere where the weather was changeable. It is the equivalent of asking 'what if' the weather is bad.

11.11 FURTHER READING

- Arthur, J.L., Frendewey, J.O., Ghandforoush, P. and Rees, L.P. (1986) Microcomputer Simulation Systems. *Computers & Operational Research*, **13**, no. 2/3, pp. 167–183.

- Bodily. S.E. (1985) *Modern Decision Making: A Guide to Modelling with Decision Support Systems.* McGraw–Hill.

- Bonczek, R.H., Holsapple, C.W. and Whinston, A.B. (1980) The Evolving Roles of Models in Decision Support Systems. *Decision Sciences*, **11**, no. 2, pp. 337–356.

- Finlay, P. N. (1985) *Mathematical Modelling in Business Decision–Making.* Croom Helm.

- Klein, R. (1982) Computer–based Financial Modelling. *Journal of Systems Management*, May.

- Mitrani, I. (1982) Simulation Techniques for Discrete Event Systems. *Cambridge Computer Science Texts*, no. 14, Cambridge University Press.

11.12 REFERENCES

(1) Brown, G. and Stephenson, J. (1972 & 1976) *BEDSOCS Manual.* Department of Computing, University of Bradford, UK.

(2) Rhodes, P.C. and Garside, G.R. (1991) Reappraisal of the use of Conditional Probability in Early Expert Systems. *Knowledge Based Systems*, **4**, no. 2, pp. 67–74.

(3) Rhodes, P.C. and Garside, G.R. (1991) The use of Maximum Entropy to Identify Unsafe Assumptions in Expert Systems. *ESQUA*, Marseille, October.

(4) Lauritzen, S.L. and Spiegelhalter, D.J. (1988) Local Computations with Probabilities on Graphical Structures and their Application to Expert Systems. *Journal of the Royal Statistical Society Series B*, **50**, no. 2, pp. 157–224.

(5) Anderson, S.K., Olesen, K.G., Jensen, F.V. and Jensen, F. (1990) Hugin – a Shell for Building Bayesian Belief Universes for Expert Systems. In *Readings in Uncertain Reasoning*, Shafer W and Pearl J (eds.). Morgan Kaufmann.

(6) Garside, G.R. and Rhodes, P.C. (1991) *Maximum Entropy for Expert Systems: the Horns of a Dilemma*. Department of Computing, University of Bradford, technical report no. CS–13–91.

Chapter 12
Concluding Remarks

12.1 INTRODUCTION

This book has outlined the nature of decisions in business. It has looked briefly at the various types of people who make these decisions and how their personality and role influences their decision making; it has proposed a general method for supporting business decisions and it has outlined existing theories which could be used to implement the proposed method.

In this concluding chapter, we will take a realistic but brief look at the feasibility of providing a general purpose Decision Support System. We will then quickly review some of the research topics which may, one day, contribute to the task of supporting decisions and we will conclude our case study and leave things tidy for Mr Keith and Mr Philip.

12.2 FEASIBILITY OF DECISION SUPPORT SYSTEMS

Consider for a moment a spreadsheet. This is a simple device, particularly in comparison with the likely complexity of a Decision Support System, but we can learn some very important lessons from it and use these to assess the likely feasibility of supporting decisions.

The first thing to note is that spreadsheets are very widely used. This is because they provides managers with a facility they need in a form which they find convenient. In other words, a spreadsheet successfully delivers a particular type of support in a form which is palatable to managers.

The second point worth noting is the lack of complexity of the type of support which is being delivered. It is unbelievably simple. A spreadsheet in its simplest form only provides basic arithmetic operators and some simple functions. The type of support which is being provided is assistance with simple arithmetic but it is very useful support indeed. Even people who are perfectly capable of doing the arithmetic themselves find the speed and convenience of using the spreadsheet well worthwhile.

A third observation is that spreadsheets are frequently used when precise information is not available and yet they are very precise devices. Managers often use figures which they know are only estimates. They also know that the figures produced by the spreadsheet have not been degraded by it. Consequently, they have as much faith in the result as they had in their original estimates.

The final, but probably the most important point to make, is that a spreadsheet does not have any inbuilt knowledge of the nature of the work which will be done using it and yet it succeeds in supporting managers, accountants, school children and many other users.

In considering the feasibility of Decision Support Systems, we should heed the strengths of the spreadsheet in the following way.

We cannot hope to support every decision specifically and yet many Decision Support Systems which are described in the literature only support a specific type of decision, i.e. whether to buy or sell shares. Decision Support Systems will have to be generally applicable in the same way that spreadsheets are. This is not a difficult concept and yet it will have to be firmly grasped before Decision Support Systems can become commonly used.

This book has described one 'architecture' which conforms with the requirement to be general but there must be many more. The building blocks, i.e. Decision Theory, Probability Theory, Utility Theory, modelling etc., which will undoubtedly be common to all, do not require inbuilt knowledge of the decision. Consequently, there is no reason whatsoever why Decision Support Systems should have to specifically address particular problems.

If sound mathematics is used to support the reasoning with uncertainty, i.e. allowing for risk and making least biased recommendations in the absence of complete information, etc., the decision maker will have confidence that the advice has been competently provided. The decision makers need not see the complex mathematics but they will need to know that it has been correctly executed. In that case the decision maker, like the spreadsheet user, will know that the outcome is as good as the information which was provided and will know how much confidence to place in the recommendations.

The above paragraphs show that Decision Support Systems could be as feasible for supporting decisions as spreadsheets are for supporting arithmetic. Spreadsheets have been an enormous success;

there are, therefore, good grounds for believing that Decision Support Systems are feasible and could become widely used if an appropriate presentation can be combined with usability.

12.3 VIABILITY OF DECISION SUPPORT SYSTEMS

The viability of Decision Support Systems will be determined by the perceived savings of making better decisions. In the case of a very critical decision, it is not difficult to demonstrate that supporting the decision is cost effective. For general purpose decision making, like that discussed in this book, the case may not be so easy to make.

The reasons for this are two fold. Firstly, constructing a general purpose Decision Support System is perceived to be a difficult and very complex task. Hopefully, this book will have helped to alleviate these fears but, even when we have sorted out all the problems, it is clearly going to be a fairly complex piece of software. However, a truly general purpose Decision Support System would have a very diverse market and hence would be a viable proposition.

The second reason that supporting decisions may not be seen to be cost effective is that most people do not accept that they make bad decisions. Consequently, most people would not consider that a saving would be made if they used a Decision Support System. This position is not easy to refute. Clearly, most people in an organisation must make fairly good decisions otherwise the organisation would not prosper. The question, therefore, rests on whether they make the best decision and whether the occasional mistake would be far more rare if their decisions were supported. The chances are that, since decision making is essentially an optimisation process and mathematical machines are better optimisers than human beings, supported decisions would be better than unsupported ones. Only time will answer this question.

A third influence could begin to affect decision making which would turn the tables in favour of supported decisions. This is more likely to occur in the public sector than in industry but industry is likely to be quick to adopt decision support once the techniques become proven. This influence is accountability. There is now more talk of citizens charters and the right of the general public to know why certain decisions were made. For example, Town and Country Planning decisions can be very contentious. At the moment the general public cannot challenge the decision on the grounds that it is illogical or was badly made. They can only challenge council decisions on the basis of procedures. If this balance is ever shifted in favour of the general public, the council will have to justify the decision. By far the best way to justify a decision would be to have a formal derivation for it. In other words, to have formally supported the decision. This sort of change, in either industry or the public sector, would quickly make Decision Support Systems viable if not essential.

12.4 USABILITY OF DECISION SUPPORT SYSTEMS

This book suggests that business control can be provided by ensuring that the higher decisions limit the choice, and influence the values, of the possible outcomes of the decisions lower down in the decision structure. This models closely the practice of industry in its human systems.

A Decision Support System based on the above would also have the advantage of allowing the user to 'rerun' the decision. This is one of the reasons why competent people use spreadsheets. It is very convenient to be able to 'tune' some figures, e.g. a budget, and it will be equally convenient to 'tune' a decision, e.g. going back and including a possible outcome which has only just been suggested. A 'rerun' feature will also be useful when a decision, which is similar to a previous one, has to be made.

Most managers avoid taking risks. If a Decision Support System can make a manager more comfortable when making risky decisions it will certainly be used. It will, therefore, be essential to provide simple methods of assessing uncertainty and risk.

The major breakthrough which brought about the success of the spreadsheet was its presentation on the screen, i.e. the Human Computer interface. A similar breakthrough is required for Decision Support Systems. If a manager friendly interface can be found, there is little doubt that Decision Support Systems will be very usable, if not invaluable, to most managers.

12.5 CONSTRUCTABILITY OF DECISION SUPPORT SYSTEMS

In this book, we have repeatedly turned to known theories when we required a formalism for part of our Decision Support System. Consequently, we must ask ourselves why Decision Support Systems are not in everyday use already. The reason is not failure to realise that decisions require support. The need to support decisions was realised several decades ago, in fact immediately prior to decision theory being developed, so we must look elsewhere for the reasons.

It is true that supporting decisions is not a trivial task. The mathematics can be quite complex and, in the days when assistance with the computations was not immediately available, this made support viable only for very important decisions. It probably also established an expectation that decision support was complex and only worth contemplating for important decisions.

This situation has now changed. Desk top computers and work stations, which can put enough computing power on a manager's desk to easily support decisions, are now readily available. Furthermore, because of office automation, many of these devices are appearing on managers' desks. It is true that the appearance of these machines has rekindled the dream of decision support but it has not yet led to widespread use of Decision Support Systems.

The reason for the failure of Decision Support Systems to emerge as a potent tool for managers does not lie with either the absence of theories nor with the non–availability of hardware. It lies with a much more fundamental issue. The truth of the matter is that, as yet, we do not really know what managers want and how to present it to them. We still have to find the right approach and the best way to solve the problem.

Spreadsheets achieved this breakthrough when it was realised that all arithmetic problems could be presented in tabular form in rows and columns. Once this was realised the need for variables, as used in programming languages, vanished because a particular value or result could be addressed in terms of its row and column. This proved to be a very easy way to express arithmetical expressions and hence financial/accounting problems and led to the general acceptance of the spreadsheet.

A similar sort of breakthrough is required for supporting decisions. This book describes systems which will achieve the goal but we have yet to discover how to present these systems to the users in a way which will be immediately acceptable. Indeed, it may even be naive to assume that, because such interfaces have been found for other systems, they must automatically exists for decision support. It may well be that a sudden significant breakthrough, like the spreadsheet, will never occur but hopefully a steady progression, such as the development of the word processor, will eventually bring about a good interface for supporting decisions.

12.6 FUTURE DEVELOPMENTS

Although much of the work required for supporting decisions has already been done, some of the current research will contribute to the ease of use and effectiveness of Decision Support Systems.

For example, the use of algebras to formalise the dialogue between user and machine will smooth the way for supporting decisions. Certainly, relational databases and their associated query languages are very much easier to build and use than the hierarchical databases which preceded them.

Reasoning under uncertainty is an area of research which will inevitably have an impact on decision making. There are two ways of approaching this problem. You can work with logic which has a formal reasoning system and try to add a method of handling the uncertainty. Alternatively, you can start with probability, which is an established technique for handling uncertainty, and try to add the reasoning systems. In practice, it has proved much easier to devise new logics than to devise new methods of handling uncertainty. Consequently, at the time this book was written, the trend was to use probability to handle the uncertainty and use logics for other problems.

Many decisions are temporal in nature, i.e. time is an important factor. The handling of time in the decision itself is accommodated within the decision diagram but the element of time within the Information Retrieval Task is not as well defined. Relational databases can easily time stamp information so that when a piece of information is retrieved the time at which it was stored, and hence when it was true, can be displayed. But, they cannot work the other way round. If you ask a relational database if a particular fact was true at a given time, it cannot answer the question.

Temporal logics are being developed to handle this situation and, since the times at which certain facts pertain may well be important for decision making, these logics will also eventually improve our decision support capability.

It would be far easier to use a machine if the machine displayed some form of intelligence so some form of natural language interface is seen as highly desirable. But, human beings have a habit of not saying what they mean. The classical example of this is the saying 'time flies like an arrow'. You and I know precisely what is meant but what chance does a machine have of correctly interpreting this statement? Time is incapable of flight. Arrows fly along roughly parabolic trajectories. This seems to have little to do with time. A machine would probably conclude that 'time flies' were something like termites and ate arrows because they liked them! So what chance has machine intelligence?

The whole issue of machine intelligence is contentious. Some people believe that machine intelligence is a long way off because computers have to be told exactly how to do a task and we cannot even define intelligence never mind give precise instructions about how to be intelligent. Other people believe that it is merely a matter of having sufficient memory to store enough knowledge and then understanding and intelligence will automatically follow.

Whichever of the above proves to be true, the consequences for the present are the same; machine intelligence is not imminent. However, this does not mean that Decision Support Systems are a long way off. Intelligent interfaces would be useful for very many tasks but we can proceed without them. For the time being it is much more practical to leave the intelligent steps for the user, to provide the searching, number crunching, etc. using the machine and to tolerate the difficulties which arise on the interface between them.

Some form of architecture for Decision Support Systems will have to be agreed if supporting decisions is to become general practice. If an architecture was developed for the method proposed in this book, the role of the various tasks would have be carefully defined as would the interface between them. But, once this was done, a person who had developed a particular type of decision formulation procedure, for example, would be able to provide the correct interface and hence make it compatible with the rest of the system. The development of various techniques would then quickly lead to very versatile systems.

It is difficult to be optimistic that this might happen, however. Certainly, experience so far in the development of computer based systems has not revealed a desire for different bodies to co-operate to this degree. The necessary level of co-operation could only arise from severe user pressure.

12.7 SUMMARY

This chapter has looked very briefly at the feasibility, viability, usability and constructability of Decision Support Systems by comparing the requirements of decision support with those of another, very successful, supportive type of application, the spreadsheet.

12.8 CASE STUDY: OUTLINE DECISION SUPPORT SYSTEM FOR R, B & H

Although the brothers have decided to retire, they still consider a useful Decision Support System for R, B & H as a good asset and an aid to improving the business prior to selling it. Consequently, they would like to see an outline of the sort of system we could offer and an estimation of its price. The latter is beyond the scope of this book but we will address the former by way of demonstrating how the previous techniques and theories could be brought together into a Decision Support System.

The first thing to consider, in accordance with the ideas expressed earlier in the book, is an overall structure which ensures that those decisions which should be made first are recognised as such and those which should be made later are made with due regard to the outcome of the earlier ones. This structure should also indicate what feedback should be considered with each decision.

It is not for us to say what the decisions themselves are. Our job is simply to provide a mechanism which the brothers will use to devise their particular structure. The mechanism which we will provide for making this structure is one which will enable them to build a multiway tree structure. It will enable them to create a node whose name will tie it to one of their decisions. This node will also store information about the type of feedback which its decision should be noting and it will store the names of decisions which are immediately subordinate to its decision. This mechanism can then be used to create a hierarchical structure with the strategic decisions at the top and operational decisions at the bottom.

Our Decision Support System will use this tree mechanism to determine which decisions are senior to the one being made. It will then retrieve the outcomes of these decisions for due consideration with the one being made. It will also retrieve the feedback which was specified. The decision maker will then be given a choice of either treating the decision being made as a multiparameter decision in which some of the parameters are the outcomes of the higher decisions or treating the probabilities associated with the decision being made as conditional probabilities which are conditioned by the outcome of the higher decisions. Whichever alternative the decision maker chooses, it will ensure that the higher decisions have been given due consideration.

The next task is to devise an overall scheme for making the decisions themselves. The system will be designed to support any decision. If the decision is given a name which is recognised as one from the overall structure then the information pertaining to that name will be retrieved, i.e. the outcome of higher decision and the feedback. If a name is given which is new to the system, the decision maker will be asked to suggest a place for it in the hierarchy. If the decision maker declines to give this information the decision will be treated as an isolated decision.

Three structuring methods will be provided. The first will allow the decision maker to split the decision into sub–decisions, sub–sub–decisions, etc.. The decision maker will be allowed to state that the sub–decisions are:

(1) Independent of each other.

(2) Exclusive.

(3) Independent except that they compete for a single resource.

(4) Dependent, in which case the decision maker must provide a hierarchy for the sub–decisions.

(5) Scheduling type decisions (in which case the system will expect to use Linear Programming but will not explicitly say so).

The brothers feel that these five cases will be quite sufficient for their purposes.

The other two structuring methods will be Payoff Tables and Decision Diagrams. These can only be used after the decisions have been broken down into sub–decisions. This restriction is for simplicity in designing the system; it prohibits the use of a sub–decision as a possible outcome in either a Payoff Table or a Decision Diagram. We will also offer them a facility to have missing probabilities estimated by the system but we had better restrict this offer to those cases where the estimates can be found using the Principle of Insufficient Reason because Maximum Entropy methods are still really experimental.

The ordering of possible outcomes will be done by either:

(1) Simple ordering on Expected Values or Certainty Equivalents.

(2) Ordering the possible outcomes for multiparameter decisions by using a function given by the decision maker which states how to combine the Expected Values or Certainty Equivalents for the different parameters into one single value which can then be ordered.

(3) Optimisation using Pruned Tree Searches.

(4) Optimisation using Linear Programming.

Again, the brothers feel that these methods will be quite adequate for their purposes.

Validation will be done by using models. These will be 'off the shelf' packages which will be bought for the purpose. The brothers think that a spreadsheet will be all that they require for making financial models and they would like a simple Discrete Event Simulation package and Directed Graph Based Expert System for the remainder of their modelling needs. They are confident that they can satisfactorily validate all their decisions with one or other of these.

All that remains is the Information Retrieval Task. We will propose a simple relational database for this and we will write procedures which will automatically store the outcome of a decision as long as the system has been told where it resides in the hierarchy. We will also write procedures which automatically retrieve this information when dependent decisions are being made. We will also provide a data entry procedure which will allow the brothers to enter information into the system and mark it as feedback for a given set of decisions. This information can then also be automatically retrieved when required.

The above system is simple and not particularly well integrated but it will suffice for R, B & H for the time being. If the business continues for a significant length of time we can study how well the system is working and decide how it should be improved.

12.9 FURTHER READING

- Andriole S. J. (1985) The Promise of Artificial Intelligence *Journal of Systems Management*, July, pp 8–17.

- Holtzman S. (1989) *Intelligent Decision Systems* Addison–Wesley.

- Neapolitan R.E. (1990) *Probabilistic Reasoning in Expert Systems: Theory and Algorithms* John Wiley & Sons Inc, New York.

Index

access to data
  concurrent, 120
  remote, 120
alternative
  possible outcome, 3
  strategies, 9
ambiguity, 7
assumptions
  and probability, 135
  minimal, 205
  of independence, 152
  used by utility theory, 220
atomic decision
  ordering outcomes of, 247
  with risk, 201
attitude
  effect on decisions, 50
attitude to risk, 208
  corporate, 225

Bacon, Francis, 55
Bayes' theorem, 149
behaviour, motivation, 83
behavioural
  attitudes, 47
  model, 48
Bernoulli trials, 233
browser, 105, 110
business environment, 17

certainty equivalence, 182, 202, 205
chance node, 171, 189
choice
  and optimisation, 4
  definition of, 3
  versus decision, 3

cognitive, motivation, 84

communication, 118
company organisation, 80

compound decision, 256
  ordering possible outcomes, 249
conditional probability, 147
  independence, 150
  use in DSS, 159
consistency, 7
constraints
  higher decisions on lower decisions, 246
  linear programming, 258
  maximum entropy, 234
continuity, 7
control, 8, 17
  a model of, 21
  loop, 22
  need for, 17
  of a business, 28
  of operations, 29
  strategic/tactical, 27
critical success factor, 32, 64
cumulative probability, 155

data, 102
  futuristic, 12
  gathering, 11
  historic/futuristic, 104
  information and knowledge, 103
  internal/external, 104
database, 12, 106, 109
decision
  complexity, 1, 31
  decomposing, 167
  definition of, 3

definition of rational, 204
making in industry, 52
making intuitively, 49
making systematically, 49
multiparameter, 247
operational, 18, 53
personal attitudes, 50
problems facing decision makers, 2
qualitative, 204
reason for support, 4
role of, 16
scope of, 20
single parameter, 247
steps of making, 55
strategic, 18, 53
structured, 53
structuring, 167
tactical, 18, 53
temperal, 167
unstructured, 53
versus choice, 3
why support them, 2
decision diagram, 171
and DSS, 184
and utility theory, 215
chance node, 171
decision node, 171
evaluating, 173, 176
exponential growth, 189
possible outcome, 171
uncertain event node, 171
use of, 174
decision maker
impulsive, 276
methodic, 276
quantitative, 276
decision making
diagram of, 60
evaluation, 57
formulation stage, 62
identifying possible outcomes, 57
observation, 55

ordering/choosing stage, 66
qualitative, 66
quantitative, 66
structuring, 55
supporting the process, 59
the process, 54
validation, 68
verification, 58
decision node, 171, 189
decision support
integrated, 1
Decision Support System
and company organisation, 80
and productivity, 80
and work redesign, 91
architecture, 33
architecture for, 312
constructability of, 309
definition of, 5
design of, 20
feasibility, 45, 306
integrated, 16
neutrality, 47
other designs, 30
the scope of, 31
usability of, 309
viability of, 308
decision theory
relevance to DSS, 157
role in Decision Support Systems, 6
dependencies, 158
desiderata, 7
direct choice, 180
directed acyclic graph, 241
dominance
outcome, 176, 177
probabilistic, 176, 178
entropy, 234
evaluating
decision diagrams, 176
payoff tables, 168

event, 134
  multiple, 142, 149
  probability of multiple, 149
exclusivity, 138
Executive Information System, 6, 13
exhaustivity, 141
Expected Value, 156, 176
  and certainty equivalence, 201
  decision diagrams, 173
  payoff tables, 168
expert systems, 297
exponential smoothing, 115

feasible region, 259
feedback, 17, 21
financial modelling, 279
forecasting, 111
  seasonal cycles, 117
  trends, 116
formulation of a decision, 62
fuzzy logic, 133

gamble
  and insurance, 209
  risk averse, 208
  standard, 205
gambling, and utility theory, 210
goal seeking, 279

human computer interface, 301

inadequate information, 131
incomplete information, 132, 230
  making decisions with, 230

independence, 142, 149
industry
  a model of, 16
  control of, 16
  resources of, 16
inflation, 80
influence diagram, 189, 241, 298, 300
  conditioning arrow, 189
  information arrow, 189
  versus decision diagram, 191
information
  data and knowledge, 103
  estimate missing, 230
  gathering, 8, 49
  historic/futuristic, 104
  incomplete, 2, 132
  internal/external, 104
  the nature of, 103
  withheld, 8
information gathering, 47, 102, 105
  demands on systems, 117
  interactive, 118
  preceptive, 48
  receptive, 48
  response time, 119
  the task of, 62
information retrieval, 109
insurance, and utility theory, 210
integrated support, 1, 16, 171
Intelligent Information Systems, 7

job enlargement, 86
job enrichment, 87
joint
  events, 142
  probabilities, 143

knapsack problem, 253
knowledge, 104
  in expert systems, 297
  data and information, 103

Lagrange multiplier, 235
least squares, 115
linear programming, 258
  problems with, 261
logic, 311
  and probability, 154
  fuzzy, 133
  modal, 133
  non–monotonic, 133

machine intelligence, 311
management
  by exception, 11
  by objectives, 12
  control, 11
Management Information System, 6, 12, 102, 105
  real time, 105
marginal probabilities, 150
Markov analysis, 286
maximum entropy, 232
  in practice, 235
minimal assumption method, 205
minimally prejudiced, 239
modal logics, 133
models, 276
  continuous simulation, 289
  discrete event simulation, 295
  financial, 279
  numeric, 279
  probablistic, 280
  use of, 277
Monte Carlo simulation, 281
motivation theory, 83
  behaviouristic, 83
  cognitive, 83, 84
  socio–technical, 89
multiparameter decision, 247
mutual independence, 153

natural language interface, 311
network, 118
neutrality of decision support, 47
node substitution, 177
  relevance of, 184
non–monotonic logics, 133

observation, 55
operational research, 265
optimising, 277
ordering/choosing, 61, 66
ordering possible outcomes, 65
ordering preferences, 201
organisations
  and Decision Support Systems, 80
  effect of supporting decisions, 90
  flatter, 81
  hierarchical, 80
  inward looking, 81
  outward looking, 82
outcome dominance, 177

payoff, 202
Payoff Tables, 167, 169
  evaluating, 168
personality, 47
planning, 17
  a model of, 21
  cascade, 23
  need for, 18
  operational, 19

strategic, 19
tactical, 19
testing a model of, 27
points to ponder
  choosing a holiday, 42
  choosing the best possible outcome, 274
  ease of making decisions, 13
  estimating missing information, 244
  management information versus decision support, 125
  models, 303
  structuring decisions, 77, 198
  supporting decisions, 13
  utility functions, 228
  validating decisions, 303
possibility theory, 133
possible outcome, 3, 7, 49, 54, 61, 156
  choosing, 8, 246
  continuous, 247
  decision diagram, 171
  discrete, 247
  evaluation of, 57
  identification of, 57
  influence diagram, 189
  ordering, 247
    continuous, 248
    discrete, 248
  payoff tables, 167
  probability of, 135
preference ordering function, 202
Principle of Insufficient Reason, 231
probabilistic dominance, 178
probability, 130, 311
  definition of, 135
  distribution, 144
  marginal values, 150
  theory, 130, 135
problem solving, 54
  scientific method, 55
productivity, 79, 80
  effect of change, 91

qualitative decision making, 66
quantitative decision making, 66
query
  language, 110
  response time, 119
  variety of, 119
query language, 110

R, B & H
  cognitive practices, 93
  control of, 37
  decision structure, 36
  Decision Support System for, 313
  introduction, 10
  Management Information System for, 122
  personal involvement sub–decision, 241
  planning, 37
  revisited, 35
  strategic decision, 160
  strategic plan, 192, 272
  transport problem, 69
  use of models, 302
  utility function for, 226
  warping salvaged yarn, 267
reasoning under uncertainty, 132
regression analysis, 112
remote data, 120
response time, 119

risk, 3, 134
  allowing for, 200
  averse utility function, 214
  aversion, 207, 209
  corporate attitude, 200
  definition of, 200
  neutral, 206
  premium, 200, 227
  seeking, 209
  versus chance, 201
rollback, 176
  with certainty equivalents, 182
  with direct choice, 180
  with outcome dominance, 177
  with probabilistic dominance, 178

scientific approach to problem solving, 55
search tree, 251
  pruning, 254
selection function, 235
simulation, 288
  continuous, 289
  discrete event, 295
  languages, 293, 296
  Monte Carlo, 281
socio–technical motivation, 89
spreadsheet, 310
standard gamble, 205
strategies, 186
structured decision, 53
sub–decision, 54, 159, 163, 167
  dependent, 250
  identifying, 56
  independent, 249
supervision, 19
supervisor, role of, 24

supporting decisions
  question why, 2
  reasons for, 4

target, 21
temporal decisions, 311

uncertainty, 3, 130, 132
  and decision support, 131
  estimating values for, 231
universality, 7
unstructured decision, 53
utility function, 202
  and business decisions, 212
  and expected value, 203
  continuously risk averse, 213
  defined, 202
  evaluating, 204
  for a person, 210
  for investors, 227
  interpretation of, 208
  multi dimentional, 211
  risk averse, 214
utility postulate, 221
utility theory, 200
  assumptions, 220
  validity of, 222
validating decisions, 276
validation, 68
validity of utility theory, 222
values, 50
  organisational, 51
  personal, 50
verification, in decision making, 55

what if, 279
work redesign, 90
working environment, 79